time of division and polarization, *Up and Doing* is a refreshing return to the lost art
lationship building. James Harmon has given us a playbook for transforming the
d through the most challenging financial markets, but it's more than that too. It's an
ring story of a wildly successful career."

ephen Ross, Chairman and Founder of Related Companies

span of Jim Harmon's interests, career moves, and priorities is reflected aptly in the
's title. With open-eyed determination, he chose areas of engagement, from invest-
banking to civic leadership, that were true to his commitment to a better, fairer
d. Whether focusing on climate change, assisting or investing in underdeveloped
omies, or just standing up to unfair policies and practices, Harmon proves again
mportance of 'doing.' The candor of his reflections and the import of his actions
nform and inspire others to get up every day and go about the work of making a
r world."

th Simmons, President, Prairie View A&M University

Praise for **Up and Doing**

"This book offers profound insights into the journey of a vete
whose global exposure, energy, enthusiasm, commitment, an
to none. In Egypt, under Jim's leadership, the economy receiv
dollars in foreign investment through the Egyptian-American
has contributed to economic and social progress as well as he
entrepreneurial ecosystem. With honesty, humor, and warm
examples of success—and a few failures—demonstrating how
section of business, philanthropy, and committed diplomacy.
understand complex market dynamics and how investing ha
positive change, *Up and Doing* serves as an invaluable and info
—Sherif Kamel, Dean, the American University in Cairo Scho

"James's career is a lesson-rich random walk. While some wor
Street winnings and coasted, Jim went to Washington, Asia, a
new frontier of investing. This grandfather and octogenarian
but he saw yet more purpose and impact to be made—with
economy, and now this book. Read it and share it."
—Roben Farzad, host of public radio's *Full Disclosure*

"From billion-dollar business deals to pathbreaking climate
Doing defies classification—much like its author. Jim Harmo
career in the service of others and gives new hope for harness
development to secure a sustainable future for generations to
—Andrew Steer, President and CEO, Bezos Earth Fund

"Harmon deftly manages the writer's trick of turning his life
one man's astonishing journey are irresistible, riotous, res
revealing of where America has been and where we're heade
—Ron Suskind, Pulitzer Prize-winning journalist and autho
and *Life, Animated*

"As the chair of the Egyptian-American Enterprise Fund,
Bank, and now as chair of the World Resources Institute
financial expertise is vital, but he is convinced that what
for building relationships—with Hollywood movie execu
in Utah, Washington politicians, Russian oligarchs, Egypt
way, he became a keen observer of personality and, as *U
really deft and lively raconteur."
—Connie Bruck, staff writer for *The New Yorker*

"In
of
wo
ins
—

"Th
boc
me
wor
eco
the
will
bett
—R

UP

AND

DOING

UP
AND
DOING

Two Presidents, Three Mistakes,
and One Great Weekend—
Touchpoints to a Better World

JAMES A. HARMON

DISRUPTION
BOOKS

New York   Austin

Published by Disruption Books
New York, New York
www.disruptionbooks.com

For ordering information or special discounts for bulk purchases, please contact Disruption Books at info@disruptionbooks.com.

Library of Congress Control Number: 2021910716

Cover and text design by Sheila Parr
Cover image credits: Mountains © iamnong / shutterstock.com;
New York City © Matej Kastelic / shutterstock.com;
Washington, DC © Sean Pavone / shutterstock.com

978-1-63331-054-4
eBook ISBN: 978-1-63331-055-1

First Edition

Dedicated to my three children, Deb, Doug, and Jennifer,
and to my four wonderful grandchildren, Dan, Mia, Piper, and Perry

Let us, then, be up and doing,

With a heart for any fate;

Still achieving, still pursuing,

Learn to labor and to wait.

HENRY WADSWORTH LONGFELLOW,
"A PSALM OF LIFE"

Contents

Foreword

MY FIRST SERIOUS ENCOUNTER with Jim Harmon was in 1999, when he was trying to make a difficult decision as chairman of the Export-Import Bank (EXIM). The Clinton White House, the congressional leadership, and every other purveyor of conventional wisdom in Washington was telling him to reject a loan guarantee for two American manufacturers supplying equipment to a Russian oil company with a dubious reputation.

The "smart" thing to do, obviously, was to drop the loan, but Harmon couldn't find anything in the EXIM charter that would justify the decision.

So Harmon did something that, in business and politics, is too rare: He stood his ground. He told his friends in the White House that if they wanted to block the loan, they should do so on national security grounds. But he wasn't going to bend the bank's rules. And for good measure, he decided to tell the whole story to me, a journalist, on the record.

I wrote in a column in the *Washington Post* a few days later that Harmon's dilemma reminded me of the scene in *On the Waterfront* when Marlon Brando's tough-guy brother tells him to take a dive in a prize fight—sit this one out, "It's not your night." I liked the fact Harmon wasn't going to sit this one out. And I've been a friend and admirer ever since.

Readers of this memoir will encounter the man his friends know so well: throughout these pages, Harmon is feisty and energetic but also reflective and self-critical. He stands by his clients and friends, sometimes beyond the point when it makes good business sense. His business partners like him for his enthusiasm and directness, and because he's just plain likable. Eleanor Roosevelt once observed: "To handle yourself, use your head. To handle others, use your heart." Readers of this book will find many examples where Harmon embodied that advice.

So often, business memoirs mask the personal pain that has accompanied success. But Harmon is the lucky person who has achieved great wealth without damaging his family, his colleagues, or his principles. He's honest in this book about some of his mistakes—the deals he shouldn't have made; the advice he wishes he hadn't given; the opportunities he missed. But that frankness only makes the larger success story more compelling.

By Harmon's account, his life as an investment banker was a story of relationship building. He liked the advisory side of the business more than proprietary trading or operational management. He wasn't a top student at Brown or Wharton, but he had a gift for making friends and gaining trust. His early mentors were old-world bankers like Herbert Wolfe, whose business sense was so canny that a young Warren Buffett would cruise by their offices hoping to pick up insight about investments.

Harmon gradually built his own network of clients, and eventually rose to lead his firm, Wertheim & Co.

Harmon's narrative is a lesson in how the advisory side of investment banking works. He explains how he came to understand (after initial skepticism) the power of Howard Schultz's vision for Starbucks and convinced Schultz to let Wertheim manage the initial financing for the company's expansion. He describes his forays into the music and entertainment businesses, including his relationship with Steve Ross as Ross became the kingpin of Time Warner. You'll see in these pages the transactional hubris of the elite as well. In one memorable anecdote, Henry Kissinger pretends that he knows Harmon to help him make a good impression on a client, and then murmurs: "You owe me one."

Making money came easily for Harmon, but he had the larger ambition of making a difference, which eventually drew him to Washington and the EXIM Bank. Harmon's proudest achievement there was expanding the bank's loan guarantees in Africa and shifting its portfolio to private companies rather than public projects. He wasn't afraid to make enemies: in addition to his politically incorrect stance on the Russia deal, he picked a fight with Senator Chris Dodd's wife (who was serving as his deputy) during the 2000 election year when Al Gore badly needed Dodd's support.

With his passion for difficult causes, Harmon embraced the thankless task of trying to assist Egypt and modernize its economy. He agreed to become the first chairman of the Egyptian-American Enterprise Fund in 2012, a year after the Tahrir Square revolution had toppled Hosni Mubarak. It was a great idea: provide American seed money to finance Egypt's entrepreneurial talent and break the dead weight of state-owned companies and government bureaucracy. There was no better advocate for this approach than Harmon.

But this good idea immediately encountered difficulty. Funding stalled during the brief tenure of President Mohamed Morsi, whose Muslim Brotherhood background caused problems in Congress. When Morsi was toppled in a counter-revolution led by General Abdel Fattah Al Sisi, Harmon continued to press the idea, now battling Egyptian government officials who wanted to steer the fund.

Harmon dealt patiently with the obstacles in Cairo and Washington. He found top-notch Egyptians and let them manage much of the enterprise fund's capital. The track record is astonishing. Among the fund's successes: Fawry, a financial-payments company whose billion-dollar IPO made it Egypt's first "unicorn"; Sarwa, a car-financing company that served Egypt's growing middle class; and Dawi Clinics, which offered affordable private health care for people who wanted more than the state-run health service but couldn't pay fancy specialists.

I'm a sucker for Harmon's stubborn commitment to projects he believes in, so I wrote several columns about the Egyptian-American Enterprise Fund's struggles and moderated a Zoom discussion in 2020 with the CEOs of two of the fund's success stories.

A final part of the story Harmon tells here is his chairmanship since 2004 of the World Resources Institute. He was earlier than most of us to recognize the severe dangers of global climate change and expanded the institute from 100 employees to about 800, with offices not just in Washington, but in China, India, the Netherlands, Indonesia, Mexico, Ethiopia, and Brazil.

Harmon doesn't describe himself this way, but he's part of the financial and legal elite that has provided money and brains for the Democratic Party (and moderate Republicans, too) over many decades. This "Establishment" gets criticism in our democracy, but Harmon's book reminds me that at its core is an ethic of public service—the idea that people who have benefited from America's blessings have a responsibility to give something back. In recent years, this roster has included political insiders like James Baker, the late Vernon Jordan, Robert Rubin, Penny Pritzker—and Harmon. It's easy to criticize this tradition of elite service, but I think it's one of America's great strengths.

Harmon distills the theme of his memoir in the wake-up he received each morning from his father, who would quote the first stanza of Henry Wadsworth Longfellow's poem "A Psalm of Life" to rouse his son from bed: "Let us, then, be up and doing, With a heart for any fate; Still achieving, still pursuing, Learn to labor and to wait."

This quintessentially American energy—a determination to make a difference in the world, day by day—animates these pages. But many American business executives are hardworking and disciplined, "achieving" and "pursuing" as Longfellow advised. I hope readers will recognize here something that's rarer in American business life. These pages describe a basic decency and compassion, a willingness "to labor and to wait" and to advocate causes even when they're impolitic and there's no reason to persist except that it's the right thing to do.

—David Ignatius, June 2021

Acknowledgments

WRITING A BOOK IS difficult. For anyone possibly thinking of embarking on this journey, I strongly encourage you to keep some sort of diary. Start today. This small investment in time will pay rich dividends when you reflect on your life and synthesize your thoughts.

In the absence of strong records, as was the case for me, I hope that you'll be blessed with a team of friends and colleagues to guide your efforts. I am immensely grateful to the many people who took time out of their busy schedules to provide me with interviews and their expertise. You all helped me to remember historical data, financial transactions, and personal events with accuracy, detail, and color, and provided helpful suggestions for how to improve my prose. My heartfelt thanks to Deb Harmon, Douglas Harmon, Jennifer Harmon, Jane Harmon, Steve Kotler, Jamie Odell, Andrea Adelman, Dan Levitan, Jim Cruse, Cornelius ("Connie") Queen, Yasmine Ghobrial, Mark Shapiro, Ashraf Zaki, Ani Dasgupta, Jonathan Lash, Andrew Steer, Ken Siegel, Krishanti O'Mara Vignarajah, Amal Enan, Bill Baldridge, Paul Wachter, Fiona Mora, Mario Aguillar, Chris Carr, and Seth Shulman.

Some people, like my friend Steve Oakes, took heroic measures, driving to another state, harvesting his records on Chappell Music from storage, and overnighting them to me. Others like Liz Cook scrutinized old budgets and historical records to help ensure that my comments about sustainability were accurate. To Liz, Steve, David Ignatius, and the many others who went "above and beyond," thank you.

Every writer needs an editor, and in my case, I was blessed with two. Many thanks to longtime colleague and friend Margaret Engelhardt, without whom I never could have completed this book. Rachel Gostenhofer also worked alongside me and helped me think through the topics and ideas detailed in these pages. The coronavirus pandemic was a lot more enjoyable with our weekly conversations about the many topics canvassed in this book.

If I have any regrets about writing this book, it's that I was forced to economize. Had I more space, I would have detailed the many experiences that I had with my longtime business partners Steve Kotler and Mark Shapiro, and recounted the many people at Hanseatic, Wertheim, the World Resources Institute, EXIM Bank, and the Egyptian-American Enterprise Fund who were instrumental to the deals and events described in these pages. To all of you who have worked alongside me in finance, government, and sustainability, I am extremely grateful.

Of all the places where I needed to economize, I particularly regret Caravel. Though this investment fund occupied twelve exciting years of my life, it gets short shrift in the book. I wish that I could have detailed the many adventures that the talented Caravel staff and I enjoyed as we traveled throughout the world making important financial and development investments together. Our work wasn't simply enjoyable and financially profitable—it was indispensable preparation for my work in Egypt. To everyone who formed part of Caravel, thank you for providing me with twelve golden years of collegiality and friendship.

Writing this book also made me focus on what's most important in my life. Without question, that is my family. I'm so grateful that my wife, Jane, stuck with me for sixty-four years of marriage, even with all of my travel and long work hours. I am so proud of Deb, Doug, and Jen, our three children. They are kind, caring, and responsible citizens. And they've given us four wonderful grandchildren. Dan and Mia are already "up and doing" with successful careers in private equity and law, both carrying on the work I began in Africa. Piper and Perry are young children as I write these words, but I hope that they will read this book one day and understand what their Bop was doing in the developing and frontier worlds.

Finally, I'd like to thank Kris Pauls and the publishing team at Disruption for transforming my labor from mere words on a screen to an actual book. After twenty years of threatening to write a book, I am boundlessly grateful that you helped me, finally, to execute.

Prologue

ONE SUNNY DAY IN September 2012, revolutionary violence erupted in Egypt. As my State Department car approached Cairo's Tahrir Square en route to a government meeting, throngs of people began hurling rocks and Molotov cocktails, destroying storefronts and other structures. Our driver stalled the vehicle, and well-meaning protestors looked inside, repeatedly motioning downward with the palms of their hands. It was a warning to me and my two colleagues, Krishanti Vignarajah, a senior aide to US Deputy Secretary of State for Management and Resources Tom Nides, and Ola El-Shawarby, a talented Egyptian financial analyst, to keep our windows fastened so that no tear gas could enter. I glanced at the cars in the distance, many of which had been overturned during the mayhem.

No one had briefed me on any unrest or violence, but perhaps we should have expected it. Egyptians had recently taken part in their first democratic elections—voting Mohamed Morsi into office. Morsi hailed from the Muslim Brotherhood, an Islamist organization that Saudi Arabia and the United Arab Emirates feared might spread to their countries, undermining their authoritarian, dynastic rule. Secular governments likewise distrusted the Brotherhood because of its violent history, its anti-Western and anti-Israel positions, and its possible links to terrorist organizations like Al-Qaeda.[1]

Nevertheless, many throughout the world hoped Morsi's election might stabilize Egypt.[2] Among the hopeful were US government officials who had renewed their interest in the region after the 2011 uprisings known as the Arab Spring. Young Arabs, across North Africa and the Middle East, were angered at government corruption, police brutality, abysmal living standards, and, in some countries, unemployment rates of over 50 percent. Taking to the streets that year, they harnessed the power of social media platforms like Facebook and Twitter, galvanizing their ranks and demanding freedom, justice, and jobs. US lawmakers, seeking ways to channel this popular disaffection away from religious fundamentalism and violence toward democracy, proposed legislation to stimulate the private sectors in Tunisia and Egypt. In December 2011, Congress passed the Egyptian-American Enterprise Fund Act.[3] It was then that Michael Froman, deputy advisor for national security on international economic affairs, informed me I'd been selected to serve as chair of this bold new venture.

In May 2012, I said yes to the offer. In addition to my lengthy career in investment banking, I'd had leadership experience in the public sector, having run the Export-Import Bank of the United States (EXIM), the government's export credit agency, for four years.[4] During this stint in public service, I had traveled to seventy-two countries and become familiar with and dedicated to helping developing economies. I could rely on my own experience and the support from the State Department and White House.

My confidence wavered on the evening of my first trip, as I sat with my colleagues at the edge of Tahrir Square, realizing we were at the epicenter of post–Arab Spring violence. We relaxed when the driver confirmed that the car had no noticeable US insignia. But anyone scrutinizing the vehicle could have made out the words "US Department of State" on the side. We nervously waited for the next two and half hours, as the chaos unfolded in the square, wishing the embassy had given us an unmarked car. As the veteran member of the contingent, I reassured the others that we'd be all right. It was hours—probably at around 10:30 p.m.—before the driver felt comfortable proceeding.

A few days later, a fresh wave of violence erupted across the region. At 9:40 p.m. on September 11, 2012, members of Ansar al-Sharia, an extremist group allied with Al-Qaeda, attacked the US diplomatic compound in Benghazi, a city about the same distance from Cairo as Chicago is from New York. Christopher Stevens, US ambassador to Libya, and Sean Smith, a US foreign service information management officer, perished in the attacks. A subsequent mortar attack killed two CIA contractors. Without delay, the United States ramped up security at its global diplomatic facilities, while the State Department evacuated US employees and their families from Egypt. Early the next morning, several marines arrived at my hotel and escorted me in an armored vehicle to the airport—a dramatic conclusion to my first trip to Cairo.

Back in the United States, I took the next few days to discuss my tumultuous visit in Washington. Senators Lindsey Graham and John McCain expressed skepticism about the prospects of the enterprise fund. President Barack Obama and Secretary of State Hillary Clinton, both of whom had no comment on the violence in Cairo, expressed hope that the protests would somehow lead to democracy in Egypt and in other Arab countries. My experience led me to remember the chants during Cairo's Arab Spring a year earlier: "Bread, Freedom, Social Justice!" Food and jobs needed to come first—political stability in the region could come only after economic stability had been attained.

To accomplish this ambitious task in Egypt—the most daunting and important task of my career—I knew that building relationships with Egyptian leaders like Morsi would be key. As psychologist and journalist Daniel Goleman has documented, people who possess emotional intelligence, or EQ, such as the ability to manage relationships, consistently make the best business leaders. Absent emotional intelligence, said Goleman in the *Harvard Business Review*, "A person can have the best training in the world, an incisive, analytical mind, and an endless supply of smart ideas, but he still won't make a great leader."[5]

I've never consciously built relationships or tried to cultivate my EQ. Like my mother and my children, I've always enjoyed forging relationships with others regardless of their race, social station, age, and cultural background. In addition to enriching my own life, these relationships have proven key to any success I've achieved as an investment banker, public servant, and environmental leader. When it comes to brokering business deals, changing the fates of nations, or transforming the energy habits of the world, we must start with human behavior. And the only way to forge consensus among people of different beliefs, ages, backgrounds, and political commitments is to develop personal relationships with them.

In many ways, this memoir, detailing the highlights of my life as an investment banker and public servant, is a story of relationship building. It includes anecdotes from early in my investment banking career—for example, when I took a chance on a then-obscure coffee company called Starbucks. I had a good relationship with a young investment banker who had a hunch the little company might do well. It details how my friendships in Utah helped me power the success of an intermountain energy giant; how my bonds with midwestern business executives led to the creation of a retail behemoth that might rival Walmart; and how my relationships with music and motion picture principals in Hollywood helped me add value to the American entertainment industry. Without my relationships with Hillary and Bill Clinton, I couldn't have addressed the 1997 Asian financial crisis, nor could I have forged bilateral trade relationships across Sub-Saharan Africa. And it's only with the continued support of my friends in the Obama and Biden administrations, as well as friendships with some of Egypt's private equity managers and businesspeople, that I'm able to help effect change throughout the Arab and larger developing world today.

But perhaps my approach to achieving impact through relationship building has been most important at the World Resources Institute, where I've served as chair for two decades. It was only through cultivating relationships among academics, heads of state, and industry leaders that we've elevated this modest institution to a world-class player at the forefront of global environmentalism. Relationship building is the only way we move the needle on climate change and global sustainability.

Because this memoir deals with my career, it doesn't address my most important relationships with my family and friends. I do not describe, for example, my decades-long marriage to my wife, Jane, nor do I relate accounts of our joys in raising our three children. I don't describe the pleasure I derive from our four grandchildren and from my closest friends. While I couldn't have attained anything near the achievements recounted in this book without their guidance and inspiration, this book is about my professional life. And writing it has been a struggle. Ever since completing my first stint in government in 2001, I've considered writing a book about my experiences in Asia, Russia, and Africa. But I could neither compose my thoughts nor sit still long enough to write them down, and I always wondered whether what I wanted to say would even resonate with readers or add value to their lives. Two decades after my initial attempt, when the pandemic forced me (and countless others) to quarantine at home and reflect, I was finally able to write.

This is a book about the role that relationships play in efforts to change the world—for the better.

The world has transformed in remarkable ways since my youth, with technological breakthroughs, global capital flows, and enhanced human talent lifting countries out of poverty and creating better societies. But our collective progress has come at the expense of human relationships. Digital technologies mediate our business and personal interactions, where we bond over text messaging, social media platforms, and digital meeting spaces like Zoom. This increasingly distanced communication has left us polarized and isolated. As many worried commentators have suggested, social isolation has reached epidemic levels, creating a climate of mistrust, suspicion, and division, and resulting in loneliness, governmental gridlock, and an appalling number of suicides each year.[6]

The polarization and strife I see in our government and business communities couldn't come at a worse time. To combat the forces of global income inequality and the scourge of terrorism and climate change, the world must collaborate like never before. We have the technology and human talent to address these problems at scale, but only if we first overcome the isolation epidemic. I wrote this book for people who, just like me, long to overcome these hurdles and bring about changes that improve the world. Whether you choose to do this through joining the government, bolstering a nonprofit, or opening a business, the formula for success remains the same: we can achieve impact only by cultivating in-person relationships. When we take the time to know other people, we recognize and appreciate our common humanity and forge change together.

As we all benefit from the many advantages that technology provides, I hope that younger generations won't give up on traveling to far-flung countries and won't conduct all their business over Zoom. Consider living abroad, joining your local school board, becoming involved in an environmental NGO, or volunteering for the foreign service. These experiences will enrich your life, as they did mine. They'll introduce you to new people with diverse perspectives and position you to have an impact. It's only by cultivating in-person relationships that we can create a stable and sustainable society for generations to come.

Relationship building is the one constant in my long career.

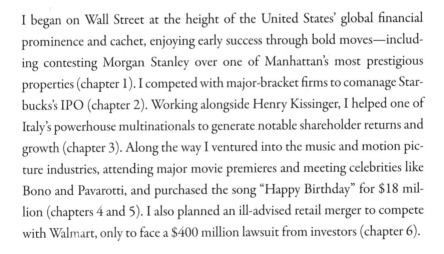

I began on Wall Street at the height of the United States' global financial prominence and cachet, enjoying early success through bold moves—including contesting Morgan Stanley over one of Manhattan's most prestigious properties (chapter 1). I competed with major-bracket firms to comanage Starbucks's IPO (chapter 2). Working alongside Henry Kissinger, I helped one of Italy's powerhouse multinationals to generate notable shareholder returns and growth (chapter 3). Along the way I ventured into the music and motion picture industries, attending major movie premieres and meeting celebrities like Bono and Pavarotti, and purchased the song "Happy Birthday" for $18 million (chapters 4 and 5). I also planned an ill-advised retail merger to compete with Walmart, only to face a $400 million lawsuit from investors (chapter 6).

After pivoting from investment banking to public service, I helped Bill Clinton gain a second term as president (chapter 7). After joining his administration (chapter 8), I worked to bolster Asian countries experiencing massive economic downturns (chapter 9), secured the first post-Soviet US-Russian oil deal (chapter 10), worked to open new markets throughout Sub-Saharan Africa (chapter 11), and created a minor firestorm upon leaving office (chapter 12). I then pivoted to the nonprofit sphere, transforming the modestly capitalized World Resources Institute (WRI) into one of the world's leading environmental NGOs (chapter 13). These diverse public and private sector experiences prepared me in unique ways for my mission in Egypt, to which I return at the end of this book (chapters 14 and 15).

This book is a wide-ranging memoir. It touches on a number of topics that may not appeal to every reader. For those interested only in finance, I recommend chapters 2–6, where I describe creating an investment banking practice with global businesses, launching IPOs, and creating special-purpose acquisition companies (SPACs) long before they became popular. For readers interested in political fundraising or public service, skip ahead to chapter 7, where I describe my career in New York municipal politics before serving in the Clinton administration (chapters 8–12). Readers interested in economic development and forging change in the developing world should navigate to the final two chapters (14 and 15), where I discuss my work in Egypt and provide a vision for lifting frontier and developing economies out of poverty.[7] But I hope all readers, no matter their background, age, or range of interests, read chapter 13. In discussing my work with the World Resources Institute, this chapter describes the cutting edge of environmental sustainability—a topic relevant to anyone interested in keeping the planet healthy and habitable.

For readers interested in helping the world to progress, but not sure where or how to begin, you might wish to trace my journey from beginning to end. Throughout my career as investment banker and public servant, advising diverse companies and serving on a number of corporate boards, participating in mayoral and presidential election campaigns, and brokering geopolitical alliances as president of EXIM Bank and a US official in Egypt, I've endeavored to add maximal value. It's the same energy I see today, the energy motivating millennials and Gen Z to create a more equitable and sustainable world.

My motivation owes a great debt to my father. As he woke me up each morning, Dad recited the final stanza of Henry Wadsworth Longfellow's poem "A Psalm of Life":

Let us, then, be up and doing,
    With a heart for any fate;
Still achieving, still pursuing,
    Learn to labor and to wait.

To me, the poem imparted a rousing, American-style optimism that powered me out of bed as a child and guided the forward march of my life journey. The stanza also described a patient energy that I've tried to inject into all my pursuits.

During moments of possibility and change in my career, I've relied on the poem's underlying philosophy of forbearance and dedication. As the poem urges, we should apply maximal effort and engagement to all our life pursuits, whether we are helping our local library, reelecting a president, or bolstering a nation like Egypt. My life illustrates, modestly to be sure, the power of patient and humble work, alongside friends and colleagues, watching as the fruits of our labor ripen in the field. I believe all of us can do well by doing good so long as we are patiently "up and doing," working our hardest to build strong, meaningful, and productive relationships with others.

1

An Interpersonal Edge

PHILIP AND HARVEY LAPIDES must have believed I was a natural businessman in 1955 when I began work at Harvey Ltd., their thriving men's clothing store in Providence. I'd always admired these two student-athletes turned haberdashers, marketing Ivy style to "Brown men" in the form of tweed button-down shirts and other fine garments, emblazoning the motto *voici le meilleur* ("the best is here") on their store literature.[8] But in truth, my work with them was not mission driven: I worked there as a nineteen-year-old undergraduate to earn spending money. My parents had come of age during the Great Depression. I hated asking them for money.

One afternoon, during a shift at Harvey's, my eyes turned to an unattractive pair of cuff links in the display window. I had often questioned Harvey's prominent placement of this men's jewelry. They were so unappealing that they hardly belonged under magnification. I pressed the issue that day. "They've been here since we opened the store," Harvey said, conceding the point. "One day someone will buy them. Unless you think you can sell them."

"I can probably sell anything you give me here," I said with youthful cockiness.

He replied that if I sold them, I could keep the money. It was the challenge, not the financial incentive, that motivated me. Within two weeks, I had sold the cuff links and impressed these two pillars of Providence.

AN INFORMAL EDUCATION

The chutzpah of my late adolescence likely owed to the example of my parents. A graduate of Yale and Harvard, my father was an impressive intellectual and attorney. As he used to say, "You aren't really educated unless you speak five languages." He spoke six. Commanding literary knowledge and worldly sophistication, he was a successful real estate investor and loved gardening, reading, and painting. When I was fifteen years old, he asked me to show some of his houses to prospective buyers on the weekends. I enjoyed the work, and the buyers liked me. Though Dad could be charming and funny—he could have everyone in stitches when he told jokes with different accents—he was sometimes a disaster with people, especially when it came to business.

When I was seventeen years old, my father made a grave human-relations error that left a lasting impression on me. He called me one afternoon with exciting news: he was set to buy a radio station on a large tract of land in Tarrytown, a village in Westchester County about twenty-five miles north of New York City. It was a great deal, he explained, and the two of us would have fun learning the radio business. He had negotiated the deal and invited me to accompany him and our family lawyer, Elmer Settle, to the closing. Once we'd convened, my father examined the legal documents and was able to ascertain the price that the seller had paid for the property two years prior. Dad's mood soured. "I think we should change the purchase price because you're making way too much money on this transaction," he said flatly.

The seller was taken aback. He admitted that he had purchased the land for a modest sum, but the terms were set in print. My father persisted, and the seller walked out.

My father was indignant in the car on the ride home, but I refused to indulge him. What did the original sale price matter, I asked, especially after he had discovered so much potential for the parcel? We could have made a lot of money and mastered a new industry together. "You're probably right," my dad conceded. "I just hated seeing him make so much." That conversation haunted me, and still serves as an example of how not to operate in life.

If my dad taught me through blunders, any success I had with interpersonal matters likely owed to the example of my mother, beloved throughout our hometown of Mamaroneck, New York. A successful business owner, Mom ran a small women's clothing boutique and later opened a second location. If the early twentieth century had been more gender inclusive, she would have operated her own retail chain. She had endless patience and generosity of spirit and took great pleasure in serving the families in Mamaroneck. As a child, I'd watch her help a young woman select just the right dress for an event, and the following weekend when her customer returned, Mom eagerly asked how the event went. My mom took a genuine interest in people, remembering their birthdays and other personal milestones. People gravitated to her warmth.

While they diverged in temperament, my parents set a great example of education and personal responsibility for my sister and me. We lived in a home with large bay windows overlooking water and marshlands. I have fond memories of taking our dinghy up the creek, its outboard motor powering me past marshlands to the open water, where the family sailboat was moored in Mamaroneck Harbor. My first real memory in this childhood home dates from 1941, when I was six years old. At this time, few families had a television set and relied on the radio for entertainment and news. One morning, as my parents entertained another couple in the living room, an emergency broadcast aired. My father told me to quiet down, a rare admonition, and they turned with rapt interest to the newscast.

My father later explained that the Japanese had bombed Pearl Harbor, the US naval base in Hawaii. To keep abreast of the war, we developed a family ritual of listening to the morning news before school. My father explained

America's decision to join the Allied forces in the invasion of Europe and how that affected every country involved. It was a valuable education about world politics, Britain's role as our ally, and the larger moral stakes involved in the outcome.

One evening four years later, as I was walking down Main Street in Mamaroneck, I encountered neighbors crying openly in the streets. My mother's store, where I was headed that day, was smack in the town center, across from our only movie theater. I routinely met her there after school, helping around the shop until she drove us home. But this day people streamed out of the theater and gathered in my mother's store, many in tears. Here in our small town was a scene playing out across the country—grief at the news that President Franklin Delano Roosevelt (FDR) had died. The great orator and leader who had shepherded America through the Great Depression while enduring a debilitating disease passed on April 12, 1945, less than ninety days into his fourth presidential term. My parents were not notably active in politics, but like many Americans, they supported Roosevelt and were crushed at his passing. We wouldn't experience such a day of mourning in my lifetime until 1963, when President John F. Kennedy was assassinated in Dallas. As with the death of FDR in 1945, Kennedy's passing sent shockwaves of grief and dismay throughout the country and around the world.

The grief attending FDR's death stood in sharp contrast with the celebrations and joy that came just weeks later, when the Axis powers surrendered to the Western Allies. Unlike my parents, whose formative years were marked by the Depression, my sister and I enjoyed a youth of postwar ease. As I made my way through secondary school, I remember sensing America's potency and strength. Following our triumph over Nazism in Europe and the Japanese in the South Pacific, our country seemed to preside effortlessly over an era of affluence and peace. Though I hadn't yet reached political consciousness, I remember the assured leadership of presidents Truman and Eisenhower and the optimism I sensed that our country could help rebuild the world. I don't remember a similar mood of confidence until the early

1990s, when the Soviet and apartheid regimes both fell, giving many the idea that Western-style democracy would triumph.

My father believed that to thrive in this new world of possibility, both his children needed to attend the best schools. My sister did a better job of meeting his expectations, attending the Baldwin School in Bryn Mawr, Pennsylvania, and then having the luxury of choosing among Wellesley, Vassar, and Smith. She chose Smith. I attended Hotchkiss, a boarding school founded in 1891, a feeder school for Yale.[9]

At Hotchkiss, we studied Greek and Latin, addressed each teacher as "professor," attended chapel for our spiritual refinement, and observed a hierarchy among grade levels, with freshman (or "preps") referring to seniors with the respectful title of "sir."[10] Unlike my sister, I lacked sufficient maturity for this environment, and instead of focusing on my studies, I sought acceptance from my peers. Mike Foster and Tom Taylor, who ran track with me and lived on my dormitory floor, defied school rules almost every Saturday night by sneaking away from their rooms after curfew for some fun and a motion picture at the movie theater. I'd soon learn that leaving campus at night is one of the gravest sins a Hotchkiss boarder can commit.

The boys continually baited me to join them, and I resisted the peer pressure, until I caved one Saturday evening (my first big mistake). In preparation for an upcoming track meet, the school had prohibited us from leaving campus that weekend so we could maintain our strength and focus. In willful defiance, the three of us snuck into downtown Lakeville and crawled into the movie theater, where, unbeknownst to us all, I had seated myself directly next to one of our teachers, Mr. Boswell. He pretended not to see me. After the movie, we raced back to the dormitory and entered into a gentlemen's agreement never to disclose anything about the matter.

That midnight, of course, Mr. Boswell entered my room, pointed a flashlight in my face, and barked: "Were you at the movie theater tonight, and if so, who were you with?" I refused to answer. The following morning, headmaster George Van Santvoord, popularly known on campus as "the Duke," convened a general assembly of all the boarders. A graduate of Hotchkiss (and Yale thereafter), the Duke became headmaster in 1926. In the decades since, he had developed a reputation as a disciplinarian and conversationalist prone to unusual gambits.[11] I remember the Duke as a colorful and austere presence. Roaming the corridors, he would grab unsuspecting boys like me by the elbows and say, "Mr. Harmon, do you think that Mickey Mouse should get a driver's license?" He expected a sincere and reasoned response and would always play devil's advocate to whatever answer we gave, telling boys with a straight face how Mickey Mouse would be disastrous on America's highways, imperiling safety and interstate commerce alike.

Hotchkiss students feared his constant questioning and probing. We avoided his table at breakfast, knowing he would engage us in intense, but equally bizarre, conversations like, "How hot is hell?" ("At one time or another, I've heard just about every one of you complain it was 'hot as hell.' Surely you knew what you meant!")[12] But we were all probably too young to appreciate him. It was rumored he counseled presidents Roosevelt and Truman.[13] On this day, however, there would be no playful discussions about fanciful topics. Instead, the headmaster solemnly summoned Mike, Tom, and me to the stage and announced that the faculty would soon vote about whether to suspend or expel us. Later that evening, the three of us watched these proceedings, which resulted in our sequestration.

Hotchkiss administered various forms of punishment and censure, but sequestration was the school's most extreme.[14] For six weeks, sequestered students withdrew from all social life on campus, sometimes taking up temporary residence in the headmaster's home. Walking the halls in silent shame, we attended classes, waited on tables in the refectory, ran the triangle (a grueling five-mile jog around the campus's perimeter and environs), planted trees by the hockey rink in the afternoons, and served on the dreaded "woods squad,"[15] one of the Duke's innovations as headmaster. Though officially involving two hours of working alongside the Duke, helping to clear the school's running trails of brush and debris, the real wood squad challenge was the Duke himself, who engaged the captive boys in discussion topics (e.g., Should the neighboring lake receive freshwater sharks? How many holes exactly should comprise a golf game?).[16]

Some boys fared well under this disciplinary regime, embodying the school's motto of *moniti meliora sequamur* ("Now that we've been admonished, let us follow better ways").[17] One such person was Paul Nitze, who endured sequestration in the early 1920s. Because two of his classmates had been sentenced to the same fate, Nitze created the Sequestered Club and commissioned triangular medals with etchings of little runners, memorializing one of the disciplinary traditions.[18] Given that he went on to become a celebrated politician and cold war strategist, serving as deputy secretary of defense, US secretary of the navy, and director of policy planning for the State Department, the punishment served its purpose. During my time at Hotchkiss, however, the punishment failed to reform me. I chafed under the enforced drudgery and complained about the injustice to the Duke and staged other small mutinies. For my senior year I was "asked not to return."[19]

I was reluctant to relay the news to my father. Without Hotchkiss, I would likely not attend Yale, thus terminating the family legacy. I mustered my courage, told my father about my misbehavior, and detailed the oppressive discipline. My father's reaction surprised me. Together we got into the car and drove to a neighboring prep school, Berkshire, which was about fourteen miles from Hotchkiss in Sheffield, Massachusetts. At Berkshire, I told Headmaster John Godman about my Hotchkiss experience and asked if I could finish my preparatory schooling there. At the time, I viewed this transition as a failure. In hindsight, it was an ideal turn of events. I broke from my father's blueprint and forged my own path to attend Brown instead.

BROWN AND BEYOND

When I arrived at Brown in the fall of 1953, my friends and I quickly realized that we would spend little time in Providence itself. Providence was not the culinary and arts mecca it is today. At midcentury, Providence was best

15

described as seedy. Other than costume jewelry, one of the city's main industries, Providence attracted scant investment and had little by way of tourism, cultural arts, entertainment, and food. This showed in its dilapidated infrastructure—its central train station reminded me of Connecticut's Stamford Transportation Center. Not dangerous like New York in the 1950s, Providence was merely unattractive. Much more fun was to be had driving to Wheaton College or Skidmore for dates or to spend an evening.

Hotchkiss and Berkshire had trained me well, so when I arrived at Brown, I could coast academically. I earned Bs with little work, and explored my interests in English literature, my academic concentration, as well as art history, later serving as the arts editor for the *Brown Daily Herald*, our school newspaper. I also pursued athletics, competing on Brown's freshman tennis team my first year and then participating in various interfraternity sports leagues in my later years. I also rushed Pi Lambda Phi, an inclusive and Jewish-friendly fraternity on campus and one of our campus's leaders in educational achievement. I was proud to join this great group of men, with whom I formed lifelong friendships. Two of my fraternity brothers and I left Brown's on-campus dorms as soon as we could, living in an off-campus apartment in the neighboring and equally rundown city of Pawtucket.

One of the first inklings that, despite my cuff links victory, I might not have been a natural entrepreneur came from observing my friend and fraternity brother Barry Merkin. While I was accumulating spending money at Harvey's haberdashery, he was becoming an entrepreneur—a smart one. At the outset of our undergraduate careers at Brown, he worked in the campus refectory to pay tuition, bussing tables and cleaning up slop. He finally came to me one day and pitched an idea: "A lot of parents," he said, "would love to give their children a birthday cake on their birthdays. I'm going to get a list of all freshmen and sophomores, contact their parents, and offer to arrange a birthday celebration for their sons or daughters for $1."

It was an imaginative proposition. Brown lacked a business school, and Providence had no entrepreneurial ecosystem to foster such ideas. Barry secured a list of all 450 or so incoming Brown students, drafted a letter to each of their parents marketing his services, and received positive responses from a high percentage of them. Barry traded his refectory work for his bustling enterprise. By the time he graduated, the business was a success, and he hatched another masterful idea: sell the venture to two incoming Brown freshmen. When it was time to apply to graduate school, he said, "I don't plan to complete the application to Harvard Business School. That's a tough application. I'm going to write them and tell them the birthday cake story."

"They'll never accept you," I cautioned. "Harvard is so strict." Against my advice, he wrote Harvard Business School and described his venture. They accepted him! As the years passed, we kept in touch, as he became an important source of business for me in the New England area.

I have often told this story to people seeking entrepreneurial advice from me. In the telling I always emphasize that I believed Barry's idea was brilliant, but I ultimately lacked faith that he could execute it. But he remained steadfast to this delivery-service vision, which financed his room and board at Brown and then granted him entry to America's leading business school. Unlike Barry, I can't say that I achieved anything notable at Brown until I joined the board of trustees many years later.

In 1957, I departed Brown for the Wharton School at the University of Pennsylvania. Compared with Providence, Philadelphia was a sprawling metropolis—harder to navigate, and more bustling and exciting. Following my graduation from Brown that June, I married my college sweetheart, Jane, and that September we set up house at Fifty-Second Street and Springfield Avenue. I took up part-time employment at a men's clothier called Eddie Jacob's. Jane and I went to the movies several times a week and explored Philadelphia's artistic and cultural attractions, while I trained my ambitions on the Wharton credential and success in business.

One memory epitomizes my experience at Wharton. My first year, I failed to complete an accounting assignment. After the first examination, the professor decided to motivate the class by announcing everyone's grades aloud. He began with the highest marks of the seventy or so students enrolled in the course, smiling and giving them due recognition. His enthusiasm waned as he made his way down the list, with each low-scoring student receiving a glance or furrowed eyebrow. A good friend of mine, who went on to become a successful New York business executive, was the second from the bottom. But the very lowest score, 37 out of 100, belonged to James Harmon. My classmates swarmed me after class, eager to meet the guy who did so poorly on a multiple-choice exam. The professor's exercise made me a lot of friends. It did not incline me to study more.

I did, however, apply myself to other courses and was interested in some of the material. But Wharton did not suit me. I thrive on classroom debates, public exchanges, or the Socratic method, not on rote memorization of facts gleaned from textbooks about taxes, mergers and acquisitions, and management practices. Harvard's core curriculum was based on case studies and classroom debate, and I would have done much better there than at Wharton, which was more analytical in orientation. As I had at Brown, I focused less on my academic training and more on my work at the haberdashery, and now on my marriage, as well as my percolating plans and ideas for how I'd make my mark in business. I departed Wharton with a master's degree in finance, but I didn't feel like I'd learned a lot.

I learned the most during the summers of 1955, 1957, and 1958 when I commuted to New York City to intern at New York Hanseatic Corporation. Kurt H. Grunebaum, a German investment banker about my father's age, cofounded this bond trading firm in the 1940s.[20] This was my first introduction to Wall Street. I still remember the routine: driving from my parents' home in Mamaroneck, New York, where I lived over the summers, parking at the railway station, boarding a train for a forty-five-minute ride to Manhattan, and then taking the crowded Lexington Avenue subway from Grand Central to 120 Broadway. This hour-and-a-half commute would later pale in comparison to my long excursions each day, where I made my way from Connecticut to Manhattan.

Wall Street today is a shadow of its prestige in the 1950s and '60s. Instead of men and women in casual wear and glued to their mobile devices, I remember a sea of men in suits packed on commuter trains. So as not to encroach on my neighbor, I learned to fold my *New York Times* just so—in clever longitudinal quarters. Investment and commercial banks, located in New York's financial district, dominated the financial community. In the following fifty years, the smartest people in finance largely deserted Wall Street, with the brightest investment bankers joining private equity firms in Midtown Manhattan, and the most talented brokers forming hedge funds based in Connecticut, New Jersey, or Midtown.

The most exciting and harrowing part of this financial services internship was working on the trading room floor. To convey this properly, I must describe an entirely different world, in which the bulk of Hanseatic's trading activities took place directly between parties in over-the-counter markets, instead of exchange trades like the New York Stock Exchange. In the 1950s, Hanseatic's trading room was the heart of the operation, as trading rooms were for many securities firms. This large room accommodated thirty-five to forty people and displayed stocks on large boards accompanied by bid and ask prices. When a broker or dealer wanted to trade, a light illuminated on what looked like an old-fashioned switchboard, leaving traders the option of plugging their line into a socket below the switchboard light, enabling them to quote a price to the interested party. On any given day, the Merrill Lynch line might flash, and I'd plug in to quote a bid or make an offer or counter-offer, depending on the stock prices displayed on the board.

My first summer as an eighteen-year-old intern, I worked as assistant to Wall Street legend Johnny Ohland and Hanseatic's most talented trader. One day, a broker from Merrill Lynch called the room, and I plugged in to the call. "How's your market in Haile Mines?" he asked. I gave him the market price displayed on the board and he responded by offering to sell me 20,000 shares at that price. I accepted.

I turned to Ohland and told him that we bought 20,000 shares. He glared at me, rose from his seat, and slammed his pencil down on the table, unleashing a litany of profanity-laced insults. Apparently, I was the dumbest guy he had ever come across in all of Wall Street. The board, I soon learned, was good for only 100 shares.

The entire room froze. Horrified by my mistake, I remember wanting to crawl into the socket where I'd plugged in my line and hide in embarrassment. Later that morning, Maurice Hart, a small man with a mustache who served as head of trading at Hanseatic, summoned me to his office. "The senior traders and I have been talking, and we're curious to know how a college-educated man like you could have done this. If Merrill had offered to sell a million shares, would you have said yes?" I was mortified.

Years later, I raised this topic with Hart again. He remembered every detail, reminding me he had never seen an error so grave. Like my experience at Hotchkiss, this was a setback. Instead of approaching the trading room with the excitement and abandon of an adolescent, I immediately changed course, now intent on every detail, and ensuring I knew everything before acting.

I ultimately rebounded from this error and, by late May of 1959, had finished at Wharton and landed a full-time job at Hanseatic. While packing up my third-floor walk-up apartment in Philadelphia, my phone rang. It was Professor Gradinsky, one of Wharton's strict and universally admired investment professors. "Mr. Harmon," he declared, "you failed to submit a report that was due months ago." His course required fourteen reports. I had, apparently, submitted only thirteen. If I did not submit this assignment, he informed me, I would fail his course and not receive my degree from Wharton.

I considered my options. What grade had I earned in the course thus far, I asked Professor Gradinsky, bracketing the final assignment. I had earned an A.

"If I don't submit this paper, will you give me a C?" I asked.

He agreed, and I hung up the phone feeling smug. I had passed the course, my degree was forthcoming, and I didn't have to interrupt my packing to churn out another tedious report. Some years later, I ran into Professor Gradinsky. He immediately recalled the story and told me he was surprised at my lack of bargaining prowess. I thought I had nailed the negotiation. Wrong: because I had earned an A in the course, he explained, he would have given me a C if I had asked for it. But he would likewise have given me a B if I had asked for that. "I hope you learn how to negotiate better in business," he said.

I remembered his words for a long time. Yes, I should have asked for a B. Ever since selling those cuff links as an undergraduate, I had experienced a healthy, if entirely unearned, sense of confidence. I had learned from observing my parents, as well as from my setbacks at boarding school and on the trading floor, trying my best to reframe them as learning experiences. But Professor Gradinsky's remarks haunted and humbled me as I prepared to embark on my first permanent job. Maybe there was more that I needed to learn about business, negotiating, and life in general.

AN INVESTMENT BANKING NICHE

When I returned to NY Hanseatic in June 1959, now as a full-time employee, I was twenty-three years old and felt the weight of responsibility to succeed. Many of my friends and colleagues were traveling the world and living as carefree single men, but I had a family. Two months after beginning full-time work, in August of 1959, my first child Debbie was born. She was a pure delight. Jane and I rented a small apartment in New Rochelle right next to the New Haven railway line, near the upscale Larchmont community as well as the hospital where Deb was born. The home's proximity to the tracks eased my daily commute but also created an inconvenience because every time the train passed, the entire place shook.

I began at Hanseatic as a research analyst working under the legendary Herbert O. Wolfe. Herb was around forty-five years old when I joined the firm. Unremarkable in appearance, with his slightly heavy build, medium height, and glasses, Herb was a brilliant analyst, egalitarian in his work behavior. He treated everyone the same, no matter their experience, pedigree, or seniority, asking us all the same probing questions about a company's real value and potential. A former mathematics instructor and microwave radar researcher at MIT, Herb took an intellectual approach to financial analysis. He loved to read annual reports and balance sheets. Among his favorite hobbies were poring over the footnotes of annual reports and chewing on a cigar. Not six years later, at the age of fifty-one, Herb succumbed to cancer. I saw him in the hospital, and he had ten annual reports on his bedcovers.

Herb's talents as a financial analyst outshined even those of Warren Buffett, who was twenty-eight years old when I began at Hanseatic. A confident and personable man, Warren often visited Herb when he was in New York. Warren frequently came sweeping into the office, waving hello to everyone, and saying things like, "You know, you're working for the second-smartest man on Wall Street."

Nevertheless, if Warren was the smartest, and Herb the second, I was struck by the frequency of Warren's visits at the firm to find out what company stock Herb was eyeing. Herb had a talent for identifying undervalued companies. In my early days, one such company was an ice-cream truck business called Good Humor, which, as we say in the business, we started buying at four or five times its most recent, or "trailing," earnings. When shares sell at x times their value, this refers to a benchmark called an "earnings multiple" or P/E (price/earnings) ratio and signifies a firm's current price versus its earnings per share. With excellent growth and experienced management, Good Humor had potential. It represented one of Herb's many successes. We also studied more complicated companies like Investors Diversified Services and New York Water Services, where Herb really came alive—the more complicated it was, the more fascinated he became.

From day one of my work at the research department, Herb asked me to become familiar with a company's "price earnings" and "price-to-book," so that I could determine why it was selling for its current price. The *Wall Street Journal* published a daily digest of earnings reports. Every morning, Herb explained, I needed to consider each company's reported earnings against its market price and determine its price-earnings ratio, its risk-rewards ratios, and other factors we needed to consider when evaluating the company.

Herb constantly probed me about different companies, soliciting my input on what to buy. Under his tutelage and disciplined observation, I developed a theory later that year that unlisted, lesser-known companies far from New York with light trading volumes often had little following and were likely to be cheap. To prove my theory, I researched companies throughout the Southwest, narrowed my selections to a handful, and proposed visiting their headquarters in search of attractive investment opportunities. Given that I was one year out of graduate school, I was surprised when Herb agreed to let me visit the CEOs of six publicly traded companies. I returned home with no purchase recommendations, but I like to believe Herb thought the trip had value in educating a young analyst.

Later that year, the firm needed a corporate finance analyst to attend a meeting of two pharmaceutical companies considering a merger. At the research department one morning, Herb asked if anyone was interested in a trip to Philadelphia. Alone among ten analysts, I raised my hand, excited at the prospect of being part of the merger discussion. I stayed up that night reading the relevant accounting reports. The following morning, I knew more about both companies than any of the attorneys present. Although the deal was not completed, I left a good impression on the professionals, who, I learned, called the president of Hanseatic to report favorably on my work. That trip taught me the importance of being prepared.

My first big break came in early 1961 when the president of Hanseatic asked me to attend a meeting in his office with Robert Futterman, a thirty-three-year-old real-estate syndicator who bought residential properties and syndicated them out to individual investors. I recognized Futterman as a talented realtor and, as a strategy to raise capital, I suggested that he consider a "purchase and exchange" offering in which investors could exchange their limited partnership interests for shares of the Futterman Corporation. The corporation agreed, and, after the registration statement became effective, Hanseatic made a market in the new shares and offered investment banking help to the newly constituted corporation. The new owners of the Futterman Corporation, like many of their industry counterparts, were experienced in buying and selling properties but not in running larger umbrella companies, and so might need our investment banking expertise.

Wall Street largely favored industrial companies and banks over publicly owned real estate companies. The real estate industry's ease of entry meant it lacked prestige. Consequently, many on Wall Street viewed public real estate companies as poorly run, reasoning that their executives lacked training in management. They neglected business fundamentals like strategic planning in favor of increasing rents or reducing building and maintenance costs. Later that year, when the Futterman Corporation encountered cashflow problems and struggled to pay dividends to shareholders, the company retained Hanseatic for financial advice.

Several years later, Futterman's lawyers asked if I would serve as president. Futterman had been consuming uppers and downers, as they were called then: amphetamines in the morning, sedatives at night. He died at age thirty-three, just months after I began to work with him. I lacked the experience to run the company, however, and declined the offer. This was the first of many decisions I would make to be an advisor instead of a principal at a company.

Instead, I created a real-estate-oriented, financial-advisory service business with relatively little competition. In lieu of taking the traditional route of providing underwriting for any of these large real estate companies, as we might have done for industrial companies, we instead followed the same formula we used with Futterman: we charged a fee for helping a company file an exchange offering, and once it was deemed effective, created a market for the new company shares, offering a fee-based advising service for those interested.

Since that time, analysts have commented on how the IPO is in trouble, as many businesses choose to avoid expensive underwriting schemes by listing their companies directly on an exchange (as tech giants Spotify and Slack have done), or through back-end runarounds like special-purpose acquisition companies (SPACs). When I read about company issuers in the *Wall Street Journal* or *Economist* devising such "new" ways to avoid public underwriting, I shake my head, recalling our doing the same thing in the early 1960s. With this method, Hanseatic became the most active market maker for national real estate companies. Before I was thirty years old, I had almost ten such clients.

This use of exchange offerings as a vehicle for real estate investment increased in visibility, and in 1965 the New School in Manhattan asked me to deliver a lecture on the topic. The organizers charged a fee to attend, and hundreds purchased tickets. As friends and clients shared their enthusiasm about attending, I became concerned. With no public speaking experience, I checked the yellow pages for a speech coach and drove to New York City before the event for coaching. "Let's go over the speech," said the instructor. I hadn't written a word.

The day of my presentation I arrived at the New School to a large lecture hall with an ample stage and no dais, and stared into the crowd, spotting many colleagues and other business associates. Somehow, I managed to explain the benefits of purchase-and-exchange offerings without embarrassing myself too much. I'm still horrified that I accepted the invitation, though in coming decades I'd become a confident public speaker. As chair of EXIM Bank many years later, I'd deliver three to four speeches a week.

Around that time, I was reading the *Wall Street Journal* on the train into the city and saw that Tishman Realty Construction, one of the country's most prestigious real estate, construction, and investment companies, was planning an exchange offering of its own. I ripped the article from the paper, stuffed it into my suit pocket, and thought it over on my way to the office. Since Julius Tishman founded this company in 1898, its success had turned the Tishmans into one of New York's real estate dynasties, akin to the Zeckendorfs.[21] In 1953, Tishman built a twenty-two-story building at 460 Park Avenue and Fifty-Seventh Street, known as the Davies building.[22] The building was now fully depreciated, meaning that the company faced an ordinary income or capital-gains rate. To avoid this tax liability, company accountants and investment bankers had already suggested that Tishman do an exchange, offering shareholders an opportunity to exchange Tishman shares for those in a new trust that would own the office building at 460 Park. If shareholders tendered their shares, this transaction would constitute a liquidation and therefore avoid significant tax liability.

After reading about this transaction in the paper, I knew I could improve it. After all, what happened if Tishman shareholders wanted to retain their preexisting shares and weren't inclined to exchange? Many shareholders at Tishman might be understandably skeptical about trading their publicly traded shares in a thriving multinational corporation for shares in a new entity that owned only one building. To avoid the risk of people clinging to the parent company stock, we could structure a "standby agreement" as follows. After pricing the new trust shares at a greater price than the publicly traded Tishman shares, the investment banks managing the offering would stand by, ready to purchase all remaining or "unsubscribed shares" in the trust for the price quoted. After conceiving the idea, I asked my secretary to call the company's chair, Norman Tishman. I got through and told him my idea. I'm amazed I had the chutzpah to call him, that his secretary connected us, and that he agreed to meet with me a week later to discuss his upcoming subscription offering.

Though I had confidence from managing a few subscription offerings, I lacked the experience of my colleagues at Morgan Stanley, whom Tishman retained at the time. Hanseatic was just beginning its investment banking business and was little match for this powerhouse. The following week, I met Norman Tishman in his office. Also present was a partner from Morgan Stanley. I remember the meeting like it happened last week, Tishman seated at his desk, his investment banker at his side, and me standing before them both, explaining how my idea would work.

Though well known on Wall Street, the standby mechanism was especially feared since the 1929 market crash. In business school, most banking and corporate finance students learned the story of Goldman Sachs and Morgan Stanley, both of them about six or seven days into a standby deal with Macy's department store when Black Tuesday sent stock prices plummeting. Following the stock market crash, many Macy's shares were left unsubscribed, either because people were frightened to spend any money or because they couldn't afford a purchase. Morgan Stanley and Goldman were legally bound to stand by and purchase remaining shares, something that nearly bankrupted both investment houses. After this harrowing event, investment bankers in America came to fear standby deals. This might be why Morgan Stanley didn't propose it to Tishman. But given the market stability of the 1960s and the cash flow from this real estate property, I was comfortable taking the risk of a standby, even though a world war or other cataclysm could intervene, leaving Hanseatic liable for outstanding shares in this new building.

Tishman and his colleague from Morgan Stanley asked for half an hour. I waited in the reception area. They then returned, agreed to the merits of the deal, and offered me a $100,000 fee for the idea. In another attack of chutzpah, I declined the offer and insisted that Hanseatic comanage the offering, with Hanseatic appearing on the cover of the prospectus next to Morgan Stanley. This was a bigger ask, and they needed a few days to confer with Morgan Stanley's partners. After all, when the prospectus graced the desks of most finance people on Wall Street, they'd see Morgan next to an unknown firm. If I could get Hanseatic on the prospectus with this leading investment banking house, it would be a major coup.

In hindsight, the Morgan Stanley partner should have laughed at the suggestion that a junior investment banker at a small house comanage an offering for his client. I'm not sure I would have entertained the suggestion if our roles had been reversed. But they both contacted me days later, ready to pay me the fee and agreeing to a comanaged deal, on the condition that Morgan Stanley's name appear on the more prestigious left-hand side of the prospectus, with Hanseatic on the right.

The deal was a success. Upon seeing the fixed price as well as Morgan Stanley and Hanseatic's support for the deal, shareholders became interested in tendering their shares. With the exchange oversubscribed, neither participating investment firm had any shares to purchase. But it wasn't the fee itself and the success of the deal that excited me. By exercising a little imagination and even more boldness in the supposedly closed and conservative world of investment banking, I had scored a major achievement. It's probably hard to imagine how open America's financial community was at that time. I'm still amazed that a junior investment banker in his twenties, working at a small firm, could call the chair of a large corporation listed on the New York Stock Exchange, and somehow persuade him, along with one of the most prestigious investment banking firms in the world, to comanage an offering. In London or elsewhere on the Continent, I could never have pitched such an idea to a large company. And in today's America, I doubt a junior associate could call up the chair of a major organization, secure a meeting the following week, and broker a deal like that. I remember walking around Manhattan in the following weeks, thinking about how wonderful it was that opportunities like this existed in America.

Seeing that I could generate income, many of my clients began asking me to invest their money. In the mid-1960s, when I was thirty years old, I formed an investment fund called Kettle Creek, named after the street where I lived in Weston, Connecticut, and many of my clients eagerly joined, entrusting me with $50,000, $500,000, or $5 million, which I managed for them in exchange for modest fees. If the investments didn't conflict with the business I was doing at Hanseatic, there was no problem or conflict of interest. Thanks to my success with Tishman Realty and other public offerings that followed, I had created the investment banking business within Hanseatic, and new businesses like ACE publishing came my way.

ACE was one of the leading US paperback publishers specializing in science fiction and non-risqué romance novels. I was intrigued in the potential I saw in the operation and sought to add value to the publishing industry. My friend Barry Merkin, of Brown's birthday-cake fame, was languishing at his job at Standex International, and I persuaded him to serve as the president. Drawing on the Kettle Creek Fund, we assembled a group of investors and purchased the publishing business in 1968. We garnered so much interest in ACE that first year that we did a private placement, and its market value increased by several multiples of its purchase price.

With the substantial income I was generating in the late 1960s, I began looking for ways to shelter it. One day, as I glanced through one of my father's favorite books on planting and nurseries, I noticed that when you buy or plant baby crops, they qualify as an expense against your ordinary income. I immediately turned to Martin ("Marty") David Ginsburg. The acclaimed tax attorney and law professor was also husband to Ruth Bader Ginsburg, the future Supreme Court justice. Marty and I were friends, and I met his wife several times, having no idea about the illustrious career awaiting her. "If I buy a large nursery," I asked Marty, "can I deduct the expense of planting seeds and baby plants from my income, and then sell the nursery as a capital gain?" Marty said he'd do some research because that scheme sounded too good to be true. The next day he called me saying, "It works!"

I began looking for attractive farms and nurseries, eventually settling on one of the largest rhododendron nurseries in the country. That weekend I took my father, who was skeptical of the tax advantage, to Sudlersville, Maryland, and we toured the multiacre nursery, admiring the magnificent plants. I borrowed a little bit to purchase the farm and proceeded to expense all my baby plants for three years. Now I was the largest grower of rhododendrons in the United States. After collaborating on the nursery business with my father, my family and I sold the nursery at a significant capital gain. Decades later, my chief of staff in government, Andrea Adelman, came running into my office. Andrea was in her first year of law school at Georgetown: "You know the story you once told me about buying the farm?" she exclaimed. "It's right here," she said, holding a textbook. Sure enough, Marty Ginsburg had written about a father-son team who bought a farm, expensed it, and sold it for a profit. It was in his multivolume textbook on tax mergers, acquisitions, and buyouts.

In 1969, Kettle Creek was doing great, ACE was worth three to five times more than we'd invested in it, I was successfully sheltering income with the rhododendron farm, and I'd created a substantial investment banking operation within Hanseatic. I'd struggled in the fifties, making mistakes at boarding school and during my internships, and I strove to find my niche in the world. But the sixties were great, and I fondly remember the thriving US economy, my community in Weston, and my growing family.

But as the sixties yielded to the seventies, the economy began to change, and my firm remained static. While Hanseatic had been an ideal place to begin a career, it was still predominantly a trading business, and I wanted to be an investment banker. In the early 1970s, I began alerting the cofounder and president, Kurt Grunebaum, that I was thinking of leaving, unless he wanted to broaden the scope of the business to encompass investment banking. It was a big ask. His son Peter was several years my senior, and although he hadn't been building a business like me, I had a feeling Kurt wanted to keep New York Hanseatic a smaller family operation.

He was a wonderful boss and mentor who hosted my wife, Jane, and me at his home each month. We were introduced to many of his European clients whom he'd also invited, drank wonderful wine, and viewed his spectacular art collection of Old Masters and German expressionists. At Christmas gatherings, he'd sometimes offer me another bonus or a painting for my own collection. I always appreciated his generosity but stayed focused on my desire to diversify the services at Hanseatic and occupy more of a leadership role. If the company didn't change, it was probably time for me to transition or "repot" myself elsewhere.

As I contemplated a move, I also began thinking about the shape of my career and my larger industry ambitions. Building wealth had proven much easier than I'd ever imagined, and infinitely more rewarding than school. Now that I understood the fundamentals of corporate finance, investment analysis, money, and banking, I saw I could make a difference in my industry. But I wasn't like my mentors Herb Wolfe or Warren Buffett, both of whom were investment experts. When Herb asked someone to go to Philadelphia to sit in on the meetings for the pharmaceutical merger, Warren thought I was wasting time. "What are you doing?" he later asked me. "Those two days are better spent studying a company and considering an investment." That's why Warren built a spectacular investment company.

Herb and Warren never wanted to work on managing relationships among clients, overseeing mergers and acquisitions, or anything in the corporate finance world. They wanted to show returns for their investors and accumulate capital. That's true of many hedge fund and private equity managers today, who find building capital and making a great fortune supremely motivating. But my interests were more in people than annual reports, which is why I gravitated to investment banking transactions and building an advisory business. Though I also wanted to realize investor returns and generate wealth for my firm, I derived my greatest personal and professional payoffs in building client relationships and helping businesses through difficult times.

By 1970, as I served on eight or nine corporate boards, had about ten corporate clients, and had a net worth large enough to retire, I began to see many of my colleagues fleeing finance for sunnier industries. While finance thrived in the strong markets and general affluence of the sixties, the market crash of 1969 heralded a more difficult decade ahead. The country became enmeshed in the bloodiest parts of the quagmire in Vietnam, began running significant trade deficits, and suffered the disgrace of the Watergate scandal. These events negatively impacted the financial community, as investment bankers saw profits evaporate as the economy entered the nightmarish era of "stagflation," when inflation occurs concurrently with economic stagnation.

As the world wrestled with stagflation, war, and economic transition, I briefly considered retiring from business to spend more time with my three children, play tennis, and increase my support for the Weston school system. But I declined this passing thought and instead spent the following years building relationships and executing transactions. What attracted me to real estate advising, print publishing, and even rhododendron farming was the same impulse that took me to a new investment banking house, where I served as a Wall Street advisor to important national companies, the subject of the next chapter. This same spirit later inspired me to help with Bill Clinton's reelection and become a public servant. This was no time to retire—my journey at "up and doing" was just beginning.

2

Westward Expansion

A SHORT WALK FROM New York City's Rockefeller Center was the 21 Club, a Prohibition-era speakeasy that hosted the annual dinner of partners at Wertheim, the financial firm I joined in 1974. A New York City icon, the restaurant was festooned with memorabilia bestowed by presidents Kennedy and Clinton, while American dynastic families like the Vanderbilts and Mellons donated the jockey statues that framed the balcony overhanging the entrance.[23] The first time I walked in, I felt as if transported to an F. Scott Fitzgerald novel, awash in the glamour of the Interwar period. With its cherrywood paneling and silk tablecloths, the place conjured old-world elegance.

For the twenty or so partners who attended this annual black-tie event, the seating assignments mattered more than the décor. If people found themselves seated in the corner, they might become what the Harmon family terms "persulted." My father coined this term—technically a portmanteau—to indicate someone simultaneously "pouting" and "insulted."

A peculiar policy also governed these annual festivities: no wives. This was a serious dinner, per the logic of Wertheim's founding generation, where men convened to talk about politics and weighty matters. One year, a man brought his wife by accident; after her cocktail, she was escorted out.

A few years after I joined the investment bank, the partners voted to allow wives to attend the annual partner dinners. But later, when I became the firm's chair and CEO, partners began to chafe at this policy, wondering if marriage was necessary for attendance, and instead whether a long-term partner or fiancée might suffice. I was able to avoid such interpersonal drama because my right hand, Steve Kotler, took pains to ensure that everyone was organized and well placed. Partners still approached me and said, "Look I'm separated right now, but in a serious relationship. Can I bring my date?" That sounded reasonable, until Steve approached me with more people, wondering if they could bring their dates. It was a mess, leaving me to adjudicate what constituted a "serious relationship." I eventually came up with a "one-year relationship" threshold but received grief for that too ("We've been dating for six months, and I might marry her!"). Didn't we have better things to focus on than this?

After repotting my ten to twelve clients and small business team to Wertheim investment bank in the mid-1970s, I routinely contended with such cultural and personality differences. As I'd come to discover, many of Wertheim's partners, rooted in classic merchant banking and old-world aristocracy, approached business in such a different way. I was a young and ambitious man looking to create a stable, client-based investment banking business.

When I arrived at Wertheim, the firm resembled a private investment club, with its partners focused on investing their own, or firm, capital. With the notable exception of Peter Schoenfeld, who would go on to create a successful global asset management firm, Wertheim lacked major revenue generators or "rainmakers." Along with my ambitious and talented colleague, Steve Kotler, I spent the next two decades at the firm aggressively soliciting new business and increasing corporate finance revenue, elevating myself to the status of resident rainmaker. As I describe in this chapter, I helped attract diverse companies like Starbucks and Mountain Fuel Supply to Wertheim, all the while transforming the firm from a mid-twentieth-century merchant bank to a modern twenty-first-century investment bank.

OLD-WORLD WERTHEIM

Following my decision to leave Hanseatic in the early 1970s, I had considered several firms to move my team and client base. I briefly thought of joining one of several bulge-bracket firms—First Boston, Merrill Lynch, Morgan Stanley, Goldman Sachs, Salomon Brothers—the most important multinational entities that dominated the investing banking world. I ultimately chose Wertheim over Goldman for the same reason I'd later choose to stay at EXIM Bank instead of moving to the Department of Treasury when serving in government: I could have more autonomy and make a greater financial and humanitarian impact at the lesser-known organizations.

At the time I joined its ranks, Wertheim was one of twenty or so "major bracket" firms, distinguishing itself from the 150-plus securities firms on Wall Street specializing in different areas like brokerage transactions, asset management, and corporate finance. That meant that Wertheim was prestigious enough to manage public offerings and compete with industry giants without being a giant itself. I could distinguish myself there, instead of competing against ten other James Harmons at a firm like Goldman Sachs.

Wertheim began in 1927 as an elite merchant bank, focusing its business on investing the wealth of its own partners and high-net-worth clients, and later on underwriting commercial loans. One of the cofounders, Maurice Wertheim, was a philanthropist, environmentalist, art collector, and chess enthusiast, who organized and personally financed a chess competition between Soviet Russia and the United States in 1946, likely hoping it might defray cold war hostilities.[24] When he died in 1950, bequeathing his valuable collection of impressionist art to his alma mater Harvard, leadership at Wertheim passed to cofounder Joseph Klingenstein. Over the following two decades, Klingenstein expanded the reach of the company's underwriting operation and created an excellent research department. Both founders, along with other firm partners, hailed from Harvard and Yale and had conservative, if not snobby, reputations. As a graduate from the lesser-esteemed Brown who had worked odd jobs throughout college, my background and overall ethos differed from Wertheim's old guard.

My first opportunity to exert some influence over this culture came six months after I joined the firm, in December 1974, when senior partner Fred Klingenstein came to my office and proposed I become a partner, offering to increase my salary and proposing a 2.5 percentage of the partnership's profits. This wasn't much of a financial enticement because, even in the economically lean years of the early 1970s, I was generating several million in revenue a year and keeping the standard nonpartner rate of 25 percent. "That's fine, Fred. Whatever you want to start me at. I'm going to do a lot of business." Though I'd be losing income, the prestige of becoming a partner my first year was more important.

Partnership at Wertheim came with perks. The firm employed a wait-staff for its partners, formally attired in black. Accordingly, every morning, a woman named Hermine waited on me with freshly squeezed orange or carrot juice, served on a silver tray topped with white doilies. There were fine midday meals, again served by Hermine, in one of the partners' four dedicated dining rooms, where I hosted guests. My long-term associate Margaret Engelhardt likes to remind me that she ate peanut butter and jelly at her office desk. But I also remind Margaret that, after I boarded a train back to Connecticut, my wife would jolt me back into the real world, instructing me to take the trash out after dinner.

A few years after becoming vice chair of the firm in 1980, I also enjoyed a company car and driver. Replacing the train with a car service was efficient, as I could speak with colleagues in London or Milan in the early hours, with no background noise or distractions, throughout my daily commute to and from Connecticut, and on my constant trips to and from the airport. My driver Tony, who zipped the Jaguar around New York City with a certain recklessness, frightened many in the vehicle. When my friend and former White House chief of staff Leon Panetta came into town, he would routinely say, "Jim, can I get Tony tomorrow?" If I didn't have a pressing schedule, I'd always agree. Leon preferred to sit up front with Tony as they seized every shortcut possible around the city.

SELLING STARBUCKS

Wertheim's research prowess, well known in the finance industry, helped me generate investment banking business and compete with industry leaders in managing corporate IPOs. Dan Levitan was a corporate finance associate specializing in the restaurant industry, and Bob Israel was a Wertheim colleague specializing in oil and gas.[25] In the summer of 1991, Bob called Dan and asked him to visit a company called Starbucks. "They're in the coffee business," Bob clarified. This food retailer was foreign to the type of industrially oriented companies that Wertheim typically advised. It was also foreign to the discerning American palate. In the early 1990s, coffee came in oversize Maxwell House cans with tin lids.

Despite his skepticism, Dan accompanied Bob to Seattle to meet Starbucks founder Howard Schultz. This was long before the internet, and Dan informally asked about the product around Seattle. "I hear this is a coffee town," he said to the hotel concierge, the taxi driver, and office assistant. "Where do you like to get yours?" Without exception, they all said that they patronized a small, fast-growing company called Starbucks. Before their meeting, Dan and Bob visited a busy coffee kiosk in the lobby of a Seattle office building near their hotel. They waited in line, ordered a coffee, drank it, and still didn't understand the appeal of the caffeinated beverage or the strange kiosk setup. But after meeting with Schultz that day, Dan discovered an incredibly passionate and innovative leader. An investment banker responsible for finding new food and restaurant businesses, Dan came to believe he'd discovered the next great sensation. Starbucks's unit economics were terrific, and it was highly successful in its initial cities of Seattle, Portland, Vancouver, and Chicago. More important, the company had a daring vision: to become a global household brand by revolutionizing a stale product category.

After Schultz asked Dan for Wertheim to compete for the opportunity to comanage Starbuck's initial public offering (IPO), Dan knew Wertheim's partners would be a tough sell. In general, most New York investors were skeptical of food-based consumer brands that began on the West Coast. And they didn't like waiting in line for items like coffee! But Wertheim was competing against Goldman Sachs as well as the "four horsemen" of 1990s finance—Alex. Brown Inc., Hambrecht & Quist Group, Robertson Stephens & Co., and Montgomery Securities—so-called because they underwrote approximately 130 IPOs a year.[26] To compete against their formidable research teams and underwriting departments, Dan knew he needed to show Schultz that everyone at Wertheim strongly supported Starbucks.

And that included my support. Dan called me one day, pleading with me to join him and John Rohs—a talented analyst specializing in restaurants—in Seattle to pitch Wertheim for the upcoming IPO. I was in London on business and eager to return home. "I don't know," I said, thinking of the business that awaited me in New York. "This is an awfully small company, and I don't even like coffee." As Dan told me about the opportunity, I decided to give my young colleague a shot, and rescheduled my flight from New York to Seattle.

We arrived for the pitch in a limo, which we'd later learn the Starbucks team found pretentious. But when Schultz's secretary gave us a tour of the roasting plant, Dan and I asked many questions about the art and science of the roasting process. I was intrigued, and apparently Schultz was looking for people to show such interest and to see the value of his methods. We'd thus made both negative and positive impressions by late afternoon when Wertheim gave the last pitch of the day. It was a long meeting, wherein Schultz and other Starbucks directors asked detailed sets of questions. Our team had prepared diligently, and Dan proved a strong evaluator of early-stage companies, seeking to discern the strength of the Starbucks team, their resilience, and a vision that would resonate among consumers.

As we'd shortly learn, Schultz's product, which the coffee mogul routinely termed the "Guinness of coffee," brought something new to the American corporate landscape. When analyzing why Japanese corporations outperformed their American counterparts at the time, many in the finance industry identified "worker engagement" as a key variable. American assembly-line workers couldn't stop assembly lines if they saw problems, while in Japan, workers had an obligation to stop them and rectify anything amiss. We all liked Schultz's more Japanese approach to his company, valuing his "part-ners" (as Starbucks refers to its employees), customers, and stakeholders as integral to his brand and vision and empowering them in everyday oper-ations. Today we're accustomed to companies needing higher callings and compelling brand identities and values, but Starbucks led this trend in the twentieth century.

After our Seattle meeting, I was eager to manage the 165-store com-pany's IPO. Though still dubious about Schultz's conviction that people of the future would "meet at Starbucks" for coffee, I was nonetheless confi-dent about the company's future growth. Fred Klingenstein disagreed and resisted our involvement because Starbucks's price-earnings ratio was high. "Why do we want to be associated with something selling so expensively? I would never buy a share at twenty times last year's earnings. It's a foolish thing to do."

"Listen, Fred," I tried to explain as gently as I could, "there's a lot of people who want to invest in companies like Starbucks. Even if you or War-ren Buffett wouldn't buy it personally, there's a world of investors who see future potential." Discussions like these epitomized the difference between Fred and me. I was interested in the deal because of the public and larger institutional investor interest in companies like Starbucks, and also because leading investment companies like Wertheim were increasingly occupying the role of marketer, curating products to offer the investing community. From his merchant banking position, Fred couldn't see this vision and was instead fixated on its price-earnings ratio and judged the transaction on whether he would commit his personal capital to it. Budding venture cap-italists like Dan represented an even different trajectory as he gravitated to mission-driven, "high-risk, high-reward" firms like Starbucks, seeing its great management, strong product, and vast market size as responsible for justify-ing the high multiple.

Four days after our pitch in Seattle, Schultz gave Wertheim the business. Apparently, my having flown in from overseas to participate underscored Wertheim's commitment to Shultz and Starbucks's directors. Demand for

Starbucks shares was terrific, and it became one of the most recognizable brands in the world. When Wertheim and Alex. Brown took Starbucks public on June 26, 1992, it sold for $17 a share and has enjoyed a compounded growth rate of 22 percent each year since—had you invested $10,000 in SBUX in 1992, it would be worth $2.6 million in the spring of 2020.[27] At the time of the transaction, Starbucks was worth $240 million, and today the global company, with 30,000-plus stores, is worth $125 billion. No one, except perhaps Schultz himself, could have predicted the market success and cult-like following the company would inspire.

Despite my own hesitations about the long-term viability of Starbucks, it was an attractive opportunity because it could elevate Wertheim to not just participate in underwriting syndicates, but to help manage them. Traditionally, when companies like Starbucks decide to launch an IPO, they select an investment bank to manage a group or "syndicate" of securities firms to distribute new shares to their customers. That distribution of the investment bank's initial purchase of shares and the reselling of them to clients is called underwriting. Following the Securities Act of 1933, the US government scrutinizes this process, requiring investment bankers to submit a preliminary prospectus of the company to the Securities and Exchange Commission (SEC).[28] Only after SEC review, ensuring a company's descriptions are accurate, its practices legal, and accounting records satisfactory, can the syndicate manager generate a final prospectus, which by law must be disseminated to every participant in the syndicate and to each buyer of the shares.

In 2018, a digital music company called Spotify avoided an underwritten offering, listing company shares directly on the New York Stock Exchange. Other technology companies have since followed suit, circumventing the underwriting process that firms like Wertheim provided for so long, avoiding significant fees but also missing the assistance investment bankers can bring to the process. This may be a new industry norm, especially after the summer of 2020, when the SEC approved a rules' change, allowing companies to avoid the IPO process but still raise new capital.[29] Venture capitalists like Dan Levitan have moved from investing in IPOs to participating in "series A" funding, capitalizing promising new companies in their early growth in exchange for equity ownership.

For most of the twentieth century, however, traditional underwriting predominated. Because of its wealth and capital, Wertheim participated in these syndicates, especially with its historic clients (who seemed to wane every year). When I arrived at the firm, however, Wertheim hadn't managed an offering in five years. I was intent on leveraging Wertheim's reputation to build a business that could compete with top-bracket firms and the four horsemen of the 1990s. Four years after I joined Wertheim, we advised Montedison, a prestigious Italian company, and later invited Goldman Sachs and First Boston Corporation to participate in several underwriting syndicates for its affiliated companies. I then capitalized on Wertheim's elevated status and deep research knowledge to manage a series of domestic IPOs like Starbucks's.

MANAGING MOUNTAIN FUEL

While corporate finance associates like Dan Levitan took their career learnings from Wertheim and applied them to the venture-capital model, I always valued advising companies as an investment banker. And one of my most important clients was Mountain Fuel Supply (MFS). Our relationship began in 1977 when Fred Klingenstein asked me to join him for lunch with the chair and general counsel of MFS, one of Utah's largest companies. A natural gas utility servicing parts of Utah and Wyoming, MFS was also an oil and gas exploration and production company.[30]

MFS's top management had traveled to New York for a two-and-a-half-hour lunch where we all became acquainted. During the meal, we formed our first impressions of MFS chair, president, and CEO Bud Kastler. At just under six feet, Bud was husky and gruff, though I sensed he was kind-hearted and fair. During the meal, he turned to Fred and said, "We'd love to have Jim Harmon visit our offices in Salt Lake City."

"Well, that's up to Jim," Fred replied, "but I'm sure he would consider it."

"Meanwhile, Fred, would you vote your shares with management in the upcoming annual meeting? That will help us against the shareholders challenging us for control of the company." As Fred and I learned over lunch, MFS was facing a proxy battle for control of the board of directors.

"I'll certainly think about it," Fred replied.

On the elevator following lunch, I asked Fred how many MFS shares he owned. He shrugged his shoulders, completely unaware of his position in the intermountain energy giant. I figured he owned a reasonable position— enough to inspire MFS managers to travel across the country to visit us. Five minutes later Fred called me on the phone saying he owned $3 million in MFS shares. I asked how he couldn't remember such a large investment. "I can't remember every million-dollar position I have," he responded. I paused, reflecting on how very rich my partner was.

A few days following the lunch, Bud Kastler asked me to consider joining the board of directors, a corporate board that I'd later learn comprised Utah's business elite, which largely overlapped with senior officials of the Mormon church, known formally as the Church of Jesus Christ of the Latter-day Saints (LDS). Almost everyone in Utah and Wyoming heated their homes with MFS gas. Unlike Con Edison in New York, however, westerners viewed utility companies as the heart and soul of their states. They had cachet. Playing an outsize role in Utah politics and institutions, the LDS church routinely installed its leaders on the MFS board.

A few weeks after I accepted the board offer, I traveled to Salt Lake City and began to learn about Utah. As I stepped into the terminal, I found delegations of families greeting loved ones returning home from missionary work. The church sends young men, and occasionally young women, abroad, where they master the language of their host country and go door-to-door proselytizing locals. Enormous crowds of people greeted these young men in their freshly starched white shirts, basking in the hugs and kisses of family members. What a great business idea, I remember joking at the time. You hire families to greet businesspeople during their travels, making them feel warmly received at various destinations.

As I moved past these airport reunions, I quickly navigated to my car, knowing that Bud Kastler's assistant, Clare Coleman, had arranged for a tour of MFS. After deplaning, however, I discovered my imagined "Miss Coleman," a famous actress, was instead an experienced, thoughtful, and intelligent businessman who oversaw the company's pipeline business. He explained the entire operation to me, including the pipelines and oil and gas exploration, and showed me the field areas where they were drilling. Over the next few days, I began to learn both about the business and the people of Utah. Like me, they worked hard, loved outdoor exercise, and didn't drink very much. Framed by the Wasatch mountains with their ample ski lodges, Salt Lake City was a beautiful place. It also had grand streets much better suited for jogging than the cramped thoroughfares of New York, Boston, and Washington.

At the company headquarters, I familiarized myself with the proxy fight I'd learned about over lunch in New York. I was long accustomed to such conflicts, which typically occur when investors are unhappy with company priorities, the perks the management have arrogated to themselves, or with a merger or acquisition managers have pursued. During such conflicts, well-resourced shareholders often solicit support from others before the annual meeting, voting in blocs to install new directors that management hasn't approved or enact new policies and procedures. That was precisely the scenario unfolding here, as a disgruntled former employee who occupied a senior position at the company had organized an effort to convince shareholders to support a new slate of directors. Helping MFS's management navigate this proxy fight was my first assignment with the company.

I asked the company for a list of institutional investors and reached out to those with whom Wertheim had relationships. In my judgment, this proxy contest or "solicitation," to use investment banking terminology, was never a serious threat to the company. To accomplish a takeover and challenge corporate management, families or corporations need to control large holdings of shares. A diffuse group of public shareholders and institutions owned most of MFS, making it an unlikely target. Management easily won the proxy fight, and afterward, people at the company often called me with questions about investor positions. With me on the board, MFS now had a friend on Wall Street who could advise on financial and shareholder matters.

This initial proxy solicitation, which established my relationship with the company, underscored Mormon dominance in the region, and revealed how the power of MFS reflected and magnified the power of the church. Among other high-ranking members, church presidents Spencer W. Kimball and Nathan Eldon Tanner served on the board. Successful proxy fights would be unlikely as few MFS investors wanted to side with outsiders, risking persecution or ostracism. I would later encounter groups of dissatisfied non-Mormons who had moved to Utah to work at the company. "We're leaving!" they'd declare, and when I asked them why, they'd regale me with stories about their low social status, or how their children weren't invited to certain events. As an MFS board member, I was in a position of authority, however, and so could only partly sympathize. Over my two decades of work in Salt Lake City, I enjoyed dinners, played tennis, and skied with many of my Mormon friends. No one tried to convert me, and I was excluded only from entering the Temple, the inner sanctum of the church reserved for church members not in arrears with their tithes.

My relationship with Mormon leaders like Neal Maxwell, the Church's most distinguished scholar, gave me a unique position in the community. Neal served on an elite governing body—the Quorum of the Twelve Apostles—which oversaw the church in much the same way that the College of Cardinals oversees the Roman Catholic Church. In addition to serving as a pillar of Mormon scholarship, Neal had a reputation for integrity, and I've always thought of him as a godly man. Neal and I grew close, building rapport at each of the board meetings. As I grew curious about church affairs, I'd ask him what Mormon conversion was like (the ceremonies are secret), and when he was curious about the stock market or a current event, I'd give him my thoughts. Though Neal passed in the summer of 2004, I still display a picture of us in my office. Years later, when I began building an investment fund called Caravel, several young people from San Francisco came to my office and saw that photo. Their entire perception of me changed, and from then on, I could do no wrong—testament to the loyalty Neal inspired.

Bud Kastler, with whom I also developed a rapport, was much different in temperament. I remember sitting in Bud's office in Salt Lake City, and when attorneys made presentations that he didn't like or said something he found disagreeable, he'd respond by saying, "That's the dumbest thing I've ever heard. Why would you even make such a statement?" He reacted the same way during board meetings. But when the board ventured outside of Utah to Wyoming, Bud joined his conservative colleagues in loosening up and even drinking alcohol. Bud was also open to new experiences. One of our directors, Bud Osmond, was a conservative man with a spectacular ranch in Wyoming with naturally occurring thermal pools. "We're all going bathing," said Bud, and in an experience I never had even in college, half the board disrobed and stepped naked into the warm waters. On another occasion, my wife, Jane's, office arranged for my corporate finance colleague Brian Sterling to take MFS members to a show of *The Best Little Whorehouse in Texas*. The bawdy production was replete with sex, foul language, and the like. Bud loved it. He couldn't wait to return home to tell everyone about the show that Jim had arranged for his Utah friends.

This spirit of friendship suffused my relationship with the company. When MFS planned a round of financing, Wertheim comanaged the transaction with the First Boston Corporation. When Bud asked me about First Boston's proposed fee, I told him I thought it was fair. "What would you charge if we did it alone with you?" Bud asked. Given our special relationship, I said I'd take whatever he wanted to pay me. The board members at MFS never forgot that.

Management also never forgot when, sometime in the late 1980s, I spearheaded a challenge against Oscar Wyatt, the famed World War II veteran, oil tycoon, and self-made billionaire. Wyatt, memorably profiled in *Texas Monthly* as "that archetype of Texas archetypes, for decades [Houston's] orneriest, wiliest, most litigious, most feared, most hated, and most beloved son of a bitch," had set MFS and its oil-rich lands in his crosshairs.[31]

An anxious Bud called me one day to tell me that Wyatt had somehow taken a large position in the company and a takeover threat loomed. After researching Wyatt's holdings in oil and gas and seeing what a formidable opponent he was, I retained Joe Flom of Skadden Arps, then the country's leading law firm in takeover litigation, and flew to Salt Lake City to defuse the crisis.

Like much of corporate America, MFS feared takeover specialists like Oscar Wyatt and Mike Milken, financiers whose aggressive tactics helped dub the 1980s the "decade of greed."[32] Though Wyatt was a serious threat, I was optimistic that Utah's public service commission wouldn't countenance his actions. In Utah, you never wanted to pick a fight with the public service commission or the church. In this case, I imagined the Utah commission would invoke its power to restrict ownership over a public utility and block an aggressive takeover from Texas. I took Wyatt aside and explained the difficulty he faced. "Do you really want to get embroiled in a long-term battle with Utah's public service commission?" I asked, telling him about the long, expensive legal battle that awaited us. To capitalize on this fear but also to give Wyatt a graceful exit, the company offered to sell him part of its gas at market price. With the threat of the public service commission battle and Joe Flom, the toughest lawyer in America, on our side, Wyatt backed down. In averting this disaster, we saved the company from certain takeover.

Normally such a defense would have cost millions in fees, but I didn't charge anything. This was one of the reasons I'd opted to join Wertheim instead of a bulge-bracket firm. As I became the firm's rainmaker in the late 1970s and '80s, I could more easily set the rules. I decided to leverage that autonomy to create special relationships, as I did with Mountain Fuel Supply.

As part of my advisory role to corporate management, I challenged the public service commission myself. Shortly after I joined the board in 1977, MFS made a significant profit from its oil and gas exploration and production businesses. Utah's public service commission, a regulatory body that determines the rates that utility companies can charge their customer bases, took an aggressive posture. "You are a rich company," the commissioners said, "and you shouldn't charge these gas rates to your customers." This activist stance struck me as antithetical to the American spirit. MFS had invested funds to produce gas for its customers, something which the public service commission tightly regulated. By a stroke of fortune, the company had also made a great return on investment (ROI) on land it had purchased in the 1920s. But that didn't obligate managers to reduce costs to customers (technically termed "rate payers"). I was convinced that rate payers couldn't possibly have a vested interest in the equity of their gas service providers' investments. The public service commission, by contrast, argued that the rate payer was part owner of the investments MFS made in oil and gas.

I testified in court on behalf of MFS and found no shortage of free-enterprise-loving, pro-capitalist conservatives in Utah sympathetic to my view. Not even the liberal bastions of Manhattan or Boston had ever attempted such an argument. Imagine, I said in my testimony, that you move to Utah and purchase a home, and suddenly you get a dividend because your utility provider made a profit investing in something else (unrelated to providing your utilities!). Many institutional investors like Prudential Financial, along with faculty at Brigham Young University and Utah State, supported me, and our position prevailed.

With work like this, I found my time in Utah both enjoyable and intellectually challenging. As I came to Utah on the weekends to ski and then worked on important company issues on Monday and Tuesday, I came to understand Utah's unique culture. Despite its mountains and open feel, Utah in general, and Salt Lake City in particular, remained a conservative place with one of the highest divorce rates in the country. Perhaps the staid culture inspired a certain rebelliousness. When we had directors' meetings in other states, many of my LDS colleagues seemed to relax, indulging in alcohol and speaking more freely. I stayed the sober course myself—never having been a drinker in Salt Lake City or elsewhere. But I hailed from the tolerant Eastern Seaboard and had never had to navigate the intense LDS social pressures.

Decades after joining the company, I made one of my more important contributions to MFS (which changed its name several times in the coming decades).[33] During my service on the board, I had helped manage every public offering of equity and debt to raise money for an expansion. But as I had also consistently noticed, some investors wanted to own shares only in the utility while others were interested in the gas exploration side. In 2010, I recommended that the board vote to divide the company in two: one part would remain a utility and the other an oil and gas business. This restructuring was the right move financially, and as I predicted, the two discrete entities would, in sum, exceed the value of the former consolidated company within a relatively short time.

A CHANGING MORAL AND ENERGY LANDSCAPE

And that's how an investment banker from New York dedicated years navigating Wertheim's old-world habits while befriending Utah's leading Mormons. I gravitated to corporate finance transactions like Starbucks because I wanted to increase Wertheim's participation in public offerings. During my hundred-plus trips to Utah, consulting on shareholder matters, testifying before the public service commission, and enjoying Utah's pristine outdoors, I fulfilled the role of investment banker and corporate advisor, helping the company achieve its goals and creating new value for investors by restructuring the company.

In building a sustainable investment banking business, I parted ways with the style and approach of Wertheim's founders. Instead of investing, like a merchant bank, I served as an agent, advising companies and helping them achieve their goals. Morgan Stanley and Goldman Sachs built their firms in this way, and it was how I approached my clients in industrial chemicals, music, motion pictures, and retail.

My experience at Wertheim and on the West Coast expanded my cultural horizons and prepared me for my later work abroad. In Utah, Wertheim's old-world–style of investment banking had to be adapted to Mormon culture, which was premised on mountain sports, religious observance and tithing, and abstention from a range of beverages (alcohol and coffee) and recreational drugs. Both Utah and the West Coast were different from hard-drinking, urban New Yorkers who exercise in expensive workout studios, and the highly caffeinated, tech-savvy, entrepreneurially minded denizens of Seattle. When I left investment banking for the public sector, I'd learn that the culture in Washington, DC, was different yet again. Instead of fixating on profit generation for end-of-year bonuses as we did in New York, Washingtonians prized the value of information, proximity to powerful people, and professional status. New York's culture of wealth differed from Washington's culture of status, which differed again from Mormons' abstemious culture. I sometimes joke that customs officials should require a passport for travel among these starkly different American regions.

The highlight of my twenty-five years of work with MFS was when I was able to unify several of these American subcultures. One day in the fall of 1995, my friend Neal A. Maxwell asked for a big favor. "Jim, I understand that US presidents regularly meet with the leaders of major American religious groups." Neal wanted me to secure an official audience at the White House for Gordon B. Hinckley, president of the Church of the Latter-day Saints (LDS).

If anyone knew of such a White House precedent, it was Neal, one of the most prominent and respected intellectuals in the Mormon church. By the mid-1990s, I'd become friends with Bill Clinton, helping his presidential reelection campaign that year and later joining his administration. Neal said: "If anybody can make this meeting happen, it's you, Jim."

Clinton welcomed the idea, and we arranged a brief meeting for Monday, November 13, 1995.[34] I remember Neal greeting me at the White House before we took our places in the Oval Office, with Neal and President Hinkley seated opposite Vice President Al Gore, President Bill Clinton, and me. After blessing the meeting with an opening prayer, Hinckley presented Clinton with several handsome genealogical tomes, detailing six generations of First Lady Hillary Rodham and Bill Clinton's ancestors (along with copies as gifts for their daughter, Chelsea).[35] Genealogies are important for Mormons. They painstakingly reconstruct their family trees in order to practice something called "baptism of the dead," which is a posthumous conversion of any non-Mormon ancestors into the faith, thereby ensuring extended families remain united for eternity.

As Hinckley detailed during the meeting, the pedigreed Gore and Rodham lineages had overlapped sometime in the sixteenth or seventeenth centuries. Bill Clinton leaned over to me, a smile on his face. "That would never happen with my family. We're White trash," he said, making a self-deprecating reference to his Appalachian roots.

This meeting, broadcast throughout Utah and the nearly ten-million-strong global Latter-day Saints community, made me look like a great friend of the Mormon church. That was true. But my larger interest was in moments of cross-cultural exchange like the one underway at this White House meeting, bridging different cultures and reaching common understandings.

But common ground is sometimes difficult to achieve, and during my time at MFS, the world had undergone drastic changes. During my first two decades of work with the company, hardly anyone focused on renewable energy or sustainability. In the 1990s, when I began working in the public sector and the NGO space, I became apprehensive about changing climate conditions. As my anxieties about the environment grew, I fused my two interests by joining the board of the World Resources Institute (WRI) and shortly thereafter becoming the chair.

Even into the 1990s I convinced myself that MFS's natural gas represented a transitional fuel, one we would quickly bypass on our journey to a postcarbon future. But the science no longer strongly supports this position, and environmental advocacy has become increasingly polarized. As I encouraged the company to make more environmentally and carbon-friendly decisions, the management became uneasy, fearing I'd taken a liberal tilt in my thinking. I decided to keep my friendships on the board but to stop advising the company. When it comes to the environment, it has been hard for me to adopt a conciliatory position: I believe now, more than ever, that we must transition to a postcarbon, renewable-energy-powered world.

One major cultural lesson I learned from Utahans was their approach to aging and retirement. When they hit their sixties, westerners tend to retire more readily than American easterners. With their close-knit families, fishing and hunting lodges, and escapes to the mountains, Mormons are exemplars of an early-retirement ethos. My friend R. Don Cash, who assumed leadership of MFS after Bud Kastler, happily retired at sixty, returning home to Texas to attend to family and travel instead of running the company.[36] Describing this decision, Don's successor Keith Rattie said, "Don's doing what most leaders would plan to do if they had the ability to choose, and that is to go out on top."[37] I have always been impressed with the ease with which western-state industry leaders have been able to retire at a relatively young age.

When I asked them about retirement, they'd simply state their work was done. "What are you talking about? There's so much more to do," I said.

"Nah, I'm ready to go fishing," they replied.

For an East Coaster like me, perpetually "up and doing," I couldn't help but take a different path. By the time I resigned from the MFS board, I felt my contributions to industry and public service were just beginning. Instead of regarding my time in Utah as a prelude to retirement, I continued my work with a powerful Italian multinational, the subject to which I now turn.

3

Montedison: A US-Italian Love Story

AFTER THE UNITED STATES emerged from World War II as the sole global superpower, perhaps nothing better symbolized American economic dominance than the New York Stock Exchange (NYSE). Most companies dreamed of listing their shares on the NYSE, while most investment bankers and securities dealers coveted a seat on the exchange. For most of its nearly two-and-a-half-century history, the NYSE, the heart of Wall Street and the larger capitalist world, was a private, members-only club, requiring a seat to execute trades on its famed exchange floor. A seat meant influence and power at 11 Wall Street, where traders scrutinized the listings on the NYSE's Big Boards, gauging the health of the global energy, health care, and technology sectors, and hoped to make vast sums for their clients.

During this postwar era of prosperity, perhaps no other country respected America's business community, financial markets, and culture more than Italy. The Italian-American relationship, strained during Mussolini's dictatorship, has remained robust for centuries. Unlike their feelings about the conservative British, the elitist French, or a US-German relationship almost irreparably damaged by World War II, Americans adored

Italy—its food, wine, and "dolce vita" lifestyle. Hollywood depicts Italy as an affectionate, sexy country that welcomes Americans. Americans flocked to Venice and Florence for art, the Amalfi coast for recreation, Tuscany for wine and romance, and Rome for adventure. Italians, in turn, had emigrated in droves to the United States, achieving success in business and politics. Almost any American who has traveled throughout Europe can attest to Italian goodwill. While the French may quibble with your pronunciation, Italians are delighted when Americans muster a morning *buongiorno*.

Shortly after arriving at Wertheim in 1974, I seized an opportunity to leverage American financial prestige into a stronger partnership with Italy when the company's vice chair and partner, Wilbur Cowett, suggested we embark on a tour of Europe. Despite Wertheim's blue-chip reputation, the firm had few clients and needed to internationalize. Wertheim's Paris office, our second stop in Europe, best symbolized the company's status and predicament. Located at 4 Place de Concorde, where the Champs-Elysées ends at the Luxor Obelisk, the Wertheim offices were close to the elegant hotels and monumental fountains that attracted tourists and the business elite. But the office saw little foot traffic and even fewer clients. Once in Paris, Wilbur and I met with Bernard Camus, personable and droll, whose father had been a leader of the Belgian Resistance. Bernard was eager for me to meet his acquaintances in Italy. I had a hunch that he could introduce me to many prospects in the Italian business world and thus could represent a major opportunity for me and for Wertheim.

On June 17, 1975, Camus introduced me to Lino Caiola, the president of Capitalfin, a holding company with four powerful shareholders, including the famed Agnelli family. Founders of the Fiat automotive giant, the Agnellis typified the country's powerful clans, wielding enormous financial, political, and cultural influence.[38] Caiola was about fifteen years my senior and greeted me with warmth, speaking perfect English. His Rome offices were near the Spanish Steps, where a monumental walkway rises from the Piazza di Spagna to the Trinità dei Monti church. His office walls were festooned with medieval paintings of a crucified Christ, and I gathered he was a devout man. In keeping with the art in his office, our first meeting was devoid of humor and small talk. Lino was nonetheless a thoughtful and friendly man who also maintained a home at Seventy-First Street and Park Avenue in New York City. Each of the investors in Lino's holding company had entrusted him with significant investment capital. And one of his most recent acquisitions, he explained to me, was a British shipbroking business called Clarksons.

Seeking to better understand how Wertheim worked and how it might add value to his operation, Caiola offered me Clarksons as a test assignment: Could I find an interested buyer? Like most US investment bankers, I had little experience in or knowledge about the shipping industry. A domain that facilitates the movement of goods and services, and the shipment and delivery of cargoes to and from international ports, the shipbroking business is highly technical and specialized, centered mostly in London.

I left the meeting, held in late 1977, determined to provide Caiola a thoughtful and independent analysis of Clarksons. Over the following six months, I conducted substantial industry research and scoured the continent for prospective buyers. I kept Caiola abreast of my efforts but couldn't complete the assignment. In February of 1978, I attended a dispiriting Clarksons board meeting in London, where we learned that business fared poorly and management wasn't optimistic about a corporate turnaround.

On November 14, 1978, Caiola and I had lunch at Wertheim's dining room in New York, this time discussing the possibility of Capitalfin selling 2.2 million of its shares in Signal Oil. Whenever it sought to purchase a company, Capitalfin took aggressive positions in its publicly traded shares. Later that year, Lino decided against that option and asked me to sell his Signal Oil shares for a handsome commission of $1 a share—a thank-you present for my efforts with Clarksons.

To appreciate what a coup this represented for Wertheim, it's important to understand "May Day" 1975, when Wall Street's commission structure changed forever, ending the postwar Golden Age of Capitalism. Since its opening in 1792, the NYSE, a beacon of global capitalism, granted fixed commissions of around 1 percent for each broker who sold shares on the exchange, a highly uncompetitive practice.[39] Into the twentieth century, the NYSE fought off the creeping forces of competition, even as institutional investors grew more powerful, threatening to take their business elsewhere if they couldn't negotiate more reasonable fees—while regulatory bodies like the Securities and Exchange Commission (SEC) clamored for change. Free-market competition eventually won on May 1, 1975, when negotiated rates replaced fixed rates for brokers. For traditional brokerage firms, this May Day signaled an actual Mayday. A number of firms disappeared overnight, with competitive discount firms like Charles Schwab eventually replacing them.[40]

Caiola granted Wertheim this lucrative commission in 1978, three years after this historic moment for Wall Street. In the new competitive-rate environment, Lino could easily have negotiated a fee of $0.10–$0.15 a share, yielding Wertheim $200,000 in revenue for the transaction. Instead of negotiating a lower fee, Capitalfin paid Wertheim a fixed rate of $1 per share, garnering the firm $2 million for the trade—all this a thank you for my efforts, albeit unsuccessful, at selling the holding company's shipbroking business. I called Wertheim's head trader, Bob Chamine, with the Signal Oil sale order, and when I entered the company's trading room, everyone stood in applause. I was embarrassed by the attention but pleased to know this transaction would bolster our firm's equity trading department, which like everywhere else on Wall Street had seen revenues plummet since May Day 1975. Having been at the firm only a year, I perceived this move would also help my position at the firm.

This episode also reinforced something I've always believed about the nature of opportunity. When an industry or domain becomes unpopular, opportunities abound. When everyone begins fleeing, I've always sought to enter, and when something seems extremely popular, I seek opportunity elsewhere. Following May Day 1975, many people acted like my friend and colleague Dennis Stanfill, who left his job at Lehman Brothers to become chair of Twentieth Century–Fox Film Corporation. I questioned Dennis about leaving the securities business at one of its worst moments. "Sure," he said, "but I'm going to do something exciting." Many securities brokers left Wall Street when it fell on hard times, opting instead to serve as chief financial officers (CFOs) of glamourous music or motion picture companies. But I remained convinced, as I do to this day, that opportunity abounds when popularity flags.

That conviction prompted me to not only build an investment banking business during the difficult decade of the 1970s, but also to develop growth opportunities in Italy, a country known more for attractive beaches than attractive securities. Though the Italo-American "love affair" strongly assisted me in building personal and business relationships, the country had a mixed reputation in the American financial community. The *Wall Street Journal*, for example, cited the Italian practice of "spaghetti accounting." By this, they referred to a general corruption within the country and to the keeping of two sets of accounting books, allowing corporate insiders to skim profits off the top. One of the reasons the American markets had such international prestige was because of their transparency. Following the Securities Act of 1933, the first piece of legislation regulating American financial markets, publicly listed companies had to file registration statements, faithfully disclosing the value of securities for potential shareholders. I always felt that while accusations of spaghetti accounting were unfair, perhaps Wertheim could add value to Italian companies by increasing the transparency of their accounting and disclosure practices.

MONTEDISON IN MILANO

My first opportunity to add value to Italian companies came in late 1977, when Lino introduced me to Mario Schimberni, the newly minted vice president of finance for Montedison S.p.A., a powerful Italian multinational specializing in chemicals and plastics.[41] The son of a barber and seamstress, Mario powered his rise through the corporate ranks with little education and outsize dedication, emerging a few years after our meeting as Montedison's chair and one of Italy's most powerful business executives. His austerity and discipline matched Lino's, though he lacked any religious component. At age fifty-three, he appeared much older than his actual eleven years my senior. Managing this company, which had been seen bulging debts for ten years, had perhaps aged him.[42] *International Management* was blunt: Montedison was unwieldly, "little more than a bloated political football, run by political appointees and dedicated more to the furtherance of state social policies than to profitable operations."[43]

Mario's hard-nosed, disciplined approach struck me as exactly what Montedison needed. To accomplish a corporate turnaround, he said during our first meeting, he needed to restyle Montedison along American lines and internationalize key parts of the chemical and pharmaceutical businesses. To Americanize the company, he needed to sell off unproductive divisions, focus on growth, and eventually eliminate government ownership. The Italian government owned about 30 percent of the company's outstanding shares, and they generated little market interest and sold at significant discounts to estimated liquidation value. To power growth, Schimberni recruited foreign talent. In addition to a cadre of talented managers, his advising team consisted of me, providing financial and corporate advice, while former US secretary of state Henry Kissinger acted as foreign policy advisor and former German chancellor Helmut Schmidt advised on European affairs.

In June 1978, the Italian behemoth gave Wertheim its first investment banking assignment, asking us to serve as the exclusive agent to sell Montedison's interest in Compagnie Néerlandaise de l'Azote (CNA), a fertilizer business based in the Netherlands. A young Montedison official informed me that Loeb, Rhoades & Co., a major New York investment firm, had controlled the assignment prior to our appointment. I called Mark Millard, a senior partner at Loeb, Rhoades & Co., whom I had never met before, and candidly explained that Wertheim now had the CNA assignment and was looking for possible purchasers of the fertilizer company. I was surprised when Mark disclosed that Norwegian aluminum and renewable energy giant Norsk Hydro had expressed interest. Most investment bankers didn't assist relative newcomers like me, especially when losing business to them.

After some research I learned that Norsk Hydro was one of the largest Norwegian companies of the time, with sizable commodity and utility business divisions, and would be a good fit for CNA. I called the company's CEO, Torvild Aakvaag, who'd served in Norway's foreign affairs ministry in the 1950s before taking a position at Norsk Hydro, and made a date to meet him at his corporate headquarters in Oslo. Like many of the phone calls and impromptu meetings I describe in this book, such communication would be nearly impossible for a young investment banker to pull off today. I made my first trip to Oslo in January 1979, just in time for the bitterly cold winter. Committed to my running schedule, I ran around Oslo Park, taking in Gustav Vigeland's monumental statuary at what would have been one in the morning in Connecticut. If I'd taken a run in balmy Rome that day, I would have been entirely alone, but here in Oslo many braved the frigid conditions and ran alongside me in the capitol's striking sculpture garden. I always felt better after a run and was now prepared for my meeting with Aakvaag.

The Norwegians had a cold climate, but I found Aakvaag and his countrymen to be warm, kind people who were especially fond of Americans. Norwegian businesspeople found Italians difficult to negotiate with, but thought Americans were straight shooters like them. Aakvaag and his colleagues were therefore pleased to be working with an American representing Italy and knew more about CNA than I expected. With no clear offering price in mind, we spent the next few months in meetings and in calls, hashing out an agreement. In the process, Aakvaag and I developed a working relationship. At the time, most successful European families wanted their children to attend US colleges. The American higher education and health-care systems were considered the gold standard, just like the financial community. When Aakvaag sought direction for his son's schools, I offered to put him in contact with people who could help. We reached an agreement for Norsk Hydro to purchase Montedison's interest in CNA that spring.

After finalizing this deal in September 1979, which garnered Wertheim a sizable $3.3 million fee, I suggested to my colleagues that we offer a $500,000 check to Loeb, Rhoades. My senior partners at Wertheim thought I was losing my mind. With no written commitment and only a single phone call of communication, I had no reason, let alone obligation, to pay Mark Millard. But I felt strongly otherwise: Millard had given me the Norsk Hydro lead, ensuring me a successful outcome on that deal, as well as a promising foundation for my relationship with Montedison. After our assistants arranged logistics for a meeting, I walked into Millard's office and presented him with a check for $500,000, the equivalent of $2.5 million today. This gesture left him deeply moved and slightly shocked. Though Wall Street prided itself on honoring unwritten agreements, it was unusual for an investment banker to split a fee like this. Such a goodwill gesture would be even more unthinkable today, as investment bankers accumulate as much profit as possible.

This deal, my first fee transaction for Montedison, marked the beginning of many more deals I would facilitate for the company over the next decade. Though I had twelve to fifteen other major clients at Wertheim, none had the international clout of this Italian firm. In the years following that initial transaction, my investment banking business with Montedison made me a frequent visitor to Milan, its corporate headquarters. With its spectacular restaurants, world-class arts, and efficient business community, Milan and I were a natural fit, and, to me, the city always represented the European equivalent to New York.

Italy taught me to appreciate life in a more relaxed and thoughtful way. Skiing, for example, was a longtime passion of mine, but the first time I hit the slopes with my Milanese friends, I was stunned to find them gradually wake up, linger over an espresso and croissants, hit the slopes midmorning, and break shortly thereafter to enjoy a relaxed lunch. What a marked contrast to Americans, who queued in line before the lifts opened, barely paused for a meal, and left exhausted at the end of the day. I embraced this Italian tempo, and instead of working late into the night, I'd often stop around three in the afternoon to visit a museum and meet with some art dealers before attending an evening performance at the opera. This more leisurely lifestyle and love of art characterized other European countries like France, but it was especially pronounced in Italy, and my colleagues were eager to embark on these activities with me. By embracing this Italian lifestyle, I also forged important relationships.

My mission for Montedison—to create a strong company that maximized shareholder value—also taught me important differences between American and Italian financial culture. Americans were much more driven by the bottom line, while Italians oriented themselves around community and friendships. Navigating these cultural differences and cultivating personal relationships occupied a lot of my time in the decade spanning the late 1970s to late 1980s. I was constantly concerned about the power and strength of the company, fixating on profits per share and market prices, while my Italian colleagues fretted about labor movements. Their preoccupation was understandable in light of Montedison's strained labor relations in the 1970s and early '80s, which had contributed to broad-based discontent among unions.[44] I navigated these differences by being present and engaging in discussions with others. With business relationships now transacted on digital platforms like Zoom, such interpersonal professional relationships would be much more difficult today.

Schimberni had never seen an American investment banker so omnipresent in Italy. He joined many of my colleagues at Wertheim who thought I might have a relationship with a woman there. They were right. My daughter Debbie spent her junior year of college in Bologna, and I often visited her, brushing up on my spoken Italian, joining her on adventures, and enjoying the city's remarkable cuisine.

Apart from recreation and indulging in the arts, my time in Italy was marked with excitement and danger. The economic turmoil of the 1970s gave rise to the Italian terrorist group called the Red Brigades. These far-left vigilantes used kidnappings, murder, and maiming to undermine the state. And though they managed to kidnap political leaders, like former prime minister Aldo Moro in 1978 and Brig. Gen. James L. Dozier (US Army) in 1981, and even tried to capture the pope, Montedison was among their main targets.[45] In 1981, vigilantes captured Montedison executive Giuseppe Taliercio and murdered him almost two months later, disposing of his body, riddled with bullets, in the trunk of a car.[46] Whenever I arrived at the Milan airport, my colleagues dressed in jeans and tattered clothing and hailed taxis for transportation, camouflaging their wealth and status to avoid a similar fate. I never took these precautions, deplaning in business attire and boarding limousines to Montedison's headquarters. "They'll never hit an American," I reasoned with Henry Kissinger one day.

"They won't know you're an American by your dress!" Henry responded.

It was probably foolish of me to take no precautions, but I naively thought that since I wasn't an Italian executive, I'd be spared.

Whether we arrived in a taxicab dressed in sweatpants or emerged from a limousine attired in Armani, we all assumed equal status as we entered the stately Milanese headquarters. The imposing front entrance of the eighteenth-century building, located along a beautiful, tree-lined cobblestone street, gave way to a series of small workspaces, with no one occupying an outsize office. The building struck me as heavy and weighty, like the discussions we'd undertake inside. Unlike most of his espresso-enjoying and arts-loving Italian counterparts, Schimberni was more Germanic or American in his approach, arriving promptly to every meeting and armed with a comprehensive agenda.

Over the course of restructuring this giant company, I enjoyed my relationships with Italian businessmen like Schimberni, who possessed a quiet wisdom and imparted important life lessons to me. One night at a business meal, I noticed that he'd finished his glass of wine. He always had one glass—and only one glass—remaining sober and in control of his faculties. That night, he hadn't eaten much and I asked if he might be hungry later. "When you get to be my age," he reflected, "you stop eating big dinners." Many years later, when I turned sixty-five, I thought back to this meal and confirmed the accuracy of those remarks. You sleep better and you're able to think more clearly if you don't overindulge in your evening meal (or in other appetites as well).

I could leverage this personal relationship when I made mistakes, as I did once in the 1980s. When Montedison had important board meetings, usually scheduled in the afternoon, I'd board an evening Alitalia flight in New York (the Concorde didn't fly to Milan), arriving with just enough time to rest before the meeting. For one important occasion, I boarded the overnight flight and found myself seated next to Romanian tennis star Ilie Năstase. We struck up a conversation as he proceeded to drink an impressive amount of alcohol. Knowing he had a match the following day, I said, "How are you going to play tomorrow? You've just put away three or four martinis."

An inebriated Năstase staggered off the plane, almost needing assistance, while I arrived at the Principe di Savoia, one of Milan's most spectacular hotels, sober and prepared for the board meeting. From my many stays at this hotel, I'd learned that if you draw the drapes and tightly shutter the wooden slats, no light can filter into the room. Needing some valuable shuteye to ready myself for a weighty Montedison discussion, I instructed the hotel concierge not to disturb me. I arose a few hours later entirely refreshed, only to discover that I'd slept through the entire board meeting.

Schimberni's assistant had called me continuously for hours but was blocked by my "no-disturb" message. Mortified that I'd flown all this way and slept through the important meeting, I was abject in my apologies to Schimberni, who worked with me for several hours, walking me through the highlights and discussing follow-up action items.

Prior to my return to New York the following morning, I scoured the newspapers to find out how Năstase had fared in his match. It amused me to discover that he'd lost the first set six–love (6–0) and won the following set six–love (6–0). The third set was a grueling athletic battle in which he lost six–four (6–4). Perhaps he and his opponent agreed to exert themselves only in the third and final set.

MONTEDISON IN MANHATTAN

To create value for global companies in the twentieth century, the best strategy was to list corporate shares on the New York Stock Exchange (NYSE). Early in 1980, shortly after Mario became Montedison's chair, I told him that several high-growth companies remained buried beneath the giant Montedison umbrella. I suggested we separate those submerged entities from this vast corporation and list them as independent companies on the NYSE, allowing shareholders to realize their true value and power their future growth. The American public and institutional shareholders could see the value of these spinoff companies, which would increase the share value of parent company Montedison. Schimberni loved the idea, and I was determined to see it through.

Our first corporate spinoff was Erbamont, which included Montedison's pharmaceutical and health sciences divisions. I was attracted to this opportunity because Montedison was one of the world's largest producers of Adriamycin, a key ingredient in chemotherapy drug cocktails.[47] Given Adriamycin's central role in chemotherapy—it was the most popular cancer drug in the United States and western Europe—I saw enormous growth potential and proposed a merger.[48] The newly minted Erbamont would control Farmitalia Carlo Erba, Italy's largest pharmaceutical company (of which Montedison had a 73 percent interest) as well as the entirety of Adria Laboratories, partially owned by Hercules Chemical, a leading chemical and munitions company in Wilmington, Delaware.[49]

Hercules Chemical also exercised market dominance in America's polypropylene (a lightweight plastic) market. Though having since achieved notoriety for their effect on the environment, plastics were enormously important at the time, profitable for Hercules and Montedison alike. In the early 1980s, my Wertheim colleagues and I proposed that each company contribute its polypropylene business divisions to a joint venture called Himont, Inc. Himont would constitute the largest chemical mixed-plastics venture on the market and would enjoy joint ownership, with Hercules and Montedison each owning 40 percent, leaving 20 percent for sale to the public. This prestigious offering attracted institutional and retail interest, and Wertheim invited Goldman Sachs and First Boston Corporation to comanage the IPO.

At the closing of the transaction, we cut a $350 million certified check and handed it to Himont's CFO.[50] This was standard at the time. Per Wall Street rules, all investors had three days to produce funds for such purchases, which in this case would be transferred to Wertheim, First Boston, and Goldman Sachs to execute the order. The CFO departed our offices, and somewhere on the subway he realized he'd lost the check. Panicked, he came rushing back downtown, unsure of what to do. It was a certified check and therefore couldn't be canceled. Imagine, I thought, that Wall Street made fun of Italian-style spaghetti accounting, yet three of America's preeminent financial institutions couldn't keep track of a single paper check. By sheer luck, a Good Samaritan who worked as a messenger found the check on the floor of Grand Central Station and casually walked into our offices on Park Avenue to deliver it. "If this happened in Rome or Milan," my Italian colleagues would later say, "they would never have heard the end of it."

Little did we know, the real Himont drama was still to come. Because Montedison and Hercules each owned 40 percent of Himont, they occupied what the financial services community terms a "standstill." To maintain equilibrium, both companies informally agreed to respect the other's joint ownership. But during a Himont board meeting one day in 1986, Mario turned to me and said: "I'm going to make an aggressive move and quietly go into the market, buying enough shares to control a 50 percent stake in Himont."

"Wow," I replied. "Hercules won't like that."

True to his word, Mario enacted his strategy, quietly accomplishing a Himont takeover. Instead of having equal representation on the board and equal say in management, Montedison had a 51 percent ownership interest in the company. The president of Hercules Chemical, a successful Italian American, was appalled. As an advisor and Himont board member, I was also surprised at this hardball move. It made intuitive sense, as most business schools taught what politicians knew instinctively: it's hard to share power.

With a few exceptions, like Goldman Sachs who had equal partners at the upper rungs, few jointly led companies prospered.

Hercules's management initially felt I'd masterminded this move, and I tried my best to broker peace among all parties while insisting on my neutrality. Though Hercules never forgave Montedison, the latter prospered following the move. Italy was thrilled to have taken over a leading chemical company, Himont's stock price increases benefited shareholders, and the company itself grew, increasing its employee count and innovative potential. It took chutzpah for an Italian businessman, who like many of his counterparts emulated American practices and held NYSE companies in esteem, to enact a takeover of a large American company. Most of us in the financial community looked on with quiet admiration, or at least respect. And, as always, the long-standing Italian-American relationship helped cushion bumps like these.

My final corporate spinoff is technically a misnomer, because in structuring Montedison's last public deal I avoided the underwriting, registration, and IPO processes. Specifically, we merged Montedison's large specialty chemical business into Compo Industries, a small NYSE chemical company on whose board of directors I served. That transaction resulted in Montedison owning over 90 percent of the surviving company, now called Ausimont. Ausimont is a textbook example of a special-purpose acquisition company (SPAC), which when merged with a preexisting public company, can circumvent the IPO process but still go public. As I write this book in 2020, SPACs have enjoyed a record year, with celebrity financiers and politicians like Ray Dalio, Chamath Palihapitiya, and Paul Ryan creating significant value using this "backdoor entry" into the public market. "The IPO is being reinvented," read a headline in the *Economist* in August of 2020, referring to companies directly listing their shares or creating SPACs.[51] The so-called reinvention is hardly new because we created a SPAC decades ago, allowing Ausimont to join Erbamont and Himont as three new publicly traded companies contributing growth for shareholders and helping Italy become a more interesting destination for investors.

HAPPILY EVER AFTER

When I consider the achievement of Montedison's corporate turnaround, my mind turns to early September 1985. Henry Kissinger, Helmut Schmidt, and I descended on Venice for an annual festival convened that year in honor of Montedison. This black-tie affair, an elaborate three-day gala, unfolded in Venice's opulent Cipriani Hotel, near Venice on Giudecca Island, as well as the Doge's Palace, the storied Gothic manor and resident of the leader, or *Doge*, of the Venetian Republic. It was the only occasion I remember Mario dropping his serious demeanor and enjoying himself and basking in his achievements.

It's hard for anyone to shine when Henry Kissinger is in attendance. The first night, I boarded a gondola for dinner at the Doge palace's dining room, meeting Helmut and Mario once inside. Turning to Henry, Mario said, "You know the famous investment banker Jim Harmon?" I'd never met Kissinger before. "Of course I know him," Kissinger replied. "I see him all the time at tennis matches." Kissinger shook my hand and remained silent until we boarded the gondola, when he turned to me and whispered, "You owe me one." I've always remembered that line. The illustrious former secretary of state Henry Kissinger had just pretended to know me and expected a favor in return.

At dinner that evening, in a spectacular room in the palace, with everyone in black-tie, Henry did something even more memorable. An enormous crowd descended for the occasion and reporters lined up on one side of the room. "Watch what Henry does now," Helmut said to me after I'd taken a seat with him and Mario near the front. Henry rose and greeted each photographer, shaking hands and engaging in small talk with all thirty or so of them. After he was done working the room, he took his seat and Helmut said: "Look at tomorrow's paper."

Sure enough, the following day each Italian paper featured a glossy picture of Henry. He'd engineered a photo-op that would be seen across Europe. Helmut, who'd led a European country for the better part of a decade, was barely pictured. Henry was everywhere, thanks to this savvy maneuver.

We spent much of the following two days playing games that Henry devised. One was identifying the three best presidents of the United States and listing the reasons. Henry enjoyed European football and narrated how each team's style mimicked their national culture: the Germans were extremely disciplined, making few errors, while the more sensual Brazilians had flair and creativity. When Brazilian theatrics met Teutonic discipline, who would prevail? Kissinger proceeded to detail an imaginative new move that Brazilian legend Pelé had engineered that would make their next match against Germany the competition of the century.

A correlation between athletics and national character had never occurred to me, but I shared my own theory about economic development with Henry and Helmut on a gondola one night. The United States represented only 4.5 percent of the globe's population, yet it enjoyed over 25 percent of the world's wealth. That unequal distribution, I insisted, wasn't sustainable. "Where's the world heading now?" they asked.

Global wealth, I suggested, will approximate the Olympic medals count in each country. At the time, the United States' share of global gross domestic product (GDP) was approximately 27 percent, while we won about 10 percent of all Olympic medals. Since that time, our athletic performance has declined as China's medal count and wealth have swelled.

The pace of change and development, we all agreed, hinged on technology, talent, and capital flows. While none of us could have predicted future technological developments or capital movements, I knew that the developing and frontier worlds represented huge potential markets. It wasn't until I migrated into public service that I saw the enormous growth of the developing world and, for national-security and humanitarian reasons, actively promoted wealth creation and private sector development in frontier and developing economies.

However compelling on their merits, our pet theories mostly revealed our professional roles. Henry nodded along about my Olympic theory, but he wasn't interested in economic development. As a diplomat he focused on national characters so he could better negotiate. He gave Helmut and me a lecture on why China was important, and how understanding the distinctive Chinese mentality could bolster bilateral relations. As the investment banker, my professional interests centered on finance, and I enjoyed speculating that China earned about 7 percent of the world's medals, but that was likely to increase to percentages in the midteens in the coming decades. As a head of state, Helmut was more interested in how technologies might impact the developing world. He was the most prescient of all three of us about coming technological developments, like enhanced communications capacities and their potential to impact emerging markets.

A diplomat, Henry was also curious. "Just explain to me, again, what you're doing with these companies, Jim." He wanted to understand corporate restructuring and how it improved the companies. His inquisitiveness was not surprising, given his distinction and achievement, and it helps explain his longevity in the political world. Despite the controversy surrounding some of his foreign policy positions, I can't name another US leader who survived the Nixon years and maintained his relevancy over the following decades. Though he hasn't occupied an office since the 1970s, Henry continues to receive speaking invitations into his nineties and still stirs controversy. During one of the 2016 Democratic presidential primary debates between Bernie Sanders and Hillary Clinton, Clinton praised Kissinger while Bernie condemned him as one of the most deceptive and underhanded people to occupy this cabinet position in contemporary American history.[52] It made headline news the following day.

Despite the attention directed mostly at Henry, I think of this gala more as Mario Schimberni's triumph. He'd survived the Italian bureaucracy, the Red Brigades attacks, and the financial challenges of the 1970s to accomplish a stunning reversal at Montedison. Not only had the company's global revenues increased to $10 billion, but it had also generated its first profits since 1979 ($250 million). And now the media was beginning to recognize what was called at corporate headquarters "la cura Schimberni" and to celebrate Mario himself.[53]

My relationship with Mario continued to flourish. A decade later, as a member of Brown University's board of trustees, I brought Mario to Providence which, with its large Italian American population, organized a parade for Mario. Crowds stood on the streets of Little Italy's central drag, Atwells Avenue, waving and cheering. Prior to his departure, Mario announced a generous gift from Montedison to Brown's chemistry department—another small chapter in this ongoing Italian-American love affair.

During my work for Montedison, US financial prestige reigned supreme throughout the world. This remained true even as financial securities brokers lost profit and prestige after May Day, as American prosperity in the 1960s gave way to stagflation throughout the 1970s, and as generally depressed economic circumstances resulted in violence perpetrated by groups like the Red Brigades. Despite the economic pessimism of the time, the world still turned to America for financial and moral leadership, trusting that its education, health-care, and financial systems would help usher in a more prosperous age.

Just as my work with Montedison began to ebb in the late 1980s and early 1990s, America's geopolitical and financial influence began changing. Digital technologies began transforming the securities business, as electronic exchanges came to replace floor-based, face-to-face trading. As the sheer number of online trading platforms throughout the world proliferated, the NYSE's symbolic and financial power began diminishing as major companies began listing shares elsewhere. In 2006, the NYSE ceased being a members-only club, itself becoming a public for-profit company. Overnight the owners of its once valuable, highly coveted seats were forced to sell, and anyone with a license could execute trades on the exchange.

My accomplishments at Montedison were possible only with the help of my investment banking partners like Steve Eppley and Ken Siegel, and because they occurred when the NYSE was the global leader in securities listings. Since the United States was the uncontested leader in global finance, I could capitalize on the time-honored Italian-American relationship. It was American financial might and Italian-American goodwill that allowed me to create significant market value for Montedison. And the value was considerable. The aggregate value of the three public spinoff companies that Wertheim created for Montedison came to exceed the *entire* value of parent company Montedison.

In creating this wealth for shareholders and increasing jobs for Italians, Wertheim also helped correct false assumptions about Italian finance, as epitomized by derogatory labels like "spaghetti accounting." Such accusations had always struck me as unfair because Italian companies were both innovative and powerful. No one in the finance world, for example, questioned the critical importance of Adriamycin to cancer therapy or the enormous value of plastics. But financial analysts did question Italian disclosure and transparency practices. By restructuring Montedison's holdings and listing them on the NYSE, we'd created a powerful Italian company, not at the mercy of the government or a powerful family, as many large enterprises in the country then were.[54] Instead, we created a series of public entities, owned by diverse shareholders, who helped maintain transparency and power future growth.

Mario Schimberni continued his bold power plays in Italy, and after another hostile takeover of financial services firm Bi-Invest, ran afoul of the Agnelli and Bonomi families.[55] In 1986, Raul Gardini, chair of a sugar and chemical operation called the Ferruzzi group, began amassing a large position in Montedison, inching Schimberni out of the company.[56] I took my exit from Montedison at around the same time, turning my attention to corporate clients in the music, motion pictures, and discount retail industries.

I'll always be grateful for the Montedison account and the fortunate break it gave me as a young investment banker. In managing the three public offerings for Montedison, I was able to apply my experience in maximizing shareholder value, concurrent with generating important returns for Wertheim. The fee income generated, together with the importance of the

Montedison business, provided an opening for the1986 merger of Wertheim with Schroders merchant bank, eventually enabling me to enter government.

But as was always the case with my life's work, the value of this experience exceeded profits and shareholder returns. Montedison increased my passion for working abroad and gave me my first inkling that I might one day help foreign countries, not just companies, to forge relationships and realize important gains. On my first trip to Italy, I began to see how building the American-Italian relationship could help strengthen Italy and began envisioning how such strong bilateral relationships could be helpful in other countries throughout the world. Montedison therefore prepared me for the work I'd take up in Russia, South Korea, Indonesia, the Philippines, Sub-Saharan Africa, and, eventually, Egypt, giving me the confidence that I could forge larger geopolitical change in the public sector. But first I would use the lessons I gleaned there in the glamourous if volatile world of the entertainment industry, the subject of the next two chapters.

4

The Surprising Profitability of Music Publishing

ONE DAY AROUND 2010, I was relaxing on the beaches of Anguilla, when Ukrainian-born billionaire Len Blavatnik struck up a conversation with me. He was one of the corporate executives who, as I liked to joke, had followed me to this island paradise. Private equity tycoon Edgar Bronfman, along with others like Blavatnik, had purchased homes in Anguilla after my family had. In truth, I had nothing to do with it, as Anguilla was becoming a fashionable place, whose secluded charms, beautiful vistas, and gourmet restaurants attracted A-list celebrities and investment bankers alike.

I'd met Blavatnik, who'd much rather be called a philanthropist and industrialist than an oligarch, in 1998, when I served in government and was negotiating a controversial oil transaction.[57] Years later, Blavatnik brought vast sums of money and his Russian cultural habits to New York City. When he vied for a $50 million townhouse on East Sixty-Fourth Street, he brought armed bodyguards to stand ready outside the meeting. The co-op board turned him down.[58] "This isn't Moscow," I told him on the phone after he called me, flummoxed by the decision. "You can't do that here."

Since then, Blavatnik had become more accustomed to American mannerisms, marrying media executive Emily Appelson Blavatnik, raising a family, and diversifying his empire. Appelson Blavatnik, I learned that day, had introduced her husband to the music industry. "I'm going to buy Warner Music Group," he told me on the beach. While I respected Len's instincts, I feared this industrial business mogul might be making a wrong move with music publishing.

When I bought the company that would become Warner Music twenty years before, I explained to him, it was cheap. As I asked him a few specifics about the industry, inquiring about the royalty income, or "net publisher's share," that he expected to generate, he shrugged his shoulders, unfamiliar with the larger industry. "Watch out, Len," I warned. "You're paying a huge price for this."

I wasn't alone in my skepticism. In 2011, when Blavatnik purchased Warner Music Group for $3.3 billion, the music business was far from its profitable heights of 1999. Many believed digital disruption had forever killed the industry.[59] Music piracy had diminished record-label profits and digital music nearly dethroned the industry's once mighty compact disc. Americans also spent on average three times less on recorded music than they did at the turn of the century.[60] One observer memorably described the music business as "roadkill on the information superhighway."[61]

Such volatility has always made me uneasy. When investors introduced me to the music industry in the 1970s, I was leery of such a high-risk, high-glamour business. But once they showed me music publishing, I realized that I'd been evaluating the music industry based only on its recording business.[62] While music recording was difficult to enter, highly asset-based, and volatile, leaving fortunes gained and lost overnight, music publishing was steady, stable, and highly profitable. Requiring almost no fixed assets, music publishing was a classic nickel-and-dime business, generating large cash flows relative to business size.

I am grateful that I pursued music publishing in the 1980s and am similarly grateful that Blavatnik didn't heed my advice decades later on a Caribbean beach. In May 2020, nine years after Blavatnik bought the music giant, the company announced a major IPO, increasing Blavatnik's net worth by billions overnight.[63] Blavatnik was prescient, purchasing this music publishing company as part of his greater ambition to create a twenty-first-century media empire. While my music goals were more modest, music publishing was just as important for me. It was among the most important industries I entered as an investment banker, introducing me to an intriguing world, and ultimately generating enough profits to allow me to internationalize Wertheim and begin my work in the government.

CHASING CHAPPELL

I began my work with the music publishing industry in early 1975, when an institutional salesman at Wertheim introduced my colleagues and me to musical theater star Jo Sullivan Loesser. Acclaimed for her role in the original production of *The Most Happy Fella*, Jo had recently lost her husband Frank Loesser, a legendary composer and songwriter who created Broadway musical hits like *Guys and Dolls* and *How to Succeed in Business Without Really Trying*. I assumed Wertheim's general prestige had made this introduction to her work possible.

In the investment banking business, representing the seller of a quality product was always better than representing the buyer. And Loesser's catalogue was clearly valuable. In selling it, I could help Jo, an energetic, slight, and vibrant woman who specialized in the artistic side of the business and needed assistance with managing her holdings and capitalizing on their financial potential. Jo's lawyers had advised her and Frank to form a music-publishing company so they could own their own music, but they had trouble marketing their songs as effectively as larger publishers. After several meetings, Jo and her attorneys retained Wertheim to sell Frank Music Corp., which controlled the music-publishing rights to the Frank Loesser music catalogue. At the time, I was friendly with Arthur Taylor, a former classmate of mine at Brown and now CBS president. Wertheim easily sold the business to CBS, and both parties were happy.

But others wanted in on this fee income. After Frank's death, a well-known New York–based therapist helped Jo to manage her grief. During their sessions, the therapist discovered Jo wanted to sell the music business, and he alerted his son, a salesperson at Wertheim. I never knew the business had come to us that way, assuming it was Wertheim's clout and prestige that aided my introduction to Loesser, just as it had with Mountain Fuel Supply in Utah. But after the conclusion of the Frank Music transaction, the therapist asked me for a finder's fee. I was astounded. This therapist sought financial reward because he was tipped off from a grieving patient who shared confidential information! I chose not to pay the therapist anything.

This successful sale led Wertheim to other music and entertainment assignments. Early in 1984, Billy Hammerstein and Phil Zimet visited our 200 Park Avenue offices. A music and motion picture industry insider, Zimet was an entertainment attorney who represented Billy Hammerstein, a music publisher and son of the late Oscar Hammerstein II, whose famous partnership with Richard Rodgers led to Broadway hits like *Carousel*, *Oklahoma!*, *The King and I*, and *South Pacific*. That day, Phil wanted to discuss Chappell Music. A small company founded in 1811 to make pianos in London, Chappell had since expanded into music publishing. Chappell's specialty in musical theater, like that of Rodgers and Hammerstein, helped transform it into the largest and one of the most prestigious music-publishing businesses in the world.[64]

Hammerstein and Zimet were familiar with our research covering the motion picture and television industries and our sale of Frank Music to CBS. That day they informed me that PolyGram record label, controlled by Dutch company Phillips and German company Siemens, planned to sell Chappell.[65] With thirty-one companies operating in twenty-three countries, Chappell was a unique and potentially lucrative opportunity.[66] But it was also a complicated transaction. Because we were unfamiliar with the industry, a team of Wertheim's corporate finance professionals, led by Mark Shapiro and Steve Oakes, spent a year performing due diligence on the transaction.

Younger readers might be envious of the position we had in the early 1980s. Chappell owned over 400,000 copyrights across the globe, and Wertheim had the luxury of considering this $100 million investment for over a year without private equity or investment banking firms competing with us.[67] In the late 1970s and 1980s, investment bankers launched powerful private equity operations, acquiring firms with both debt and capital equity like Chappell. But large private equity giants like KKR & Co. and Blackstone were in the early stages of building their businesses, allowing me this unique opportunity that would be impossible today.

If I had been more of a risk-taker, I could have persuaded Steve Kotler and several other corporate finance colleagues to leverage our position in Chappell and form a private equity business of our own. Such a move could have positioned us with the likes of Blackstone and Apollo, and we could have amassed the same fortunes as their managers did. But I had clients like Mountain Fuel Supply in Utah, Montedison in Italy, and the motion picture industry in Hollywood that I loved working with, and which represented recurring sources of income. A move to private equity would have been a major financial gamble and resulted in a somewhat less interesting and meaningful life.

It was with a more "up and doing" spirit that I explored music publishing for much of 1985 and began to learn the intricacies of copyright protection, royalties, and licensing arrangements. When successful music groups like the Beatles create new music, their publishers receive royalty income for the duration of the copyright. As owners of a certain percentage of the rights, these music publishers generate small fees each time artists record or perform their music around the world, or whenever it appears in a motion picture, corporate advertisement, and the like. When Elton John sold a million records, Chappell received $500,000, and when Hebrew National advertised products with a piece from *Fiddler on the Roof*, Chappell received $100,000.[68]

These recurring revenues rendered this conservative bastion of the entertainment business a banker's dream. In a bad year, music publishing grows 3 to 4 percent, and in a good year, 7 to 12 percent. That's why I called the industry "almost recession-proof" in a 1987 interview with the *Los Angeles Times*, telling the *New York Times* that same year it was "recession-resistant."[69] With the exception of major catalogue acquisitions, furthermore, these businesses were largely self-financing. They also derived a substantial amount of free financing from the float generated by the three- to twelve-month lag between the receipt and disbursement of royalty revenues. US intellectual property law had recently strengthened the business as well. Beginning on January 1, 1978, a few years after my introduction to the industry, copyright protection for all works extended to the life of the composer or author plus seventy additional years.[70]

This business model has remained remarkably stable to the present day. In 2020, for example, Goldman Sachs predicted that the global music industry would lose a quarter of its revenues due to live-event cancellations and other disruptions associated with the Covid-19 pandemic.[71] But that same year, music catalogue sales did a brisk business, with investors and publishing companies courting musicians and successfully persuading artists like Rick James, Barry Manilow, and Stevie Nicks to part with all or, or at least portions, of their catalogues.[72] In December 2020, the industry inked the most lucrative and mythic deal of all when lyricist, civil rights icon, and Nobel Prize recipient Bob Dylan sold his 600-plus catalogue of songs to Universal Music Publishing Group.[73]

As I considered the Chappell deal, I especially gravitated to the company's independence. Of the four top global music publishers of the 1980s—CBS, Warner Music, EMI, and Chappell—Chappell was the only one not related to a major record company.[74] This provided the company a competitive advantage by allowing the composers music revenues that could not be linked to, or "cross-collateralized" against, recording contracts, merchandising arrangements, or live-performance deals. Instead of doing recording and promotion in-house, Chappell offered its artists autonomy and flexibility.

I also found the stature and richness of the company's portfolio almost overwhelming. Once a publisher of letters, Chappell contained original missives from Beethoven, King George IV, and Charles Dickens in its archives. A Beethoven letter addressed to one of his students in 1819 speaks to the company's reputation in the nineteenth century. "Chappell in Bond Street," says Beethoven, referring to the company's historic London location, "is now one of the best publishers."[75] Among the company's 400,000 copyrights numbered icons like Gilbert and Sullivan, Noel Coward, and George and Ira Gershwin, while its contemporary artists included Elton John, Rod Stewart, Michel Legrand, and Bob Geldof.

After more than twenty years as an investment banker, working as a corporate advisor, I finally felt ready to become the principal at a company. In mid-1985, Wertheim organized a group of investors and reached an agreement to purchase Chappell for $103 million. My corporate finance colleagues, Steve Schechter and Steve Oakes, were critically important in arranging the debt financing of $75 million and assembling a distinguished group of investors (Creditanstalt, Bank of Boston, and the European Banking Company), two US private equity firms (Boston Ventures and Warburg), and an international group (Pincus Investors and Electra Investment Trust PLC in London) to join us for the purchase. I knew that our $30 million investment would pay rich rewards if we managed it right.

Aside from the United States and the United Kingdom, France was Chappell's largest market, and it threatened to overturn the deal. Because French copyrights represented almost 17 percent of the total price, the government required public approval for the sale. The French ministry of finance approved the deal, but the ministry of culture denied it, suggesting that only French nationals should purchase a French subsidiary of Chappell.

On October 28, 1985, I met with Jack Mathieu Émile Lang, France's minister of culture, in his stately seventeenth-century Parisian office. Arriving thirty minutes late, the minister attempted to conduct the meeting in French, although he commanded nearly fluent English. With a few of his colleagues in attendance, Minister Lang began in a theatrical fashion, lecturing me about why French music couldn't possibly have American ownership.

I reminded the minister that French nationals hadn't owned Chappell's French companies for over a century and that PolyGram, a Dutch-German company, currently controlled the catalogue. If he could find a French music group to purchase the country's stake for the same price we offered—$17 million for 17 percent of the catalogue—then all would be fine. "But if we don't gain your approval," I said, and absent a French buyer, "we will exercise our rights under the purchase and sale agreements, and ownership will revert to PolyGram."

His response, in an English-French pidgin, was that French soldiers had died during World War I and World War II singing songs in the Chappell catalogue. Though highly political, his remarks revealed a European respect for older music and national pride for his country's artistic heritage. I nonetheless reminded him about the different roles the Germans and Americans played in World War II. "If French soldiers died while singing this music," I insisted, "all the more reason Americans should own it, and we shouldn't give it back to the Germans."

I thought it was a decent point, but the negotiations remained tense. Minister Lang really didn't want to sell the music, and I really didn't want to lose the French portion of the catalogue. This ranks as one of the more annoying and unpleasant meetings of my life. "You have a month to find a French buyer," I announced as I left his office, "otherwise we'll give it back to the Germans."

CHAPPELL WARNER

After the French reluctantly granted approval and the deal closed, I knew that to build the company, we needed to nurture its human capital. I was thus grateful that the deal came with Freddy Bienstock, a slight, chubby man of Swiss descent who had broad international experience in the music industry. I liked Freddy from our first meeting. He had a Henry Kissinger–style accent that made him sound even more intelligent than he naturally was.

His knowledge of Chappell and enthusiasm for acquiring new talent and catalogues impressed me, and his sense of humor put me at ease.

As Freddy argued after the sale, Chappell wasn't aggressive enough in pursuing new acts and relied too heavily on the older revenue streams of artists like Cole Porter, Gilbert and Sullivan, and Rodgers and Hammerstein. Absent more creativity, the company wouldn't maximize its value and improve its standing in the industry. Freddy ventured into nightclubs and other music venues each evening to scout new talent. He believed that Chappell needed leaders to model this type of proactive behavior. "Jim, there are some good people at Chappell, and I wouldn't change the management. They just need leadership."

The more I evaluated the possible contenders, the more Freddy seemed like the ideal person to assume such leadership. It would be hard to find someone more committed to the industry in general and Chappell in particular. After coming to America from Switzerland in 1939, following a brief stint in Vienna, a teenage Freddy often passed by Chappell's headquarters near Times Square to see his cousin, a Chappell Music executive. Freddy began working there as a fourteen-year-old stockroom clerk, rising through the ranks to song plugger (or promoter), before striking out on his own, acquiring diverse music catalogues and managing sales of artists like Elvis Presley in movies. In 1984 we asked Freddy, who would have a 15 percent stake in the Chappell transaction, to serve as CEO of the company. It was a dream come true for him. He happily began directing the company he'd begun working at as a teenager forty-two years earlier.[76]

In the years to follow, Freddy exercised strong artistic leadership. One of the reasons he could do so was because Chappell was the only leading music publisher that was privately owned, meaning it didn't have to worry about quarterly earnings reports—an advantage that many contemporary companies have since embraced. Since the mid-1990s, the number of publicly traded companies has plummeted. In 2018 Warren Buffett and Jamie Dimon (CEO of JPMorgan Chase) observed that "the pressure to meet short-term earnings estimates has contributed to the decline in the number of public companies in America over the past two decades." The economy has suffered as a result. "Short-term-oriented capital markets," they wrote, "have discouraged companies with a longer-term view from going public at all, depriving the economy of innovation and opportunity."[77]

When it came to securing emerging talent, Freddy leveraged Chappell's capital funds to make long-term decisions. One night in the late 1980s, for example, Freddy called me and said, "Let's go to Ireland so we can sign Bono." Freddy was convinced that this artist, whom I'd never heard of, was going to be sensational in the next five years.

"Five years, Freddy," I replied. "What returns will we have over the five years?"

He told me to forget about any short-term return on investment—we needed to sink several million into future sensations and wait for them to mature. He was right about Bono, and when we went to Nashville, where he seemed to know everyone, he turned to me and said, "This guy's going to be great." We then signed George Michael—another Freddy success story. I never pretended to be an expert in music, always reminding Freddy that I'd once predicted the Beatles wouldn't amount to much. He'd still throw recordings my way saying, "You've got to listen to this. He will be the next star." Knowing my limits, I'd circulate the recordings to the younger people in my office and share their opinions with Freddy.

I supported Freddy's long-term artistic judgments, while still reminding him that we had investors interested in shorter-term profits. Luckily, I could show our investors strong balance sheets. Music publishing produced significant cash flow. If we made a deal with someone like Bono, we could pay him an initial lump sum and amortize the balance, meaning we could gradually write off the cost over the span of years. Instead of high earnings, we thus reported good cash flow, which made us attractive to investors.

In early 1987, Warner Communications approached me to buy Chappell, suggesting a merger of two of the largest music publishers in the world. Understanding the newly competitive private equity environment, Warner structured an advantageous package, offering us $200 million in convertible preferred stock in Warner, enabling investors to defer the capital-gains hit that would have accompanied a taxable cash transaction. The offer was approximately ten times our equity investment two years prior, and the convertible preferred was an attractive security that increased in value. If you invested $1 million in the original deal, you received $7 million two years later, and within five years, that would double to $14 million. You only paid taxes when you sold the convertible or received dividends.

Everyone was elated with the Warner transaction except Freddy. He loved running Chappell and didn't want to sell. I understood. Though he'd amassed wealth and status, Freddy dreamed of running Chappell for the rest of his life. Warner offered Freddy an honorary position after the deal, but the experts in Warner's publishing department looked down on him. Freddy continued working in his own music business called Carlin and collaborated with his brother and daughter on important projects. But I was always saddened to think Freddy felt I'd abandoned him. After having worked closely together for three years, everything changed with us.

The CEO and chair of Time Warner and Warner Communications, Steve Ross, was a formidable man who was universally beloved in Hollywood. (Beware that this book features another Steve Ross, the real estate magnate and environmentalist, my other good friend and colleague, who appears in chapter 11.) Before becoming a leading agent in Hollywood and buying Warner Brothers, Steve Ross worked in the funeral business. He knew how to manage people in grief and had a unique interpersonal gift in understanding human nature.

One day during negotiations between Time Inc. and Warner, Steve drew on such wisdom when explaining the differences between the WASP and Jewish worlds of entertainment. He told me when we ventured to *Time*'s headquarters, the WASPs that ran the company would serve us alcohol and that we all needed to have some. "But when they come here," Steve said, "we serve them cookies. Liquor dulls the senses, but sugar makes you happy." Before negotiations, his offices contained the most beautiful array of cookies and ice creams. We all left these meetings having gained some weight but with smiles on our faces, and then proceeded over to Time Inc. to begin sipping scotch.

When negotiating my fee for the merger of Time Inc. and Warner, Steve did something unusual. I quoted him a $3 million fee to merge the companies. "Jim, we will pay you $4 million." No client had ever proposed to pay us *more* than our asking fee. When I looked perplexed, he told me how great a job we did for the deal and how much we deserved $3.5 million. "In the next two years," he then said, "I'm going to ask you to make contributions to different organizations that I think are important for the world. And I expect that you'll make them from this extra $500,000 reserve of money." It didn't initially make sense to me, but on the walk back to my offices, I saw the logic.

This reserve of funds helped Steve run a powerful company like Warner. Whenever Steve received a call from the chair of the American Heart Association or some other worthy organization, he could always give them money without question. He didn't have to consult a committee or discuss it with his managers because he'd built up this surplus fund with people like me. I consulted with my lawyers. They'd never heard of such a practice. It was a gentleman's agreement. Though I wasn't legally bound to do the charitable transactions, I felt great about contributing to worthy causes. Later that year Steve called me and asked Wertheim to increase its annual contribution to Mount Sinai Hospital, which I happily did.

When Steve approached me to buy Chappell, he showed his interpersonal edge. After I told him I could sell Chappell for $225 million, he offered me $200 million. "I'd like you to stay around," he added. I told him that I'd love to advise him and become more acquainted with what he was doing in the motion picture business. "I'd like you to be more than an advisor," he responded. "I'd like you to be chair of Warner Chappell Music." As I walked from our meeting at Rockefeller Center back to my offices at Wertheim, I realized this was also a smart business decision. If he was going to pay me a significant purchase price, he wanted to ensure my enthusiasm about what he was doing. "You did a brilliant deal, and in two years' time you've made a fortune on this business. I'm not going to pay you anything," he said.

"Instead, I'll ask you to take this title. If in two years you aren't happy, you can leave." That was fine with me. With record profits and a chair for me, it was a well-packaged exit for us at Chappell and also assured us some of Warner's future investment banking business.

After this 1987 transaction, we became well known in the music publishing world, and the following year I oversaw an important and intriguing transaction as chair of Warner Chappell. It began in 1988 when the owners of Birchtree Group, an international publisher and distributor of educational music, suggested a meeting. Birchtree resembled any number of small music clients that we'd advised since the Jo Loesser transaction, and I didn't attend the first meeting because it was a small business. One of my partners was present at the meeting, however, and he later told me: "This company is family owned, easy to deal with, and has a fascinating story."

The story blew me away. In Louisville, Kentucky, during the 1890s, two sisters, Patty and Mildred Hill, kindergarten and Sunday school teachers, wrote the melody to what would become the most popular song in the English language.[78] Patty's students greeted the school day by singing:

Good Morning to You
Good Morning to You
Good Morning Dear Teacher
Good Morning to All[79]

Believing that songs were an important part of a child's education, the sisters published "Good Morning" in *Song Stories for Children* (1893), which they promoted that year at Chicago's World's Fair and for which they secured a copyright. The students at Louisville Experimental Kindergarten School innovated with that melody, singing "Happy Vacation to You," "Good Bye to You," and the famous "Happy Birthday" variant, which took off in popularity across the country. Birchtree owned the copyright to the beloved "Happy Birthday," which generated about $1 million a year in licensing fees and accounted for around 85 percent of the company's profits.[80]

Despite the profits Birchtree garnered from its prize song, the company lacked the resources of larger companies like Warner to protect its copyright, ensuring that every time the song was played or performed (whether on Broadway or at a restaurant), it collected a licensing fee.[81] In 1988, we paid $18 million for the Birchtree Group, becoming the proud new owners of "Happy Birthday to You."[82]

Warner Chappell was supposed to control the copyright until 2030, but in 2013, long after I'd completed my work in the music industry, Jennifer Nelson, a documentary filmmaker who was making a movie about the song, received a $1,500 licensing charge.[83] She sued Warner Chappell, challenging the company's rightful ownership of the song. The music industry watched closely as the judge scrutinized the evidence, observing that the teachers published a song with the identical melody but different lyrics than the one currently copyrighted "Happy Birthday." In 2015, Judge George H. King of the United States District Court in Los Angeles declared Warner Chappell's copyright invalid, meaning the company could no longer collect the then $2 million in revenue it garnered each year in licensing fees.[84] In 2016, the company paid $14 million to reimburse people who had paid royalties on the song in the past.[85]

"Happy Birthday" now belongs to the public domain. Fear not next time you publicly perform the song at a restaurant or at your child's birthday party.

When I discovered that a song like "Happy Birthday" could be owned, I took Freddy aside. "Look what we've done with 'Happy Birthday,'" I told him. "There must be millions of people the world over who'd love to purchase a song." The possibilities seemed endless. If a fiancé wanted to buy his betrothed something meaningful, why not allow him to purchase her part of a romantic song like "South Pacific" or "I Love Paris"? Maybe a parent wanted to give her Christmas-loving child a fraction of "Frosty the Snowman" or "Jingle Bells" for a holiday treat. Some might afford a 25 percent investment, while others might purchase 2, 5, or 10 percent. Every time the song played, the partial owner would get a personal thrill and generate recurring dividend income. Freddy was skeptical, and when I circulated a memorandum at Warner Chappell suggesting that my revenue-generation scheme could transform us into a multibillion-dollar company, my colleagues were appalled.

Their reaction reminded me of when I was in business school and conceived of a similar idea: advertisements on railroad freight trains traversing the country. We could plaster advertisements for Coca-Cola or a presidential hopeful in phosphorescent paint, I thought at the time, and as the train swept the country, onlookers could see the ad. I contacted an artist while at Wharton Business School, we mocked up some designs, and I met with the New York Central Railroad's CFO. "I'd like to lease the sides of your freight trains," I said, quoting him a price and telling him I'd assemble a creative team. He rejected the idea because he felt it would cheapen the countryside, in some way, to have Coca-Cola plastered to the side of the train car. Now, of course, every square inch of real estate, from city buses to personal vehicles, serves as canvases for advertisers.

Music industry insiders universally disliked my song ownership idea, suggesting that the fractional sale of such artwork would degrade the product itself. Composers and lyricists, they reminded me, sold their royalty income only when they encountered financial difficulties. "If the music publisher sells a fraction of what he has to the average Joe, people won't come to publishers again," Freddy said. Facing unanimous disapproval, I dropped the idea. I've never wanted to upset the creative side of any industry. But I still believe the idea is a potential gold mine.

And so is music publishing. As I write this book, the profitability of the industry has only increased. Interest rates are at historic lows, meaning music royalties are like bonds, increasing in investment value the lower rates decline. Whether it's my acquisition of Chappell music and "Happy Birthday" in the 1980s or the Chappell IPO and Universal's acquisition of the Bob Dylan catalogue in 2020, the industry continues to be robust and vibrant. But don't get me wrong. The internet has changed the music industry and the motion picture industry, the subject to which I now turn. To maintain their relevance and profitability in today's climate, rife with disruption, entertainment industry insiders will come to entertain schemes like the fractional sale of songs. That's an idea whose time, I predict, is soon to come.

5

More Fun Than Profitable: Making Movies in the 1980s

ONE DAY IN THE MID-1970s, an executive from Lucasfilm movie studio gave me a call. "You're a layperson with average tastes, so we'd like to arrange a movie screening for you." Though mildly insulting, his evaluation of my tastes was accurate. The closest I came to artistic savvy was my wife, Jane, a gifted theatrical producer. The screening was for a space-opera odyssey that George Lucas had written and directed called *Star Wars*.

After my long commute from Connecticut, I shuffled into a small screening room at the southern tip of Manhattan at nine o'clock in the morning, a little disheartened. Part of the pleasure I've always derived from cinema is social: I love watching the responses of other moviegoers and seeing what they find funny or compelling. Instead of sharing in common laughter and applause, I sat motionless and alone in this cold theater for several hours that day. When the final credits rolled on the screen, I walked back to my office at Wertheim at One Chase Plaza and called Lucasfilm's office. A movie executive asked what I thought of the film. "I thought it was dumb," I said. "I don't think it's going to do very well."

In the years since, studio executives have endlessly delighted in playing this tape back to me. As we now know, *Star Wars* met with wild acclaim from its launch in May 1977 and has since become one of the most popular franchises in entertainment history, setting records in merchandising and special effects alike.[86]

I've protested in the years since, jokingly challenging others to go to a theater in the early morning, alone and sober, and identify the next cinematic sensation. But there's no denying that I was on the wrong side of history with my predictions about this film. Whether it was the next great band or the next great blockbuster, I've been unable to predict new tastes and popular trends, focusing my energy instead on adding financial value to the entertainment industry. Both the music and motion picture industries were glamourous and exciting, but I was uneasy about their volatility, or what I sometimes referred to as "the amplitude of the financial fluctuations" they experienced.

Such volatility was even more pronounced in motion pictures than it was in music recording. Movies like *Star Wars* were rare. Wonderful scripts with A-list celebrities and decent distribution networks routinely bombed in the box office, losing film companies significant money. Motion picture studios also routinely produced several big hits, generating lots of money as well as popular adoration and critical acclaim; the following year, however, that same studio would release several flops and lose its popular luster, leaving executives anxious about how to make ongoing debt payments.

I had faith in the artistic abilities of movie creators but was never optimistic that the public or the market would reward this talent, let alone produce consistent returns for investors. When working in the film industry in the 1980s, I therefore tried to flatten the curve and somehow tame or "manage" the volatility of this important industry. My real investment in motion pictures was nonfinancial, as I remained committed not to profits, but rather to the cinematic artists and the beautiful cultural products they gave the world.

CONSISTENTLY VOLATILE

My journey with motion pictures began in April 1972, when I met Richard Bloch in his Beverly Hills office. Richard was president and majority owner of the Phoenix Suns basketball team. Bloch was partners with Tucson-based Donald Pitt, developing buildings for lease to large companies like IBM.

A tall, athletic man, Richard competed in equestrian events and was interested in sports and the arts. But it was his big smile, outgoing personality, and love of people that attracted me when we met that spring, and we would develop a close friendship over the following two decades. Many real estate developers who accumulate capital eventually gravitate to more glamourous businesses.

This began for Richard in 1968, the year he cofounded the Phoenix Suns, bringing the first sports franchise to Arizona.[87] In the coming years, I'd see Dick, as I came to know him, at basketball games in New York and Los Angeles. On one such occasion, sometime in the mid-1970s, I flew to Phoenix to join Dick and his wife, Nancy, to see basketball great Connie Hawkins perform his on-court magic. Hailing from the Bedford-Stuyvesant neighborhood of Brooklyn, Hawkins began dunking at the age of eleven and would exert a strong influence on future legends like Michael Jordan and Julius Erving.[88]

Connie also had a reputation for being eccentric, which I discovered that game day, as we stood courtside watching the coach motion to speak with Dick. After a brief exchange, Dick returned and informed us of a problem. Hawkins was convinced he couldn't perform athletically that day because he hadn't been intimate with a woman the night before. He believed, apparently, that sexual relations before a game relaxed him and boosted his performance on the court. With a look of mock horror on her face, Nancy exclaimed, "Don't look at me!" We all collapsed in laughter.

Though Dick had been successful in real estate development and running the Phoenix Suns, he was also partially based in Los Angeles and dreamed of entering the film industry. Dick took a significant position in the publicly owned Filmways, a midsize Hollywood studio that produced several successful television shows including CBS's *The Beverly Hillbillies* and *Mister Ed*. After Dick became CEO of Filmways in 1976, he wanted his studio to produce feature films. In April 1978, when American International Pictures (AIP) retained Wertheim to help sell the company, I immediately thought of Dick and Filmways.

AIP's cofounder, Sam Arkoff, known in the industry as the godfather of beach party and teenage-werewolf movies, was ready to retire. Short and stocky and always armed with a cigar and strong opinions, Arkoff produced more films with the best directors (Francis Ford Coppola, Martin Scorsese, Brian DePalma) and stars (Jack Nicholson, Robert DeNiro, Charles Bronson, Nick Nolte, and Peter Fonda) than nearly anyone I can recall.[89] He was a true Hollywood character. But his business was suffering. While AIP had traditionally enjoyed financial success with low-budget, youth-oriented summer pictures, Universal's release of Steven Spielberg's *Jaws* in June of 1975 was an enormous success, making it difficult for midsize outfits like AIP to compete.[90]

I made the introduction, and in early summer of 1979, Filmways purchased AIP for $4.5 million. Directly following the sale, AIP released *The Amityville Horror*. Based on a book with the same title, the story centers on the supernatural experiences of a family who bought a home in Amityville, Long Island, the site of a gruesome murder. The film was a commercial success—grossing over $85 million, it ranked among the most lucrative independent films of all time (and the second most popular of 1979, trailing only divorce drama *Kramer vs. Kramer*).[91] And though it rose to classic status in the horror genre, most critics panned the movie, while others questioned the authenticity of the events on which it was based.[92] Artistic merit aside, the timing of this movie so close to the sale was most fortunate. The transaction may never have closed if the film had been released earlier.

But seeing that Filmways was still struggling, taking on more debt and on the brink of bankruptcy, I hatched an unorthodox idea. It involved the purchase of an insurance company. Why would the directors of an entertainment company want to buy an insurance company, and why would the board of a steady, conservative insurance business want to become involved in the volatile entertainment industry? Let me explain my reasoning. I'd served on the board of Union Fidelity Life Insurance Company (UFC) since the late 1960s and had managed the company's initial public offering. UFC was an innovative company, and I became active in building the business, attending each quarterly board meeting in Philadelphia. Founded by brilliant marketer Harry Dozer, this outfit created a new product category in the direct marketing of insurance. Instead of analyzing preexisting conditions or delving into the traditional complexities of health insurance, UFC simplified the entire process. If its policyholders ever went to the hospital, UFC paid them a per-diem rate, allowing them to cover medical costs and maintain their family incomes while temporarily out of work.

UFC policies were popular, and because they were direct-to-consumer, the company didn't sink costs into insurance agents, leading to its steady growth throughout the 1960s and early '70s. During the market volatility and climate of stagflation thereafter, UFC shares declined to well below their book and market value by the mid-1970s. Seeing the stock drop from $15–$20 a share to $3–$4, Harry became depressed, and I talked with him about selling the company or relinquishing his shares. I now had just the buyer for him, and in 1977, Filmways bought Harry's controlling interest in UFC and proposed a merger of the two companies. Though some of UFC's shareholders contested the merger and others raised objections, all parties eventually emerged happy. Filmways paid Harry $28–$29 million so he could retire, leaving the struggling film studio with control of a company it could continue to grow and eventually sell. Using the talented people working for Dozer who remained committed to the company's success, that's exactly what they did. Under the Filmways umbrella, moreover, UFC didn't experience the market fluctuations of a standalone company.

Even with a profitable insurance subsidiary and a motion picture and TV-production company, the Filmways conglomerate was still indebted. Since its founding in 1952, the company had struggled in the movie business. Even by midcentury, mounting production and distribution costs made movies less financially attractive than ever. If you lacked the big studios' financial heft, it was harder to guide and grow the company. Dick asked me to run the company several times, and I declined.

By 1980, Filmways was insolvent. For the fiscal year that ended February 28, 1981, Filmways lost $66.3 million, marking the worst performance in the company's history. Its total debt exceeded $100 million and three major bank lenders agreed to extend the repayment of $38.5 million for three months. We needed to sell UFC. In late 1980, Wertheim hosted an auction for the insurance company, announcing that we would accept bids. I'll never forget the day. Dozer and his fellow UFC officers, along with my team, were anxious because bank lenders were clamoring for their money, and we weren't sure if anyone would bid. I worried this might represent the first bankruptcy of a major client of mine.

By midday we received a bid for $100 million from a Chicago-based insurance company called Combined Insurance Company. Luckily for us, Combined Insurance had no idea it was our only bidder. I entered the conference room and, in one of my gutsier business moves, flatly rejected the bid. "We need $110 million," I told the Combined group. After deliberating, Combined Insurance upped its offer to $105 million, and after pretending to think it over very carefully and compare it to other offers, we accepted. Filmways had purchased Union Fidelity Life Insurance Company for $35 million and two years later we sold it at a $70 million gain. Shortly thereafter, Filmways reduced its bank debt from $117 to $30 million and acquired some limited solvency. Best of all: we avoided bankruptcy.

The struggle exacted a toll on Dick. His pastimes included riding horses, and after our victory he said, "I don't want to try and rebuild this again." On paper the Filmways conglomerate looked strong following the UFC transactions. The company had a skeletal domestic distribution system, a library of about 500 feature films and 300 television shows, a publishing business called Grosset & Dunlap, and several other assets. But it also had no attractive business on the horizon. Filmways lost $20 million over 1981 and was once again near bankruptcy by early 1982. Though I didn't occupy a seat on Filmways' board or own any of its shares, Dick's company was a client and I really wanted to help him escape the struggle to survive in the motion picture industry.

When Orion Pictures expressed interest in this flailing studio early that year, I was relieved. Though Orion was also a midsize company, one of its founders, Arthur Krim, was already a legend in Hollywood, and his team of film greats like Eric Pleskow, Mike Medavoy, and Bill Bernstein had been successful together at United Artists (UA) studio.[93] During their four years at UA, the studio won ten Best Picture Oscars, including *One Flew Over the Cuckoo's Nest*, *Rocky*, and *Annie Hall*, and finished number one at the box office for two of those years.[94] They also made Francis Ford Coppola's master-piece *Apocalypse Now* and were working on Martin Scorsese's *Raging Bull*, a film that movie critics later voted best movie of the decade. Arthur, Eric, and Bill left to form Orion in 1978, and now they wanted to leverage the Film-ways catalogue and distribution capacity to transform the company into a major Hollywood player. If anyone could build a new studio, it was Orion.

Upon taking control of Filmways and reincorporating as Orion Pictures Corporation on August 31, 1982, Orion began a major transformation. It divested all of Filmways' nonentertainment assets, including its unprofitable Grosset & Dunlap publishing business and its radio equipment manufac-turer called Broadcast Electronics. Orion fired more than eighty employees, replaced forty with their own recruits, and borrowed $52 million from the Bank of Boston and Chemical Bank, of which $28 million was used to pay off Filmways' debts.

PEOPLE OVER PROFITS

This was the time when I could have, and perhaps should have, left the motion picture industry. With Filmways under great management and with no personal investment, I could exit this troublingly volatile industry. My other investment banking clients like Mountain Fuel Supply, Montedison, and Ames Department Stores were a lot more profitable. But nothing was as much fun as the pictures. Every month Orion seemed to release a new film with major stars. For the pure pleasure of the industry, my relationships with the principals, and my intellectual curiosity about the films, I stayed on, joining the board of Orion and providing all of the financial help I could.

Orion's formidable chair, Arthur Krim, was politically active and hosted spectacular fundraisers and soirées with his wife, Mathilde, an AIDS activist and outstanding scientist. Arthur was twenty-five years older than me, but we were like brothers. Like me, he loved the excitement and creative energies of the motion picture industry, without being creatively inclined himself, and was more interested in producing quality work than making money. We also both became involved in the Democratic party, with him playing the role of fundraiser for Lyndon Johnson that I would later play for Bill Clinton. He and his wife attracted a broad-based group of people at their spectacular New York townhouse, hosting parties that resembled nineteenth-century French salons.

I naturally took to Orion and its ethos. United Artists, Warner, and other major motion picture studios claimed credit, listing every producer, director, or actor in the opening or concluding credits of their films. Orion was unique in the industry in giving credit. You never see Orion principals like Krim, Pleskow, Benjamin, or Mike Medavoy, head of production at Orion, appearing in final film credits. Though they served as producers, directors, or so forth, they subordinated themselves and their roles, allowing the quality of the products to occupy center stage. As Medavoy reflects:

Arthur, Bob, and Eric were always willing to share credit, and they taught me how important that was. Hollywood is a jungle where everyone fights to survive and get ahead, and it's easy to fall under that spell. Most people take credit for any success they can while begrudgingly giving it to others. In our most unique of all Hollywood partnerships, taking credit was never an issue. Everything was done under the auspices of the company and our reputations lived and died as a group.[95]

Though Warner and 20th Century Fox had greater resources, capital, and distribution capacity, Orion won an outsize number of awards. This focus on creativity and the product, instead of personal credit, gave them an edge.

And so did their willingness to promote artists like Woody Allen, whom Orion championed despite his modest commercial success. Many in the industry appreciated Woody's art and his Oscars. But his work appealed to a niche following in New York, Los Angeles, European capitals, and France, where he commands a huge following. Whenever I told investors that Orion was producing a Woody Allen film, they expressed no excitement. That's likely because Orion lost money on his films, even as the studio remained committed to producing them. And I could understand why, because of the spectacular artistic value of his work. He was constantly using motion pictures to tell important stories that enriched audiences.

Sometime in the mid-1980s, I purchased an apartment at 930 Fifth Avenue, and when Arthur Krim introduced me to Woody, I discovered he owned the penthouse suite directly above my unit. I also discovered a unique relationship I shared with Woody and Luciano Pavarotti—we were all born on or near October 12, 1935. Woody didn't care about this birthdate coincidence, however, and was instead focused on our building's prohibition on dogs. His love interest at the time, Diane Keaton, sneaked her miniature dog into the building using her pocketbook as a disguise. When others in the building informed the management, the superintendent intruded on Woody's privacy, entering the unit for an impromptu inspection. "We have to ask the board to vote on allowing dogs," he said to me.

When the co-op board rejected Woody's canine proposal, he circulated one of the funniest letters I've ever read. It wasn't meant to be funny and the tone was entirely serious, describing the importance of having a dog in your life. When I saw Woody in the elevator, he typically kept his head down, not wanting anyone to recognize him. But after the dog fiasco with the co-op board, he and I would chat in the elevator about how unfair this building was. I soon capitalized on this rapport, as I thought Woody could help Wertheim raise money in a public offering for Orion.

When financing or fundraising, I've always believed the nouveau riche are better targets than the Rockefellers. By that I mean that old money sources, like the Vanderbilts and Fords, have established foundations and multiple committees that make fundraising challenging. The nouveau riche, like oil tycoon Len Blavatnik and tech pioneer Bill Gates, are faster to respond and excited at the prospect of glamour and recognition of their generosity. The same is true when attracting investment for a Broadway show or a motion picture.

Sensing Woody might be an ideal prospect, I approached Arthur to ask Woody to consider speaking to a group of investing institutions. "Everyone will come," I insisted.

"I can't use Woody that way," Arthur replied. "Besides, he'll never agree." Sure enough, Woody rejected the idea. But remembering his writing talents with the co-op board, I asked Arthur to petition Woody to record a video for the event. Woody agreed, proceeding to give another highly entertaining performance. Once again, his seriousness was extremely funny, as he insulted his audience. "I wouldn't want to be in your business," he said, referring to investment banking and finance, "and I don't think you understand motion pictures at all." Only Woody could deliver such insults and charm the entire room. The investment bankers representing various institutions loved the video, and it helped raise us a lot of money.

Woody, who always struck me as an unusual character, has since become mired in controversy, as revelations about his private life have surfaced. I've always found him a brilliant and entertaining artist, with a terrific sense of humor, if odd personal mannerisms. Geniuses often don't get along with the average person and sometimes have troubling idiosyncrasies. Because the building wouldn't budge on dogs, Woody sold his spectacular penthouse, and we lost touch.

Woody might have helped our coffers, but in the first two years under Orion Pictures' new management, the stock price soared in anticipation of great hits to come. But those hits weren't forthcoming. This surprised me as I watched the studio's amazing films every month. (The Motion Picture

Association gave access to prerelease films to those on the board of major studios, like me.) Though I wasn't a major entertainer, I took advantage of these prereleases, showing the movies to my friends and to Wertheim's corporate finance department, where about twenty-five of our thirty people regularly attended to see early screenings of *Amadeus*, *Cotton Club*, and *Hoosiers*.

Arthur and Eric were worried about Orion's 1986 release called *Hoosiers*. After the movie screening, I said, "I'm not a good judge, as you know. But I loved it and I'm convinced that others will too." Here I showed unusual prescience because this movie, detailing the triumph of a small Indiana basketball team, captivated much of America. *Amadeus* was also an enormously successful film about the life of Mozart, and I invited my friends and colleagues, music enthusiasts or not, and they loved it. The direction, lighting, staging, and cinematography were so artistic and beautiful—one of Orion's triumphs. *The Terminator*, released to much acclaim and box office success almost a month after *Amadeus*, I called "junk."

Other films, like *The Great Santini*, which Orion released in October 1979, left me uncertain. In the film, Robert Duvall plays a military man who has a hard time transitioning to civilian life. One of the scenes especially stuck with me. Duvall's teenage son plays basketball with him, as his two sisters and mother look on from the house. When the boy wins twenty-one points, clinching his victory, Duvall is so mean spirited, he yells at the boy, taunts him by throwing the ball repeatedly at his head, and calls him "a little girl."

As my father used to say, "I don't want to go to the movies and leave feeling worse. I've spent the whole day on law cases, and I don't want to pay four dollars for pain." Dad's words resonated as I watched this painful movie scene. Many in the country probably feel the same way, wanting to feel happy or even inspired after watching a show.

And that's how I always felt about the talented and lovely Jane Harmon, my favorite theater producer by far. Though a great producer, my wife had mostly local experience until the 1970s, when she worked on a David Mamet production called *A Life in the Theater*, garnering experience with director

Gerald Gutierrez. Her career took off, and she eventually produced *Driving Miss Daisy* with Playwrights Horizons, a not-for-profit off-Broadway theater dedicated to supporting contemporary artists. Alfred Uhry, a fraternity brother of mine from Brown, wrote the script.

Jane immediately saw its potential and scored a major casting coup when Morgan Freeman agreed to play the lead. It debuted at Playwrights Horizons to terrific reviews. After it achieved success touring throughout the country and then abroad, Jane began broaching the idea of a cinematic adaptation. Despite the buzz, several motion picture companies turned her down. Leveraging my relationship with Steve Ross, the chair of Warner to whom I sold Chappell Music, I gave him rave reviews about the production. He'd seen the show off-Broadway and took it up with his motion picture division. But a few days later he called me with bad news, saying the division refused it. Lesson learned: just because you know the chair, you don't always get your way.

Jane secured the cinema deal herself. Terence ("Terry") Steven Semel, chair and co-CEO at Warner Brothers, came to New York to see the show. As they spoke after the show, Semel said, "I'm going to do it. I love it." They persuaded Freeman to play the lead, securing Jessica Tandy and Dan Aykroyd as well, and produced one of the best films of 1989 (according to Gene Siskel), a movie that has remained popular to this day. I loved the quarter-century relationship between an ornery Jewish widow named Daisy (Jessica Tandy) and her affable Black chauffeur, Hoke (Morgan Freeman), and thought that their friendship was inspiring, especially during the fraught time in American history in which the film is set.[96] Many in the Black community, however, came to think that Freeman's character was subservient and the film's message of racial reconciliation naive.

I spoke with my friend Ruth Simmons about the movie. Ruth was president of Brown University at the time, the first Black woman to be president of an Ivy, and I was supporting their Africana Studies program. I admired Ruth's story. She was the youngest of twelve children and her father was a sharecropper. She became a well-known academic with an illustrious career.

Our discussion of the movie led us to a broader exchange about Brown University confronting its past. The university's founder, John Brown, made his fortune as a slaver, and there was increased pressure and interest in the university community formally reckoning with this history. Ultimately, I found it beautiful that this quietly humorous film could spark such an important discussion. To me, that is what all great art seeks to do.

On March 26, 1990, Jane and I attended the 62nd Academy Awards ceremony at the Dorothy Chandler Pavilion—one of the rare nights in my life when half the people in the audience I knew from business, and the other half were friends in the arts. Freeman himself became a family friend and visited our home in Anguilla. When announcing Best Picture nominations, Kim Basinger said, "We've got five great films here, and they're great for one reason: because they tell the truth."[97]

I couldn't have been prouder that evening as the film received nine nominations, ultimately winning four Oscars. Jessica Tandy won for Best Actress, the oldest actress before or since to win this category. Alfred Uhry received recognition for Best Adapted Screenplay, rendering my old housemate the only American who would go on to win the writer's trifecta of a Tony (a play), a Pulitzer (dramatic writing), and an Oscar (best screenplay).[98] And in addition to another Oscar for Makeup, the film won the coveted Best Picture that year.

As an investment banker, my pride in Jane extended to the commercial success of this film. Unlike the films in which I took part, this play-turned-movie produced enormous revenue globally. I compiled all of the performance revenue and subsidiary income to discover that this production, which cost $150,000 to produce off-Broadway, generated total revenue, including film, cassette, digital, and international and domestic subsidiary rights, in excess of $500 million. I was delighted that Semel had the foresight to see its potential and that Warner shared in some of this profit.

Every year I spent in the picture industry the financial volatility only increased. The glamour of the industry proved my saving grace because every time we encountered financial trouble and began to worry about debt requirements, highly capitalized people or outfits like Orion appeared, willing to take over. I quickly learned that the glamour of owning a movie studio or producing a great picture was so great that I didn't need to worry. When we needed to raise equity, I'd turn to heavyweights like industry mogul John Kluge and his partner Stuart Subotnick, and they'd save the company each time. Alleviated of most financial stress, I could simply enjoy the company of creative people and the films they produced.

Over my six to seven years in the industry, I was happy that I saved Filmways from bankruptcy, ensuring that thousands remained employed. The UFC sale and acquisition, which in turn facilitated the Orion acquisition, enabled the company to avoid bankruptcy, save money, and retain jobs. Though I cared deeply about these jobs and people, I never invested my own capital, as I had in Chappell, and instead let those more smitten with Hollywood's vaunted mystique invest their own wealth when times were hard.

There were rich social dividends in the motion pictures business. These studios produced quality work that enriched the lives of American moviegoers and burnished the country's artistic canon, motivating me to remain in the industry from 1982 to 1988. But I'm glad I didn't spend my lifetime with Hollywood. I would have inevitably had a bankruptcy (and probably an ulcer). In the late 1980s, I left Orion's board and exited the industry. By 1986, as I ran a multinational finance firm, I became enmeshed in a mega-retail debacle. In perhaps one of the great ironies of my life, it wasn't the glamourous motion picture industry, but rather the conservative world of affordable retail, in which I experienced my first bankruptcy (my second serious mistake). Unlike the film industry, furthermore, I had significant personal capital as well as my colleagues' investments in this retail merger. Despite the unending volatility of the movie industry, I never personally felt the fluctuations and, instead, largely enjoyed the journey. With Ames Department Stores, the subject to which we now turn, the impact was personal and deeply felt.

6

A Big Retail Failure

THE BIGGEST MISTAKE OF my entire career began shortly after a board meeting in 1987. The meeting itself was routine—the standard Ames Department Stores gathering of board members, meetings I'd attended for two decades. At the company's Hartford, Connecticut, headquarters, we spent five to six hours focused on the financial numbers of this discount store chain with sandwiches and coffee at our elbows.[99] But on this occasion, when the discussions concluded, Herbert Gilman, who had joined the company his two brothers had founded in 1959 and now served as chair and CEO, asked me to his office. There, Herb delivered some devastating news: he had terminal cancer.[100]

I was stunned. Like his two older siblings, Herb was a disciplined man. He refrained from drinking and smoking and didn't carry one extra pound. His cancer had progressed to stage four, he told me, and he would soon need to retire. At the time, I didn't know much about cancer. I figured it resulted from smoking, genetics, or working in an industrial area. Herb's case threw me because none of these applied. His two brothers, Irving and Milton, who had stepped down together in 1980, had found out the day before me.[101] Faced with this prognosis, Herb now focused on his succession. "When I can no longer serve," he asked me that day, "will you accept the chair of the company?" I responded by saying that I'd do what was best for the company as well as for its employees and shareholders.

Though this was a financial and business decision, it also felt personal and emotional. I'd been advising Ames since 1967, when I'd joined the board of directors. It had been my first experience serving on any board, and I was proud of the success I'd witnessed, and in some way helped Ames accomplish, in the twenty years since. During that time, we'd steadily and responsibly scaled the company, expanding its footprint throughout New England and along the mid-Atlantic seaboard.

As I also discovered that day, while Herb had spent six to eight months visiting oncologists throughout New England, he'd also been scouting for a CEO replacement. A few weeks after our meeting, I decided to accept his offer, thinking that I'd serve as an interim chair until the new CEO was ready to assume the position. I also took comfort knowing that this was a "nonexecutive" chair, meaning that I wouldn't be involved in business operations like merchandising. As an investment banker, my strengths were in analyzing people and their companies and forecasting strong investments. But I wasn't an entrepreneur and had no idea how to operate a business like Ames any more than I could run Starbucks, Orion, or Chappell Music.

Nonexecutive chairs performed duties in which I excel, like coordinating corporate operations with institutional investors, helping management grow the company, and advising on nonrecurring decisions. Unfortunately, during my first year of occupying the nonexecutive role of chair, the company made a fateful decision about one such nonrecurring business action: a large acquisition. This resulted in the biggest failure of my career—a failure that all these years later is still painful to write about and one I never imagined would occur in the staid and conservative world of discount retail.

A PLEASANT RETAIL GRIND

Norman Asher, a chubby and gregarious partner at the Boston-based Hale & Dorr law firm (now WilmerHale), introduced me to Ames Department Stores in 1966. About ten years my senior, Norman was a formidable tax and corporate attorney and a dear friend. We developed a rapport early in my career, and Norman became my champion in Boston, referring countless clients to me, visiting me at Wertheim, or hosting me at his law office and delighting me with his easy sense of humor. With Norman's help, Ames, a modest discount retailer largely run by three straight-shooting Midwesterners, went public in 1967. Listing Ames shares on the New York Stock Exchange was a thrilling coup for a family that had grown up with no electricity and heat and whose parents had mortgaged their childhood farm so they could open their first discount store in 1958.[102]

I discovered just how down-to-earth these brothers were during my first board meeting. From my house on Kettle Creek Road in Weston, the commute was only an hour. When I pulled up to this old building surrounded by an ample and desolate parking lot, I was a little surprised. As I entered the offices themselves and noticed their simple (you might even say "shabby") quality, I was even more surprised. Could this possibly be the headquarters of a public company? It was the opposite of the slick and stately offices of the cosmopolitan superstars of Wall Street.

Of all the warm greetings I received that day, I especially remember that of cofounder Milton Gilman, the most dominant of the brothers. Hardworking, honest, and dedicated, Milton epitomized the best attributes of the Greatest Generation. Among the first parents drafted to the war effort in 1942, Milton joined the Eighty-First Armored Medical Battalion and helped liberate the Mauthausen concentration camp in Upper Austria.[103] After returning to civilian life, he started the family business with his brothers, which by the time I joined had expanded to twenty locations. Ames served an important and valuable niche in these twenty towns, I began learning that day, becoming the largest retailer by offering national brands in these communities at markdown prices. Everyone in these twenty towns and small cities knew Ames and loved the stores. For me, the intimate and rural setting of these stores recalled my mother's retail shop in Mamaroneck when I was boy—an efficient and warm place that the community adored. Just like my mother, these men knew the daily sales data of each store and hired employees committed to teamwork and to developing relationships with customers.

Ames's business model was impressive. Employing a similar strategy to Woolworth in the American South, the brothers studied preexisting department store data in other communities, and when small or independent operations fared poorly, they offered to acquire them. The brothers knew how to customize each store layout and inventory based on customer data from years prior. They also had a knack for judging local tastes and offered just the right national names in shoes, shorts, and other product categories, selling this merchandise at everyday discount prices.

The company's board also attracted me because it was a team of equals. Each brother took a nominal salary and reinvested capital into the company itself, husbanding every penny in their effort to build new retail stores. As true company insiders, each board member was more involved in the decision-making and operations than at other companies. In the months following that first board meeting, as I visited these stores and watched the brothers operate, I felt confident about how they ran the business.

All three brothers raved about how honored their mother and father would have been to know that their sons had created a company that made it onto the vaunted New York Stock Exchange. But corporate management wasn't experienced enough to guide their newly minted public company. Their provincial approach and outlook marked a strong contrast to my other clients, like Montedison in Milan, whose managers were sophisticated about geopolitics and generally savvy about financial markets, or my glamourous music or movie studio clients in Los Angeles, who had a broad knowledge of world events. I was well-positioned to help Ames navigate financially. Up to this point, they'd counted on their lawyer Norman and their accountant Mel Rosenblatt, who cared for them like family. After joining the board, I became the company's Wall Street advisor, helping management negotiate financial challenges and advising on major shareholder matters.

You could say that my first two decades with Ames were predictable (perhaps, at times, even dull). That's because it was a smartly run and almost formulaic business. Ames ground out one store after another, honing its fundamental business skill at learning exactly what merchandise and layout decisions increased sales. When management opened a new store, I had confidence in its abilities and didn't feel the need to visit the location or study the local retail geography. After converting a new store to the Ames model, management intuitively knew how much it would cost and how long renovations and merchandising changes would take and could nearly predict the profits it would generate in the first, second, and third years. The biggest problem Ames encountered was something called "shrink," an industry term referring to inventory loss. "Shrink" still afflicts retail operations in the digital era and usually happens when a store manager makes markdowns and fails to record or report them, or in cases of shoplifting, fraud, or simple accident. Ames wrestled with missing and unaccounted-for inventory for most of its existence.[104] Shrink problems sometimes suggested poor management in the industry, and Mel called the brothers day and night to discuss instances of shrinkage and how to manage the fallout.

After Milton and Irving retired together in 1980 and Herb assumed leadership, the company expanded from taking over small stores to acquiring small chains. Herb was a little more adventurous and less conservative than his predecessors, but he still adopted the same approach with chains as he did with individual stores, knowing just how much he needed to widen the aisles, and what new merchandise the chain should introduce. Under Herb's leadership, Ames increased sales and earnings every year, garnering respect for the company in the financial community. The company also expanded into variety chains, like five-and-dime or dollar stores, and even began venturing into urban markets, with their different customer bases.

Despite how busy I was during this time with music, motion pictures, Montedison, and Mountain Fuel Supply, I maintained a close relationship with the Gilmans and happily discharged my role as Wall Street advisor. I updated them about what the financial community was saying about the company and interpreted the financial community's needs or inquiries for them. I often rewrote the first drafts of their quarterly or annual reports, maintaining their down-to-earth style but modifying the language for a financial community audience and so it conformed to the general retail reporting practices of the time. I never wanted them to sound like Wall Street insiders, and my goal was to let their low-key culture shine, even as I modified and elevated the language a bit. That was my approach with Ames as I attended meetings, coached them on speeches, and played a role in helping them appraise the strengths and weaknesses of acquisitions. I also advised and protected the brothers personally. Herb, for example, might call me and say, "I'm buying a new home and need $250,000 for the purchase. Can I sell some of my Ames stock?" I'd analyze the last time he'd sold any shares and advise him about whether he'd have to publicly disclose the sale and if such publicity was a good idea.

I was sometimes uneasy when Ames wanted to make a larger acquisition, but I never spoke up too much, remembering that I was a trusted advisor more than a lawyer or accountant. I was hesitant, for example, about the G. C. Murphy acquisition, for which Ames paid nearly $20 million in 1985. As a late-stage and larger acquisition, it was an unusual purchase. Based in Pennsylvania, G. C. Murphy operated both discount and variety stores. The acquisition doubled Ames's sales to $1.7 billion and expanded operations into fourteen states, but it also significantly increased company debt. In the first three months following the purchase, Ames closed or sold 139 unprofitable stores, converting the rest to the Ames model. Despite my initial hesitation, this acquisition went much better than I expected.

A PERFECT RETAIL STORM

Herb's terminal cancer diagnosis came a few years after the G. C. Murphy success. He made aggressive plans for succession, asking me to become chair right away, because he trusted me, while landing on Peter Hollis as the new CEO. A retail industry insider, Hollis had worked at the Bradlees division of Stop & Shop before specializing in discount retail, serving as executive vice president and president of the Fishers Big Wheel chain. Hollis was also general merchandise manager and senior vice president for thirteen years at Zayre Corporation, a more diverse and urban retail discount chain that was roughly the size of Ames.[105] Despite their common experience in retail, Peter was different from the Gilmans. Peter had sophistication and polish, and, unlike the Gilmans who had no detectable hobbies, he enjoyed skiing and classical music.[106] When management agreed to hire him as CEO, I thought they'd made a solid choice.

Though saddened by news of Herb's cancer diagnosis and retirement, I believed Peter wouldn't fundamentally alter the company, committed as he was to maintaining its thirty-year culture of teamwork that discouraged superstars.[107] And I was happy to play my part alongside Hollis, serving as chair until he was experienced enough to assume my role. Though I would continue to serve as the company's advisor to the financial community, my position changed from a public-relations perspective. At the time, it was prestigious to serve as the chair, even the nonexecutive chair, of a public company. Because I could make strategic decisions and hires, being chair was also considered powerful. As the face of Ames in the financial community, I spoke about the business to institutions that solicited my opinion on the latest acquisition as well as my thoughts on Hollis.

After I became chair, many competitors approached me with offers about a merger or Ames sale. To explore such a possibility, I visited Walmart's headquarters in Bentonville, Arkansas, gauging company founder Sam Walton's interests in expanding into Ames's core markets like New England. Arriving on Saturday, I was just in time for the company's famous weekly rally.

Give me a W!

Give me an A!

Give me an L!

Give me a Squiggly!

Give me an M!

Give me an A!

Give me an R!

Give me a T!

What's that spell?

Wal-Mart!

Who's number one?

The Customer! Always![108]

Like many, I found the cheer, which Walton famously adapted from a Korean tennis ball factory he'd once visited, equal parts energetic and unsettling.[109] I'd long admired Walton, who, since opening a small variety store in 1962, not far from the headquarters in Bentonville, had become one of the country's largest retailers.[110] Walton had a disarming demeanor and cracked jokes, but I could tell he ran the company in a stern fashion. When we met, three or four senior officers accompanied us, and none of them said a word as Walton dominated the discussions, explaining the company's merchandising and larger strategy. "When you are ready for a deal," he said, referring to an Ames acquisition, "let me know."

I departed Arkansas that day with Walton believing I was ready to negotiate a sale. But I never explored the possibility. In truth, I liked serving as chair of such a big company. Instead of selling to Walmart, I was confident—overconfident—that Hollis and I could help build Ames so it could compete with Walmart. In hindsight, these delusions of retail grandeur represented a marked lapse in judgment.

Six months into my service as chair, Hollis expressed strong interest in buying the Zayre discount chain. I asked my partner Steve Kotler about the idea because he was the banker for Zayre, and Steve told me that it would be a welcome opportunity because he believed the parent company was selling it at a discount to its liquidation value. Knowing the company's proven strategy for converting chains to the Ames model, I was receptive to the idea. Having spent thirteen years with this chain, Hollis seemed uniquely positioned to accomplish this merger. He had an intimate understanding of the Zayre operation, customer markets, employees, and so on. But great potential aside, I was also hesitant. Zayre was financially troubled and would constitute Ames's largest acquisition ever—doubling its size.

When Peter broached the acquisition idea to Ames's senior management, everyone became excited, and the sale closed soon thereafter. On September 15, 1988, Ames announced its purchase of Zayre's discount unit division, something the financial community hailed as a spectacular investment and brilliant coup.[111] Ames stock soared upon news that this 348-store retailer would add Zayre's 388 stores to its portfolio.[112] The size and scale of the proposed merger was staggering: with the Zayre acquisition, Ames would become the fourth-largest retailer in the country, trailing only Walmart, Kmart, and Target.[113] Everyone in operations was thrilled to be part of such a large retailer, believing they were acquiring a chain about which the new CEO had an intimate, insider understanding.

As we planned and executed this 1988 purchase, the American economy was entering an uncertain period. In the late 1980s and early 1990s, savings and loans associations (S&L) began faltering, having either strategized poorly or squandered their clients' deposits on dubious real estate investments and hefty corporate compensation packages.[114] According to then-president George H. W. Bush, this had cost the American economy an unrecoverable $100 billion, sending negative rippling effects into the larger economy, hitting particular sectors like banking, oil, construction, and real estate particularly hard. Aside from department stores and Walmart, many retailers filed for bankruptcy. Caldor, a northeastern discount chain once dubbed the "Bloomingdale's of Discounting," began suffering around this time. Unable to compete with larger chains, Caldor would soon file its first Chapter 11 bankruptcy protection.[115] Bradlees Inc., another struggling chain of 136 stores, filed bankruptcy protection the same year, struggling under mounting debt and unable to compete with megaretailers like Walmart.[116]

In this difficult economic climate, Ames's acquisition strategy proved faulty. About ten months following the purchase, Hollis decided to change the names of all Zayre stores to Ames. As part of the Gilmans' playbook, it sounded reasonable at the time. But unlike preexisting stores that had come under the Ames umbrella, Zayre stores were largely based in urban areas and had significant Black and Hispanic customer bases. Unlike their rural counterparts in the Northeast and mid-Atlantic region, these customers had never heard of Ames before. Along with changing the name, Hollis also modified Zayre merchandising, swapping out discount staples that appealed to urban minorities for the high-end brand names that resonated with a White and more rural demographic. But Zayre's customer base gravitated to urban fashion, not the shorts that sold well in Hartford or rural North Carolina. Urban customers, moreover, were accustomed to periodic sales, while Ames customers were habituated to the company's "everyday low cost" model. Traffic in Zayre locations evaporated—this was a store that none of its customers could recognize.[117]

These rebranding, advertisement, and merchandising decisions took a devastating toll. Within months, store volumes dropped by 15 to 20 percent, compounding the poor sales prior to the acquisition. The financial community learned of these troubles and the stock began to drop, declining from $30 to $1.62.[118] Investors lost money, and Ames senior management lost faith in Peter Hollis. What we'd once regarded as a brilliant move, we now saw as a disaster. In one news piece, memorably titled "Ames Got an Excedrin Headache After Swallowing Zayre Chain," a commentator captured the problem perfectly: "By buying Zayre, Ames was no longer a laid-back organization operating fairly small, quiet stores for a mostly captive rural audience." Instead, Ames/Zayre was now "a major player operating 680 stores in intense, fast-changing urban settings amid heavy competition."[119]

Worse, like Bradlees and Caldor, Ames was now saddled with debt. The Zayre acquisition had cost $1.3 billion, including a significant amount of debt.[120] As sales volumes plunged, Ames had to pay interest payments on the massive loan every month. Ames filed for Chapter 11 bankruptcy, and the Gilman legacy was forever tarnished. The company that had earned a reputation for textbook acquisitions now served as a textbook case in M&A failure.[121]

Different securities firms approached me to speak on this matter since I was the public face of Ames on Wall Street. I spent a fair amount of 1990 trying to explain our circumstances to the financial community, detailing why we'd all thought that Peter Hollis had been the right leader and why the Zayre acquisition had struck us as a great business decision. As I tried to control the story, however, the negative multiplier effects only increased. Zayre locations continued to shutter, and those that remained open were forced to sell their merchandise at punishing markdowns. The financial community grew even more fearful and shareholders began unloading their stock.

Focusing all of their energies on trying to save Zayre, moreover, management neglected Ames's legacy stores. Removing its most talented human capital from the basic business only compounded the problem. Zayre and Ames, for example, used different computer systems. According to best practices in mergers and acquisitions, the acquiring company converts the acquired to its system.[122] Instead of following this practice, managers decided to change both systems simultaneously, something one observer likened to "changing horses in the middle of the stream while juggling crystal goblets."[123] The resulting technical glitches led to late payments on supplier invoices.[124] Word spread throughout the financial community that Ames might not meet its debt obligations. Before long, bankers and suppliers lost confidence in the business, refusing to extend credit to Ames/Zayre for fear they wouldn't receive payment. Ames/Zayre struggled to find the cash to stock its shelves. When retailers don't have credit for merchandise, they can't operate. The economic impact of the S&L crisis, combined with Peter Hollis's ultimately poor operating judgement in this massive acquisition, proved too great to overcome.

When stockholders lose money so quickly, strike-suit specialists usually descend, poised to sue directors and companies. The corporate leader in such litigation, who earned titles like "the most hated man in the boardrooms of corporate America" and "the king of torts," was Melvyn ("Mel") I. Weiss, the founder of New York–based Milberg Weiss.[125] Known for lavish parties, private jets, and adorning his home with Picassos, Mel had created the largest class-action operation in the United States, employing hundreds of lawyers, accountants, and FBI personnel that went after Philip Morris, Aetna, Enron, and other large or beleaguered companies. Now it was Ames's turn. I remember meeting with Mel and found him to be a reasonable man who patiently walked me through his strategy. As he explained, his team had gathered small shareholders into a lawsuit directed against Ames, but not against me or Wertheim. All the plaintiffs asked, Mel insisted, was that Wertheim return the $20 million fee it had charged for advising on the Zayre acquisition.

I should have accepted these terms and immediately refunded the fee. But my Wertheim partners objected. They felt they deserved compensation for their hard work advising on the deal. "We didn't do anything wrong," they insisted, pinning blame on Hollis's failure to manage the acquisition. To return the fee, they reasoned, was an admission of guilt. I could see their point of view, but still objected. Relative to the size of our firm, this fee was inconsequential. And because I was chair of Ames, any negative publicity from the lawsuit and its fallout would impact me personally. Refusing to part with the fee, we'd sealed our fate. Another law firm pursued the case. When plaintiffs couldn't find a New York law firm to sue Wertheim, Washington-based lobbying giant Patton Boggs filed a new lawsuit for $400 million naming not only Wertheim but also me, Ames's former chair, James Harmon!

On October 14, 1992, just after news of this lawsuit broke, I severed all ties with Ames—having already resigned the chair, I also resigned from the board of directors.[126] Most lawyers and investment bankers knew that this astronomical sum was meant to garner bad publicity and to frighten me and my lawyers. But the press capitalized on it, running salacious headlines about the lawsuit. My friends joked with me saying, "Jeez, Jim, I didn't know you had a spare $400 million." Philanthropic organizations like Lincoln Center also called me suggesting that if I were going to have to part with $400 million, why not give them $100 million.

Once the Patton Boggs lawyers began deposing me and my colleagues, my partners at Wertheim knew the lawsuit would be an overwhelming commitment of time. We decided to settle, returning the $20 million fee. Patton Boggs took a generous share of that sum and returned the balance to Ames, which rebuilt itself and emerged from Chapter 11 a year later under new management. Peter Hollis resigned following the bankruptcy, and Stephen L. Pistner, who'd earned a reputation as a demanding and tough executive who could accomplish corporate turnarounds, took the helm.[127] It looked like Ames might escape the fate of Caldor and Bradlees when an industry publication awarded it "turnaround of the decade" in 2000. But debt and competition from megaretailers like Walmart led to the liquidation of its assets and the closure of all its stores in the summer of 2002.[128]

FAILURE'S SILVER LINING

Though the entire affair only cost Wertheim its negligible $20 million fee, the ill-fated merger and bankruptcy cost me reputationally. When I assumed the nonexecutive role as chair of Ames, the financial following I'd amassed over the years only grew. I'd invested with several instruments, like my Kettle Creek fund, and had responsibly guided the investments that others entrusted to me. These same individuals, as well as large institutions, followed my lead and purchased Ames at anywhere from $12–$20 a share. They believed this was Jim's latest investment opportunity and figured that I wouldn't have become chair if I wasn't optimistic about this company's future. Investors also loved the larger story: Wall Street insider Jim Harmon and retail superstar Peter Hollis combined their joint expertise to double the size of this company, ensuring future profitability.

By the time of the shareholder lawsuit, the stock had plummeted from $35 to under $3 a share. People rightly complained that I had purchased my Ames stock when it was only $2 a share. I didn't lose anything in this mayhem. But the major institutional investors had bought in following news of the acquisition when shares sold for $15–$20 each. Their financial pain was compounded when they learned Wertheim had refused to relinquish a $20 million fee for a deal that had cost them so much. They were rightfully upset, and I felt guilty.

This embarrassment haunted me for years. After a career spent serving as an advisor and only reluctantly as a principal, as I had with Chappell Music, I regretted my decision to become chair of Ames. In hindsight, how could I possibly lead the fourth-largest retailer in the country? And how, only a year into this major decision, did I possibly support the Zayre mega-acquisition? These were some poor business judgments that kept me up at night. My family still remembers my distress over the fiasco.

As a conservative businessman, I shouldn't have agreed to both replace Herb and acquire Zayre within a year. Instead, I should have assumed the role and kept the operation as it was, building Ames in the key markets in which it excelled. I should have also considered the larger banking and real estate crisis at the time, not to mention the extensive retail bankruptcies, and waited for the country to recover before pursuing such a large acquisition. Then, following an economic rebound and after Hollis had proven himself as a leader, we might have entertained the topic of such an acquisition. If I'd agreed to serve as chair and my colleagues at Ames had insisted on the acquisition, I should have resigned immediately, choosing instead to stay on the board and help advise, instead of presiding over this decision.

But though the episode still brings me sadness all these years later, it taught me an important lesson about failure. When undergoing personal crises or business failures like this, people tend to obsess, believing the impact to be vast—that the entire world is watching in judgment. Often this isn't the case. When I traveled to London to meet with Wertheim's new partners at Schroders plc that year, no one asked me a thing about Ames. They wanted to know only about the future. Five years later, in 1996, as the White House vetted me for a position in government, I braced myself for questions about Ames. Teams of people had descended on my homes in Connecticut, New York, Florida, and Anguilla, studied my medical records, scrutinized my investments, and interrogated my neighbors about what kind of person I really was. The topic of Ames never arose. Years later, I asked Bill Clinton about it, and he said, "If you were on twenty boards and had a problem with one, why would we focus on that? Your other nineteen did well, and that's an amazing record." No one in the business community or in government ever questioned me about it again.

Some even regarded this failure as an asset. A half-dozen retailers or so retained Wertheim in the 1990s, figuring that the Ames experience had taught us a lot about retail. Lane Bryant, a retailer specializing in plus-sized women's clothing, approached Wertheim and we managed the sale of the company. When I met with a different kind of retailer, Howard Schultz, only several months after the $400 million lawsuit was dismissed, he and his colleagues at Starbucks agreed to let Wertheim manage his IPO. Howard spent an entire day asking me questions about my career, but he never once broached the topic of Ames. Years later, after we'd developed a rapport, I asked him why he never raised the question. "If you experienced what you did at Ames," he said, "I bet it made you a whole lot smarter. I figured you'd bring that knowledge and experience to Starbucks."

One of the lessons I learned from this failure is that even a conservative businessman like me can get swept along by a new manager or CEO, blindly trusting their expertise instead of doing my usual due diligence. I was fifty-three years old and should have known better. But I was chair of an international investment banking firm, had achieved success running Chappell Music and advising clients like Montedison and Mountain Fuel Supply, traveling the world on a Concorde. Clearly this had given me an oversized ego, as I believed I could purchase a massive retailer and it would succeed just like these other ventures.

Such an experience has given me empathy for those undergoing hardship. Many of my friends, in the months following their divorces, have believed that every time they entered a room, people were speaking and gossiping about them. I remind my recently divorced friends that they might feel sensitive and even embarrassed in the short term, just as I was after the Zayre acquisition and the lawsuit. But in the court of public opinion, my mistake or failure faded because it wasn't habitual. The same holds true for them.

Ultimately this experience in leadership failure would benefit me as the memory of being chair of Ames would fade. Shortly before this episode, I became chair of Wertheim Schroder, the subject to which I now turn. But that didn't last for long, as I had my sights on the public sector and became chair of a public institution, where my decisions would impact more than just institutional investors. They would affect entire countries.

A Time of Transition

IN JANUARY 1991, I began training for my first marathon. I consumed many books on the topic of running and became friends with a terrific group of marathoners in New York City. We often met in Central Park, circling the reservoir and the roads in the park as we prepared for the challenge and developed camaraderie.

No matter where I was in the world that year, I was diligent about my running schedule, much to the consternation of colleagues and investors who found the whole idea strange. When I stayed at the Berkeley while on business in London, I ran in Hyde Park. When meeting at Saint-Jean-Cap-Ferrat on the French Riviera, where I had many finance transaction meetings, I was the only one who ran. I got lost in Tokyo while running, unable to navigate to my hotel because I didn't speak Japanese; I braved the frigid cold in Moscow, running past heavily armed policemen guarding the Kremlin. "You really do a foot race?" one of my Italian colleagues asked in confusion. "Americans are crazy, running in the streets in their underwear."

Midway through my training, in July 1991, my father passed away. The entire Harmon family grieved, but the event cemented my resolve to complete the marathon in November. Having reached a ten-minute-mile pace, I was squarely in the middle of the 25,000 or so pack of runners that crisp fall day, crossing the finish line at just under four hours and twenty minutes.

This marathon had a larger symbolic value to me. I came to think of the race as marking a transition to a new life, the metaphorical training for a new challenge. After decades of intense and fulfilling work in the private sector, I knew I wanted to pursue something new, something that might make a greater difference in and impact on the world.

EXPANDING WERTHEIM

By the time of the marathon in November 1991, the most important business transaction of my career, which ultimately enabled my major life transition, was the merger of Wertheim with British merchant bank Schroders. In late 1984, Fred Klingenstein expressed his desire to sell his family's nearly 40 percent interest in Wertheim. At the time, Wertheim's partners controlled the remaining 60 percent interest, and I had the second largest share after Fred. The news wasn't surprising. After about four or five years at the firm, I had realized that Fred didn't really like managing people, disagreed with some partner decisions on corporate finance transactions like the Starbucks IPO, and would have preferred investing his family's capital and leading an asset-management firm.

Steve Kotler and I proposed that the partners purchase the Klingenstein interest, but Fred wanted an institutional buyer that could invest capital and attract more global business. Fred approached Morgan Stanley, whose managers presented the idea to London's S. G. Warburg & Co., the United Kingdom's foremost merchant bank. This bank had a storied history that would appeal to Fred. Siegmund Warburg, who founded the bank in 1946 with industrialist Henry Grunfeld after fleeing Nazi Germany, became the dominant banking figure in postwar London and an architect of European financial integration. His investment bank had contributed to the economic recovery of Britain and western Europe and, some might say, helped spur twentieth-century globalization.

I'll never forget Siegmund Warburg's lifelong obsession with graphology. For Warburg, a person's handwriting could reveal profound and penetrating insights about a person's character and business proclivities.[129] Before hiring a merchant banker, Warburg submitted a writing sample to Zurich-based graphologist and psychologist Theodora Dreifuss, who evaluated the prospective employee.[130] Warburg performed a graphological analysis of our team at Wertheim, and I never saw the results. But I imagine they were positive because Warburg felt comfortable supporting Wertheim and my becoming chair and CEO. A few years later, I remember telling this story to Bill Clinton. "I think there's something here," he said. "We should start doing this for every cabinet officer."

After negotiations with Warburg and Co., we agreed on a $200 million acquisition price for Wertheim, comprising a package of cash, equity in publicly traded common shares, and convertible debt. Fred, Steve Kotler, and Wertheim president Bob Shapiro boarded the Concorde for the formal signing and announcement of sale at London's Ritz Hotel. The Ritz was founded in the early twentieth century and needed more upkeep than the newer Savoy, Berkeley, and Claridge's. But when we entered the Ritz's boardroom, my grudging comparisons fell away: my colleagues and I saw a long table that could have accommodated forty or so people, and in front of each place a plush chair, a magnificent setting of china, and sparkling champagne flutes. The four of us greeted the twenty or so representatives from Warburg in this ceremonial setting. They all stood, ready to applaud the signing.

Upon reviewing the deal, however, Fred became distraught. Warburg's chief executive, Sir David Scholey, had overvalued his company's securities, anticipating a price increase following the announcement of the merger. We all had reason to have faith in David, whom Warburg himself had designated heir-apparent prior to his death several years earlier. But we were all surprised at the security valuations.[131] Had Steve and I been leading Wertheim, we would have taken David aside and negotiated satisfactory terms. This was not Fred's style. Incensed about the securities prices, Fred politely walked around the room, shook every Warburg representative's hand, and boarded the Concorde back to New York the following day. I had closed many deals, large and small, but I couldn't remember a transaction failing at the signing after principals had flown 3,000 miles for the occasion. The Warburg partners were stunned, or to borrow my Dad's phrase, "persulted," at this unusual behavior. I was always saddened that we weren't able to close the Warburg deal, but so pleased that I have maintained friendships with some of the partners, especially Oscar Lewisohn, a dear friend, now for decades.

Later in 1985, some months after the Warburg fiasco, I was returning from London, again on the Concorde, and seated next to Alva O. Way, an international businessman who had served as CFO at General Electric and was now chancellor of Brown. "So, you're back in London," said Al. "What's going on?"

"Every time I come back here," I said, "I think about this failed transaction we just did." Then I told him the bizarre story of the Warburg deal.

"I've got the answer for you. I have an even better partner." That day, Al was returning from a board meeting with Schroders plc, a successful British merchant bank with an excellent asset-management business. From this fortuitous discussion among two friends came the biggest milestone of my professional life. Al introduced Wertheim to Schroders, the negotiations moved much faster than they had with Warburg, and we arrived at a better deal, ultimately selling Schroders 50 percent of Wertheim but maintaining control of the business. All credit for this transaction is due to Steve Kotler for structuring and negotiating the terms.

The transaction closed in July 1986, the name of the firm changed to Wertheim Schroder, and I was now the chair and CEO. This marked a turning point. During the 1960s, I had enjoyed success in the market but always behaved conservatively, careful to ensure I could provide for my family's long-term future. During the economic turbulence of the 1970s, I was successful in business but conservative with my money. As I told the *New York Times* in 1987, "I've been married to the same woman for 30 years, I've been an investment banker for 30 years, I've even lived in the same house for 25 years."[132] But by the mid-1980s, however, I'd experienced two liquidity events: the lucrative sale of Chappell Music and selling half of Wertheim. As a fifty-year-old CEO of a global investment bank, I now had capital and status.

I started to enjoy the fruits of my labor for the first time, indulging my love of art. Earlier in the 1980s, I had expanded my modest art collection, purchasing a Robert Motherwell, the abstract expressionist I'd appreciated ever since Professor George Downing mesmerized me with his lectures at Brown. Following my liquidity events, I expanded my interests from abstract expressionism to a nineteenth-century Romantic period centered in Barbizon, France. I became more involved and aggressive at art auctions, purchasing Barbizon School artists like Jean-Baptiste-Camille Corot and Jean-François Millet.

After one Corot purchase, which I won in an auction, I sent the painting to a specialist for cleaning. After fifty years of accumulating tobacco from cigarettes and other toxins, the painting was dirty. Several days later, while I was at work in my Wertheim office, the specialist called me and said, "Stop what you're doing and get here now!" As I discovered after racing over to the art studio in a cab, the newly clean painting was spectacular. I'm glad it wasn't cleaned before the auction or it would have increased the price substantially.

In addition to enlarging my own collection, I sponsored emerging talent. In the late 1980s, one of my London-based art dealers introduced me to Gillian Ayres. From her studio in Wales, Gillian created colorful and playful abstracts that bore influences of Jackson Pollock and Henri Matisse. I purchased several of her paintings and later sponsored a one-person show for her in my Manhattan apartment. Her popularity increased as gallery and museum spaces featured her work, and she came to be regarded as one of London's most significant postwar painters.

Following the Schroders transaction, I also began investing in my quality of life and explored real estate opportunities. Jane and I had always loved beaches. In 1987, Jane visited the Caribbean with one of our Weston neighbors, and the two women returned home regaling their husbands about a little-known island called Anguilla, southeast of Puerto Rico. They said it was spectacular, quiet, and ideally located—not as remote as the Grenadines, but lacking commercial-flight access. To get there, you had to fly into St. Maarten and board a ferry. Such travel exertions kept the place secluded.

After Jane and I visited the island together, Jane was determined that we buy a house there. I imagined it would be a headache. Luckily, an engineer named George, who worked at the island's luxurious Malliouhana Hotel, was midway through building a house. We liked the house so much we purchased it in 1988. It has been our beloved family refuge ever since.

Construction on the Anguilla house finished just in time for my oldest daughter's wedding. In the 1980s, Debbie met her college sweetheart, Robert ("Bob") Allen Seder. Bob would go on, eventually, to work with Anthony Fauci at the National Institutes of Health (NIH). When Deb said she wanted the wedding at the Pierre Hotel in New York City, I immediately tendered a $25,000 deposit. But then a few months elapsed, and Deb wanted to change course.

Months later, Jane began preparing for the nuptials at our home in Weston, planning a platform to stage the ceremony. Fortunately, we didn't embark on construction because three or four months passed and Deb announced, once again, she and Bob wanted to postpone. They were a busy, "up and doing" power couple, Bob juggling medical school and residency, and Deb at business school and the beginning of her career. She would go on to become the cofounder and CEO of a very successful real estate private equity firm. At the time, she and Bob couldn't find the time to plan the festivities.

After these two false starts, my wife and I told Debbie she was on her own. Six months after that, she began planning a spring wedding in Anguilla.

I'd only see my deposit again, the manager of the Pierre told me, if he could find a replacement to rent the room at the same time. So Jane and I visited the hotel in November, the day we'd reserved it for Deb's wedding, and found the room completely vacant. But the management had prepared an elegant table for two with a bottle of wine and two crystal glasses. That night, over one of the most expensive bottles of wine we'd ever had, Jane and I toasted our daughter and her future marriage to Bob, whenever and wherever it would take place.

Debbie finally arranged a beautiful event in Anguilla, which took place in the late spring of 1989. A hundred or so guests attended, all of them staying at the Malliouhana for a long weekend of swimming, snorkeling, and beach time. At the wedding celebration itself, my dad made two toasts that everyone loved:

"If you had to pick an island, couldn't you have picked Manhattan?"

"The six words ensuring a happy marriage: 'Yes, dear, you may be right.'"

Two years later, in January 1991, we all celebrated Dad's eighty-fifth birthday at his home with Mom in Florida. Complications from Parkinson's disease had taken a toll. That July, amid my fevered preparations for the marathon, paramedics rushed him to the hospital near my parents' apartment in Rye, New York. My mother called me on the morning of July 4 telling me Dad was in terrible pain, and I raced to the hospital. Unable to bear the thought of my father suffering, I told the doctor to discontinue the heroic measures then underway to keep him alive. My sister, Carol, was angered and resentful when she learned of my decision. She hadn't been able to say her final farewell.

My mother was even more of a concern. Having wed in 1927, shortly after my dad graduated from Yale, she had enjoyed sixty-four years of marriage. I thought she would struggle after Dad passed. But she thrived instead. With a close circle of friends, my mother blossomed in her eighties and nineties, doing more socially than many people I knew who were in their sixties. We had a spectacular ninetieth birthday party for her at New York's Carlyle Hotel. Much to my surprise, she called me in her nineties, telling me about gentlemen who asked her out on dates, and wondering if I would grant her permission to go. "You don't have to ask me, Mom," I said. "If you like him, you should go out with him." She continued on this way until the age of one hundred, passing at age 103.

With these many personal and professional changes, I still felt I was undergoing a transition but hadn't made any decisions about the form it would take. People around me sensed a transition was underway too. At one point, Al Way said, "It doesn't seem to me that you'll be doing this for another ten years." I told him the truth: I yearned to do something different, but I wouldn't leave my investment banking firm so soon after the merger. My partners looked to me for leadership, and I needed to wait until everyone was happy and taken care of before repotting myself elsewhere.

MARKET MAYHEM

In the fall of 1987, barely a year into my tenure as chair and CEO of Wertheim Schroder, I had to exert such leadership when Black Monday devastated Wall Street. The weekend leading up to this crisis couldn't have been calmer as I planned a trip to Providence to attend a Brown University trustees meeting.

Sometime in the mid-1970s, Brown University president Howard Swearer had visited my offices at 200 Park Avenue, asking me if I'd like to become more involved with my alma mater. He arranged a day for me to meet some of the faculty, students, and administrators so that I could learn more about the present-day university and where I might be of value. It was an enjoyable day as I met with faculty and posed questions about the problems at Brown and what they would like changed.

After that day in Providence, I drew the same conclusion about Brown that I would later make about the World Resources Institute. Brown had an extraordinary return on its equity value. Its modest endowment, the leanest in the Ivies, produced outstanding students and talented faculty members. I could help by building the basic equity base of the endowment, powering future growth and even better results. Brown had undergone a revolution in the late 1960s and early 1970s and some of its decisions, like removing its core curriculum requirements, had given me pause. But I couldn't argue with the results I saw that day as well as President Swearer's great leadership. Brown's success in the early 1970s, I joked, had retroactively made my own degree more valuable.

Swearer proposed my involvement take the form of joining the board of trustees, which I happily did. At the time, many of the other members either lacked the experience or interest in aggressive or creative fundraising. I introduced the school to new revenue sources, convincing Montedison executives, who'd never heard of the school, to make a donation to the chemistry program. The trustee meetings never energized me, but I always liked conversing with students, seeing interesting programs and institutes sprout up, and meeting with President Swearer and, later, President Ruth Simmons.

For the two weeks or so before my trustee meeting in the fall of 1987, my general unease about the markets had heightened. Inflation had started to increase while growth slowed. The Federal Reserve had steadily increased interest rates that year, in a series of moves from January to August, and in the first weeks of October, bank and mortgage rates spiked. I worried that these events could herald a global crisis that would affect the oil market, like the disruption we'd experienced in the 1970s, leading to regional unrest and geopolitical instability.

As chair of a global investment firm, I knew there was nothing I could do. I kept checking around the firm, and people reassured me, saying, "We've been through this before." Analysts in Wertheim Schroder's trading and research departments looked up to me, thinking I'd done something brilliant to occupy the role of chair and that I had the last word on market conditions and market timing.

October 19, 1987, as I drove from Connecticut to a trustees meeting at Brown, the Dow Jones plunged 508 points, losing 22.6 percent of its value.[133] On this day, forever known as "Black Monday," Wall Street experienced the biggest decline in its history—nearly double the decline of 1929.[134] To give readers some perspective on how cataclysmic this was, imagine waking up tomorrow to news that the market had fallen 22 percent. The Dow Jones, worth 35,000 the night before, had suddenly lost 6,500–6,800 points. Uproar and even chaos would descend as individuals and institutions saw the values of their retirement accounts and company stock plummet.

Though by nature an optimist, I greeted this news with dread. If markets continued to decline at this rate, we would cease to have a market at all. I felt uneasy during the trustee meeting in 1987, fretting during my lunch with President Swearer and constantly taking breaks to call the firm. After returning to the office, I scrutinized the firm's balance sheets. Until this time, I'd given this task to the finance team and hadn't looked too closely. It wasn't uncommon for investment banks to have some leverage, a term referring to the amount of borrowing relative to base equity. As I gazed at the balance sheets, I remember saying to Steve Kotler, "This makes me really nervous. Could this be 1929 all over again?"

I called Georg "Gowi" Wilhelm Gustav von Mallinckrodt, a famed German merchant banker and the chair of Schroders, our partner firm, reaching him during a trip to Asia. "I need a loan for $25 million, and I need it this week," I said, urgency in my voice. As a practical matter, we never needed the money, but the loan would serve as an insurance policy. Given the generally dreary circumstances, our clients or counterparties might be unable to pay us. He agreed, and I hung up the phone, grateful I had a partner with these resources. I'm sure that Gowi wasn't thrilled to see this market and financial instability across the pond. But his act of faith bolstered confidence around the firm. No matter what happened in the market, our partner stood ready to lend, generously, on a day's notice.

At the Christmas party that year, everyone was still unnerved. The room felt gloomy, with people realizing how national or geopolitical events could impact markets, which in turn impacted their personal economic circumstances. Many told me they'd had difficulty sleeping, wondering if they would make enough money to stay afloat. I circulated through the room, speaking to everyone, and later that night gave an "up and doing" speech to a sea of terrified faces. I told everyone I was confident we'd weather the storm and reminded them all that we had an amazing partner in Schroders. I felt young, energetic, and certain that a bright future awaited. If we could just keep building more clients, like Starbucks, Chappell Music, and Mountain Fuel Supply, we could provide sustainable income to each person there.

President Ronald Reagan offered the same reassuring sentiments to the American public, and thankfully we were right. The market rebounded within months of this fall, and in only several years' time returned to its pre–Black Monday levels.[135] Some pin the blame for the crisis on a dramatic, but necessary, market correction, while others cite improper understanding and regulation of options, futures investments, and other quant-driven investments that had come to dominate Wall Street trading in the prior few decades.[136] Whatever the cause, the financial world wouldn't experience another such cataclysm until 2007–08, when a much worse calamity ravaged the stock market and economy alike.[137]

As the years of my leadership at Wertheim Schroder passed, and as I enjoyed two major liquidity events and helped the firm overcome the Black Monday crisis, my longing to embark on a major life transition only increased. After arriving at Hanseatic with nothing but an MBA and working my way up to chair and CEO of a multinational investment firm, I'd accomplished much more than I'd ever imagined. More important, I'd accomplished my mission at Hanseatic and Wertheim: to build a sustainable investment banking business and increase value for a wide variety of clients. I'd also learned a lot about working with people from different backgrounds and cultures. Though I loved these multicultural environments and the challenge of each new client, I was ready for something different.

Whether you are president of Brown University or the United States, it's always been my belief that a decade is an ideal length of time to lead an institution. I would abide by this axiom myself, rounding out a decade of leadership in 1995, when I formally entrusted Wertheim Schroder to Steve Kotler. I began exploring different interests in the early 1990s, gravitating to fundraising for worthy politicians like New York City mayor David Dinkins and President Bill Clinton, the subject of the next chapter. Just as I had sensed when preparing for the marathon, a different future awaited me, and I began to think about service in the public sector.

7

Reelecting Dinkins and Clinton

ONE EVENING IN 1993, I joined New York City mayor David Dinkins for a speech in Brooklyn's Bedford-Stuyvesant (called "Bed-Stuy") neighborhood. David and I arrived with a police escort to an outdoor platform, and before a packed crowd, I gave a brief introduction and campaign pitch. We need to reelect David Dinkins, I told the audience, the 106th mayor of New York City and the first African American to occupy the office. I talked about David's service in the US Marines, his education at Howard University and Brooklyn Law School, and our need for campaign funds to oust Rudy Giuliani. "I know you might not be accustomed to political giving," I told the crowd, "but every dollar counts."

As David approached the dais to deliver his address, I glanced at the 1,000 or so people in the audience and didn't see a single White face. At the time, I had no idea that Bed-Stuy was a vibrant center of African American culture, nurturing artists like Jay-Z and athletes like Jackie Robinson. I also had little inkling that the neighborhood was known for its dilapidated housing projects, poverty, and record homicide rates.

After concluding his speech, I said my goodbyes to the team, stepped down from the podium, and began walking toward the subway entrance. David caught my arm. "You're not going anywhere," he said, calling over a police car that escorted me back to Manhattan.

The moment reminded me of several decades prior, when Henry Kissinger expressed shock that I chose not to camouflage myself to avoid the Red Brigades, who routinely knee-capped Italians in business suits like mine. I was engaged in a similar moment of naiveté. Over the course of becoming acquainted with David, I'd realized that despite my decades on Wall Street, I was just a Connecticut commuter, unfamiliar with the outer boroughs as well as the larger challenges facing the city.

That's not the only reason I was an unusual choice to serve as David's finance chair, helping him build a war chest for his 1993 reelection bid against Rudolph Giuliani. As a registered Republican and investment banker, I looked nothing like his election team or constituents. But that made me an asset: I could attract more conservative voters in the city and improve David's standing in the business and Jewish communities, where his popularity was weakest. David's mayoral campaign marked my entrée into politics, preparing me for presidential fundraising and enabling my transition to the public sector.

A NEW YORK CULTURE WAR

I met David Dinkins on a New York City Partnership trip to London in May 1992. Founded by David Rockefeller in 1979, the Partnership invited the leading executive officers ("partners") of major investment banks, accounting firms, and law practices to join its ranks. The organization approached me in the late eighties, after I became chair and CEO of Wertheim Schroder, and I attended some events, especially bipartisan ones on subjects like taxes. In 1992, Bob Tisch, a member of the Partnership's board, asked me to join a delegation to Europe under the auspices of Mayor Dinkins to develop and encourage European investment in New York City's businesses.

132

The Tisch family was a self-made New York dynasty. Sons of middle-class Russian immigrants, Bob and Larry began amassing real estate in the mid-twentieth century before expanding into offshore drilling, insurance, and other industries.[138] The Tisch name then became omnipresent in the city, appearing on hospitals and New York University's prestigious school of the arts.[139] Larry, a Wertheim client, served as CEO of CBS's television networks. His sibling Bob now told me that I'd be valuable on this trip given my partnership with a leading European investment bank. "Schroders's investment in Wertheim is exactly what we'd like to replicate in the city," he explained.

I agreed to join the London delegation and arrived at our first dinner a little late, entering the hotel banquet hall to find twenty-five business executives already seated. I eyed one open seat and asked if it was free. "Yes," replied the man seated nearby. "No one wants to sit next to the teacher."

I sat down next to this personable man who introduced himself as David Dinkins and came to enjoy his relaxed, gregarious personality. Many politicians are personable, but David really put me at ease. He began our discussion by giving me a briefing of everyone in the room. "That's Bob Tisch," he said, pointing. "He runs Tisch hotels." After performing that exercise for everyone present, I learned more about David and discovered some common interests we shared, like tennis.

The delegation's next stop was Paris, and I had two tickets to the French Open. I suspected that David would enjoy the event and extended an invitation. Looking pained, he said, "I'd love to, but it would be the wrong thing to do." Imagine the press getting ahold of pictures of Jim and David at this elite tennis competition while they were supposed to be doing important work on behalf of New York's business community.

I ordered my favorite London-menu offering that night: smoked salmon and grilled sole. When David inquired about the order, I told him that this fish agreed with me. He smiled and ordered the same thing.

That evening in London marked the beginning of my decades-long friendship with David. Back in New York, we competed regularly in doubles tennis. David typically paired up with a strong female, often a former professional, while he assigned me a reasonable player that was never in the same league. One day, I arrived at the court with sports attorney and agent Donald Dell. The former Davis Cup captain, companion of tennis legend Arthur Ashe, and acclaimed doubles champion from the 1960s, would be harder to defeat. As usual, David had paired with a strong female and prepared to face off with me and Dell, who had great hand-eye coordination but didn't like to move around the court. Seeing how delighted the mayor was to win the first set, Dell took me aside and said, "This is embarrassing. If we lose today, the tennis world will hear all about it. Stop playing social tennis and focus!" We rallied for the second set, and everyone decided to call the match a draw. It was a diplomatic way to end the competition.

In early 1993 my professional relationship with David began in earnest when Joe Flom, senior partner at Skadden, joined me for lunch at Wertheim's dining room. Flom was especially knowledgeable about corporate takeovers and acquisitions, and I had retained Joe on a number of matters over the years. That day I figured he wanted to discuss a case. Instead, Flom said, "How would you like to be the finance manager for David Dinkins's reelection campaign?" I was inclined to do it. "This won't be easy," he added, "because you have to raise at least $12 million to compete with Giuliani."

During my business career, I had singled out three New Yorkers so disagreeable in temperament and character that I avoided them entirely. The first individual, not even a New Yorker, was George Steinbrenner, the principal owner and managing partner of the New York Yankees. He treated his players and colleagues badly and had an unappealing personal style. Second on my list: Donald Trump, the real estate developer and reality television personality who, much to my consternation, later became US president. Throughout my career, I avoided all contact with the man. Rudolph Giuliani was third on my list for being a mean-spirited prosecutor and attorney.

But my aversion to Giuliani was largely unrelated to my support for David. My view was that helping to fund the reelection of the city's first Black mayor was intrinsically worthwhile. As Joe and I discussed that day, my status as a longtime registered Republican would help the effort. (Years later, Bill Clinton made the same observation, praising me for being a Republican and bringing other fiscal conservatives into his campaign—all before requesting that I immediately change party affiliation.)

What they didn't know was that I registered as a Republican because I wanted to join the board of education in Weston, Connecticut. It was a lot easier to take a leadership position on the board at my children's school as a member of the GOP. Ideologically, I was a Rockefeller Republican—conservative on economic issues, like free markets and balanced budgets, but progressive on human rights and social issues. But Flom and I knew my real value was as a fundraiser.

Reelecting David would prove challenging. During Dinkins's first term, Rabbi Menachem Schneerson, leader of the Chabad-Lubavitch movement, led a motorcade through Crown Heights, Brooklyn. To keep pace, a Hasidic driver ran a red light and careened over a curb, striking and killing Gavin Cato, the seven-year-old son of immigrants, who had been playing on the sidewalk. Long-simmering tensions between the Hasidic community and Black immigrants erupted into what *Time* magazine described as the most violent race riot since the assassination of Martin Luther King Jr.[140]

The Orthodox Jewish community decried the mayor's response, blaming Dinkins for the ensuing riot and looting in Crown Heights. This criticism followed Dinkins for years. Bringing a class-action lawsuit against him, the Crown Heights Jewish community cited his role in the "murderous, anti-Semitic rampage that engulfed the Brooklyn community of Crown Heights for four days."[141] This denunciation spilled out to the public, with many claiming to be incensed that David didn't leverage his stature in the Black community to curtail the violence or use the authority of his office to command a stronger police reaction.

The riots complicated the election landscape. While Giuliani capitalized on the hardening of the Orthodox Jewish community against the incumbent mayor, David still had strong support among Manhattan's elite, more moderate Reform Jews—including business dynasties like the Tisch billionaires and the Rudin family, which controlled a big real estate group. They accompanied us on the delegation to London. Other businesspeople still believed that David wasn't sympathetic enough to New York's commercial interests. The contest eventually came to resemble a municipal culture war, as Republican prosecutor Giuliani tapped into the inherent racism of some ethnic neighborhoods in Brooklyn, Queens, and Staten Island, while David inspired a more ethnically varied coalition of Black voters and liberal progressives based in Manhattan.

On July 5, 1992, I joined David Dinkins on my very first trip to Israel, a critical visit given the mayor's flagging support among New York's powerful Orthodox Jewish community. Teddy Kollek, the one-time aide to David Ben-Gurion who went on to become mayor of Jerusalem, greeted us warmly. Prime Minister Yitzhak Rabin called Kollek "the greatest builder of Jerusalem since Herod the Great."[142] So did Shlomo Lahat, the legendary mayor of Tel Aviv, who did as much to bolster that city as Kollek did Jerusalem.[143] Heads of state Shimon Peres and Prime Minister Rabin especially impressed us. With intelligence and diplomatic skill at moderating people, Rabin struck me as brilliant the moment I met him. Both he and Peres seemed mission driven, not politically motivated, and didn't manifest many of the weaknesses I saw in American leadership.

It was an exciting time to be in Israel. I witnessed new business developments underway and sensed the place would become a powerful country, diverging from its neighbors in North Africa and the Middle East to approximate a contemporary Scandinavian democracy. Several years after my visit, the country experienced a devastating loss when a right-wing nationalist assassinated Rabin, partly in opposition to the peace accords that he had helped broker in Oslo.

UNCERTAIN DEFEAT

Back home, I worked diligently with the reelection team, hoping to ensure the first Black mayor of New York had the funding to compete against Giuliani. Fundraising for David proved challenging. At our events, like the rally in Bed-Stuy, many supporters could afford to give only about ten to fifty dollars. Most of my Manhattan friends were lawyers and investment bankers. Commuters like me, they were largely uninterested in municipal politics. My politically engaged friends were mostly real estate developers and either gravitated to the Republican party or had qualms about David's first term as mayor. I understood their position because if I hadn't known David personally, and if Flom hadn't approached me to serve in his campaign, I'm not sure I would have.

During the campaign, I became close with David's team. Bill Lynch was our campaign manager. A rumpled, heavyset man, then in middle age, Bill was also a keen political strategist and New York insider who had assembled a diverse coalition to secure David's 1989 primary victory over incumbent mayor Ed Koch and the eventual defeat of Giuliani. Our key political advisor was David's attorney, Peter Johnson, a litigator whose father was a politically engaged senior partner at a leading New York corporate litigation practice. The firm typically supported conservative Republicans, but they all loved David. Peter was a brilliant advisor, able to rewrite David's speeches in minutes, modifying just the right word or phrase to make it flow and appeal to our audiences. Professor Ester Fuchs, an urban politics and policy specialist at Barnard (before moving to Columbia), was a great addition to our team.

Of all the strong human capital David had, Harold Ickes, the namesake son of FDR's secretary of the interior, made the strongest impression. Charismatic and tough, Ickes was the most progressive member of the team, including David. Years later, when we both served in the Clinton administration, I saw Ickes leave a White House meeting, furiously storming past me without a greeting. Clinton had just issued his controversial decision to reform the welfare system, and Ickes was in a rage, having just exploded at the President. Such was Ickes's unwavering commitment to policy over politics. During the Dinkins campaign, I made an impression on him as well, as he'd never seen an investment banker working day and night on political fundraising.

In advance of the election, we somehow managed to raise $12.5 million, roughly the same as Giuliani. Seeing David well-capitalized and up about 2 to 3 percent in the polls, my confidence increased. But the more seasoned Lynch and Ickes shook their heads, saying, "We aren't up by 2 percent." As they explained, when a minority candidate runs, White voters mischaracterize their preferences by a factor of 2–4 percent, unwilling to state their actual intentions to pollsters. In 2016 this message resonated when I found it also applied to women running for office. Donald Trump won the national election that year despite polling predictions heavily favoring Hillary Clinton.

I remember gathering in a hotel with David on election night in 1993, hoping along with his supporters that we would prevail in this, his second electoral contest against Giuliani.[144] But NY1 television station called the race for our opponent. In 1989, Giuliani lost by 50,000 ballots; four years later, he won by 53,000.[145] Many pundits invoked the AIDS and crack cocaine crises, racial unrest, and David's budget cuts as explanations for this loss.[146] From my perspective, David's flagging interest in the business community played a role. But given David's advantage of incumbency, the strong Democratic leanings of most registered New Yorkers, and Giuliani's mediocre campaign, I believe the loss was attributable to David's lack of leadership during the Brooklyn race riots.

The day after the defeat, I reserved a table at the Four Seasons in Midtown Manhattan's Seagram building so I could debrief with David and offer encouragement. New York's elite loved this spot, and the maître d' was pleased the mayor would be dining there. But the lunch proved painful as a stream of well-wishers approached the table, expressing their condolences. It was like someone had died. We were expecting a reporter to join us for an interview with David over lunch. But his paper called to explain they were interviewing Giuliani instead. I understood entirely when David said he wanted to go home. I walked back to my office at Wertheim, shaking my head. What a sad day it was for David.

FUNDRAISING MANIA

Despite the defeat, my work in the Dinkins campaign attracted the attention of Democratic party insiders who thought I could be helpful in national fundraising. Sometime over the course of David's reelection campaign, Harold Ickes took notice of my dedication and began quietly drafting me for a future role in a second Clinton administration.

My relationship with Clinton began a few months after the election, in June 1994, when the President invited Jane and me to attend a White House movie night. Movie night was a venerable White House tradition since 1942, when FDR converted a cloakroom into a theater, using it to practice speeches and to screen movies before a select audience, including members of the cast and the film director.[147] These gatherings accommodated forty or so people at several tables overlooking the White House gardens. During these social events, noteworthy guests, cast members, and Hollywood industry types enjoyed easy conversation.

For our first movie night, Jane was seated at one side of the President and a journalist sat at the other. To my surprise, he and I spent a lot of the evening in conversation.

Unfortunately, Clinton had chosen to screen *The Wolf*, a romantic horror film whose plot, writing, and special effects I found dismal. The film's stars, Jack Nicholson and Michelle Pfeiffer, were present that evening. I managed to suppress my reaction to the movie. I excused myself during the intermission and entered the hallway, where I ran into Hillary Clinton. "Who picks the movies?" I asked her.

"The President does," she replied, explaining how he vetted a list before each occasion.

"I'm not impressed with the selection so far," I said. "I wouldn't have sat through this movie if I'd been in a theater."

"Don't tell me. Tell him," she responded. We enjoyed a good laugh.

In the months to follow, the White House social secretaries extended regular invitations to movie night, but having learned my lesson with *The Wolf*, I always researched the movie before I agreed to attend. Clinton, meanwhile, was introducing me to key members of the Democratic party like Bob Nash, the White House's director of presidential personnel, and Vernon Jordan, one of the most prominent political figures in Washington, DC, and Clinton's close friend.

Always my sponsor and advocate, Ickes asked me to join a high-profile business delegation to China in August 1994, led by Secretary of Commerce Ron Brown.[148] It was a pivotal moment in US-Sino relations, as the Clinton administration had just granted China most-favored-nations trading status, despite the country's human rights record.[149] The Chinese treated our delegation like royalty, and we were able to see the latest business developments in this emerging superpower.

Though the business leaders accompanying me cinched billions in transactions that trip, I did not promote my investment banking business. While I suggested that a few people speak to my colleagues at Schroders, my focus was on deepening my relationships with public servants like Ron Brown, the country's first Black secretary of commerce. Beginning that trip, Ron and I became close, and he frequently visited me in New York. "I think you should replace me as secretary of commerce next term," he often said, "and I'll take over as a chair of Wertheim Schroder." It was an ideal solution for an investment banker contemplating a move to the public sector and a public servant who wanted to make some money. Tragically, however, Ron died on April 3, 1996, when his plane, headed for another trade mission to explore investments in the former Yugoslavia, crashed into the mountainside in Dubrovnik, Croatia.[150]

Months after returning from China, in December 1994, I joined a United States Agency for International Development (USAID) mission to Haiti, as one of eight or nine election inspectors. The impoverished country was in tumult following the 1991 military coup that deposed President Jean-Bertrand Aristide, the nation's first democratically elected head of state. Haiti's bleak poverty stunned me, and I struggled to reconcile the fact that the Dominican Republic—with its vibrant, tourism-oriented economy and strong national leadership—shared the same island.

I vividly recall the first day of the trip, putting a bottle of water to my lips, when Brian Atwood stopped my hand. "The only thing safe to drink here," Atwood cautioned, "is carbonated water." He pointed out the window, and we looked below to the driveway, where locals and hotel staff alike filled plastic bottles from an open hose. We traveled Haiti in an armored vehicle, Pakistani army members serving as our guards. An intelligent and personable diplomat, Atwood was leading this mission, and immediately went on to teach at Brown University's Watson Institute.

It was clear that Haiti's leadership, and the American business community, were providing little economic and humanitarian assistance to Haitians. Sensing violence and instability, most businesses fled the country in the late 1980s and early 1990s, including Rawlings, a baseball manufacturer, which relocated its facilities to Central America. This lack of opportunity had rendered the island lawless, and there were areas where, even in the company of professional soldiers, it was too dangerous for us to visit. No matter where we ventured, crowds of children begged for money. I departed with a rare sense of hopelessness. When serving in government years later, I visited some of the most impoverished places in Sub-Saharan Africa, but I never witnessed anything resembling Haiti's poverty and human misery.

After China and Haiti, I focused much of my professional attention on fundraising for Clinton's reelection, taking particular interest in the campaign's White House coffee klatches. Between January 1995 and August 1996, the President held 103 such intimate coffees, where guests could meet over coffee with the President.[151] Prior to the meetings, I told each of my invitees that I expected them to contribute to the Democratic National Committee. Critics alleged that the money we raised from these meetings, totaling $27 million, was part of a formal fundraising program and therefore in violation of campaign rules.[152] As our lawyers would later argue, these voluntary contributions occurred after each event, with money never changing hands on government property.

For these coffees, I invited people like the convivial Howard Schultz, whose IPO Wertheim Schroder had just comanaged, and Tom Werner, who owned the San Diego Padres. A television producer and business executive, Werner would later purchase the Boston Red Sox. He was one of the nicest and most easygoing clients I'd ever worked with, and he had selected Wertheim Schroder over several bulge-bracket firms to help him sell the Padres in the early 1990s. The Padres were losing games, morale was low, and, to cover his losses, Werner refurbished the team roster, trading some of his players for new talent.

On opening nights of the San Diego Padres' season, Werner sometimes invited television stars to perform the pregame national anthem. One year in the mid-1990s he asked Roseanne Barr to sing. She proceeded to belt out the entire anthem not only off-key but also with her hand grasping her crotch. Werner was embarrassed. A few months later, I flew to San Diego with my son Doug, who knew California from his graduate school days at UCLA and was a baseball aficionado and keen judge of people. When we arrived, we were saddened to see the San Diego stadium almost empty. A front-page headline in a local paper blared: "Let's trade Tom Werner and his family instead of trading baseball players."

"I paid $75 million for this team," Werner said to me in exasperation, "and I'll sell it to you for a song. Why don't you manage the team for a few years, find a buyer, and give me the first $75 million from the proceeds." My friend was desperate to sell. I declined the opportunity, but some months later helped him sell the team for $78 million instead.

I made my largest contribution to the Clinton reelection campaign by introducing people like Schultz and Werner. They attended the coffees, contributed to the campaign, and hosted their own fundraisers for the President in Seattle and Beverly Hills, respectively. The coffees still remained my favorite fundraising vehicle. They were fun on the one hand, while on the other inspired robust and engaging conversations. Clinton usually picked the theme or topic and then opened the floor, allowing everyone to pose a question, offer a perspective, or snap photographs for souvenirs. Over relaxed discussions of national policies and world events, Clinton came alive. The meetings often ran over their allotted time, causing a secretary to enter and announce, "The President is due for a meeting. We've got to cut this off here."

Early in my fundraising efforts I took no credit for the funds I generated and instead gave it to others, thinking this would boost morale and help with donors' career advancement or placement in future administrations. When I asked my friend Howard Schultz to host a fundraiser, we attracted a new crop of West Coast donors. Unlike today, Seattle wasn't a big money town and represented a minor fundraising base compared to heavyweights like New York, Washington, DC, Chicago, and Los Angeles. But for this important event in an emerging market, I took zero credit. I did the same for the White House coffees, as the invitation lists were informal and remained unlisted in the official records.

My style diverged markedly from that of Virginia governor Terry McAuliffe. Terry was one of Clinton's best friends, and his fundraising prowess had elevated him, at the age of twenty-three, to the post of national finance director in the Carter administration.[153] "Jimmy," he'd call me up, "let me tell you about my new fundraising idea." His notion was to invite ten people to a special White House event, complete with lunch with Bill or Hillary, a tour of the grounds, a nice dinner, and a movie. A full day at the White House, he figured, surely had a $1 million price tag.

"I don't have the faintest idea about who would pay $1 million for anything," I responded, reiterating my interest in finding potential donors and inviting them to the coffees. McAuliffe remained dedicated to attracting such funds and targeted different industry organizations, asking them to pool $1 million in fundraising money, and then select one lucky person for a White House Day. He thus approached the head of the Plaintiffs Bar, an association representing certain litigation specialties, and offered him the deal, and then Terry went on to do the same with the medical associations.

I was uneasy with McAuliffe's aggressive fundraising. "This is getting a little crazy," I said one day. "Next thing I know, you'll tell me that someone can go to Camp David for the weekend, and you'll charge them $5 million." McAuliffe loved my "brilliant idea." After hanging up the phone, I walked into Steve Kotler's office and told him how Terry had grasped ahold of my facetious idea. We shook our heads.

By the mid-1990s, I was a regular at the White House, had participated in several trade delegations, and could sense that the Democratic party was considering me for service. Dinkins's reelection campaign—and his defeat—were instrumental in this journey. If David had won the 1993 mayoral election, he'd planned on appointing me deputy mayor for economic affairs in his administration. I would have accepted this position and led a much different life, remaining in New York and focusing my attention on running the city.

I reflected on this in 2014, the next time I visited Brooklyn. As I walked through the neighborhood, bound to see my daughter's performance at Red Hook Park, I reflected on how much South Brooklyn had changed since the Dinkins campaign. The place had transformed from a rough-and-tumble waterfront spot to a tranquil and posh community that was an easy commute to Wall Street. I arrived at the park's coastal pier at around four or five in the afternoon, just as the sun began to wane. The water was calm, the spring temperatures were balmy, and because it was a weekend, the entire place had a relaxed vibe. Jen's dance company had converted the pier into a performance space, with Manhattan in the background and boats moored in the foreground.

This setting was no accident. A talented artist like her mother, my daughter routinely choreographed and directed site-specific pieces like these. Each of Jen's seven dancers that evening performed in tandem with the sun. As it traced its way across the horizon that evening, they made gestures to the sky, signifying their own autonomy and freedom as well as harmony with the natural world. I was delighted when, after the performance ended, the dancers introduced themselves to me and expressed their appreciation for Jen. These hours with Jen and her dance troupe marked one of the most charmed and beautiful moments I've spent with my children.

Throughout the early and mid-1990s, I balanced my political fund-raising efforts with my investment banking work, managing the Schroders merger, and serving on about six or seven different corporate boards. By 1996, I spent about half of my time on public policy, talking to people like Ron Brown about work in government, or facilitating and sometimes hosting political fundraisers like the White House coffees. As Clinton's reelection grew nearer, I stopped working in the firm entirely, preparing Steve Kotler to take over as I became a senior advisor to the President. My transition was now complete: I had left the private sector and prepared for work in the United States government.

8

Rudderless and Leaderless

RUDDERLESS. LEADERLESS. CORRUPT. In the spring of 1997, this was how the media and certain members of Congress described a federal trade-finance agency called the Export-Import Bank of the United States (EXIM). President Bill Clinton had appointed only financiers as EXIM chair, some alleged, and the organization was unethical, violating federal labor laws by lavishing half the staff with retention bonuses.[154] To many critics, EXIM was no more than a corporate welfare agency, enriching the GEs and Boeings of the world, and ought to be disbanded.

Whether they wanted fresh leadership or the dissolution of the flailing institution, many critics reached a similar conclusion: the last thing EXIM needed was another Wall Street alumnus and Clinton crony to take the helm. "If the President nominates Wall Street veteran and Democratic donor James A. Harmon to run the agency," warned a *Bloomberg* piece, "Ex-Im's troubles could multiply."[155] But that's just what Clinton did, tapping me to be the eighteenth president and chair of EXIM and attracting even more ire from congressional Republicans and a skeptical media.

On November 5, 1996, Bill Clinton won a historic second-term victory, becoming the first Democrat to achieve reelection to the presidency since

FDR. But he entered Washington under a partisan cloud. For the first time in sixty-six years, a Democrat occupied the executive branch while Republicans, under the leadership of firebrand Newt Gingrich, controlled the House of Representatives.[156] Growing partisan divisions as well as adverse publicity surrounding Clinton's fundraising excesses came to engulf EXIM, a nonpolitical government agency that FDR created in 1934 to support the US business community's sale of products and services abroad.[157] When I arrived in Washington, I witnessed how this independent agency, with 440 employees and a $726 million budget, had become enmeshed in the larger partisan stalemate and rancor that would characterize Washington during Clinton's second term.[158]

To an outsider, this might seem like a daunting way to begin my time in public service. After accepting the position as chair and president of EXIM, I not only operated in this hostile climate, but I also encountered a series of crises involving my confirmation in the Senate, the reauthorization of the bank itself, and the securing of funds to maintain the bank's administrative costs. But repotting myself in the public sector was the best professional decision I've ever made. I've never experienced more joy, challenge, and excitement than when I came to Washington, cultivating relationships on the Hill and learning the intricacies of how governmental power operated.

In my first sixty days in Washington, I needed to save the bank from dissolution and mend its tattered reputation, all before addressing a global financial crisis. But as I had learned in the private sector, and would later discover while working in Egypt, the best time to invest in industries, agencies, and countries is when they are in disarray. If I could keep the bank operational, I somehow knew that it could have an important impact on the American business community and the larger developing world.

A HOSTILE CLIMATE

I first contemplated serving at EXIM in early January 1997. As I met with Ester Fuchs, my friend and colleague from the Dinkins reelection campaign who was visiting me that day, I received a call from Vice President Gore. Sensing this might be a delicate matter, Fuchs left my office. "Before we get started today," Gore began, "let me take down your email address."

"Hold on a second," I said, placing my hand over the receiver. "Do we have an email address?" I asked my assistant Michelle. My friend Al Gore was always the first to adopt new technologies and among the first public servants to understand and broadcast the perils of climate change. Gore overheard my question that day and dived into a lecture on this new form of digital communication called "email."

He then explained that President Clinton planned to nominate me as chair and president of EXIM Bank of the United States (EXIM). I had initially expected the secretary of commerce position. But I'd learned that the White House was gravitating to Bill Daley, a longtime Democratic supporter and the brother of Chicago mayor Richard M. Daley, a major Clinton fundraiser. "I'll think it over," I responded to Gore. Like most people, I wasn't familiar with the EXIM Bank and needed to study this agency to determine whether it was a good fit.

As I hung up the phone, I recalled a recent conversation that I'd had with Vernon Jordan. "Don't negotiate," Jordan had advised me. "When the administration offers you a position, raise your right hand and go to work." Besides, he continued, if you do a good job, even more attractive positions will arise. I wasn't interested in jockeying for positions or ascending the public service ranks but decided to take Jordan's counsel. EXIM Bank served an important role in the US corporate community, providing trade-financing solutions for companies selling goods and services abroad. My work in the private sector had prepared me to work at an agency like this. I also had a hunch that if I joined a smaller agency instead of a larger cabinet bureaucracy, I could have more autonomy and exercise more influence. I called Gore and said that, if nominated, I would accept the offer.

Once again following the counsel of other Washington insiders, I asked the White House to announce my nomination only after the FBI completed its vetting process. I'd already relinquished my seats on all corporate boards, like that of Mountain Fuel Supply, and had begun divesting many of my assets like that of Latin Communications, a company I'd chaired since 1995. Latin Communications was a growing Spanish-language media group that owned *El Diario*, the United States' oldest and largest Spanish-language newspaper. Over the course of campaigning for Dinkins, I'd learned that the Hispanic population in America would exert increasing influence in national politics. Had I not entered public service, I planned to use Latin Communications as a base to build a Hispanic media operation that would help develop and channel that political influence.

Two weeks into the vetting, the FBI called to inform me that, contrary to my paperwork, James Harmon wasn't born on October 12, 1935, in Manhattan. I called my mother to double check, and she insisted that these details about my birth were accurate. The FBI thought I was failing to disclose important details about my life, but the story proved more embarrassing. "Check to see if 'James Hamburger' was born at the hospital and date indicated," I responded. Long ago, I'd learned that my father had changed our surname from Hamburger to Harmon following his graduation from Harvard Law School. During class, Dad often sat next to a young man with the last name of "Frankfurter." When professors did roll call and said "Frankfurter, Hamburger" in rapid succession, the class erupted in laughter. As the FBI discovered, I was born Hamburger and later became Harmon.

I wouldn't learn any further details about the vetting process until a cold winter night in 1999, when the FBI delivered a large report on the investigation to my suite at the Jefferson Hotel. Senator Chris Dodd had told me I could file a Freedom of Information Act request to see the dossier. After I followed his suggestion and received it months later, I settled in for hours of reading about what my former colleagues and neighbors had to say about me.

The FBI had dispatched four teams to New York City, Connecticut, Florida (where I own a condominium), and, to my surprise, the small island of Anguilla. Many of their recorded interviews were unsurprising, like the Wertheim employee who remarked how conservative I was with his year-end bonus. Many of our neighbors in Anguilla, who lived in modest homes near my beach house, concluded that Jim Harmon must be a shady financier if the FBI was trailing him to the Caribbean and inquiring about his character. But the biggest surprise was the report of a real estate partner of my daughter Debbie. When asked about James Harmon, he said, "I can only tell you that if I had to pick a father out of everyone I've met in my entire life, I'd pick Jim." I was moved nearly to tears that he held me in such esteem.

As I cleared the vetting process in April 1997 and graduated to Senate confirmation, the mood in Washington continued to deteriorate. In 1994, Newt Gingrich had joined Texas representative Dick Armey in authoring a legislative agenda known as the "Contract with America" that had catapulted the Republicans to victory in Congress.[159] Because of larger ideological changes, or what political scientists have called "sorting," among the American electorate and its representatives, the differences between the Republicans in Congress and Democratic consensus-builders like Clinton grew ever more stark.[160] This larger partisan divide came to coalesce around Clinton and Gingrich, both politicians from the South. Their personal hostility and aggression resulted in a protracted government shutdown at the end of 1995 and the beginning of 1996. Unlike previous shutdowns, which had been infrequent and brief, this one involved two parties that couldn't agree on a common set of data projections. I still remember the constant barrages of Republicans, insisting on using the Congressional Budget Office's more pessimistic revenue projections, and the White House wanting the more optimistic Office of Management and Budget numbers.[161]

Historians remind us that American history is replete with intense personal animosities, like that of Alexander Hamilton and Aaron Burr, as well as eruptions of anger and even violence. By the mid-twentieth century, however, lawmakers had largely retired fistfights, duels, and threats, and settled on a set of civil norms.[162] I was shocked to see the disintegration of some of these norms and the depth of personal animosity fueling many political conflicts. In my thirty-eight years on Wall Street, I'd never witnessed anything approximating the hostility that I saw in Washington. Such widespread anger and hatred would continue to develop, especially when an even more polarizing president, Donald Trump, came to office two decades later, culminating in an armed, deadly insurrection at the US Capitol on January 6, 2021, as Congress certified the election of President Joseph R. Biden.

The White House prepared me for a difficult confirmation process in the Senate and assembled a small team to guide me. Paul Carey, a White House special assistant to Clinton who liaised among the Senate Banking Committee and my staff, was indispensable.[163] While I knew that the partisan divide would complicate my confirmation, I had confidence in my record and my ability to answer any question at the hearing.

That confidence wouldn't fray until my first mock trial, when a number of attorneys role-played senators on the banking committee who would conduct my hearing. Apparently, everyone was afraid to tell me how poorly I performed. My answers made the audience of staff members cringe, setting members of the White House on edge. According to my future chief of staff, I was "terrible."[164] Bill Clinton took his chief political advisor Doug Sosnik aside, suggesting to him that I meet with his speech coach Michael Sheehan, a brilliant advisor and one of the world's best communications specialists.

Sheehan began our training by posing a few questions about my career and qualifications to lead EXIM Bank. After giving him some direct and candid replies, he stopped me: "If anything is unclear or occupies a gray area, you refrain from commenting and say that you would like to ask your counsel." Apparently, I was too practiced in the straight-shooting SEC-style investigations from my investment banking days. Sheehan familiarized me with "Washington speak," a way of communicating that prioritizes a message or agenda to impart to your audience. The art of imparting that agenda involves staying "on message." When asked about my thoughts on climate or the foreign trade deficit, I offered slightly different answers each time, just to vary it up. Bad idea. In Washington speak, redundancy is a virtue, and I began to learn the art of blunting the truth and giving more rehearsed, if dull, answers.[165]

As a technique for staying on message, Sheehan instructed me to draw a rectangle on a piece of paper and to write a preferred reference or "talking point" at each of its four corners. My corners had the following talking points to support my candidacy for EXIM chair: "experience working in foreign countries"; "experience managing an organization with multiple stakeholders"; "experience with labor"; and "thorough understanding of budgets." I was dubious about this approach, thinking that these four points couldn't possibly address the array of questions that committee members were likely to pose. But after a bit of practice, I was amazed at its effectiveness. If you watch expert testimony on the Hill, many employ some version of this technique, infuriating the person posing questions by staying on message. To this day, if I'm preparing for a difficult meeting, I take out a sheet of paper, draw a rectangle, articulate the four items I want to stress that day, and return to them throughout my meeting.

Jane accompanied me on that first session with Sheehan. She'd just received a Tony nomination for her production of *Last Night at Ballyhoo*, and CBS was set to broadcast the fifty-first annual Tony awards ceremony at Radio City Music Hall on June 1, 1997. This was yet another high point in Jane's career in theater, similar to the acclaim she'd garnered for *Driving Miss Daisy* at the Academy Awards earlier that decade. But she'd contracted Lyme disease from deer ticks on our Connecticut property. With part of her face temporarily paralyzed, she was sensitive about appearing on national television. Sheehan was terrific with her. While conversing with her for several minutes and studying her face, he taught her how to position her body to achieve friendly camera angles. After one hour's time, Sheehan had infused both of us with confidence. Jane did brilliantly on television, and after a few more sessions with Sheehan, I was more focused and on message.

Because I was the first noncabinet appointee awaiting confirmation before the Senate Banking Committee, my White House team seemed especially anxious. I was surprised when, prior to the hearing, members from the White House suggested I invite my children, grandchildren, close friends, and mother to attend. If everyone expected a confrontation, I asked, why should I subject my family to such unpleasantness? They persuaded me to bring them along, and I'm glad I did, because I sailed through confirmation. After much preparation, the hearing was a lovefest.

I initially attributed the success to my reputation and experience. But it turned out that my vice chair, Jackie Clegg, was also up for confirmation that day. As I discovered shortly following the hearing, Jackie was then the girlfriend of Connecticut senator Chris Dodd, an influential member of the Banking Committee. Though this relationship had helped us during the process, given that no one wanted to anger the romantic partner of this powerful senator, this situation struck me as a conflict of interest. How can a member of a congressional committee with oversight over the agency objectively evaluate the candidacy of an agency leader when they are romantically involved?

White House officials had broached the topic of Clegg several months earlier. "Have you thought about your vice chair?" several asked, telling me about someone named Clegg who had served as chief of staff for my predecessor Ken Brody. These officials told me of her friendship with Chris Dodd, reiterating her reputation for being difficult, and sometimes impossible, to manage. But she had been a congressional staffer for many years and worked at EXIM for the past five. "I can't imagine having difficulty managing someone like that," I said at the time, echoing my enthusiasm for having a vice chair so experienced and well connected. While she proved advantageous at the confirmation hearing, I should have heeded these early cautions about a potential problem. My decision to retain Clegg would later haunt me.

WORKING THE HILL

My official tenure at EXIM began with my mother, children, and sister all venturing to Washington, DC, to see me sworn into office by Vice President Al Gore. I was especially moved that David Dinkins was in attendance. He had been a stalwart supporter, and in March of 1997 had written *Business Week* magazine countering the negative press surrounding my candidacy. "I have known Jim Harmon for many years," said David, "and he is a man of great intellect and integrity, and one who has an excellent grasp of international finance and world affairs. These are the credentials which make him ideal for this post."[166]

While preparing for the confirmation in April and May that year, I had studied the history and loan experience of the bank, received daily briefings about geopolitical developments related to our loan exposures, and was prepared for work. Instead of beginning work on running the bank, as I longed to do, I turned my attention to a pressing matter. Every four or five years, Congress must reauthorize every agency, and EXIM was now due. EXIM's reauthorization ultimately fell to me, its newly minted chair, who was just becoming acquainted with the bank himself. Shouldn't reauthorizations take place when the agency or department chair had been in office at least six months or a year? Just as I was familiarizing myself with the bank and considering various financing ideas, I turned my attention to operational and stakeholder concerns. Specifically, I had ninety days to convince a polarized Congress to reauthorize the agency.

To save the bank, I needed to master the intricacies of "working the Hill." The Hill, a term referring to the highest end of the property line in Washington, DC, where the House of Representatives and Senate are located, encompasses the 535 members of both chambers of Congress along with their three thousand–plus staff. During my first few days in Congress, I watched senators discuss the day's agenda while walking side by side with their experienced staff, asking them how they should vote on different bills. Staffers provided informed and reasoned cases for voting yes on an immigration bill but no on a budget proposal. Congressional staffers are much more capable than many outside government realize.

Like every other agency and department, EXIM came equipped with a congressional affairs division of three to four staffers. These staffers are indispensable because, as they say in Washington, DC: "The President proposes, the Congress disposes."[167] "It's nice to make speeches," Bill Clinton always told me, "but Congress has the last word." When you're worried about the budget, facing a controversy, or, in my case, needing reauthorization, you rely on congressional staffers. They help you face questioning on the Hill. Clinton nominated Sandi Jackson as director of EXIM's congressional affairs. The wife of Illinois congressman Jesse Jackson Jr., she was a skilled politician and city alderman.[168] She did a wonderful job advocating for the bank. Later, I was sad to see Sandi and her husband, Jesse, plead guilty to campaign fraud. My chief of staff Andrea Adelman also helped me liaise with the Hill. One day, after I returned from a vacation in Anguilla, she stared at me and candidly said that I appeared so suntanned that I looked like I had been on vacation for months.

Appearances loomed large when working the Hill. You must avoid looking sun-kissed and refreshed, I discovered, because it suggests you haven't been working very hard. I also learned to leave my double-breasted suits, monogrammed shirts, and cuff links in New York City. Meetings on the Hill weren't investment banking affairs, and I needed to dress down.

Negotiating power dynamics proved even more important than appearances. Rule number one: never antagonize Mitch McConnell, the fearsome leader of the Republicans, as my predecessor had done. If you upset McConnell, my staffers warned, a parade of horrors will befall you. He'll slash your budget, make you testify at different hearings, and otherwise complicate your life. The first time I met McConnell on the Hill, he said, "I hope you'll do a lot better than the last guy." He then walked away, not allowing me to explain my vision for the agency.

Jackie Clegg, Andrea Adelman, and EXIM congressional affairs officer Bill Hellert spearheaded the reauthorization effort. Jackie began her career as an aide to Utah senator Jake Garn before moving over to EXIM and becoming close with Senator Dodd. When I first met Jackie, she struck me as young, serious, and moderate in her opinions. Andrea had also come to EXIM by way of Capitol Hill, where for seven years she was an aide to Representative Sam Gejdenson, a Connecticut Democrat.[169] Because Andrea was a seasoned staffer on the House side, Jackie knew the Senate, and Hellert had great relationships with everyone, they made a formidable team.

On day one of the effort, they presented me with the bios of everyone on the Hill who had business with EXIM, along with an overview of the 435 districts these members represented. By way of strategy, they'd also generated a color-coded map, with each member highlighted in green if they were positively disposed to EXIM, yellow if they were neutral about the bank, or pink if they had a financial or ideological problem with us.[170] This reminded me of preparing for a merger or acquisition in the investment banking world, familiarizing myself with every employee detail, product description, and balance sheet. Over the following forty days, we personally visited about three-quarters of the House and Senate.[171] It was a lot of fun as I rehashed my life story to congressional members every day and learned more about the backgrounds and goals of our country's leaders. They sometimes encouraged my efforts and other times unleashed a barrage of criticism about my predecessor.

EXIM was unpopular on the Hill in part because of certain past leaders. My predecessor, a Wall Street executive named Kenneth Brody, was popular on the Hill. After a long career in banking, he'd become a Clinton fundraiser, focusing on the 1992 New York primary race.[172] After three years at EXIM, Brody was disappointed when the chair of the World Bank went to James Wolfensohn instead of him.[173]

On New Year's Eve 1995, in the final year of Clinton's first term, Brody resigned as EXIM chair, leaving his vice chair, Martin "Tino" A. Kamarck, a business executive with close Clinton administration ties, as his heir apparent.[174] Tino's wife, Elaine Kamarck, had an illustrious academic and professional career. Now at the Brookings Institute, Elaine had helped to found the New Democrat movement that propelled Clinton to victory and was Al Gore's chief of staff before becoming a lecturer at Harvard's Kennedy School.[175] Many congresspeople on the Hill, including Mitch McConnell, opposed her husband Tino's elevation to chair. According to a General Accounting Office watchdog report, EXIM had violated federal law by granting retention bonuses to two hundred or so of its employees.[176] Clinton infuriated McConnell by granting Tino a recess appointment, elevating him to chair when Congress wasn't in session and therefore unable to vote on the confirmation.[177] Fed-up senior policy makers considered discontinuing the agency. Members of Congress openly discussed either dissolving EXIM or merging it with a sister organization focused on foreign trade.[178]

Leadership aside, EXIM Bank was much diminished from its peak influence and stature. In the 1950s and 1960s, EXIM was a key agency for promoting American business abroad, guaranteeing the financing for roughly 10 percent of all US exports.[179] This when national GDP was largely domestic and the sum of American imports and exports represented around 8 to 9 percent of the country's GDP. But with the worldwide move from fixed to floating currencies at the Bretton Woods conference in 1944, global price fluctuations diminished as free currencies self-adjusted to supply and demand, encouraging an efflorescence of global trade.[180] Today, exports and imports represent roughly 30 percent of American GDP and EXIM guarantees only around 1–2 percent of them. EXIM has lost market share to commercial banks, which have internationalized their operations and financed major exporting deals on behalf of US business.

When I came to office, "Tea Party" Republicans and certain progressive Democrats alike accused EXIM of being a corporate welfare agency, directing money or subsidies to multinational corporations instead of small businesses.[181] There was a kernel of truth to this charge, or at least the contention that free markets, instead of governments, ought to do the work of EXIM. I'd scrutinized the bank's balance sheets and knew that while it guaranteed loans from emerging economies, it also financed transactions like China's purchase of Boeing airplanes. In principle, I could understand someone objecting to that transaction because China could afford to pay for its own equipment. China didn't need the subsidized interest rates EXIM Bank provided.

But such a criticism failed to consider that the United States was competing against European rival Airbus, which received handsome subsidies from the French and German governments. Accusations of corporate welfare disregarded these larger geopolitical stakes and the competition our large companies faced. As I reminded the congressional representatives and senators on the Hill, EXIM Bank existed to support the US business community's exports. Without guaranteeing loans to countries that couldn't afford our domestically produced goods and services, without granting subsidies to help our own companies compete, we would lose jobs and harm our economy.

I was able to avoid partisan crossfire and make my case for EXIM's continued importance by developing friendships on the Hill. David Dinkins was close friends with Congressman Charlie Rangel, a Democrat who represented Harlem and was also the first Black chair of the House Ways and Means Committee. Through them I met Jesse Jackson Jr. and California congresswoman Maxine Waters. I appeared before the Congressional Black Caucus throughout my time in government, sometimes several times a month, asking them how I could support Black-owned exporters and keeping them abreast of my future work throughout Africa.

Because I was a businessperson coming from the financial community, many Republicans saw me as more moderate. My friendships within the Republican party advanced considerably with the help of Barry Gottehrer, a journalist, sportswriter, and old fraternity brother of mine. A liberal Republican, Gottehrer had served in New York City's mayor's office before moving to national politics and joining the lobbying corps in Washington, DC.[182] One day, he introduced me to Sonny Callahan, a Republican congressman from Alabama with the coveted status of "cardinal." In overseeing and directing federal government spending, the House Appropriations Committee is so powerful that the chairs of each of its twelve subcommittees are dubbed "cardinals." New to Washington, I had no idea what "cardinal" meant— the term sounded vaguely religious to me—and simply enjoyed Callahan's demeanor and persona. I had little inkling of how much Callahan's status as chair of the House Appropriations subcommittee on state, foreign operations, and related programs would later help me.

I marveled (and sometimes cringed) at his frequently amusing, if politically incorrect and off-color, stories. Callahan frequently tussled with the President, once declaring that every time a foreign leader with a turban joined Clinton at the White House, the President opened a bottle of wine, wrote the person a check, and then came to Sonny, instructing him to appropriate the funds. In response, Callahan said he himself planned to don a turban, visit the President, and, over a glass of wine, request money for American seniors and taxpayers, instead of foreign leaders.[183]

Callahan extended an invitation to dine with him and his colleagues one evening at what looked like a rundown bar. I stepped inside and said, "I'm here to attend a dinner with Sonny Callahan." The host pointed past the main dining area to the back of the building. I walked back, as directed, only to encounter an incredible scene. In this smoky back room, the 1920s had come alive. There I found seven or eight men in business suits drinking hard liquor, puffing on cigars, and telling off-color stories about women. I spotted the heavyset and gregarious Callahan, who in his thick southern drawl introduced me as the "token Democrat." When asked about my role, I grabbed my precious opening to brief them on EXIM before taking my leave, having nearly succumbed to the backroom cigar smoke.

When I told Bill Clinton about the event, he encouraged me. "We need someone who knows them well." After word spread that I was friendly with Callahan, Madeleine Albright called me and said, "I'm going to the Hill. I have a very important budget item, and I'm wondering if you'll go with me." I declined the invitation, out of judiciousness. I didn't want to come across as doing the Democratic party's bidding. In addition, I was mindful of EXIM's important budget needs. I needed to preserve my relationship with Callahan, who I knew would be helpful in coming years. Callahan ultimately proved a fiercely loyal friend who later publicly defended me.

Barry Gottehrer brokered other relationships for me, one day suggesting that I join the entire Republican congressional caucus. Criticized for not having relationships with any Democrats, the Republicans believed I could be an ally, especially after Callahan recommended me as a sound and sensible businessperson. They convened one day in a ballroom, and I sat on the stage with House Speaker Newt Gingrich, Senate Majority Leader Trent Lott, and House Majority Leader Dick Armey. "Once in a while, the Democrats find someone who's actually doing all right," said Gingrich, who proceeded to detail my background in the business community. I immediately wished I was recording this terrific introduction.

I turned to Lott and confessed I was a bit anxious because I hadn't prepared any remarks. With that introduction, Armey whispered, "You could talk about baseball and they'd be happy." I felt completely at ease as I approached the podium, telling the group that they were the politicians and that I was just a simple trade-finance guy. EXIM might have had some troubled leadership in the past, I suggested, but it now had someone who cared deeply about American businesses and exporters. My comments pleased everyone, and Gingrich draped his arm around me as he escorted me out, saying, "Are you sure you're not a Republican? That was great!" I told him I'd actually been a Republican for most of my life, and that made the Speaker even happier.

I established a similar rapport with leading Democrats, especially after Andrea Adelman arranged a meeting with California's Democratic congressional delegation. It was an overwhelming experience because while some states have one representative, and many have a handful or so, California had a stunning fifty-three representatives in its delegation, by far the largest in Congress. When I entered the meeting room, I wasn't prepared for the sea of forty Democratic faces greeting me. But I capitalized on the relationships I already had, like that with Jane Harman, the senior-ranking California Democrat who led the delegation. Once before the podium, I thanked everyone for the kind introduction and then deadpanned, "In the interests of full disclosure, you should all know: I've been sleeping with Jane Harmon for thirty-five years." Silence engulfed the room.

"Point of information," said Jane, rising from her seat, "Jim's wife is also Jane Harmon." That impromptu joke set the mood for a cordial meeting that left Jane, my wife, and me laughing for days. Because of routine encounters like these, working the Hill was a sincere pleasure, reminding me of rushing my fraternity in college.

But interpersonal danger sometimes lurked. As we ascended the White House stairs one day, I locked eyes with the mayor of Pittsburgh, who was exiting the building. "How do you know him?" asked Andrea Adelman.

A few years back, I told her, Major League Baseball had contacted Wertheim. After we'd successfully sold the San Diego Padres, they wanted us to sell the Pittsburgh Pirates. Paul Wachter, my investment banking colleague at Wertheim who ran our West Coast operations and specialized in sports transactions, accompanied me to Pittsburgh. Together we met with the Pirates' ownership group. Paul referred to these twelve or so men as "Knights of the Roundtable" because they ran powerful organizations like Pittsburgh Plate Glass, Carnegie Mellon, Heinz, and Westinghouse Electric. "The mayor wants to meet with you," they told us.

The following day we met the mayor and his deputy. Once we took our seats on a sofa, the mayor said, "You're going to sell the team to John Rigas." The Rigas family had been Pittsburgh royalty ever since John cofounded Adelphia Communications—at the time of our meeting one of the most successful cable companies in the United States.

The Pittsburgh trip marked the beginning of due diligence, and we didn't yet understand the local market. But we did know that the mayor had attended college with John Rigas and that rumors were rife that New Yorkers were descending on Pittsburgh to relocate their beloved Pirates. Paul and I nodded along politely, suggesting that we had no intention of relocating the team and we'd certainly prioritize Rigas during our search. But we reminded him that we had a fiduciary duty to the owners and would select a buyer that was best for them.

"You're not hearing me," said the mayor, an edge in his voice. "You're going to sell this team to John Rigas."

"How would it look in the *Wall Street Journal*," I replied, "if it comes out that the mayor of Pittsburgh forced us to sell the team to his college roommate?"

The mayor rose to his feet, sprang across the coffee table separating us, and shoved me in the chest. His deputy followed suit, leaping up and shoving

Paul. The commotion spilled over from the mayor's office into the vestibule. A terrified assistant darted out of the way as I broke my fall on her desk.

We exited the building dumbfounded, and a little sore, making our way back to the posh Duquesne Club to debrief the Roundtable knights. Physical violence in a business meeting was a first for Paul and me. We shook our heads at each other, certain we'd lost the opportunity. But no sooner had we greeted the owners at our table than one of them stood up and began clapping. "Anyone willing to fight for our team is OK with us!" he exclaimed. The others agreed with gusto, and we managed to complete the sale—to someone else.

"Are you going to say hello to the mayor?" asked Andrea.

"No, I'm not," I replied emphatically. "I hope he doesn't recognize me!" I needed to do a better job managing relationships in Washington than I had in Pittsburgh.

Though my bipartisan friendships gave me more confidence as EXIM's reauthorization date approached, my advisory team remained anxious. They worked hard for forty days, and when the morning of the senate hearing arrived, White House staff briefed me with some urgency on what the senators on the banking committee might ask. After our visits on the Hill, we'd transformed the color-coded chart of congressional representatives and senators with many of the once neutral yellow and hostile pink names now shaded in green. But the bank's reputational crisis, created by my predecessors and exacerbated by the partisan tension on the Hill, loomed large. If we failed reauthorization, I would be more than the eighteenth president of the EXIM Bank—I would be the infamous last president too.

Jackie and Andrea were thus delighted to report that Congress reauthorized EXIM Bank with unanimous support in the Senate and surprisingly strong support in the House. Though unhappy about the leadership of my predecessor, congressional representatives supported EXIM's continued existence, especially its mandate to keep American exporters competitive abroad. I was relieved that many on the Hill could see past the partisan loyalties and even suspicions of corporate welfare, determined that EXIM would not simply survive but also grow and thrive.

A DIFFERENT STYLE OF LEADERSHIP

But I first needed more money. Government budgets are typically twofold affairs: program budgets deal with money needed to support the business or work—in our case supporting exports—while administrative budgets cover employee salaries and other expenses. Likely fearing scrutiny on the Hill, my predecessor had applied for a woefully inadequate administrative budget. As I scanned the numbers, I realized this budgetary shortfall posed another major crisis: we didn't have enough money to reach the end of the fiscal year ending on September 30.

As I grappled with this crisis over several weeks' time, Jane and I went to the National Cathedral to attend the wedding of Karenna Gore, Al and Tipper Gore's beautiful daughter, to Andrew Schiff, a dashing primary-care physician from New York. About two hundred people attended the nuptials on July 12, 1997, and as I glanced into the crowd, I saw members of Congress and the executive cabinet as well as personal friends from the Gores' home state of Tennessee. When thinking of magnificent churches, Americans often imagine London's Westminster Abbey or Paris's Notre Dame Cathedral. With its spectacular façade and vaulted gothic interior, the National Cathedral belongs among the finest churches in America and possibly the world.

Later, at the vice-presidential mansion on Embassy Row, President Clinton led me around for part of the evening, introducing me to members of Gore's staff and reconnecting me with longtime friends like Peter Knight. Knight had served as Gore's chief of staff while he was in Congress and then played a decisive role in the 1996 reelection campaign. Though the setting was spectacular, and I'd enjoyed some time on the dance floor with Jane, my mind was on EXIM and our budgetary problems. Bill Clinton leaned over: "How's it going?" he asked. "You having fun yet?" It's a droll expression in Washington, and one that Clinton and my EXIM colleagues would often ask in the coming years.

In truth, I loved forging relationships on the Hill, but didn't think of it as fun. "Fun is when you ski down a beautiful powder slope or swim the beaches in Anguilla," I responded. "I find some of my challenges enjoyable, but I wouldn't use the word 'fun' to describe them."

"Well that's too bad," he said. "You should be having a good time."

"I didn't come to Washington to have fun," I countered. "I came here to solve problems. And I appear to have walked into a hornet's nest." Amid the music, dancing, and celebratory champagne toasts, I was cautious of talking shop. But when President Clinton then inquired about how he could help, I couldn't resist. I plainly told him that we were running out of administrative funds. Send me a memo next week, he said, and he would help.

Early the following morning, I ventured back to my office and wrote a detailed memorandum about our urgent budgetary needs. A lot of important information arrived on Clinton's desk on Sunday nights, and I wanted EXIM on top of the pile. On Monday morning, the President read the memo and forwarded it to the Office of Management and Budget (OMB). The funds we needed materialized. When EXIM staff learned that the new chair had solved our administrative budgetary problems because he had a personal relationship with the White House, our flagging morale began to lift.

With the institutional and financial future of the bank in place, I began to settle into my life in Washington. Unlike many members of Congress and agency heads, I didn't rent a home or apartment and instead signed a lease at the Jefferson, a five-star boutique hotel located about half a mile from my EXIM office and the White House. A stately and conservative place, the Jefferson had a quaint feel, and I was happy that, unlike the Four Seasons, its ninety-nine suites and smaller common areas couldn't accommodate a convention crowd. My suite on the third floor was just above Bob Rubin's, a man I knew from Wall Street when he was a senior partner at Goldman Sachs and who now served as Clinton's treasury secretary. Bob and I conducted life at the Jefferson as we would in our own homes, entertaining people for dinner and cocktails, and this greatly enriched my time in Washington.

My tennis buddy Donald Dell introduced me to the athletic club across the street from the Jefferson and I became a member. Every morning, I'd either work out at the club or enjoy a beautiful run, setting out from the hotel, making my way through the nation's monuments, and rounding back through the Smithsonian galleries. Whenever I faced a battle, these monuments and the history they represented gave me a psychological lift. Having lived most my adult life in a small town in Connecticut, I'd never lived among monuments, and I appreciated the weight of history and seriousness they inspired in me.

After my workout, I'd make my way to EXIM's office, which was about two hundred yards from the White House. From my office window, I could see Lafayette Square framing the iconic government headquarters. Before heading to the Hill, I'd often stroll through the Square. Sometimes I sat on a bench to gather my thoughts before a meeting or simply reflected on a pressing matter as parents with strollers passed or people playing chess congregated in the background.

With the confirmation, reauthorization, and budgetary crises behind me, I could finally focus on running the bank. With the help of Clegg and Adelman, I turned my attention to our considerable human capital, devoting several weeks to meeting the staff and asking them about their roles. According to one EXIM veteran, "Nobody had ever done that before."[184]

Just as I had done countless times as an investment banker, I needed to establish a workable management structure at the bank.[185] All fourteen division heads reported directly to the chair or vice chair, creating inefficiencies and bottlenecks. I asked each divisional head to detail how they managed and operated their units, and based on their feedback, did some reorganizing. We replaced the fourteen divisions with a more efficient M9 structure and began setting performance goals and accountability structures for those in leadership. Staff at the bank, I began to suspect, received promotions because of seniority instead of performance, meaning some unskilled managers may have ascended the ranks.

As we began implementing a more skeletal and meritocratic management structure, I asked some personnel to leave. To manage the retention-bonus fallout of my predecessor, EXIM's interim chair had hired two men from the private sector whom I quickly asked to resign. We needed the extra budget, and I had the banking and finance background to run EXIM without them. I also encouraged the talented executive vice president to seek a new employment opportunity. An organization of fewer than five hundred employees didn't need an executive vice president, and I didn't want another layer separating me from the career public servants at the bank.

With so many personnel changes underway, I was especially grateful for Jim Cruse, Mark Shapiro, and Margaret Engelhardt. Having served at the bank since 1970, beginning as a country economist before moving on to policy matters, Cruse was not only the bank's foremost intellectual, he was also an embodiment of its institutional memory. By far the most knowledgeable person on the history and inner workings of the bank, Cruse was the institution's elder statesman and I couldn't have discharged my role without him. Around ten years my junior, Mark Shapiro had studied philosophy at Brown and earned law and business degrees from Columbia before becoming a student of corporate finance. After moving to Wertheim, he proved an excellent leader with a gift for mentoring investment bankers. He later replaced Steve Kotler as head of the firm's corporate finance department, where he thrived. I was surprised and relieved when Mark expressed interest in joining me at EXIM Bank. With him and my trusted assistant and confidante Margaret by my side, I knew my transition to Washington would be a lot easier.

By law, EXIM Bank has certain immutable structures, like its five-member bipartisan board of directors, usually comprising two Democratic and two Republican appointees and one chair (appointed by the majority party). Just as was the case for the boards overseeing the securities and exchange commission and the federal reserve, EXIM board members are political appointees, sometimes lacking financial qualifications. Instead of having subject-area expertise, as was customary on corporate boards, EXIM's board members had strong interpersonal knowledge and Washington connections. Chairs of independent public agencies, I soon learned, have more power than in the private sector, as board members largely defer to them for instructions and assignments.

During my first six months in office, I became acquainted with Jackie Clegg, my number two in command and member of the board. Having worked closely with Jackie during the reauthorization, we had a solid rapport, and I tried to give her prestige assignments that I felt appropriate for a vice chair. In November 1999, for example, I asked Jackie to travel to Vietnam to reinstate EXIM's programming there. After Vietnam's long period of isolation following the war, the United States sought to reestablish diplomatic and commercial relations. EXIM's program marked a milestone in the larger normalization of US-Vietnamese relations, and Jackie, a talented public speaker, represented the bank and the country well.

Rita Rodriguez, who'd served on the board since 1982, had assumed the role of acting president and chair in the spring of 1997.[186] In addition to serving on the board and managing the power vacuum left by my predecessor, Rodriguez headed the bank's policy group, coordinating the agency's work and strategy with the Paris Club, Berne Union, Organisation for Economic Co-operation and Development (OECD), and other international bodies.[187] Had I been able to select board members based on experience and financial acumen, Rodriguez would have been a top choice. With a doctoral degree from NYU's Graduate School of Business and deep knowledge of the bank, she was highly intelligent, had great interpersonal skills, and was beloved among the staff. She never interfered with my decisions and offered consistently helpful advice.

My third member, Maria Haley, was a Clinton appointee. She had a long history with President Clinton, working with him on his gubernatorial campaign in 1978 to transform the sleepy state of Arkansas into a more economically vibrant place that attracted business.[188] She honed her expertise on small business promotion and export development in the Arkansas government and then joined the Clinton White House. Haley, born in the Philippines, eventually became a director at EXIM and a board member in 1994. She had assisted me during the confirmation process, detailing EXIM's small business programs to counter claims of corporate welfare, and later traveled with me to Africa, where we worked together on Sub-Saharan initiatives.[189] With her private sector experience in international marketing before joining government, she was a major asset when it came to small businesses and was helpful whenever matters related to Arkansas or Democratic politics arose.

Julie Belaga, a Republican from Connecticut, rounded out the board. Having served in the Connecticut state legislature for ten years, she'd run for governor in 1986.[190] After losing her gubernatorial bid, Belaga sent her résumé down to Washington, DC. President George Bush appointed her regional administrator of the Environmental Protection Agency in Boston. I respected Belaga's conviction that environmental protection and economic development could be mutually reinforcing, instead of mutually undermining. That understanding formed the bedrock of my future environmental work at the World Resources Institute. Based on her political experience and background with the environment, she served as a board member and COO.

I found the title "chief operating officer" to be something of a misnomer in government. In the private sector, a COO plays a critical role in management and operations, including what business an organization should conduct and what companies it should acquire. In government, COOs have a more administrative, human resources role—evaluating staff, intervening when problems arise, and determining compensation for senior employees, including the general counsel and accounting office. Honest and pragmatic, Belaga executed her role well and was trusted among the staff.

After implementing key management changes and familiarizing myself with the board of directors, I drew my attention to the bank's mission, immersing myself in EXIM's balance sheet and diverse credit exposures. I began brainstorming ways to increase the bank's support of creditworthy exporters while opening new export markets. Roughly 75 percent of EXIM's loan guarantees in the developing world, I was surprised to discover, went to governments instead of private sector entities. My work in international investment banking had demonstrated the increased importance of the private sector in creating jobs, democratizing wealth, and achieving important innovations. The Iron Curtain had recently fallen in Europe, and China was developing its own version of the private sector, further positioning the world for increased privatization.

Part of my mission at EXIM, I established early on, was to help fund the private sector purchase of US goods and services, hopefully encouraging the Europeans and Japanese to eventually follow suit. Whether it was privatizing Montedison or internationalizing Wertheim, my business life had encouraged private ownership. I've always believed that governments serve indispensable roles, especially in combatting global scourges like terrorism and climate change.

But the success of nations depends on robust private sectors, where on average, people are more imaginative, creative, and hardworking than their public counterparts. In strong private sectors, people have jobs, become financially and personally "invested" in the economy, and are more likely to enact democratic reforms instead of succumbing to political or religious extremism. Private sector growth was good for the global economy, international democracy, and US national security, and I was determined to alter our balance sheets from sovereign or "public" funds in favor of private sector businesses in frontier and developing economies.

Arriving at EXIM in Bill Clinton's contentious second presidential term, when his stalemate with Gingrich had peaked, I had little inkling of what life in Washington would be like. Thus far, I'd only repotted myself at different firms and traveled throughout the world brokering diverse finance deals. Moving from New York to Washington, and shifting from the private to the public sector, represented an extreme form of personal repotting. And that's what made it an invaluable growth and transformation opportunity.

When young people approach me for advice, I don't recommend that they become investment bankers or even work in foreign development. But I always recommend that they spend several years in Washington. I give them a brief outline of my time in government and detail how public service could have a similarly transformative potential for them. A college education is extremely valuable, but my time in Washington gave me a doctorate degree in life itself.

When I arrived in Washington, I didn't expect to have as much fun as I did forming relationships. Nor did extreme polarization keep me from making bipartisan friendships. Not only that, I enjoyed doing so. Part of this owed to my circumstances. I was then in my early sixties, a successful career behind me, so I came across as nonthreatening, uninterested in jockeying for competitive public sector posts. Because I had a business, not political, background, most Republicans and Democrats had little trouble seeing me as a neutral representative of the private sector. But I still believe my effort at building relationships proved key. If others in government launched charm offensives like the one we launched during my first six months in office, they too could develop relationships with almost anyone on the Hill. They would also enjoy themselves and achieve important outcomes in the process.

Once repotted in Washington, I anticipated an entirely different set of obstacles. Instead of wrestling with my confirmation and EXIM's budgetary concerns, I sailed through both. The confirmation hearing resembled political theater thanks to the presence of my vice chair, and I solved the budget problem by accident, simply by leveraging my relationship with the President at a wedding. To my surprise, however, I arrived on the job needing to justify the continued existence of the agency, cheerleading for an organization I'd just joined. After securing reauthorization and the funds to keep the bank operating, I then needed to institute managerial discipline at the organization, rebuild the morale of 440 employees, reestablish EXIM's battered reputation on the Hill, and begin to develop my own vision for the agency. Over the next few years, I did just that, receiving classified briefings every morning, traveling to over seventy countries, and learning the intricacies of US democracy and foreign diplomacy.

But I had barely settled in, enjoying a brief lull in the chaos and planning for a private sector–oriented future, when a crisis erupted in Thailand. This global financial crisis, to which I now turn, would be the greatest test of my leadership to date. Over the course of this crisis, EXIM's decisions affected more than the destiny of companies; they determined the fate of entire countries.

My parents, Belle and Bert Harmon.

Already up and doing at age 3.

My sister, Carol, and me as children in matching outfits and later as adults enjoying the beach.

My daughter Deborah.

My daughter Jennifer.

With my son, Doug, for a
ski trip in Vail, Colorado.

The first Wertheim partners' dinner at the 21 Club in New York, December 1974.

Bottom row, from left: Jen Harmon and Mia Seder; middle row, from left: Deb Harmon,
Jim Harmon, Doug Harmon, Christine Harmon, Dr. Robert (Bob) Seder; top row: Dan Seder.

Steve Kotler, my partner and right hand at
NY Hanseatic and Wertheim & Co.

Joseph Flom, partner at Skadden, Arps,
Slate, Meagher & Flom.

From left: Dan Levitan, Wertheim & Co.; Howard Schultz, Starbucks; and Doug Harmon.

Prime Minister Margaret Thatcher.

From left: David Dinkins, Harold Ickes, and Bill Clinton in New York prior to his 1992 presidential election win.

Reverend Jesse L. Jackson Sr. and David Dinkins.

Then-HUD Secretary Andrew Cuomo and Congressman Charles Rangel in Washington, DC.

In the hot seat at my Senate confirmation hearing for chair of EXIM Bank, 1997.

My view at the Senate confirmation hearing: Senator Chris Dodd, Senator Paul Sarbanes, and Senator Al D'Amato.

My family attended the confirmation hearing and had the opportunity to meet Vice President Al Gore. From left: Doug Harmon, Dr. Robert (Bob) Seder, Deborah Harmon, Belle Harmon, James Harmon, Vice President Al Gore, Dan Seder, Jane Harmon, Jennifer Harmon, Carol Feit Lane, Fred Lane, Sheila Baker, and Isabel MacDonald Baker.

Confirmed by the Senate as chair of EXIM Bank, I am sworn in by Vice President Al Gore while Jane holds the Bible.

Jane and I enjoy holiday festivities at the White House with Vice President Al Gore and the Clintons.

EXIM Bank staff gather for an official photo at the New Executive Office Building in Washington, DC.

Vice President Al Gore.

Russian president Vladimir Putin.

Russian minister of finance Mikhail Kasyanov.

Leonard Blavatnik and Putin.

The EXIM Bank legal staff.

EXIM Bank leadership with Secretary of State Colin Powell. From left: Maria Haley,
Jackie Clegg, Secretary Powell, James Harmon, Julie Belaga, and Dr. Rita Rodriguez.

Ghana president Jerry John Rawlings.

Ukraine prime minister Viktor Yushchenko.

Uzbekistan minister of finance Rustam Azimov.

Taking time for a bit of fun on a camel ride in Uzbekistan.

Leading the fight against climate change at World Resources Institute. From left: WRI president Andrew Steer, Elizabeth Cook, James Harmon, former president Jonathan Lash, and board member Dan Doctoroff.

New York City mayor Michael Bloomberg, with Stephen Ross and Jonathan Lash, at an event for World Resources Institute.

From left: Andrew Steer, Pamela Flaherty, and Hillary Clinton.

The original board of the Egyptian–American Enterprise Fund with the Egyptian Ambassador to the United States. From left: (standing) Sherif Kamel; Hythem El-Nazer; Ambassador Mohamed Tawfik; James Harmon; Tarek (Terry) Abdel-Meguid; (seated) Dina Powell; Naveen El-Tahri; James Owens.

In conversation with Egypt president Abdel Fattah Al Sisi.

Jane and me with our children, Doug, Jennifer, and Deborah, at a Harmon Family Foundation board meeting.

9

Saving Asia

IN MIDSUMMER OF 1997, I learned of a troubling development in Asia. As my EXIM team briefed me, Thailand's official currency, the Thai baht, had plummeted on July 2. The resultant financial devastation unleashed a chain reaction beyond the Indochina peninsula, quickly and severely damaging Indonesia and South Korea while also harming the Philippines, Malaysia, Hong Kong, Laos, and even Vietnam and China. Stock, debt, and currency markets precipitously declined throughout Asia, resulting in unemployment, bankruptcies, regional instability, and human misery.[191]

Given the pace of globalization and today's highly integrated financial system, we've grown accustomed to such crises creating domino effects across the world. For most of my career in the private sector, however, international investment and global integration weren't as extensive, rendering most financial crises more isolated and self-contained. But just prior to my arrival at the bank, the world appeared to be changing. The Mexican peso crisis of 1994–95 had threatened to spread throughout Latin America. It was only because of a decisive US-led intervention, with the help of major global economies and the International Monetary Fund (IMF), that we confined the devastating poverty and recession mostly to Mexico.

Following my briefing on the Thai baht, I convened a meeting of EXIM's senior staff to discuss Asia and the likelihood of this financial contagion spreading further. Given the magnitude of the crisis, as well as EXIM's credit risk in these struggling countries, I asked the team if we should schedule a trip abroad to assess the situation. Silence ensued. Finally: "What would we gain by visiting?" one of my colleagues asked. "Won't they just ask for more funding?" someone else wondered.

Moments like these reminded me that the public sector was a different world entirely. While scheduling trips was second nature to an investment banker like me, public servants operated differently. For their careers to advance through government, they needed to be highly knowledgeable but also discreet and conservative. My team also had a more expansive perspective than mine, having witnessed financial downturns, like the Mexican peso crisis, while I'd assumed my role at EXIM just months prior. If every chair reacted to every crisis with a visit, they must have thought, we wouldn't be able to conduct the business of EXIM Bank. America's financial security wasn't in jeopardy, we concluded at that meeting, because few countries—whether stable or in crisis—wanted to imperil their standing with the United States by defaulting on loans.

Throughout the fall of 1997, as I continued to receive briefings from the Central Intelligence Agency, State Department, and EXIM on financial developments in Asia, my assessment began to change. Despite IMF relief packages as well as important visits from US Treasury and State Department leaders, the economic turmoil showed no signs of abating. EXIM's overall risk exposure in Asia also began to alarm me. Of the nearly $100 billion that different countries and private sector entities owed EXIM, Asian countries represented roughly a quarter of that risk, or "exposure," cumulatively topping $25 billion. As commercial banks in Asia stopped extending credit in their countries, the number of US businesses exporting products and services decreased.

With Asian economies floundering and US business interests threatened, I came to believe that EXIM had the financial power and moral responsibility to act. I therefore assembled a team to visit South Korea, the Philippines, and Indonesia in January 1998. Besides China, these three countries represented our highest risk exposures in Asia, and two of them, South Korea and Indonesia, had been especially damaged during the crisis. While abroad, I planned to meet with government and business leaders, personally assessing the creditworthiness of individual businesses and countries. My presence in Asia would, I hoped, reassure jittery private investors, foreign ministers, and heads of state that EXIM was open for business, while also helping me to develop an intervention strategy that protected US business interests and helped Asian countries recover.[192]

A LONG-STANDING AMERICAN ALLY

When I deplaned with my EXIM colleagues in South Korea, I wasn't prepared for the media attention that would engulf us. With their assertive and at times aggressive behavior, the South Korean media reminded me of the paparazzi in London. They were never violent or angry, but no one managed their access or cordoned them off behind ropes as in the United States. I hadn't prepared any remarks for the live television crew that greeted me on the tarmac, so I spoke extemporaneously, telling eager reporters that we'd come to evaluate economic developments and to try to help.

The magnitude of South Korea's crisis was stunning, especially for such a robust and technologically advanced country. Market declines had hurt equity investors, while currency declines had troubled all parts of the economy, leaving average citizens unemployed and bankrupt. In December 1997, the IMF had extended a $60 billion loan package, but as I determined on day one of my visit, this had done little to calm markets.[193] No credit was available for the purchase of goods and services (US or otherwise).

From my first meeting with President-elect Kim Dae-Jung, a thoughtful and experienced leader whom I met in the presence of a dozen or so cabinet members, I felt more at ease. I'd been briefed that the President-elect, a former socialist, might resist financial austerity, but I found his strong relationship with labor to be advantageous. Kim reassured me that his government was committed to financial transparency and reform, and I left the meeting thinking South Korea was fortunate to have his leadership.

In South Korea, EXIM's exposure centered on aircraft. US multinational Boeing, the largest aerospace company in the world, emerged from World War II to become America's largest exporter.[194] When I arrived at the bank, aircraft fund guarantees represented over 25 percent of EXIM's total loan exposures. Many Asian countries purchased Boeing planes for their domestic airlines, though European rival Airbus would eventually compete just as strongly. In South Korea, two large airliners—Asiana and Korean Airlines—constituted $1.8 billion in risk to EXIM. At the time, I believed that it was EXIM's $1 billion-plus exposure in the bankrupt Asiana that represented the single most serious risk to the bank. If the airlines defaulted, we would assume the aircraft as collateral, meaning that EXIM would basically own the South Korean airline industry!

As I considered the airlines and met with more business and government leaders, I marveled at how hardworking and responsible South Korean citizens were. In one touching moment, I visited a bank and witnessed South Koreans placing family jewels into government coffers. Confused by the scene, I asked a team member to confirm what I was witnessing, and he appeared just as humbled as I was looking at people parting with their precious heirlooms. Even as many couldn't afford their mortgage payments and worried about feeding their families, they nonetheless donated their jewelry and sentimental keepsakes to help the nation. Never before or since have I seen such an emotional and selfless response to national hardship.

When evaluating companies in the private sector, I always considered their cultures and the talent and capacity of their managers. Applying the same approach to South Korea, I concluded that the country's culture of self-sacrifice and hard work, along with strong management talent in the form of President-elect Kim, made it eminently worthy of American support.

Situated at the border of the communist world, South Korea had long served as an exemplar of private enterprise and democracy. With the help of allies like the United States, the country had graduated from a frontier to an emerging market and was now becoming a highly developed economy—one of Asia's extraordinary success stories. The United States had invested a stunning $50 billion in South Korea since 1950, and they were worthy of more investment now.

When the economies of trading nations like South Korea are in free-fall, they need credit infusions to help businesses purchase raw materials and spare parts. Absent funds for these essential items, companies can't make products and the economy ceases to function. As the crisis had come to overwhelm South Korea, and skittish investors withdrew their support, South Korea's banks became insolvent, leaving domestic manufacturers unable to borrow funds to purchase raw materials from the United States. EXIM wasn't powerful or well capitalized enough to lend money directly to large importers and often worked with local banks to facilitate deals.[195] Even before my return home, I began consulting my program heads to devise a lending program to capitalize South Korea's banks and thereby kick-start an economic recovery.

I was reminded about America's strong and almost sentimental relationship with South Korea a year later when I returned to the country with President Clinton. After a short stop in Tokyo, Air Force One took us to Seoul. Jetlagged and a little exhausted, the President and I entered an auditorium where thousands of South Koreans had assembled, welcoming us with warmth and playing the US national anthem. The earnest enthusiasm of the performance reminded me of how much the South Korean people valued the United States and how grateful they were for our support against North Korea. Overcome with emotion, I must have teared up a bit, prompting President Clinton to turn around, drape his arm around my shoulder, and declare: "Wow, I have an emotional banker."

A CRISIS IN CONFIDENCE

Though this all transpired before widespread cellular-phone technologies and social media platforms, word of my travels spread quickly throughout Asia. By the time my EXIM team and I arrived in Manila, the second stop on our tour, nearly everyone we met knew of our trip to South Korea.

The US-Philippine relationship had been strong since WWII, and EXIM Bank was the only export credit agency to remain open during the country's civil unrest and recession of the mid-1980s, when President Ferdinand Marcos was deposed. Our strong bilateral partnership in part created the delicate diplomatic situation I encountered during my visit. Secretary of Finance Roberto de Ocampo and Gabriel Singson, Central Bank governor, both expressed disappointment that the United States had not tackled the Asian financial crisis more aggressively. Private sector leaders, usually more outspoken and pointed in their criticism than their more diplomatic public sector counterparts, delivered a blunt evaluation. As the president and CEO of a major purchaser of US telephone equipment warned: continue to neglect Asia, and the problem will migrate to US markets.

Such critical sentiment, which I believed was understandable though overstated, didn't extend to President Fidel Ramos, with whom I enjoyed a warm and friendly meeting. We discussed how the Philippines had dutifully adhered to IMF financial requirements for some thirty-five years, and that within that time span, the country had passed a staggering 135 reform laws. Despite the financial crisis, President Ramos insisted, the country hadn't closed any financial institutions. The basic takeaway from my meeting with him and other Filipino leaders: don't lump the Philippines with South Korea and Indonesia—their economies fared much worse.

My lasting impressions from my trip to the Philippines were of personal encounters like these. As we greeted one another, President Ramos shook my hand as a photographer snapped pictures at a distance. After our meeting concluded, the President handed me a framed photograph of our meeting with his signature and an engraved note reading, "Thank you, Chairman Harmon, for meeting with me." Since that meeting, such plaques, commemorating the visits of foreign dignitaries, have grown more popular. But they were rare at the time, and as I navigated the tense and difficult Asian crisis, this thoughtful gesture made our time even more memorable than the warm discussion I had enjoyed with South Korea's President-elect Kim.

Over conversation in the Philippines, I also had one of my more memorable discussions about free enterprise and capital markets. One of the businesses that EXIM supported in the country, a large, mixed conglomerate, had recently become a public company whose share price was increasing. During my conversation with this company's CEO, he had a Eureka moment: "What you're saying about the value of my company makes sense. I can actually make more money with my shares than I can from skimming profits off the top." It might sound crude or basic, but this powerful Filipino executive had just awakened to a realization that I believe is critical for the future of global commerce. Capable and diligent people, working within the capitalist system to build value in their enterprises, can experience greater market success and wealth than those engaging in cronyism or corruption.

The Philippines was in the strongest position of the countries on the tour, and I departed feeling encouraged. Despite peso depreciation and stock market declines consistent with the rest of Asia, the Philippines didn't need a bailout. EXIM had a little over $2 billion in Filipino exposure, diversified throughout the telecommunications, electrical power, and aerospace industries. But the country had solid fundamentals in place to ensure a return on EXIM's credit guarantees. After the IMF intervened following a 1982 property-development collapse—the country's equivalent to Thailand's baht crisis—the Philippines had exercised financial discipline, giving it the economic fundamentals to surmount the current obstacle. As I sat talking with Central Bank governor Singson, the peso's then-current value, at a little over forty-three pesos to the dollar, was at "panic" lows because of the general crisis in Asian currency markets, and not because of any structural weaknesses. After assessing its currency stability, interest rates, and unemployment, I concluded that the Philippines was suffering only a crisis of confidence.

As I left, I remembered the advice of Tim Geithner and Larry Summers, who said to visit Thailand, not the Philippines. While these top administration advisors knew Asia's economic situation more thoroughly than I did, I was focused on our diplomatic relationships. American and foreign dignitaries had bypassed the country altogether during the Asian crisis, leaving a vital Southeast Asian ally feeling neglected and isolated. But a crisis in confidence is still a crisis, and the Philippines needed more attention and assistance from its long-standing American ally. The US embassy in Manila reinforced my convictions about the need for this visit, calling EXIM's time an unqualified success that was important in lifting morale.

At the time of my visit, the Philippines represented a pleasant hiatus between the deep and extraordinary feelings elicited by the South Korea visit and the concerns prompted by my trip to Indonesia. This general ease and optimism make it even more surprising that a year following my visit, the most dramatic event of the Asian crisis would unfurl with a Philippine Airlines carrier. It began when Bob Morin, the head of EXIM's aircraft finance group, notified me that Philippine Airlines, a company I'd believed to be highly creditworthy in January 1998, had experienced some internal corruption and now owed EXIM money. I listened closely because Morin was a highly skilled professional and, based on my experience with him, likely among the world's leading experts on aircraft financing. "Unless we set an example and show that this isn't acceptable," Morin warned, "we'll have a $3–$4 billion setback." Morin was a risk-taker like me. His proposal: seize the airline's fleet of Boeing airplanes in San Francisco, reroute the passengers affected to other flights, and stow the aircraft in the Arizona desert until the company paid up.

I agreed with the plan, and the Justice Department and FBI seized the aircraft. During my initial trip to Asia, I'd pegged South Korea's Asiana Air as EXIM Bank's greatest exposure bar none. As a risk to our balance sheet, the airline fleet in the Philippines now far outpaced Asiana and reminded me of the country's still-lingering corruption. In the 1970s, President Ferdinand Marcos and his wife, Imelda, accrued massive wealth and power through showing favoritism and privilege to an inner circle of friends.[196] Such crony capitalism was endemic to the archipelago nation, and it remained pervasive after Marcos fled in 1986 (although President Ramos insisted otherwise). EXIM's analysis revealed that the problems at Philippine Airlines weren't part of the Asian crisis, but were rooted instead in internal corruption and labor problems.[197]

The story attracted press attention and not just because of the hijinks involved with aircraft seizure. As I commented at the time, "We have a very important added mission to encourage reforms."[198] As the aircraft incident demonstrated, EXIM Bank would guarantee loans in creditworthy countries where reforms were underway but wouldn't support sovereign funds or businesses that lacked transparent governance and bookkeeping. By proactively encouraging policy changes, I was admittedly expanding the boundaries of EXIM's mandate, which was to support American jobs through guaranteeing the financing of US exports.

Gestures like this inspired media outlets like the *Asia Wall Street Journal* to comment that "James Harmon has played the hero in Asia's economic crisis, and he has played the bully."[199] The American ambassador to the Philippines agreed, calling me at two in the morning in a rage after learning of the seizure. The reader can decide whether my "reformist zeal," as one headline phrased it, made me a financial bully or a public servant committed to the well-being of the US business community and larger Asian world. But one thing is certain: this episode marks an example of the expansion of my objectives—even a certain "mission creep"—that would come to define my role and legacy at EXIM.

A BENEVOLENT DICTATORSHIP BUCKLES

My third and final stop was Indonesia. With a population exceeding 200 million, the vast and far-flung island-nation was the most troubled country I visited. After thirty years of stability and economic progress under Suharto's benign dictatorship, the country now faced a staggering monetary crisis. Within nine months of the Thai baht's collapse, Indonesia's rupiah had fallen by 75 percent, and stock markets plunged about 70–80 percent. Eager to participate in the strong economy, many private sector entities had borrowed short-term money to finance long-term projects. After a liquidity crunch followed the currency plunge, Suharto's government raised interest rates to prevent capital flight, sending businesses and individuals into a tailspin. Absent something like the United States' Chapter 11 restructuring procedure, bankruptcy, massive unemployment, and hardship spread throughout the country.

Morale was low when I joined my colleague Barbara O'Boyle, head of EXIM's project finance group, to meet President Suharto. At the time of the meeting, rumors and intrigue beset the country, while the international press speculated about Suharto's sickness, incapacitation, and death. There was talk of a coup d'état.

During our meeting, Suharto appeared frail but not ill, striking me as a man under a great deal of pressure. When I told him he looked better than most of the press indicated, he complained about the inaccuracy of the reports about him and his country's economic status. He was concerned about unemployment and the monetary crisis provoking a political crisis that would destroy the country. He'd reached an emergency funding agreement with the IMF. But those meetings had been tense. Worse, an unfortunate photograph of President Suharto with IMF head Michel Camdessus was circulating in the press. Suharto is seated, signing a document, his head bowed, while a dominant Camdessus stands beside him, watching, his arms crossed over his chest. To onlookers, this posture made it appear that Suharto signed the agreement under duress.[200]

My approach to diplomacy, as with investment banking, centers on building consensus and developing rapport. "The United States is invested in Indonesia, and I am too," I told Suharto, detailing how my daughter Jen had studied Indonesian dance in the early 1990s while living in Bali. She also continued to draw on this important style and its techniques as she taught dance in the United States. Suharto seemed touched that I knew something about Indonesian culture. It was an informal connection. But it was sufficient. He appeared to have concluded my concern was genuine. His mood brightened, and he invited me and my family to return to Bali for vacation.

The record indicates that we met for twenty minutes, but it seemed much longer. Having devoted most of the meeting to establishing a rapport with the Indonesian president, I concluded by reiterating EXIM's support for Indonesian development and business. "EXIM has been active in Indonesia since 1950," I told him, "and I look forward to another fifty years of fruitful cooperation." But I also countered his accusations of media misrepresentation, encouraging more transparency and enhanced disclosure so the world could understand what was truly happening. In hindsight, neither of us understood the depth of corruption and cronyism running rampant in the country.

EXIM's exposure in Indonesia was the greatest of all the countries on the tour, amounting to almost $4 billion, and I departed the country concerned, lacking a simple solution to its problems. Unlike President-elect Kim, who had the confidence of the labor force and the larger business community, President Suharto seemed too frail, and his position too politically volatile, to be effective.[201] A political battle loomed, and when Suharto stepped down several months after my visit, the depths of state corruption began to surface.

MISSION CREEP

After I returned from Asia, EXIM initiated a $1 billion short-term lending program to fifteen creditworthy though temporarily insolvent South Korean banks. With this capital, the banks could extend loans to companies wanting to purchase raw materials and spare parts from the United States. Issuing these "letters of credit"—the official mechanism by which we brokered this transaction—was a risk. Though EXIM rarely lost money on short-term lending programs, my colleagues were concerned about financing insolvent banks. I understood their reluctance because when I examined these banks' balance sheets and saw their accumulated debts and receivables, I too was frightened. But the Roosevelt administration created EXIM to take risks like these, serving as the "lender of last resort" when private institutions like Citicorp couldn't stomach the uncertainty. If EXIM failed and South Korea defaulted on these loans, the bank, along with the larger export credit financing world, would suffer a great setback. But if we succeeded, we could stabilize a great economy and help initiate a larger economic turnaround across Asia.

After taking a calculated risk and initiating the loan program to South Korea in February, my team and I worked to structure similar such deals in the Philippines, Indonesia, and Thailand. I also longed to exert even stronger leadership in stemming the Asian financial crisis. Without the support of other countries, Asia might not rebound and the crisis would continue to infect the world like a contagion.

With the support of my colleagues at the bank, I planned a meeting of the Group of Seven (G7) credit agencies, along with fifteen others, to address the crisis. This marked a departure from precedent, as our respective partners often competed rather than cooperated on the world stage. But I believed a multilateral effort could prove psychologically and financially beneficial. By coordinating a response, we could demonstrate international solidarity in stabilizing markets and encourage Asian countries to continue purchasing from G7 exporters.[202] Practically, I'd also hoped to inspire other countries to create a pool of funds so we could extend EXIM's short-term lending programs, as well as supplement IMF programs already underway, thereby helping Asia recover even quicker.[203] Foreign ambassadors responded to my idea with surprise verging on shock. "We've never done this before," they remonstrated. "On whose authority do you convene this group?" They were accustomed to meetings where policy was discussed, not to convening during an international crisis to develop solutions as a group.

"It doesn't matter," I responded. "We have to help Asia." During times of crisis, US presidents and cabinet members have been accused of overreach as they attempted to solve global problems. Nevertheless, the world looks to the United States for leadership, so when my colleagues abroad suggested this proposal was overreach, I encouraged them to think of it as leadership.[204] I convinced the head of Japan's export credit agency to preside over the gathering with me. Representing Asia's regional power player and the world's then second-largest economy, Japan had a vital leadership role to play.

We settled on London to host two separate G7 meetings. Europeans and Asians are accustomed to traveling there, and the location wouldn't pull focus from the event, as a meeting in the United States threatened to do. In late February, barely a month after my Asian tour, the heads of the G7 export credit agencies, along with thirteen or fourteen other agency heads, converged on London. Without realizing it at the time, this meeting raised the profile of these obscure agencies to a diplomatic or finance ministry level, resolved to meet and act during global crises. The first such coordinated export credit agency meeting was a partial success, helping to calm investor fears and demonstrate solidarity.[205] But while the Japanese agreed to match our $3 billion in loan guarantees to Asia, the Europeans refused to commit, saying they needed to consult their finance ministries before moving forward. Many of the European agency heads didn't want to risk a default and didn't commit to a global insurance program.

Though I didn't achieve the coordinated international response that I'd desired, our "return on relationship" proved excellent. The decision to break with the tradition of my more risk-averse predecessors and embark on the 1998 Asia tour, instead of transacting business from Washington, was crucial, allowing me to develop relationships with Filipino, Indonesian, and South Korean heads of state and business leaders. By talking with people, we gained concrete insights about these troubled economies and more accurately diagnosed their needs.[206] Sometimes these needs were financial (the case in South Korea), and sometimes they were psychological (the Philippines). I'm therefore pleased that, instead of heeding my colleagues' advice about visiting Thailand, I opted for the Philippines, hoping to increase their morale and resolve as they faced a national crisis of confidence. And I'm also happy I broke with my colleagues again and, instead of lecturing Suharto about financial malfeasance, found common ground with him through my daughter Jen's love of Balinese dance. EXIM's decision to host the coordinated export credit agency meeting in London, instead of the United States, and the decision to comanage it with Japan led to my building a strong relationship with the chair of the Japanese export credit agency. Japan's decision to match the US funds went a long way in confronting and helping to resolve this international financial crisis.

Following these national and multilateral efforts in relationship building, EXIM's response to the Asian financial crisis proved successful. EXIM's programs and initiatives, totaling $5–$6 billion in guarantees throughout Asia, proved successful within five to six months after my initial trip. After providing South Korea with an initial $1 billion infusion, the country paid us back, and we rolled it over again, this time graduating the country from a short-term to a medium-term loan program. With a strong economy prior to the crisis, South Korea terminated the program in 2000, having demonstrated a classic V-shaped recovery.

Having adhered to the IMF guidelines for decades, the Philippines proved a disciplined country and—the airlines heist aside—was also a program success. Indonesia gave us mixed results. Its banking system was in such disarray it couldn't implement the program in 1998. This owed to the unstable political landscape—over my time at EXIM, I met with four different Indonesian presidents—as well as corruption. But Indonesian defaults represented a small percentage of the disbursements we made in what proved to be an immensely successful program. Overall, EXIM's losses as a percentage of disbursements (that is, the disbursed funding for equipment or airlines) were less than 2 percent. Few private sector finance companies have such a strong record. That figure speaks to the hesitation countries have in defaulting on the United States. But it also reflects the importance of the programs we were gutsy enough to implement at EXIM.

The Asia program reenergized the bank's staff. Morale at EXIM had suffered after the setbacks of leadership, reauthorization, and budget shortfalls. But as word of our short-term program with South Korea spread throughout the bank, EXIM staff became energized and excited. As I came to work on Saturdays and Sundays, accustomed to working weekends from my time in the private sector, I began to find I wasn't alone in the office. When I asked my chief of staff about why everyone was so excited, she confirmed their general interest in the Asian programs and how exceptional it was for staff to work on weekends.

This energy was selfless. I say that because we initiated the lending program in February, and I didn't hear any feedback or results for months. By September or October, I began to get a little nervous and asked the head of EXIM's short-term insurance program about how the South Korean loans had fared. In the absence of publicity, I figured it had turned into a nightmare. "We're doing great, Mr. Chairman!" he replied, brandishing a list of some 2,400-odd transactions covering the purchase of raw materials and spare parts for South Korea, with each one marked "paid." *No one defaulted.* If a person or team had achieved such success in the private sector, they would have widely publicized the feat—probably because such people would enjoy profit participation or at least a financial bonus.

Unmotivated by year-end bonuses, raises, or promotions like their private sector counterparts, EXIM staff worked nights and weekends because of their commitment to the mission. Though I was impressed by this selflessness and grateful for the enthusiasm and morale boost that this programming had provided, I knew that an absence of benchmarking was unfortunate. Without institutional memory at an agency like this, such programming couldn't be memorialized and therefore remobilized during future crises. Luckily, EXIM had people like Jim Cruse, who ensured that the South Korean transaction wasn't forgotten. Future chairmen remobilized our Asia crisis template when addressing the Great Recession of 2008–09.

After the South Korean lending program, I was just as energized as my staff. My trips to Asia, and especially the fanfare we received in South Korea, made me realize that I operated in a part of the US government that helped countries. I wasn't like the IMF that did excellent work throughout Asia but always insisted on conservative behavior, like high interest rates, to control currency declines. I was more like a friendly doctor with medicine who entered a country and helped everyone feel a little better. "You should enjoy this," Bill Clinton said to me. "You are the one dispensing the money. It's no surprise they love you and greet you like a head of state."

With less than a year at the bank, I had implemented a novel and aggressive lending program, leaving me astounded by the impact the EXIM agency could have. Instead of consulting layers of bureaucracy or securing interagency approval, as I would have done in the Commerce, Treasury, or State departments, I made decisions about the Asian crisis on my own. Because my program involved finance and not policy, I needed no consensus or permission.

Sometimes this autonomy surprised me. During my tenure, the bank made a loan to Saudi Arabia for $5 billion to purchase aircraft. I remember asking Bob Rubin, US secretary of treasury and my neighbor at the Jefferson Hotel, if he approved of this deal. "I don't know anything about what goes into a decision like this," he responded. When I asked him if I should consult others in the government, he couldn't think of anyone. As I kept the Treasury Department and White House abreast of my decisions, I enjoyed even more autonomy than when I was chair and CEO of Wertheim Schroder. Every major decision at the investment bank required the consultation of partners, committees, and investors. As head of this government agency, I had responsible and well-informed colleagues who cautioned me when they thought I was making a misstep, as many did when I wanted to work with insolvent banks in Asia. I considered their advice, all the while having a greater appetite for risk and a strong conviction about the future success of the Asian programs. Though I never wanted to damage EXIM's reputation, I risked losing billions of dollars because I believed that struggling Asian countries would rebound. More important, I also believed that such action was the morally right thing to do.

As senior officials at the bank reminded me, these programs throughout Asia marked a departure at EXIM. Because the bank was a "lender of last resort," previous chairmen had never proactively approached a crisis like this. Not only had I proactively—some might say aggressively—intervened, risking capital in short- and medium-term loan packages, I also took international leadership, encouraging the world's leading countries to join me. Along the way, I'd seized a country's fleet of Boeing aircraft, signaling to many that the new EXIM chair was leveraging his position to create reform in Asia. They were right. "It would be very bad," I said to reporters at the time, "if we came through this whole crisis and didn't have reforms."[207]

Globalization had increased the world's collective interdependence and risk, and I believed this required a new style of leadership. By the late 1990s, increased capital flows, technological developments, and advanced human capital—three items Henry Kissinger, Helmut Schmidt, and I had identified in Italy decades prior—had all served to democratize global wealth. This had allowed frontier economies to become developing countries, and developing countries to graduate to advanced industrial power status.

But new opportunity also brought increased potential for harm. The Asian financial crisis had demonstrated that theories of domino effects and contagion, once confined to the spread of communism during the Cold War, now applied to financial markets. A crisis in Thailand had created a severe problem throughout Asia. Though Asia rebounded, this crisis would also spread to Latin America and eastern Europe and reverberate throughout Europe and the United States. Most important for EXIM's purposes, the crisis would next spread to Russia, where I now turn. In Russia, I was forced into a much different, but equally important, test of my leadership at EXIM.

10

Tyumen Oil: A Morality Tale

IN AUGUST 1998, THE ASIAN financial crisis reached Russia. Skittish from the downturn that had begun in Thailand a year prior, foreign investors had already begun avoiding Russian markets, decreasing the value of oil, the lifeblood of the Russian economy. With its lean coffers and currency pegged to the US dollar, Russia struggled to compete in the global economy.

After seven years of steady economic progress in his country, Russian president Boris N. Yeltsin responded by devaluing the ruble, sending foreign capital fleeing and markets tumbling. Russian banks suddenly became insolvent, pensions and life savings evaporated, and Russia declared a temporary suspension or "moratorium" on paying off all foreign debt. Months after the Asian economies began to recover from their financial crisis, Russia was now in trouble. I was determined that EXIM could help Russia's economy through this crisis, just as we'd done in South Korea and as I would later do in Egypt.

This marked a pivotal moment in Russian history, and, heeding the advice of my friend Rahm Emanuel, I didn't want to let this crisis "go to waste." In helping Russia navigate this financial hardship, I wanted to join other US officials in encouraging the country's transition to a stable, rules-bound, market economy, thereby forging a stronger post–Cold War US-Russian bilateral relationship.

THE WILD EAST

Like many observers in the West, I'd hoped that the Russian debt moratorium wouldn't upend the US-Russian relationship, which had progressed substantially over my lifetime. I came of age during the Cold War, when two superpowers waged a seemingly interminable battle between American-led democracy and Soviet-style communism. During my youth, early adulthood, and investment banking career, the United States and Russia also engaged in a nearly five-decades-long nuclear arms race, as generations grew up fearing the imminent destruction and the annihilation of their communities and even the planet.

Such a threat always loomed. In 1965, when Jane and I moved into our house in Weston, Connecticut, we didn't have the finances or expertise to do any landscaping. My dad, whose green thumb and love of gardening had inspired my rhododendron nursery purchase, gladly came to the rescue, helping me plant a vegetable garden. "Look what I'm doing, Jimmy," he said. "When the Russians come, they're not going to be interested in investment banking. You're going to have to grow your own produce." His comment was partially tongue-in-cheek, but it still spoke to the anxiety of the era.

Dad's comments came at the height of Cold War tensions, following the erection of the Berlin Wall (1961) and the American domestic craze for building "fallout," or bomb, shelters. The idea was simple enough: if a Soviet or US leader detonated a nuclear weapon, families could take refuge in reinforced-concrete underground rooms, designed to protect people from a nuclear blast and the ensuing radioactive materials in the environment. My property in Connecticut has an underground pump house, and one day, when a technician came to service it, he told me that its cement construction would make it a great bomb shelter. I shot him a skeptical glance, but, unlike my dad, he was entirely serious. When the Berlin Wall collapsed in 1989 and the Soviet Union began fracturing into independent states in 1991, I remember feeling a sense of exhilaration. The ideological war and threat of nuclear winter now seemed over, as a new era of opportunity and human progress had finally dawned.

When I arrived at EXIM six years after these momentous events, the world seemed to share in this general excitement and enthusiasm for a post-Soviet Russia. Yeltsin had worked diligently to grow the private sector, and the American business community felt Russia represented a profitable market for US goods. In its attempt to foster a post-Soviet transition to stable markets, the US government established eleven enterprise-assistance funds throughout the former Soviet satellite states, hoping to inculcate free enterprise and help spur private sector growth. The US government wouldn't employ the enterprise model again until the Arab Spring uprisings two decades later, when I would become chair of the fund in Egypt. Then, as now, enterprise funds are rooted in the conviction that it's only by bolstering the private sector that countries can achieve freedom and avoid totalitarianism, military dictatorship, or religious extremism.

Despite Yeltsin's reforms and the enthusiasm of the West, Russia's evolution to a market economy was not seamless. During the era of Yeltsin-led privatization, a handful of Russian entrepreneurs, often referred to as oligarchs, accumulated major positions in formerly state-owned companies. They used a variety of tactics to accomplish these takeovers, including approaching employees at recently privatized companies and offering to buy their stock for a fraction of its actual value. Unaccustomed to working in a market, many Russian citizens didn't know the value of the shares they'd recently received and figured the money was better.

Throughout my time in Russia, I would get to know many of these powerful Russian magnates, including Mikhail Khodorkovsky. A tough but sympathetic character, Khodorkovsky became the richest man in Russia largely owing to his oil and gas holdings in Yukos, one of the country's largest and most successful companies. He eventually ran afoul of Putin. I had a critical meeting with him prior to his decade-long incarceration. Other power players were more cautious, like the well-read, intelligent, and charming Mikhail Fridman, who cofounded Alfa Group in 1991 and served as chair of Tyumen Oil—ventures that would occupy center stage in my work with Russia.

Some observers hoped this period of oligarchic wealth and monopolistic control would end as Russia progressed to more equitable wealth distribution. Others were more critical, seeing their activities as exacerbating wealth inequalities, leading to widespread unemployment and the resurgence of epidemic diseases, poverty, and human tragedy.[208]

By the time I joined EXIM, these oligarchs had amassed enormous wealth just as the country was transforming from eternal foe to potential friend and reliable trading partner. I believed EXIM had an important role to play in that transformation. That's one of the reasons why I broke with agency precedent and made Russia my first trip as EXIM chair instead of our neighbor Mexico. This probably aroused the consternation and mild annoyance of the White House and certain people on the Hill. Many of them were skeptical about Yeltsin's programs and still associated Russia with the Soviet-era crimes of Stalin. Only one of my predecessors at EXIM had visited Russia. I made four trips.

In my enthusiasm for elevating Russia's importance and assessing opportunities to improve its economy, I was fortunate that EXIM had Washington's top Russia experts. They included diplomat and scholar Michael McFaul, later the US ambassador to Russia; Stephen Sestanovich, a renowned scholar and US foreign policy expert on Russia and the former Soviet Union; and Steve Glazer, an attorney at EXIM. At the end of my first or second day at EXIM, I stepped out of my office and a man extended his hand, introducing himself as Steve, asking, "May I walk you home to the hotel?" He had studied my movements, apparently. Is this an EXIM lawyer or a CIA officer? I wondered.

Steve Glazer became my leading partner on all matters Russia, giving me learned finance expertise as well as practical advice about how to navigate my time in-country. As soon as I announced my intentions to visit Russia, the US government descended with briefings that mostly emphasized the country's adverse economic conditions, corruption, undisciplined judicial system, and oppressive taxes. But Glazer emphasized the positive, believing, with me, that Russia had enormous business potential. "Everything is bugged in your room," he warned me, telling me not to discuss anything delicate on the phone or in the car. And be careful about how much vodka you drink, he cautioned, because the CIA wouldn't be present to water down my drinks.

My wife, Jane, chief of staff Andrea Adelman, and EXIM attorney and Russian expert Steve Glazer accompanied me to Russia in November 1997, five months after I'd joined EXIM. In addition to touring the Kremlin and meeting with distinguished heart surgeon Leo Bockeria, who directed the Bakulev Institute for Cardiovascular Surgery, where EXIM had supported a $59 million project for medical equipment, we also met with Alfa Bank.[209] Though already a leading commercial bank in Russia at the time, with whom EXIM had begun a relationship earlier that summer, Alfa expressed its desire to become a superregional bank.[210] Perhaps to that end, I learned in my briefing materials, it had just purchased a 40 percent stake in Tyumen Oil, Russia's third-largest oil company. At the time, Tyumen asked EXIM to restructure some of its deals with Alfa, making it the major borrower in the transactions. My team's decision to work with Tyumen was pivotal to my work at EXIM and soon led to a high-profile conflict full of intrigue and scandal.[211]

We then flew to Kazan, the capital of Tatarstan. One of the twenty-one republics making up the Russian Federation, Tatarstan was in the heartland, near the Volga River.[212] Following the disintegration of the Soviet Union, Tatarstan negotiated a deal with Russia that ultimately gave it freedom to conduct its own economic affairs but not autonomy over its foreign policy.[213] I remember a freezing day, snow falling, and a Russian government plane that was uncomfortable and elderly. With its well-worn turbo props, it reminded me of American aircraft from the 1950s that one now sees as museum pieces at regional US airports. The condition of the plane reflected the country's economic standing in 1997. As the oligarchs began seizing increasingly strong positions in previously state-owned companies, little money remained for investment or infrastructure spending.

We landed on a private Kazan airfield to a friendly delegation of Tatar leaders eager to welcome a US contingent that wanted to do business in the region. EXIM had been a financial catalyst in the years prior, having already financed an oil modernization project and a petrochemical plant. It was considering guaranteeing a $27 million transaction for equipment to a Kazan medical facility.[214] On all government flights, I represented the "president" of the expedition and deplaned first so that I could greet local press and any dignitaries who awaited me.

As I descended onto the tarmac, extending my hand to the mayor and his officials, I noticed the compacted ice on the airfield. We were fortunate indeed that our well-worn aircraft hadn't careened into a snowbank as it landed. As I smiled and posed for pictures with the mayor, I looked behind me to see my wife, an accomplished ice skater, flat on her back. Her stylish shoes weren't meant for these conditions, and she'd slipped. I smiled at her and said, in jest, "I can't take you anywhere." Her spill on the ice in Tatarstan still gives us a laugh. We carefully guided her over the ice sheets as she held a large bouquet of flowers. We later enjoyed a beautiful evening at the opera, where we sat in the presidential box, and felt increasingly confident about the Tatar business community.

Throughout the trip, as I met with First Deputy Prime Minister Boris Nemtsov and Governor of the Central Bank Sergei Dubinin, along with leaders of commercial banks and chambers of commerce throughout St. Petersburg and Moscow, I conveyed the message that EXIM wanted to work with Russia in a constructive, friendly manner. Russia needed US equipment and reasonable financing terms to revitalize nearly every part of its economy, and during that trip I was particularly keen to identify Russian regions with potential for economic growth, so the bank could focus its work there.[215] "Everywhere I went," I reflected to my team at the time, "I encountered a quiet but confident determination to create a real market economy with real competition and real opportunities to succeed."[216] I departed the country motivated to increase our assistance in Russia and begin operating true project financing as we did throughout the rest of the world.[217]

THE TROUBLE WITH TYUMEN

By mid-1998, about six months after my first trip to Russia and following my tour of Asia, I realized that Russia had major economic problems. While EXIM's programs, along with help from the IMF, had helped Asian countries to jump-start their economies following the 1997 Thai baht crisis, financial turmoil continued to spread to places like Russia's commodities markets. With one-third of the world's natural energy reserves beneath its soil, Russia produced 9 percent of the world's oil, making this commodity a cornerstone in its economy.[218] With the price of oil plummeting to $10 a barrel in the spring of 1998, $4 below Russia's break-even price of $14, the government was left with little choice but to devalue, or "float," its currency and announce a moratorium on all debt so it could restructure its holdings.

This crisis only strengthened my resolve to help Russia. At the time, the country wasn't strong enough, and its financial infrastructure not developed enough, to attract foreign direct investment. It needed commercially oriented agencies like EXIM to bridge that gap, channeling funds to build a private sector economy. Of all the federal agencies operating within Russia—as I explained to President Clinton after returning from that first trip—EXIM was best suited to help Russian private sector entities, while advancing our foreign policy goal of democratizing Russia and liberalizing its economy. Since our 1994 reopening in Russia, EXIM had guaranteed over $2 billion in exports throughout the oil and gas, mining, health care, and telecommunications sectors. We had begun working with Russia's troubled banking industry in 1996.[219] Our repayment record across these sectors remained excellent.

Prior to my arrival at EXIM, Steve Glazer worked with our attorneys to institute a project finance mechanism that would prove pivotal to bolstering the development of the Russian oil industry. His method was similar to those that Exxon and other industry heavyweights had deployed to ensure a return on their investments in the developing world. The process was straightforward. Once geologists certified that a company had proven reserves of oil and gas, company owners could monetize those reserves as collateral against which to purchase oil and gas drilling equipment. The company could then use the income from its sale of oil and gas to pay off these equipment loans. Working with a capable law team, Glazer devised a way for EXIM to use the same process, guaranteeing loans of US companies exporting drilling equipment.

Throughout the summer of 1998, I scrutinized one such deal that appeared especially promising: securing the sale of drilling equipment to Russian oil giant Tyumen. Before approving the Tyumen deal, which had been initiated before I started at EXIM, I needed to ensure that it was environmentally sound and creditworthy—two requirements for all projects that EXIM supported. Per the deal, a few suppliers (including Halliburton, one of the world's leading manufacturers for oil and gas exploration equipment) agreed to sell Tyumen $500 million worth of machinery. Tyumen, in turn, agreed to secure the loan with a lien on the property and a promise to pay with proceeds from future oil and gas. I personally reviewed the data with our credit department, ensured that the technology used would do the least amount of harm to the local environment, and traveled to Russia again to meet with Alfa Bank senior managers to discuss the deal and probe its creditworthiness. In late 1998, EXIM's board of directors had voted to approve the transaction, and in early September we had forwarded it to the Hill for a thirty-day congressional review.

Unbeknownst to us at the time, British Petroleum (BP), Britain's largest company, had invested approximately $500 million in Sidanco, a large Russian oil operation that controlled important production fields in western Siberia. Although Sidanco produced only 380,000 barrels of gas and oil a day, a small percentage of BP's 2 million gallons per diem, this was nonetheless a bold investment for BP to take in this chaotic, post–Berlin Wall environment.[220] And it resulted in failure, at least in the short term, because Sidanco couldn't pay its debts and filed for bankruptcy in 1999. Bankruptcy proceedings were treacherous affairs in Russia, with Alfa Bank insiders like Mikhail Fridman. Russians were likely using hardball tactics to "persuade" BP to part with Sidanco, while favoring Tyumen Oil, in which Alfa had a large ownership stake. At a bankruptcy auction, Tyumen wrested control of Sidanco for $180 million. BP chair John Browne, whom the press dubbed the "Sun King" for his business acumen and daring but calculated financial risk-taking, was angered he'd been outmaneuvered in the deal, which he believed was worth more than what Tyumen paid for it.[221]

Determined to block EXIM's transaction, BP engaged in a strong-arming offensive of its own. Enlisting the services of lobbying giant Patton Boggs and financier George Soros, also an investor in the Sidanco oil fields, BP spent a small fortune lobbying EXIM and the executive branch of government.[222] And it was brutal. If I didn't back down, lobbyists warned me, embarrassing things about me would surface in the press, and Congress would increase its oversight of my agency. Lobbyists walked the halls of EXIM talking to our directors, showing them pictures of Russia's brutal war against the Chechens, and conflating our transaction with support for this conduct.

Chechnya was a sensitive topic during Clinton's second administration. According to certain media outlets and foreign observers, the White House's enthusiasm to advance America's relationship with Russia had led it to overlook the Kremlin's brutal conduct against Chechen separatists.[223] Now attuned to such criticism, which was exploited in this lobbying effort, the White House applied significant pressure for EXIM to retract the Tyumen loan guarantee, citing Russian corruption along with its horrible human rights record in Chechnya.

Prior to this transaction, I had little direct knowledge of the corporate lobby's power in Washington. Global corporations like British Petroleum, I soon learned, could hire multiple lobbyists and pay them millions to unleash large armies of staff, many of whom were former government employees and cabinet members. These heavyweights leveraged their connections and large sums of money to help their clients. Case in point: heading BP's lobbying offensive, I later discovered, was the former roommate of a top US policy official.

Perhaps the lobbying campaign's most egregious tactic came in the form of a "confidential" and "classified" memo from the Central Intelligence Agency (CIA). The agency had an office at EXIM, and most mornings the agent directing the office visited me with a briefing. Because these briefings contained sensitive information, I was allowed to read them but not to retain any physical records. One day, as I was on my way to the airport to visit Russia, a CIA agent presented me with a confidential report. "You've got fifteen minutes with it," he told me, accompanying me to the airport while I read.

While mostly dealing with innocuous topics like Alfa Bank's management and corporate structure, the report also contained a section detailing the corruption of the business magnates associated with the Tyumen transaction. It documented instances of rape, abuse, and all manner of sinister behavior. I read it through three times, cover to cover, struck that the White House had gone to such lengths to stop this transaction. Thanks to the investigative work of *Washington Post* journalist David Ignatius, we now know that the CIA didn't author the report. British Petroleum hired former KGB officers to write it and then gave it to the White House, who forwarded it to me via the CIA. The CIA and White House were playing hardball with memoranda like these that implied that I was backing the thugs at Alfa Bank.

The Russian oligarchs always reminded me of J. P. Morgan, Andrew Carnegie, John D. Rockefeller, and any number of other nineteenth-century American industrialists and financiers. These groups of well-connected and shrewd entrepreneurs, given pejorative titles like "oligarch" and "robber baron," amassed enormous wealth and acquired monopoly control in their industries, usually strong-arming their way to attain it and engaging in ethically dubious behavior. During my later trips to Russia, I met with Alfa Bank principals like Len Blavatnik, my future neighbor in Anguilla, and the powerful and imposing Mikhail Fridman. I routinely sat there, representing the US government, with a strong-willed Russian billionaire, a firearm visible in his pocket.

These discussions, much like the Russian bankruptcy auction of Sidanco, reminded me of any number of Drexel's dreaded private equity takeovers in the 1980s. Many in the financial establishment, me included, disliked Drexel's aggressive tactics. But Drexel still outmaneuvered its competition in a way similar to Alfa Bank and, critically, didn't do anything considered illegal in Russia.

When I offered such comparisons and spoke about the aggressive but still legal tactics that the Russians had employed in the bankruptcy proceedings, my colleagues in the White House objected. Secretary of State Madeleine Albright, for example, countered such claims by saying that we needed to set an example and teach the Russians better behavior. "Even if it wasn't strictly illegal," she said, "we shouldn't reward such conduct by funding this project that hurt British Petroleum." But I stood firm based on the merits of the deal. Because oil secured EXIM's investment, we had judged it to be a creditworthy transaction that adhered to EXIM's mandate to support the American business community and to protect the environment.

More generally, the transaction would help the reeling Russian economy, increasing privatization-led growth in the country, and it even stood to bolster the US-Russian diplomatic relationship. It was also a historic deal, representing the first export credit agency transaction since Russia declared its moratorium on debt repayments—and the largest-ever US loan to Russia's private sector. Given the deal's adherence to EXIM's charter, as well as my larger policy objectives bordering on "mission creep," I stood firm in the bank's decision.

To further counter EXIM's support of the transaction, certain White House officials began suggesting that the transaction wasn't in the national interest. The invocation of the national interest changed the terms of the debate, which came to center on the 1978 Chafee Amendment to the Export-Import Bank Act of 1945. According to this amendment, the president has the power to veto any bank transaction deemed to support international terrorism, nuclear proliferation, environmental degradation, and human rights abuses.[224] The President issued an executive order one year later, delegating his authority to invoke "a Chafee" to the secretary of state, who must consult other agency heads including the secretary of commerce, before doing so.[225]

When anyone broached Chechnya or Russian corruption when speaking about Tyumen, I replied by daring the White House to "Chafee me." My experience in Russia and my evaluation of the economy had led me to the opposite conclusion, which was actually twofold: first, Russian companies and powerbrokers needed to see American exporters as reliable suppliers for EXIM to help the country and, second, the United States had to achieve its foreign policy objective of developing a stable market economy in Russia.[226]

But the pressure continued, and in November 1999 a bipartisan group of House representatives expressed their strong reservations about Tyumen. In a letter signed by fourteen congressional representatives, ranging from Texas Republican Ron Paul to Gary Ackerman, a New York Democrat, members expressed concern, citing Tyumen's "likely illegal activities under Russian bankruptcy law" and certain illegal activities under US law. EXIM's actions, they warned me, would ultimately complicate US foreign policy objectives that centered on helping the country develop a legitimate, capitalist system.[227]

But I also had allies in the fight, like Halliburton chair Dick Cheney, whose equipment figured prominently in the Tyumen transaction. Halliburton and EXIM had enjoyed a long and productive relationship as the bank had worked over the decades to guarantee loans for its equipment throughout Africa and Latin America. "You're going to lose," Cheney said in my office. "You might have the support of half of Congress, but you cannot beat the system and win against the executive branch." With decades of insider experience in Washington, Cheney knew how government power operated. During that meeting, Cheney offered to withdraw his request for $500 million in loan guarantees.

"I appreciate it, Dick," I replied, "but withdraw the request only if you believe it will create blowback on Halliburton. Don't do it on my accord." I emphasized, "If the White House doesn't like the deal, it can Chafee it."

Cheney, who would become a friend, was one of my many unlikely allies in this struggle. On my second visit to Russia, when this conflict was in full swing, I walked into an auditorium and received a standing ovation, with everyone in attendance enthusiastically welcoming me. I was embarrassed by the attention and worried about the optics in New York and Washington. A year or so later, a member of Putin's inner circle came to my office to say, "I have a message for you from President Putin. He would like to meet next time you are in Russia. You don't have to tell anyone about it." It was a suspicious offer, and I passed it along to the CIA, which forbade any rendezvous. Still, it was apparent that the leadership in Russia along with important US exporters appreciated that someone in Washington championed their interests.

On December 22, 1999, the White House issued a Chafee to block the Tyumen deal. As the *Los Angeles Times* reported, "The Clinton administration blocked $498 million in loan guarantees to Russia on Tuesday, in a striking signal of displeasure with Russian economic corruption and an indirect protest of its brutal military campaign in Chechnya."[228] Relief washed over me. If Secretary of State Albright determined it was in the United States' national interest to block this deal, then the matter was resolved. The timing couldn't have been better, as I was headed for the beaches of Anguilla for the Christmas holiday, where I planned on drinking a rum punch and putting this episode behind me.

Only weeks later, we learned BP had met with Alfa Bank executives, who agreed to pay the company a $200 million "advisory fee." On March 30, 2000, after the White House received word of this deal, it lifted the Chafee, with Albright confirming that Tyumen had "cleaned up the corrupt business practices that led her to delay the transaction in December."[229]

This about-face came just days after the Russian people elected Vladimir Putin as president. The White House welcomed the President-elect's platform on investor rights and foreign investment and, with BP mollified, reauthorized the Tyumen deal.[230] While hopes for the Putin presidency were misplaced, EXIM's successful transaction with Tyumen formed part of Russia's comeback from the 1998 ruble crisis. By 2000, we'd averted the worst economic projections for Russia, including hyperinflation and 10 percent declines in GDP, as the world began purchasing oil again and Russia started (modestly) diversifying its economy, enabling the ruble to rebound.

In the days following the Chafee lift, I left my EXIM office and sat on a bench in Lafayette Square, reflecting on what it all meant. When I began work at EXIM, I shared in the world's larger enthusiasm for a post-Soviet Russia.

In keeping with my usual practice, I had leveraged personal relationships to help make a difference in the country. I'll never forget when Mikhail Kasyanov, Russia's minister of finance who would later become prime minister, visited EXIM with an entourage to discuss a deal on Russian hospital equipment. When discussing the financing terms, he appealed to my sympathy, describing the hardship that children at this hospital endured and how the Russian state didn't have the equipment necessary to diagnose and treat their ailments. We were ready to ink the deal when he told me that EXIM's standard interest rates were too high. "I don't think you should charge the same amount for sick children as you would for oil drilling equipment," he said.

"I'd like to talk with you alone," I said. With his nearly native English, we didn't need interpreters, and I cleared the room of my EXIM colleagues and his entourage. It was unusual to conduct a meeting alone with a head of state, but I thought this would prove optimal for our relationship. Since my days in investment banking, I've found that people often play to audiences; in the absence of such an audience, you can have a more genuine and productive conversation. "What do you think a fair rate would be?" I asked him. Although taken aback that I would negotiate, he took a moment to consider and asked for a reduction from 7 to 6.5 percent. "That seems reasonable," I replied. "I'm going to take it to my board." In truth, I knew I would honor this modest reduction in children's equipment costs. This was a fantastic deal for Russia as well as American suppliers eager for the business. It also marked the beginning of a long-term relationship with this man. Once again, I marveled at how an agency like EXIM allowed me the autonomy to forge personal connections and broker deals without undergoing a cumbersome interagency review process.

Sometimes my attempts at establishing personal rapport and forging common deals, as I attempted to do with President Vladimir Putin, ended in failure. I initially met Putin in September 2000 when he appeared for the official signing of the Tyumen Oil deal, and we met again in 2003, when he visited Columbia University and the New York Stock Exchange. Unfortunately, the Russian president's behavior between our two visits had undermined my attempts to foster foreign direct investment in Russia and to broker deals like Tyumen. After leaving government, I tried appealing to Putin's sense of fairness.

By 2002, Russian oligarch Mikhail Khodorkovsky had accomplished the most significant feat for Russia's post-Soviet economy. Committed to transparency, shareholder protections, and best practices in governance, Khodorkovsky transformed Yukos into one of the most important and technologically proficient companies in Russia.[231] Yukos's profits soared, Khodorkovsky became the richest man in the country, and US credit agencies rated Yukos as the most creditworthy private corporation in Russia.[232] But in what international journalists and The Hague would characterize as a blatant act of state-sponsored theft, Putin issued trumped-up fraud charges against Khodorkovsky, imprisoned him for a decade, and illegally appropriated tens of billions in shareholder value from Yukos.[233] While telling the President I had much to commend him for after his first year in office, this massive loss to foreign shareholders "has seriously affected the perception of the rule of law and protection of minority interests in Russia"[234] I'm not the only one who has failed in his appeal to Putin's fairness and integrity.

Whether I achieved common understanding, as with Kasyanov, or failed to do so, as with Putin, I nonetheless aimed to broker creditworthy deals to help Russia's progress to free markets in general, as well as help it overcome the 1998 currency crisis in particular. But as the Yukos debacle helps to illustrate, progress in Russia has remained mixed. Participation in the economy remains low, and the country's leader, having granted himself perpetual rule, now resembles a tsar from Russia's premodern past.

Russia's unfortunate state is partially understandable. One reason for the failure of larger US policy objectives in Russia is because our government expected too much, too soon. It took the United States over one hundred years to develop securities laws, bankruptcy protections, and other financial infrastructure to earn the trust of investors. If our stable financial framework took this long to build, why did we expect Russia to accelerate this process in four or five years? I would raise this same argument later, when working on economic development in Egypt. The Arab Spring uprisings, just like the fall of the Soviet Union, gave us hope for a better future. But for the United States to expect that the former command economies in the East or military dictatorships in the Middle East would quickly become exemplars of Western democracy was and remains unrealistic.

The more I reflected that day, the more faintly sick I felt about the Tyumen transaction. A foreign corporation had successfully lobbied the White House, whose members worked to do the company's bidding instead of supporting the US business community and the larger Russian economy. In serving the interests of this company, the White House had invoked the Chafee Amendment, a mechanism intended to stop foreign government abuse, and deployed it to terminate a private transaction for the first time. By broadening the scope of the Chafee to stop a private creditworthy transaction, I believed the White House had created a dangerous precedent.

After BP received its $200 million payment, furthermore, the White House revoked the Chafee, proving that the Chechnya argument had been a red herring all along. If White House officials had really cared about corruption or human rights abuses in Chechnya, they wouldn't have terminated a financial transaction involving oil and then immediately reversed course. That action did nothing to stem the tide of violence in Chechnya or overcome the corruption plaguing Russia. In fact, it had done the opposite. In our effort to teach the Russians a lesson about corruption, we'd corrupted our own system.[235]

A year later, John Browne, the BP chair, confirmed my conclusions when we met in London. In a remarkably candid discussion, Browne admitted the Russians had outsmarted him, though still he insisted there was rampant corruption at Alfa Bank. He'd lost $400 million for his shareholders with the unfair and corrupt loss of Sidanco and was intent on recouping this money. His efforts included aggressively lobbying the White House to quash the Tyumen deal and then returning to the Russians at Alfa Bank, offering to help with Washington in exchange for an "appropriate payment."

As I sat on the bench contemplating the degree of corruption in both of our systems, I realized how Washington had proven extremely complex, with foreign governments and lobbying efforts all complicating major transactions. In many respects, congressional term limits create a similar type of pressure for election fundraising as quarterly earnings reports do in the corporate world. Both fostered a troubling short-termism. On balance, however, the US private sector was more ethical than the political world by a fair margin.

Shortly after the affair, journalists from the *Washington Post*, *The New Yorker*, *Harper's*, and the *Harvard Business Review* approached me, encouraging me to write about this story. Though I answered questions for the press, I've largely avoided detailing the entire affair until now. I don't regret any of the actions I took, but more than twenty years later, I don't feel good about what happened.

But I do feel proud about the work I did in Sub-Saharan Africa, to which I now turn. While Tyumen Oil had its elements of scandal and was laden in corruption, my work in Africa inspired even more media attention and controversy. In Africa, my mission creep would achieve its highest expression, as I accomplished my most important work for EXIM Bank.

11

An Investment Safari in Africa

THE NEW CHAIR OF EXIM just began a junket to Africa, reported Al Kamen, Washington's leading gossip columnist. It was October 1999, just before four EXIM staff and I visited Ghana, Nigeria, and South Africa. "The quintet," continued Kamen, "is flying two legs—Ghana to Nigeria and Nigeria to South Africa—in the comfort of a private Lear Jet. What was wrong with commercial airlines?"[236]

To answer Kamen, traveling north to south in Africa was nearly impossible. After trying to book our travel on safe roads, train services, or available commercial flights, my travel specialists at EXIM had deemed this trip impossible. I therefore decided to charter a plane at my own expense and treat my team to a safari before beginning our work together.

Throughout my time at EXIM, some spurned such use of private planes, while others dubbed my energetic efforts as "investment safaris" and "mission creep." There is some truth to these statements because when it came to Africa, my approach was aggressive, or what I like to term "progressive." I became the first EXIM chair to visit southern Africa, expanding the bank's market reach from Latin America and Asia to the entire African continent.[237]

My Africa strategy focused on growth in all markets and sectors. When I began at EXIM, I was surprised to learn that we were open for business in only thirteen African countries and supported less than $40 million a year in exports to Sub-Saharan Africa, substantially trailing our European competitors' volumes. I was intent on opening throughout the continent, especially in the forty-eight countries comprising Sub-Saharan Africa. Unlike the North African countries in the MENA region (typically including Algeria, Egypt, Libya, Morocco, and Tunisia) with long-standing trade and economic relationships throughout Europe and the Middle East, the greater Sub-Saharan region was vastly underserved.

My goal was to cement important deals with long-standing Sub-Saharan trade partners like Ghana while also creating new markets throughout the region and in long-neglected countries like Nigeria. I also wanted to increase business volumes by continuing the bank's focus on large industrial parts, oil and gas equipment, machinery, motor vehicles, and aircraft, while expanding into more niche areas occupied by small- and medium-sized (SME) businesses. My efforts in Africa, culminating with important, Africa-focused legislation in the US Congress and a controversial program I devised to address the AIDS crisis, represented some of my most important work at EXIM.

TRADE NOT AID

My work in Africa owes a great debt to the Clintons, both Bill and Hillary, who awakened the national interest in Africa's cultural treasures and economic importance. In the spring of 1997, Hillary Clinton embarked on a lengthy tour of Sub-Saharan Africa, the longest ever by a president's spouse. With her daughter Chelsea, she traversed 18,000 miles, visiting schools, museums, and palaces, and peering into "The Door of No Return" that slaves saw in Benin before beginning their harrowing passage to the United States. They toured villages ravaged by AIDS and witnessed the majesty of the Serengeti plain.[238]

Clinton discussed this trip with me while I was dealing with EXIM's reauthorization. Though preoccupied at the time, I remember her asking me to visit Africa. "I don't know about your schedule, but get to Africa as soon as you can. Africa hardly buys anything from the United States." She wasn't exaggerating. US exports to Africa accounted for a scant 1 percent of our global total.[239] EXIM's record reflected this trend, as Africa made up only 2–3 percent of the bank's aggregate $58 billion business exposure.[240]

In the spring of 1998, President Clinton took a historic twelve-day trip to Africa, also setting records as the longest such trip of any US president. Calling for an end to stereotypes and misconceptions about Africa, as well as free markets and democracy in the region, Clinton inspired his administration to focus on the continent. "It is time for Americans to put a new Africa on our map," President Clinton said during a speech in Ghana.[241] Secretary of Commerce Bill Daley, Transportation Secretary Rodney Slater, Secretary of State Madeleine Albright, Energy Secretary Bill Richardson, and Labor Secretary Alexis Herman, along with other federal agencies like EXIM, were thereafter inspired to focus on growing US commercial and cultural relationships throughout the continent.

Galvanized by this stirring call, I was the first US senior leader to follow President Clinton's tour to Africa, embarking on my trip two weeks after his return.[242] Two weeks was what I term the sweet spot in presidential travel. My first trip with the President had been to Mexico in January 1998. Following a speech, I distinctly remember queuing in line with Hillary Clinton, Madeleine Albright, Bob Rubin, and about seven or eight other cabinet members. Facing us several feet away were our Mexican governmental counterparts. We each had five minutes allotted to speak.

After the minispeeches, I remember walking outside with Albright and Rubin, asking them if our time was over. When you go with the President, they told me, you get only five minutes. Though I traveled with the President many other times, and enjoyed each occasion, I resolved thereafter to travel *after* him whenever I could. That way, the energy and publicity of his trip could provide a positive context for conducting my own business.

I planned my inaugural trip to Africa, which I took in April 1998 to Zimbabwe, South Africa, and Namibia, to understand why we had such slim business volumes on the continent and to seek out new markets for US products. As my team prepared me for Zimbabwe, I anticipated abundant opportunity. When I imagined Zimbabwe, I thought of the country's agricultural wealth, elevating it to the breadbasket of Africa, as well as its magnificent climate and cultural talent. Despite its rich minerals and abundant agriculture, my briefings suggested, the 1997 currency crisis had battered the country, raising inflation to 30 percent the following year and exacerbating poverty.[243] The average life expectancy was forty-one years. In my early sixties at the time, I remember finding this figure shocking.

After landing in Zimbabwe, I was immediately struck by the poverty. I didn't fear theft or violence, as I might have in Johannesburg or New York City, or revolutionary protest, like I'd later fear in Cairo. Instead, I saw human hardship everywhere I looked. When Mugabe assumed power in 1980, he'd expanded living standards and literacy among the country's formerly disenfranchised Black citizens, transforming the British colony of Rhodesia into the democracy of Zimbabwe. In 1995, only several years prior to my visit, the World Bank had praised Mugabe's regime for helping the country reach important milestones in literacy and economic renewal, and many regarded him as a hero for his efforts at redistributing wealth.

But Zimbabwe was changing, and so was the President's reputation. My first night in country, I stayed in a hotel in Bulawayo, the nation's second-largest city, as drummers played outside all night long. The music was beautiful, and everyone enjoyed themselves, but I got little sleep. The following day, Ambassador Tom McDonald, a thoughtful Midwesterner, escorted me to a parade in honor of Mugabe. Seated about twenty yards from Mugabe, Ambassador McDonald rose to his feet and attempted an introduction: "The chair of America's Export-Import Bank is here, and Zimbabwe wants to do more business with them. Won't you come and say hello?"

"I don't say hello to anyone from the United States," Mugabe replied. The ambassador was embarrassed that Mugabe spurned me because he harbored a grievance against the United States. But we still had a productive time discussing business opportunities throughout the country. A few years later, the depth of Mugabe's tyranny, financial mismanagement, and human rights abuses came to light.

South Africa, another stop on my tour, was a mature and developed economy, representing EXIM's largest export market in the region. My drive through Johannesburg, however, showed me how harrowing and dangerous parts of it could be. The taxi drivers rolled through traffic lights, afraid to stop because people routinely jumped onto vehicles, muscled their way inside, and robbed passengers.

My briefing materials indicated that many European countries had been slower than the United States to recognize the evils of apartheid, a system of institutionalized racial segregation that Nelson Mandela had helped abolish only a few years earlier. Many Europeans, the briefings indicated, had continued with "business as usual" in the country. The United States, by contrast, had agitated against this regime in its universities, and many US companies had embarked on a wide-ranging consumer boycott of White-owned South African businesses. I figured this situation was likely more complex than the briefings suggested, as European countries were former colonial powers and had objected strenuously to apartheid while maintaining long-standing business relationships in the area.

But as I'd later tell Nancy Pelosi at a subcommittee hearing that she was chairing, I still thought that America's principled anti-apartheid stance would be more helpful for business. "In South Africa," I said, "where I thought our sanctions policy during apartheid would now benefit US businesses returning to the market, I found our firms to be at a great disadvantage. European firms had simply used the sanctions period to cement their own positions in the South African economy."[244]

I could easily change that status quo, I realized on my visit, because a diverse business community welcomed me throughout the country, eager and filled with energy to do whatever business they could. And as Deputy Governor James Cross, of the South African Reserve Bank, observed,

European export credit agencies may have had more established relationships in the country than EXIM Bank, but such agencies did small business volumes with SMEs.[245] This struck me as an ideal niche to expand the US presence in South Africa and in the neighboring Sub-Saharan African countries more generally.

I found the third country on the tour, Namibia, to be beautiful, clean, and organized, exactly what I'd expected of a former German colony. I remember waking up in the US Embassy my first morning and lacing my shoes for a run. When Ambassador George Ward saw me, he delivered a stern warning. "You don't know your way," he said. "You could run into animals." He sent security officers to run with me, and I enjoyed a beautiful morning jogging through magnificent, lush foliage. Unlike Zimbabwe, where wealth was racially stratified, Namibia was more egalitarian, with most enjoying a higher quality of life than many neighboring countries. Namibia's hardworking ethos reminded me of South Korea, while its streets reminded me of Switzerland, and its climate of South Africa. This was an underserved market, brimming with potential for US businesses.

MARKETING AMERICA

When I returned from my first trip, I was impatient to begin work on Africa, especially focusing on stimulating trade in the long-neglected Sub-Saharan region. Africa, I said at the time, "is truly an untapped market—maybe the last of the great untapped markets."[246] I saw enormous opportunities to increase US jobs while helping a series of frontier and developing countries improve their economies. The World Bank had forecast a 4.2 percent growth rate in Africa from 2000 to 2020, while government subsidies and other business barriers had steadily decreased, fueling even greater foreign direct investment (which had quadrupled from 1990 to 1997).[247] Africa's time had come, and if American businesses didn't capitalize, they would lose out.

America's commercial posture toward Africa in the 1990s nonetheless reminded me of the 1970s, when I served on the board of a medical company that manufactured equipment for rehabilitation. One day, the chair told me that a large Nigerian company had approached him to buy crutches and other orthopedic equipment. "But who would sell anything to Africa?" he asked. "We'll never get paid." I urged him to investigate further and perhaps talk to the Nigerian ambassador, or to someone in Washington or New York, to inquire about the legitimacy of this company and its creditworthiness. "It's not worth the trouble," he said. "We've got a lot of other orders." He then told me that I could pursue the case personally if I felt so moved, but I was busy running my businesses and we never executed the order. Throughout the 1970s and 1980s, this typified the American business perspective in many sectors, with some not pursuing opportunities in Africa because they feared losing money.

Unfortunately, my tour to Africa and my survey of EXIM's balance sheets revealed that such thinking about Africa's supposedly inhospitable business climate persisted. And some of it was justified. In the 1990s, there was little creditworthiness throughout Sub-Saharan Africa.[248] Africa's famine, political instability, and poor market fundamentals produced what the *Washington Post* called a "horrible repayment record," especially in the countries of Sub-Saharan Africa, which accounted for $1.1 billion of the $1.9 billion in debt owed to industrial economies in 1999.[249] Despite support from the Clinton White House and the Congressional Black Caucus, skepticism about Africa reigned on the Hill. The first enterprise fund in Africa, founded about seven years prior to my tenure at EXIM, had failed and lost taxpayer money. Sadly, investigators uncovered corruption in that fund and many congresspeople and business leaders alike gravitated to the stability of European and Asian economies.

My first trip to Africa convinced me that creditworthy opportunities abounded throughout the continent. But I still needed to market Africa to US business manufacturers and service providers, showing them that EXIM was open for business there and ready to assist their expansion into these exciting new markets. I embarked on a speech tour throughout the United

States and leafleted American embassies and business roundtables with literature explaining how EXIM Bank worked and its willingness to guarantee creditworthy loans throughout the continent.[250] Private sector buyers in Africa deserved this advocacy because the African continent was poised for expansion across a wide range of industries like energy, aerospace, and telecommunications. Its beautiful landscapes, cultural treasures, and legendary wildlife also made it an ideal place to expand taxi services, airlines, hotels, and other components of a vibrant tourism industry.[251]

But because I initiated these efforts in government, conducting business in Africa also entailed significant bureaucratic hurdles. Though I was accustomed to great latitude at EXIM, this freedom didn't extend to creating new EXIM relationships across Africa. Instead of simply developing programs, as I'd done throughout Asia, and engineering transactions, as I'd done for Russian oil giant Tyumen, I needed to first (re)open EXIM banking operations throughout large swaths of Africa prior to conducting any business.

These openings required a complex interagency process involving the Treasury, State, and Defense departments, as well as EXIM economists and the White House. Collectively, they all determined whether a country was creditworthy, and if so, whether it qualified for short-, medium-, or long-term loan-financing programs. Just as with its exceptional team of Russian specialists, EXIM had strong economic analysts, perhaps as talented as any in the US government. Over a period of thirty years, EXIM had become a center of global economic analysis, with fifteen to twenty economists, many of whom had top training and in-depth specialties in different regions and countries. Their country knowledge rivaled that of their counterparts at the World Bank and IMF, and I was fortunate to receive their frequent briefings about these countries, their economies, and the credit risks each posed.

The interagency process nonetheless proved tedious and required lobbying my own risk-averse economists. I still recall the long days in my office, with me explaining why I wanted to do more business, and them countering with all the reasons why we shouldn't. "Mr. Chairman," they might say, "we can't just change the rating on Mozambique because we want to."

We did everything we could to open these countries. With Angola, when its credit report returned with government economists declaring that it wasn't quite creditworthy, we advocated for a nonthreatening short-term reopening. When the economists returned with Zimbabwe's multiple risks, even citing the frightful life-span statistics, we provided a business plan for the country in which the United States didn't lose any money. "Nothing is creditworthy in Chad," I remember my team advising us, telling us about how dictator Hissène Habré had made such business relationships impossible. Their reservations were understandable, and I knew the public sector incentive structure didn't reward the type of risks I wanted to take. But I'd taken an even greater financial risk in South Korea. The countries of Sub-Saharan Africa were equally worthy of US help.

SELLING AMERICA

Once EXIM began opening throughout larger swaths of Africa, I broadened my focus from attracting US capital flows to the continent. Unlike in Asia and Russia, where people were familiar with EXIM's programming and larger mission, I had to introduce EXIM to African companies and countries accustomed to working with European financial institutions.[252] Having honed my marketing skills in investment banking, my transition to the public service, where I marketed US products and services throughout the world, proved a natural fit for me. Although I embarked on such marketing and branding efforts throughout the central Asian republics and in Latin America and the former Soviet Union, I felt these efforts were most important in Africa, since it represented a vast and underserved market of nearly 800 million people. As I traveled to Africa in the coming years, I devised some creative strategies to encourage more business there.

Many countries in Sub-Saharan Africa, for example, favored local currencies when borrowing money. If they assumed a debt in US dollars and their own currencies declined, their revenues would also fall, making it harder to repay loans. This risk was greater for SMEs given their smaller financial reserves and increased risk of bankruptcy. In August 1999, EXIM authorized the first foreign currency exchange in its history, guaranteeing loans in South African rand instead of US dollars.[253] Following this program's implementation, countries could borrow rand to purchase pumps, solar panels, and airplanes, dramatically increasing EXIM's business volumes in South Africa and Sub-Saharan Africa more generally.

Ghana was another regional power where EXIM Bank was open for business and where we guaranteed two important transactions. Ghana was an easier sell for our economists, who'd joined the global business community in promoting the country because of its strong leadership and long history of compliance with IMF and World Bank programming.[254] When I landed in Ghana, I felt like I was in Europe, walking streets lined with cyber cafés and speaking with university-trained, tech-oriented entrepreneurs. I'd later travel to Silicon Valley and tell investors about this vibrant emerging technology ecosystem and EXIM's enthusiasm for encouraging an African dotcom in the country and across the continent more generally.[255] I became close with the country's leadership, including Ghana's ambassador to the United States, Koby A. Koomson, who was especially proactive on behalf of his country. The minister of finance was an Ivy-educated man who had an unusual and endearing style, ending every telephone conversation with "God bless."

In the fall of 1999, I met with President Jerry John Rawlings, a burly and outgoing man with whom I also became close starting with that trip. After meeting in his offices in the capital city of Accra, President Rawlings directed my delegation to a large helicopter, ready to fly Ambassador Koomson, Minister of Environment Victor Gbeho, and my team to the Keta Sea. EXIM was considering a loan guarantee for a seawall to preserve the country's coastal environment. Had I known we were boarding a helicopter, I might have consulted with the embassy about safety. This was far from Marine One, and even more of a risk than the aging turbo prop that took me to Kazan, Russia. Helicopters tend to have poor safety records compared with other aircraft globally, and I had the sudden feeling as we departed, flying low over jungle brush, that any bad weather could easily send us careening into the terrain below. At one point, President Rawlings took the helm of the helicopter, something that didn't inspire more confidence.

My team had briefed me about sea erosion and failed reclamation efforts at Keta. Flying above the coastline was a different experience entirely.[256] With the aerial view provided by the helicopter, I could visualize the ocean eating away at the shacks that bordered it, as well as schools and agricultural areas that were all nearly submerged. With this visceral experience of erosion, I became even more committed to the seawall. As we landed on an outcrop on the edge of a cliff overlooking the water, people enthusiastically greeted us, eager to tell us how this erosion inflicted harm on their communities and how much they needed the wall. I still have a picture of President Rawlings and me at the edge of the cliff, peering over to the sea below.

The ambassador and president were smart salesmen for their country. Ambassador Koomson had already researched the US exporters that could provide the products and services to accomplish this project. The Keta seawall was a classic example of a mutually beneficial transaction. US exporters could ship goods and services without fear of default because of EXIM's guarantee, and the seawall itself would save vital ecosystems and housing developments, all the while stimulating the regional economy. Over lunch that day in the President's beautiful home, my team and I discussed this project and a slew of others that would help his country. In May 1999, EXIM announced a $93 million loan for the Keta Sea Defense project.[257]

As happy as I was to support this massive infrastructure project, I was equally happy to bolster smaller operations. As my team passed a group of women fishing during that visit, I immediately inquired about what they were doing. This wasn't on my official itinerary, and I asked the driver to make an impromptu stop so we could introduce ourselves. I walked out to find about twenty women anglers hard at work. Immediately impressed by how industrious they were and their substantial catch of fish, I looked to a man who seemed to be in charge of the operation. "How much do you generate in revenue for a business like this?" I asked him. Since everyone spoke fluent English, the women spoke up, saying their catches were great, but most of the fish spoiled during transit to local markets.

This operation, comprising three generations of women, needed refrigerated trucks to ferry their inventory to inland markets before the fish went bad.[258] For this operation, we eventually guaranteed $1.2 million for refrigerated storage containers that cost $20,000–$25,000 each. Projects as diverse as the seawall and the refrigerated containers made Ghana the African equivalent of South Korea: a model partnership with a stable, creditworthy country.[259]

Nigeria had a more checkered history than Ghana, and I was determined to commence EXIM operations and ensure important transactions there. It was one of the most complex and overwhelming countries I experienced in Africa.[260] With the largest population of any country on the continent, hovering around 116 million at the time, the word "chaos" best describes the cities I visited there. Urban traffic patterns were a nightmare, traffic congestion suffocating, and beggars omnipresent. The country's reputation for corruption is legendary, with American leaders and civilians alike receiving royalty scams and other Ponzi schemes emanating from the country.

But during my tenure at EXIM, Nigeria was changing, and President Clinton was keen to develop our bilateral relationship and attract foreign investment to the country. I learned of his enthusiasm in August 2000, when we accompanied his delegation to the nation's capital city of Abuja. After Air Force One landed, we boarded separate cars, with Clinton's entourage headed to the national assembly, and me off to a poor village to check on a company EXIM was financing. The driver expressed concern about a limousine visiting this remote place, but I went nonetheless and met up with Clinton later in the evening, sitting in the front row with Madeleine Albright and a few other members of the cabinet, as he addressed the Nigerian parliament. That evening, President Clinton spoke with humor, pathos, and just the right tempo about the importance of Nigeria to West Africa. "The world needs Nigeria to succeed," he said to national assembly members who'd only taken office a little over a year prior, following the cessation of military rule. "Nigeria is a pivot point on which all Africa's future turns."[261]

Clinton referred to Olusegun Obasanjo, who in May 1999 became the first civilian to occupy national leadership. EXIM had just reopened in the country following its transition to democracy, and the future of Nigeria seemed auspicious. Obasanjo's thoughtful questions and emphasis on transparency inspired great confidence during a meeting I had with him and Secretary Albright following Clinton's speech. Likely jetlagged from the trip, Albright brandished her meeting notes and proceeded to read them to the President like a speech. I sat quietly through this awkwardness until it was my turn. I then explained very simply my message to Obasanjo, and how EXIM and Nigerian businesses could productively partner.

As we discussed, Nigeria was poised for a new chapter in stability and economic growth, especially with the President committing to the reforms needed to attract foreign direct investment.[262] But democracy isn't enough and the relationship was still complicated because, while EXIM Bank had to contend with a fair amount of outstanding loans in Nigeria, it was harder to appraise the value of this country compared to a nation like Ghana, which had a history of creditworthiness. By the time of its transition to democracy, Nigeria relied on oil for 80 percent of its revenues, was in arrears on its debt by $3.5 billion per annum, and had a history of corruption.[263] But Nigeria's banks were strong, and the President made international headlines by advertising his idea of a "democracy dividend." No matter what happened to Obasanjo, who I knew might be voted out of office, I liked to think of EXIM's programs as forming part of his democracy dividend.[264] After reopening EXIM in Nigeria, the bank approved credit for eleven Nigerian banks and then guaranteed finance projects as diverse as gas pipelines and broadband internet installation.[265]

While conducting such work in Africa, I was routinely chagrined by the operational inefficiencies and lack of coordination among US agencies. During a trip to Mozambique in 1999, for example, I was delighted to announce the first opening of EXIM there since 1969.[266] But as I went to meet the Mozambican president, I found the chair of the Overseas Private Investment Corporation (OPIC), our sister organization, leaving his office before me. OPIC was another agency in the US government responsible for encouraging equity investments across the world, with an emphasis on helping US businesses within emerging economies. But because OPIC formed part of the foreign policy establishment and was under the State Department's aegis, while EXIM was commercial in orientation and operated independently, our two organizations existed as independent fiefdoms that didn't communicate, much less coordinate.

It was especially disconcerting that I saw this happen in Mozambique, one of the world's poorest countries that, if managed right, could represent one of Africa's major turnarounds.[267] As we brushed shoulders that day, I appealed to OPIC's president: given that OPIC and EXIM both belonged to the same parent company, the US government, and had overlapping missions in Mozambique and across the world, we should consult one another, share information, and devise strategies in the future. I wanted to tell him about the rand program EXIM had implemented and enlist his help in aiding American firm entry into Mozambique, a market where Portuguese and British companies occupied significant market share.[268]

OPIC's chair and associates felt I was behaving in an aggressive manner. When I told Vice President Gore, presidential chief of staff Erskine Bowles, and a few others about this story, proposing that we merge agencies, everyone agreed in principle. But they wouldn't pursue it because there would be an outcry if Congress lost the ability to appoint people to diverse agencies. I softened my proposal, suggesting that we streamline operations instead of consolidating them, perhaps moving the agencies into the same building and introducing some formal communication between us. Still, some on the Hill accused me of empire building.

AID FOR AIDS

Though some in government and business expressed reservations about certain commercial transactions that I pursued at EXIM, I never encountered international and wide-ranging blowback until my program began to finance drugs to treat HIV (human immunodeficiency virus), which causes AIDS.

After returning from one of my trips to Africa in which I toured several underserved hospitals, I asked an EXIM director about the possibility of including pharmaceutical purchases, like antiretroviral HIV medication, within a larger loan package. When financing a hospital or clinic in Africa for $300–$400 million, could we attach $20 million extra for pharmaceuticals? As it turned out, EXIM had never implemented such a program because most of the applicants asked only for construction equipment.

I was inclined to pursue this idea because HIV/AIDS was ravaging Africa. At the time, 13 million had died from the disease on the continent while nearly 25 million had HIV.[269] Sub-Saharan Africa increasingly represented the epicenter of the contagion. At only 10 percent of the global population, Sub-Saharan Africa had a stunning 71 percent of all HIV/AIDS patients. As I wrote in the *Washington Post*, "Who would not be horrified by the statistics coming out of Sub-Saharan Africa? The HIV/AIDS pandemic threatens to bring decades of slow, hard-won progress to an abrupt end."[270] Africa needed to address a "resource gap" afflicting the continent, and here I believed EXIM could provide what the public sector calls "additionality."[271] After the White House and my friends in the Congressional Black Caucus expressed enthusiasm, I went to work on developing a proposal.

On July 19, 2000, EXIM officially committed $1 billion for twenty-four Sub-Saharan nations that could include a drug package in their EXIM loans when constructing new hospitals and clinics.[272] EXIM announced the program at an emotional, standing-room-only press conference, with journalists from the *New York Times*, *Washington Post*, and other major outlets in attendance. People struggling with AIDS described the pain and hardship the disease had caused them, and how grateful they were to the Clinton administration and EXIM Bank for providing relief. Most of us in the room were near tears. Ghana's ambassador to the United States, Koby A. Koomson, whom I describe above, called our program "a noble beginning."[273]

The HIV/AIDS program was controversial, and criticism came from unlikely sources. My son-in-law, Bob Seder, a scientist and leader in malaria research, worked for Anthony Fauci, a physician-scientist-immunologist who was then head of the National Institute of Allergy and Infectious Diseases. Bob arranged for the two of us to meet. During a friendly meeting, Fauci gave me an informative lecture about the international AIDS-relief landscape. "You have to understand," he said, "that AIDS is a global problem with many powerful organizations overseeing it. You'll have problems if you work outside of the system." Many organizations, I discovered that day, protected this niche in the health-care world, and when outsiders like me launched AIDS programming, the establishment expected to be consulted.

It wasn't just the international AIDS bureaucracy that felt brushed aside. Mathilde Krim, wife of Arthur Krim, a friend and chair of Orion Pictures, expressed similar sentiments. She'd been working on HIV/AIDS for nearly two decades. "Why didn't you talk to me?" she asked, explaining that she could have used her contacts to help with the program.

Others criticized the deal itself. Namibian politician and physician Kalumbi Shangula wrote an impassioned op-ed in the *Washington Post*, suggesting that EXIM's program would cause the poorest parts of Africa to become even more indebted. Commenting on his country's decision not to enter the program, Shangula said,

> If HIV drugs were a cure, many African countries would consider accepting the Ex-Im Bank offer. But given the duration of treatment required and the increasing number of AIDS patients, assuming a loan to purchase antiretroviral drugs does not make sense for developing countries, many of which are already burdened by foreign indebtedness. It does not make sense for Namibia. It would mean plunging ourselves into perpetual debt from which we would not be able to extricate ourselves.[274]

Others echoed Shangula's sentiments, suggesting that countries should have had hospitals and pharmaceuticals provided not as a loan with interest, but as part of an aid package. Commenting on the program, Joelle Tanguy, executive director of Doctors Without Borders said, "In my mind, grants—not loans—would have made much more sense."[275]

After launching the program, I'd anticipated strong competition to lower drug prices in the region. "I would call it a drug war in the best interest of the recipient," I said at the time.[276] But in addressing the criticism of adding to African debt and calling on more donors, I still looked to the balance sheet and felt justified.[277] Global aid organizations donated $300 million annually to the fight, while according to the United Nations, $3 billion was necessary for prevention and treatment efforts, not including the price of pharmaceutical drugs.[278] I knew the mood in Congress, and it didn't favor international aid; other aid-based agencies, like USAID, couldn't accommodate several extra billions in their budgets for drugs. With this epidemic raging, all I could see was a resource gap that I wanted in some part to address, whether it came in aid or loans.

Because the loan was tied to hospital construction, and African nations built only three to four new hospitals a year, the program didn't have extensive reach. And because I launched it during my last year in office and hadn't properly consulted with the AIDS establishment, it didn't continue after my departure. But the program increased international awareness to stem the tide of this scourge. Calling on sister export agencies to join, just as I had during the Asian crisis, I increased visibility in the international community and helped save lives in the process.[279]

I later embraced the term of "mission creep," applied to my leadership at EXIM after I launched this pharmaceutical program, as a badge of honor.

But the first time the phrase arose, I tried hard to deflect. David Carter, EXIM's vice president for media, conducted public relations work at the bank, trying to bolster EXIM's brand among the press. Carter arranged for me to visit the *New York Times*'s towering offices on Forty-Second Street one day in the late 1990s, and I remember sitting in a bleak and windowless conference room with several of my colleagues. Over the course of describing the programs and initiatives underway at the bank and my larger objectives as EXIM chair, one journalist turned to me and said, "This is true mission creep. This bank is headed toward becoming an aid agency."

This was the first evocation of the term "mission creep," and it caught me off guard. The man hadn't suggested this referring to my work in South Korea, the Philippines, central Asia, Latin America, or even the Tyumen Oil deal in Russia. He referred to my work in Africa, especially my spearheading of the AIDS initiative. His description was apt, as my sympathy for these countries had motivated my African mission. But I had to deny this label, as it would be disastrous for EXIM Bank to appear as an aid organization on the Hill and larger press. If I let this get out, EXIM might not survive its next reauthorization.

I therefore redirected the conversation, underlining how I occupied the nonpolicy, commercial side of government and recommended deals based only on their creditworthiness, with a view toward bolstering the US business community. To underscore my point, I told the journalist that if he examined the percentage of our losses compared to our overall disbursements, we were at 1–2 percent, better than many financial organizations in the private sector.

But in many ways, I consider mission creep a moot point. Bolstering US jobs through supporting exports—my mission at EXIM—created positive multiplier effects, including growing the private sectors of developing and frontier economies, increasing national security across the globe by averting the allure of extremism, helping to rectify gender imbalances, and achieving a host of humanitarian objectives like improving the lives of Africans dealing with a deadly disease like HIV/AIDS. My humanitarian inclinations and sympathy were beside the point, especially when, unlike an aid organization, I was beholden to the American taxpayer and the larger business community and could show great financial returns for both constituencies. By the time I left government, EXIM loan guarantees roughly matched African development assistance, making the two much more in harmony than at odds.[280] EXIM's ability to create these financial and non-financial returns underscored my belief that private sector growth is key to prosperity and democracy, and it's this philosophy that I would later bring to my work in Egypt.

EXIM proved especially successful in its work throughout the Sub-Saharan region and among SMEs, both areas of my strategic focus with Africa. My strategy of opening up Sub-Saharan countries with short-term loans and then gradually advancing them to longer-term ones worked profitably for the next two decades at EXIM.[281] After introducing the rand currency program, South African businesses did much larger trade volumes, and we began occupying the coveted niche of securing loans to SMEs. In 1999, EXIM was proud to announce its first large transaction with Namibia in the bank's history, helping its airlines modernize and expand throughout Africa and Europe by guaranteeing a Boeing deal for approximately $100 million.[282] And despite the economic crisis that Robert Mugabe inflicted on his country, we still forged deals with the Zimbabwean business community. In particular, we helped a small Dallas-based internet and telecommunications company expand into the country, increasing the US telecom and digital presence in Zimbabwe and the larger region.[283]

Many critics suggested that even as we created important new markets, EXIM's portfolio leaned heavily toward aircraft and large oil and gas projects. Many countries in Sub-Saharan Africa were transforming from agrarian, commodities-based economies to stable, self-sustaining industrial economies. To assist in this process, EXIM guaranteed many aerospace deals. While some of them went to leaders of countries, other deals, like EXIM's approximate $5 million guarantee of Cessna aircraft to Zambia, went to help doctors and health-care workers reach remote parts of the country.[284]

But critics still called us "Boeing's Bank" because this company represented roughly 40 percent of all the exports we supported. This was perhaps the most unfair criticism leveled at EXIM.

When I began in government, I was astonished to learn that Boeing had thousands of subsuppliers in every US state. When you conduct business with Boeing, you aren't so much working with a major multinational as working with the thousands of small businesses that subcontract with Boeing. These small companies are invaluable to countless communities across the country. Without Boeing securing large deals and winning the business necessary to build planes, the US manufacturing sector and national economy would suffer.[285] And absent this "Boeing small business program," we would lose international market share to formidable European rival Airbus and begin to trail China, our foremost global rival. As long as our competitors subsidize their own exports, agencies like EXIM must level the playing field to keep America competitive.

My mission to bolster private sector growth always prioritized SMEs. Though I was proud of the major pipeline projects and the Keta seawall, I was equally pleased to announce smaller deals we did in Kenya and South Africa, in some cases guaranteeing loans as modest as $250.[286] It's also why I proactively sought out small businesses, like when I asked my team to stall the car so we could investigate the entrepreneurs in Ghana angling in the surf. Through transactions like these, large and small, we increased our trade volumes in Sub-Saharan African tenfold over my tenure.[287]

My time in Africa formed a small part of the US-led success story on the continent.[288] In 2000, at the conclusion of my tenure at EXIM, Congress passed the African Growth and Opportunity Act (AGOA), which EXIM Bank personnel helped to draft. This legislation addressed President Clinton's call to create a new Africa by eliminating tariffs, quotas, and other barriers on 1,800 items.[289] This legislation created jobs and sent investors into Africa, with Ugandan president Museveni suggesting a few years later it was one of the West's best acts toward Africa following independence.[290]

This legislation was in the spirit of my work at EXIM, stimulating business creation abroad while helping US exporters. As always, this important work rested on relationship building. Some relationships were a sincere pleasure, like with Ghana's minister of finance, a fellow banker with whom I had an easy rapport, and President Obasanjo, who aspired to create a stable, long-lasting democracy in Nigeria. Others proved more difficult. In South Africa I didn't find the warm welcome I had anticipated following US solidarity through the apartheid era, and in Zimbabwe, President Mugabe shunned me for being American. Other relationships I mismanaged. In my zeal to address the AIDS epidemic, I failed to consult important friends and stakeholders, something that ultimately curtailed the power and reach of the Sub-Saharan AIDS pharmaceutical program. Despite my own missteps and the suspicion of American help among certain heads of state, African businesses and nonprofits universally welcomed us. It was these diverse relationships—spanning the women angling on the beach in Ghana to the South African SMEs who benefited from the rand exchange program—that cemented preexisting commercial alliances across Sub-Saharan Africa and increased our business penetration in new markets.

We made significant commercial progress in four years. When I arrived at EXIM Bank, the country did business in thirteen African countries, and when I left, we were open in all countries for traditional finance, and all countries, save one, for project finance.[291] When I began at EXIM, the bank supported $40 million in exports to all of Africa. When I left, we did over $1 billion in Sub-Saharan Africa alone! This expansion in markets and trade volumes proved important in helping these countries to participate in the global economy, all the while bolstering American business.[292] Even with what many deemed a risky exposure in the Sub-Saharan market, our losses throughout the continent still held steady at around 2 percent, the same margin as in Asia.

When it came to Africa, EXIM took some of its greatest financial risks and achieved some its best financial and humanitarian returns on investment. It was also the most gratifying work I undertook. Unlike my having to wrangle with the White House and BP lobbyists over Tyumen, or address financial crises in Asia, my time in Africa was simply welcoming, and I approached it with a genuine desire to help. But as I completed these transactions, the end of my time at EXIM drew near, and I encountered a major interpersonal problem, to which I now turn. But though I'd depart EXIM Bank under a small cloud of controversy, nothing could overshadow my legacy at EXIM, of which Africa represented the crown jewel.

12

My Third Big Mistake

ON SEPTEMBER 13, 1998, Doug Sosnik, a senior political advisor to President Clinton and close acquaintance, gave me a heads-up. President and First Lady Clinton were flying to New York the following day and wanted me to join them. The President was delivering a speech to the Council on Foreign Relations that focused on the global financial crises afflicting Asia, Russia, Latin America, and elsewhere, and he wanted my input on his remarks.[293]

Normally, one of the President's secretaries would have called me three to four days in advance of such trips. But I agreed to go on short notice, and my driver Joe picked me up at the Jefferson Hotel extra early the following morning so we could arrive at Andrews Air Force Base in time for Air Force One's departure at ten o'clock. Unfortunately, our car broke down on the side of the road. I promptly hailed a taxicab. "I've got to hurry to Andrews Air Force Base because I'm flying with the President," I told the driver, who looked at me with a smile of disbelief. Apparently, he didn't believe that the guy with a broken-down car would soon be wheel's up with the President.

The taxi somehow got to Andrews before takeoff, and I stepped onto the tarmac only to discover that the plane, typically full of press and other cabinet members, was entirely vacant, except for Bill, Hillary, and a handful of staff and airline crew. The tension in the cabin was palpable. Hillary had defended her husband the entire year, calling charges against him a "vast right-wing conspiracy" and predicting that they would "slowly dissipate over time under the weight of [their] own insubstantiality." But Kenneth Starr's impeachment investigation against the President had now taken a devastating turn. Presidential intern Monica Lewinsky had at this point testified twice before a grand jury, and just days before our flight, the House Judiciary Committee received the infamous Starr Report.[294]

I tried to discreetly navigate to the back of the plane, hoping to bide my flight time inconspicuously reading reports and news articles. But just after takeoff, a White House staff member approached me and said, "The President would like to review his speech with you." I made my way to the President's airborne office, greeted Bill and Hillary, and sat down midway in the office, between Clinton at his desk, and Hillary, seated on the far end of a couch. They both looked sleep-deprived, exhausted, and wounded.

I was stuck in this difficult personal moment. Part of the speech involved EXIM's work in Asia, and I tried to focus on assisting with that, framing the President's language about the administration's response to the financial crisis. The industrialized world, the President wanted to convey, had a moral responsibility to strengthen struggling countries. And although US-led efforts had helped curtail the economic devastation in Asia and Russia, much of the developing world was still reeling, having plummeted from the middle class to poverty in a matter of months.[295] Crafting such language was normally a joy, but this flight was uncomfortable and awkward.

After landing in New York, the Clintons and I boarded a limousine motorcade to the Council on Foreign Relations at Sixty-Eighth Street, just off Park Avenue. But both sat on opposites sides of the car next to a window so they could greet the crowds, and I was in the middle.

After hearing the President's stirring and motivating speech about American leadership and economic renewal, I headed directly to my New York apartment. Jane greeted me as I walked in, saying, "I'm so glad you're here. I need you to take out the garbage and clean up because we have company tonight." As I was emptying the trash and engaging in last-minute tidying, I thought about how odd the day had been. When you are young and imagine that one day you'll ride with the president and the first lady on Air Force One and accompany them in a limo through crowds of people in New York City, you probably don't envisage my experience that day. And you probably don't think you'll return home at the end to clean the house!

President Clinton accomplished a great deal in office by creating a powerful economy, achieving foreign policy milestones in Africa, and securing the ratification of the General Agreement on Tariffs and Trade (GATT, now the WTO) and the North American Free Trade Agreement (NAFTA). Unfortunately, the Lewinsky affair broke in his second term, and he left office under a cloud.

Like Clinton, I exited my office under a small cloud of my own. As I transitioned out of government in 2001, EXIM Bank was in good financial shape, morale was high, and I'd expanded the market for US exports in Asia, Russia, and Sub-Saharan Africa.[296] With the staff and I having achieved so much, it was unfortunate that my experience ended with a typical Washington episode that I describe in this chapter. Though I regret the way that I managed the situation, it did not cast a negative shadow over my time at EXIM. In fact, I left government in June 2001 grateful for the experience and confident that I would eventually return for an even more important mission.

CROSSING SWORDS WITH A SENATOR'S SPOUSE

My drama at EXIM centered on my vice chair. As I've described, a White House official broached the topic of her serving in this role before my nomination (chapter 8). "The person that the White House is considering is quite controversial," they'd told me at the time, tactfully alerting me to a potential problem. The last two EXIM chairs had also cautioned me about Jackie Clegg.[297] Instead of heeding their collective wisdom, I thought that a young woman with strong Senate experience and a close relationship with Senator Dodd could be helpful. Senator Dodd and I had developed a friendship and we enjoyed playing golf together.

As I've described, Jackie was helpful in the confirmation proceedings both with her guidance and because it was apparent that none of the senators conducting the hearing wanted to cause difficulty for Senator Dodd's companion. My chief of staff and I then worked the Hill for the next few months, touting the benefits of the bank so we could secure its congressional reauthorization.

My first three years with Jackie passed mostly without incident. After dating for several years and after cinching a fourth term, Christopher Dodd wed Jackie Clegg on June 18, 1999, in a small ceremony at the groom's home in East Haddam, Connecticut.[298] I later hosted a party at the Jefferson Hotel in celebration of their marriage.

I was aware that Jackie wasn't beloved among some of the EXIM staff, to use a British understatement, but we had a workable relationship. I relied on her intelligence and experience in all matters on the Hill and, busy with my work, didn't devote much time to managing her. In hindsight, that made me a good public servant but a bad politician and manager. In addition to giving her prestige assignments, like reopening EXIM's operations in Vietnam, I also routinely consulted her on matters involving Congress.

When board director and EXIM stalwart Julie Belaga announced her retirement in 1999, I was sad to see her go. Throughout her tenure as COO and director, Julie had demonstrated excellent interpersonal skills and managerial acumen. She'd deftly managed any disputes that arose and maintained reasonably good morale among the staff. Jackie asked to fill the COO position several times but many at the bank expressed reservations. After all, in smaller agencies like EXIM, the chair often assumed the duties, if not the title, of COO. In light of this custom, as well as Jackie's lack of management experience, some suggested that I give her the title of COO but retain the responsibilities for myself. Once again, I chose not to heed this advice, selecting Jackie to occupy the vacant COO position in title and responsibility. In hindsight, this was an error in judgement.

The frequency of the conflicts with the vice chair increased after the COO appointment. On numerous occasions I heard of conflicts she had with different departments, and she also began subtly undermining my efforts. Many at the bank believed that she had notified *Washington Post* reporter Al Kamen about the private plane I chartered for the October 1999 trip to Africa because of a personal dispute she had with Gloria Cabe, a thoughtful, experienced advisor on my staff whom Jackie strongly disliked. Jackie was unable to build relationships with a number of key officers in the bank, and I was unable to reconcile the differences she had with them. The tension and the drama were impacting the entire organization.

A later meeting with Jackie proved unproductive and disagreeable. I then decided to assume the title and responsibilities of COO.

My actions caused a firestorm. White House personnel and members of the Hill inundated me with calls, demanding that I rescind my decision about the COO position and make peace with Senator Dodd's wife. The White House chief of staff called me twice, and despite his confrontational tone, I tried reasoning with him, detailing the violations. "I don't care if she murdered someone," he replied. "Chris Dodd is essential to our campaign, and if you care about the election, you'll reinstate her immediately." The commerce secretary called my counselor Clyde Robinson and said, "Tell your boss that he just bought a one-way ticket to New York."

At the end of September, I attended an event at the home of West Virginia senator Jay Rockefeller. There I met Andrew Cuomo, secretary of housing and urban development (HUD), Jack Quinn, former White House general counsel, and Tom Downing, a former Virginia congressman. They all proved helpful. After discussing the situation, Andrew hosted a lunch for me and Jackie a few days later and offered her the position of assistant secretary in his department. Jackie, I discovered at the lunch, had no interest in joining HUD, and instead wanted EXIM's chief technology officer (CTO) title, in addition to vice chair, along with a formal email announcing her new positions to the bank.

Though I wanted to conclude this drama as swiftly as possible, I thought that assigning the CTO role to Jackie would have made a mockery of the bank and this important function. It also would have generated problems for the bank's incumbent CTO and created confusion among the staff. After more wrangling and further pressure from the White House, I agreed to make Jackie chief of the technology committee, on the condition that she provide weekly status updates to me. Jackie accepted the offer, which I formally announced throughout the bank.

At the time, I was annoyed at myself for allowing such interpersonal drama to blemish my legacy at the bank. But I also felt I had a responsibility to the bank and its employees to do the right thing. My relationship with Jackie continued to deteriorate and became intolerable. We were unable to resolve our differences. She left the bank and did not return. I fault myself for failing to build a stronger relationship with her during the first three years. It is important to add that the system itself was at fault. Allowing a senator to have oversight of an agency where his or her relative is working in a senior capacity is a serious conflict of interest.

But I still assume ultimate responsibility for this matter. I made mistakes throughout the process, beginning with White House warnings about making her vice chair, as well as others' reservations about promoting her to COO. Over the course of my four years with Jackie, I should have done a better job mentoring her.

On November 7, 2000, a few months after this fiasco, Al Gore lost the election to Republican George W. Bush, the governor of Texas and eldest son of the forty-first US president, George H.W. Bush.[299] I prepared to resign my post, as all agency heads customarily did after administrative turnover. That December, Vice President-elect Dick Cheney called me to discuss this matter, mentioning that before the new administration could appoint my replacement, my vice chair Jackie Clegg would serve as interim chair. "That would be a big mistake," I told Cheney, briefly explaining how she'd been absent from the bank and that her assuming leadership would cause an uproar among the staff.

At the time of Cheney's call, I was on my way to Anguilla to celebrate the winter holidays and put the episode out of my mind. My first night in Anguilla, however, as I was relaxing on the beach, my wife came to tell me that Vice President-elect Cheney had called for me again. "I'd rather talk to him tomorrow," I said. Jane thought that I should take the call, but reluctantly told him I wasn't available. Early the next morning, Cheney called me from Wyoming.

"After lengthy discussion with the President, we'd like you to continue serving," Cheney told me. "I have an ideal position for you overseeing EXIM and OPIC and a variety of other commercial organizations in government." The incoming team needed someone from the prior administration, he said, and I was just the man. When I told him I'd consider it, he responded by saying that at the very least, I had to continue serving as chair until the confirmation of my successor. He'd done some investigations on his own and didn't think Jackie should assume leadership of the bank.

I agreed to consider Cheney's offer. If I were really looking to continue my career in Washington, I would have accepted Rahm Emanuel's suggestion that I become deputy to Larry Summers at Treasury. But I now longed to do something new that would allow me to continue to make a difference in the developing world.

In agreeing to remain as chair for an additional six months of the Bush administration, I violated a long-standing rule from the private sector: never stay after a hostile takeover. Though I had good relationships with Cheney and Secretary of State Colin Powell, I accomplished very little in the months ahead.

Nearly every time I attended a meeting, I overheard people saying, "Here comes the Clinton guy," and then smile and laugh. Some even said it to my face. "You know, guys, I really don't think EXIM Bank or any of the work I do here is political," I responded. The new crowd nodded in agreement, but they still didn't want to do business with the "Clinton guy." Many senior staff and agency heads have documented how difficult their working environments can be when they remain in office after a turnover.

In my final few months, Vice President Cheney asked me to meet with

Mel Sembler, someone the new administration had tapped for my replacement. Mel had been a prominent Republican fundraiser for decades and would later serve as ambassador to Italy. We met soon thereafter, and as I showed Mel around the offices, I found him to be a personable man with a great sense of humor. "I only have two questions for you," he said. "First, do people stand when you enter a room?"

"No one has ever stood for me in this job or any other time in my life," I responded.

"Second," he said, "could I work three days a week in Washington and spend the rest of my time in Florida?" I told him I worked twelve-plus-hour days, seven days a week, and still felt behind. Perhaps he was more efficient than me, but I couldn't imagine doing this job effectively any other way. He thanked me heartily for my candor and left.

About forty-five minutes later, Cheney called me and said, "Jim, what did you say? I can't believe he just turned down the position!" It all worked out, because the administration tapped Mel as the new US ambassador to Italy, and appointed former pharmaceutical executive John Robson, an eminently capable leader, to serve as EXIM chair.

THE EXIM LEARNING CURVE

I officially departed government in June 2001 feeling grateful. Whether I was working in the beautiful EXIM offices or traveling to one of the seventy-plus countries I visited during my tenure, I found my work as chair to be intellectually challenging and meaningful. With my daughter and son-in-law, and two of my grandchildren living nearby, I also enjoyed my time in Washington.

I left the bank having accomplished my larger goals. When I arrived at EXIM, I was surprised to discover that nearly 70 percent of transactions went to government-owned enterprises, with only 30 percent reserved for the private sector. I was determined to reverse this. Following the disintegration of the USSR and the debt crises of the 1980s, governments

MY THIRD BIG MISTAKE

worldwide ceded their sovereign ownership of power plants, airlines, mining concessions, and the like to their private sectors.[300] By the time I departed, EXIM reflected these trends in global privatization with 70 percent of our funding allocated to the private sector, and only 30 percent for exports to government-owned enterprises. In accomplishing this substantial redirection of capital, our losses stayed roughly the same. Other export agencies throughout Europe and Asia have followed this trend, gravitating to more private sector loans and guarantees. Given my career commitment to the development of the private sector, this represents one of my proudest accomplishments at EXIM. To maintain their importance in future generations, I believe EXIM should consider privatizing some of its activities like the European and Japanese export credit agencies.

At EXIM, I learned that export credit agencies, little known except among trade finance groups, can accomplish outsize feats in the world. When I convened the G7 export credit agencies to help with the Asian financial crisis and when I negotiated with big pharma companies to lower their drug prices for those suffering with HIV/AIDS, I learned how powerful American-led influence could be. With engaged leadership and workforces, along with a spirit of cooperation and multilateralism, small agencies can make outsize impacts.

This lesson is important for young people considering government service. You don't have to serve as secretary of state or president to make a difference. In fact, it's harder to make a difference in large departments and agencies, with their multiple layers of bureaucracy and their close scrutiny by Congress. At EXIM, my colleagues and I made global decisions on our own authority. If you work hard, stay focused, and use a bit of imagination, smaller and lesser-known governmental agencies and departments are ideal places to forge change in the world.

More experienced people can make a significant difference. One of the reasons I exercised bold leadership at EXIM and indulged in mission creep was because I'd already had a fulfilling career in the private sector and wasn't concerned about status, jockeying for positions, and ascending the public service hierarchy. If I had been thirty-five or forty, I would have been too preoccupied about my career to have made such gutsy decisions. But in my sixties, I cared principally about the mission. As I've frequently said, it's constructive to appoint older, private sector alumni to government, because they often aren't beholden to voter blocs or money and will therefore do the right thing.

Some will inevitably find strong leadership uncomfortable, especially in Washington. When I first arrived at the bank, I asked a friend for advice about how to thrive in my new setting. "You'll know you've been successful if, when you leave, nobody knows who you are," he replied.[301] Washington, according to journalist David Ignatius, was a "play-it-safe town." My principled stances in favor of the Tyumen and HIV/AIDS transactions reveal that I didn't take my friend's well-meaning advice. And for that I received criticism.

Many remained unhappy about the pace of change at EXIM during my tenure. As *Project Finance* magazine pointedly stated it, "No-one at Ex-Im is willing to comment on such a radical departure from past mission method. But Ex-Im is already unrecognisable from the conservative institution of the mid-1990s."[302] I couldn't disagree with these observations entirely because my motivations, especially in Africa, were partly humanitarian. I wanted to improve African hospital and clinic facilities as well as help stem the tide of AIDS sweeping the continent.

Criticism for my efforts was matched with approval as well, including from the capable and talented diplomat Susan Rice, who became a friend of mine in government. "I don't understand how you brought this agency back to life," she said. "EXIM has a pulse!"

And I wanted to ensure that the pulse continued beating. In January 2017, just before President-elect Trump assumed office, his son-in-law Jared Kushner called me. "Should we keep the EXIM Bank or not?" he asked.

"If you want to compete against the Chinese," I responded. Though I knew this would play well—the Trump administration would express concerns about Chinese competition—it was also an honest answer. In my third or fourth year at EXIM, I recounted to Kushner, China's export credit agency had contacted me. They'd followed my work on the Asian crisis and wanted to send some of their personnel to shadow our staff and learn more about how we operated. I initially welcomed the idea before asking about logistics. To my shock, Beijing wanted to send forty people, almost 10 percent of our staff. The Hill and White House were appalled, and I had to decline the offer.

But even without shadowing EXIM in person, China had observed us from afar, and since the time of my tenure at EXIM, had captured significant market share in the developing and frontier worlds, where they continue to make strong inroads with financing programs. At the time the Chinese approached me, EXIM Bank supported $14–15 billion in US exports, while the Chinese supported around $1–2 billion. In the ensuing decade, the Chinese surpassed us, supporting hundreds of billions compared to our $15 billion. If we don't meet the challenge of China, I told Kushner, we'll lose an enormous geopolitical battle. I learned that to his credit, Kushner spoke with the President, and the administration decided to support the bank, appointing Kimberly A. Reed, a talented attorney with experience at the Treasury Department, as chair.

Though gratified that EXIM continued to exist, I longed to leave Washington after the "hostile takeover" in 2000 and return to New York. I joined the board of Rothschild Bank in Paris and rejoined Questar's (formerly Mountain Fuel Supply) board.

A year later, on a beautiful morning in September, I'll never forget having breakfast at the Rainbow Room atop Rockefeller Center, discussing my thoughts about a career transition with Dan Zelikow. Dan had served as one of Bob Rubin's deputies at the Treasury Department when I was at EXIM, and he'd become a good friend who would later work with me in Egypt.

As we enjoyed our meals and the panoramic view of the city, I saw Dan's face blanch. He'd seen a plane collide with one of the World Trade Center towers. We could barely take in the surreal moment before personnel from Rockefeller Center escorted us down the stairs and out of the building, having disabled the elevators as a precaution. Only when I returned to my office and turned on the television could I see the magnitude of the disaster. I'll never forget the horrific sight of people jumping to their deaths from the upper floors of the towers, preferring to die upon impact rather than burn alive. And I'll never forget the heroism of the city's fire and police departments, losing their lives to save those trapped in the smoldering towers.

To my surprise, the chair of Germany's export credit agency called me that day, making sure my family and I were unharmed and expressing their sadness and astonishment that terrorists had struck New York. The gesture reminded me how we can overcome tragedy only with the help and support of community. After I hung up the phone with these former colleagues who were now friends, my mind returned to when I was six years old and saw my dad appalled to hear on the radio in our living room that the Japanese had attacked Pearl Harbor, killing more than 2,300 American servicemen and civilians.

As I continued exploring different career possibilities in the coming years, I was especially interested in using my government experience to help developing countries. In October 2004, I joined David Halpert, a gifted young portfolio manager at Prince Street Capital, to invest in frontier and emerging markets. The Caravel Fund began with only a handful of employees, including a portfolio manager, analyst, and chief financial officer, and a slim volume of funds from family and friends.

Though circumstances looked inauspicious in 2004—with oil prices at record highs, short-term interest rates rising, and geopolitical risks worsening—I found that global investors were looking beyond such cyclical risks to a longer-term growth story unfolding in many emerging markets. With a diverse group of experienced specialists, including Katiana Guzman MacNabb, Caglar Somek, Jamie Odell, Beidi Gu, and, later, Kareen Laton,

Caravel invested in many of the countries with which I'd become familiar at EXIM, while also exploring new markets like Rwanda and Pakistan.

One summer evening in July 2007, as I enjoyed a pleasant evening on the porch with my son, Doug, I began to realize that difficult times lay ahead. "Have you been following what's going on in these high-risk, secondary mortgage markets?" he asked me. I'd always felt a professional kinship with Doug. Doug and I were both advisors at heart. Doug has a very successful career and—because he served as an investment banker for the real estate industry—was highly knowledgeable about the mortgage market. Like many in the financial investment banking sector, I tended to focus on the corporate world and wasn't as well versed in real estate and securitization. I grew increasingly alarmed as Doug told me about his recent surveys of the markets and how he had seen institutions grant high-risk mortgages to nearly anyone. Negative leverage was creeping into the US financial system. "We're headed for some serious trouble," Doug said, using the metaphor of a swelling balloon ready to burst, and it could have a huge impact on the stock and bond markets.

I began to understand how prescient Doug was a few weeks later in Florida, when I struck up a conversation with my mother's housekeeper. I'd walked into Mom's condo to find her housekeeper, always in good spirits, positively beaming. When I asked why she was so happy, she told me that she was a homeowner. She had secured a 100 percent loan to purchase a home, and many of her friends, all immigrants from Jamaica, had done the same. They never thought they would qualify as homeowners and were elated. I was thrilled for her, but worried about major US financial institutions offering loans without any equity investment. Of course, just as Doug predicted, these subprime mortgages created a global catastrophe. The US housing market collapsed, major financial institutions like Lehman Brothers shuttered their doors, and the Great Recession (2007–09), the worst downturn since 1929, devastated the global economy and threatened to upend financial markets.[303]

In its thirteen years of existence, this was probably Caravel's greatest setback. But we rebounded and continued to invest for nearly a decade more, until I became preoccupied with other pursuits and, seeing looming market declines on the financial horizons, made the difficult decision to return money to investors. Thanks to the fund's CFO Joe Rivera and Margaret Engelhardt, who had risen to partner and chief administrative officer, we closed the fund and returned money to investors on May 31, 2017.

Over the course of its life, Caravel's funds grew to over $800 million and generated a cumulative net return of 243.7 percent. More important, the fund also helped demonstrate that capital flows to developing countries can result in more efficient markets and democratic reforms. Since beginning the journey with Caravel, we've seen considerable progress across many of the countries in Caravel's investment universe, including but not limited to Bangladesh, Georgia, Indonesia, Kenya, Mexico, Peru, the Philippines, Poland, Sri Lanka, and Vietnam. The future of the global economy as well as world peace depend on continued investments to the frontier and developing world.

My time in Washington and the continuation of the work at Caravel proved energizing and deeply rewarding. I loved traveling the world and doing good by the US taxpayer and international investors, all the while bolstering the private sectors of developing countries. I also continued to nurture my connections on the Hill, developing strong relationships with members of the House and Senate who were interested in the Middle East and Egypt, where I would eventually specialize when I returned to public service. But I was also intent on branching out of the public and private sectors alike. In 2004, I began my journey with a nonprofit called the World Resources Institute, the subject of the next chapter. My time in government had heightened my awareness about the perils of climate change, and the time I would devote in the coming decade and more to doing environmental work gave me enormous gratification and fulfillment. The best investment we can make is an investment in the environment.

13

Decarbonizing the World

IN 2020, AS I WROTE this book, the world celebrated a milestone in environmental philanthropy. Amazon founder and CEO Jeff Bezos created a $10 billion Earth Fund, the largest climate-change initiative in history, promising to allocate funds to any activist, nonprofit, scientist, or NGO that could help combat climate change.[304]

The World Resources Institute (WRI), an environmental nonprofit where I have served as chair since 2004, submitted two brief proposals for Jeff Bezos and his partner Lauren Sánchez to consider.[305] If allocated money from the Earth Fund, WRI proposed two major initiatives: first, Climate Watch, a satellite-based system to monitor all land-based carbon emissions across the world and, second, a program to electrify all of America's school buses by 2030.[306] I wasn't optimistic about our odds because no WRI board member or officer had any special relationship with Amazon or Bezos himself.

We were thus gratified and surprised when Bezos named WRI one of its first five $100 million Earth Fund recipients. Bezos immediately disbursed the funds in the form of Amazon shares, and within thirty days of the announcement, we had sold the stock and had an extra $100 million in our coffers. In all my years in fundraising, I have never seen capital disbursed this quickly. In the often dreary and sad march toward environmental sustainability, this windfall marked a rare moment of optimism and joy. Perhaps tech billionaires like Jeff Bezos could help overcome the most difficult and intractable problem facing humanity: climate change.

As news of the grant energized the rank and file of WRI, I reflected on what a milestone this represented for the organization. When I arrived at WRI in 2001, it had 120 full-time staff on the payroll and a $20 million annual budget. I often scrambled for months to secure $25,000 grants to fund our basic programs. Two decades later, we could now attract the attention of the wealthiest man in the world, who in two-and-a-half months' time had given us the funds and heightened visibility to empower and expand our mission: to keep the planet habitable for current and future generations.

The grant also validated my general approach to leadership at WRI, focusing on developing and enhancing our relationship with the private sector. As an investment banker and public servant, I've always strived to grow the private sector, as I strongly believe it is a linchpin of democracy, freedom, and prosperity. But that doesn't mean that governments aren't also vital, especially when addressing global crises like climate change. That's one of the reasons I embarked on my environmental work in government, as I describe in this chapter, and then continued it at WRI, a nonprofit institute.

To the anxiety and chagrin of some of my colleagues at WRI, however, I routinely met with oil, gas, and real-estate company executives, actively courting private sector captains of industry to our board. Since the heyday of the environmental movement in the 1970s, relationships between environmental advocacy and the larger corporate world have been strained. During my twenty-year journey of leadership at WRI, working to expand the power and reach of this leading environmental organization, I've focused on attracting a diverse range of stakeholders to sustainability. We need everyone's help to create a sustainable, postcarbon world.

COMING TO CLIMATE CONSCIOUSNESS

My journey with environmental advocacy, which ultimately led me to WRI, started at the beginning of my tenure at EXIM. In 1995, EXIM adopted environmental guidelines for each of its finance projects. Since the passage of these rules, the bank has scrutinized the environmental impacts and social risks that each project proposal entails. When submissions prove creditworthy but adversely affect air quality, water safety, waste management, or the involuntary resettlements of people, EXIM declines financing for the project.[307]

A few months before I became chair of the bank, EXIM's board declined to support China's Three Gorges Dam, the largest dam and electrical generation project in world history. It was a sensitive decision. Chinese leaders attached symbolic and ideological importance to this project. "Blocking the Yangtze is a great moment in the modernization of our country," said President Jiang Zemin, who'd recently taken power after the death of Deng Xiaoping in February 1997. "It vividly proves once again that socialism is superior in organizing people to do big jobs."[308]

But while Chinese authorities celebrated the dam as the greatest engineering marvel since the Great Wall, Vice President Gore along with other government officials joined a host of environmental groups in expressing concern about the project's environmental impact.[309] In addition to compromising cultural heritage sites, the dam created silt drainage problems, sewage contamination concerns, and involved the hasty resettlement of many inhabitants.[310]

EXIM's decision to decline support for the project angered the Chinese, as well as US manufacturers who lost business to our more environmentally lax foreign competitors. Jim Owens, the future chair and CEO of Caterpillar, the world's largest construction and mining equipment manufacturer, called me directly to appeal the decision. "I know your history as an investment banker," Owens told me in his low voice, "and I'm surprised by this," he added in his characteristically cool manner. I sympathized with Owens. He'd devoted a large part of his career to relationship building with Chinese bureaucrats precisely so he could secure a massive deal like this.[311] On the call, Owens described his efforts and how many jobs this decision would cost American companies.

There was also blowback on the Hill. Early in my tenure, two senators representing the states of the disgruntled exporters who'd wanted to participate in the dam project, met me in the corridors of the Dirksen Senate Office Building. They'd just emerged from a hearing and people busily walked by in both directions. In a rather aggressive manner, both senators scolded me about negatively impacting the American worker. I had one year to persuade the other six members of the G7 to adopt similar environmental guidelines. Without G7 buy-in on EXIM guidelines, they threatened, they would amend the bank's charter and eliminate the guidelines themselves. Having been at the bank for only a few months, I needed way more time to resolve a crisis like this. "We don't care how you do it. Just make it happen."

I believed strongly in the importance of these environmental guidelines, so I initiated an international lobbying effort to harmonize environmental standards across the G7. In the first meeting of G7 export credit agencies, convened in my Washington office several months after my meeting with the senators, I encouraged my international counterparts to join EXIM in supporting only those projects found to be sustainable—environmentally and socially. "If we keep polluting the world," I said rather dramatically, "my grandchildren are going to suffer." The CIA later intercepted the French ministry's reactions to my emotional plea, and I remember phrases describing me as "kind of a nut" and even "environmental kook." All of the countries voted against me, six to one, declining the adoption of environmental guidelines.

I continued the struggle. "When other countries preach green but subsidize dirty," I said in an op-ed to the *Washington Post*, "we all lose."[312] Alaska senator Frank Murkowski wasn't convinced and in a rebuttal op-ed expressed his anger that EXIM had declined the Chinese megaproject, dismissing the bank's concerns as "feel-good environmentalism."[313] As EXIM had declined support for the megaproject, he insisted, our fellow G7 allies had cheerfully taken it on, hurting US exporters.

To assist in this environmental effort, I began drawing on the many NGOs and nonprofits that populated the nation's capital. After my long career in investment banking, traveling the world and meeting with diverse clients, I felt prepared to do financial work in the public sector. But NGOs play a much larger role in Washington than in the private sector, and I had no background on or preparation in dealing with them. I had initially imagined environmental nonprofits as thoughtful, gentle, and almost academic in approach, much like think tanks that wrote papers and presented their cases in measured and scholarly ways. This was a misperception, as many of these organizations I encountered on the Hill were powerful outfits with aggressive litigation and lobbying departments.

NGOs like Greenpeace also engaged in increasingly confrontational and theatrical tactics. This was an era of ecological civil disobedience as groups staged sit-ins from trees that loggers threatened to cut, Greenpeace defaced industrial property, and the Natural Resources Defense Council (NRDC) tried to embarrass its opponents in efforts to win.[314] I'll never forget when World Bank president James Wolfensohn gave a press conference in Helsinki in March 2001, and two environmental activists smashed a pie in his face.[315] Part of this behavior stemmed from the confrontational mood in Washington, with Newt Gingrich's partisan style poisoning the larger environment. But part of this anger represented infighting among the NGO players, all competing with one another for a small number of grants and fundraising dollars. "What a pity," I remember saying to Al Gore. "There's such bright young talent in the NGO world, and they're tearing one another down."

To cultivate a less confrontational and more collaborative approach with the NGO environmental community, I began a brown-bag lunch series in 1998. To this weekly or bimonthly event, I invited representatives from the NRDC, Greenpeace, Conservation International, and the World Resources Institute to join EXIM staff for informal discussions. This gesture surprised many leaders, as did my desire for their frank assessment of the social and environmental impacts of our projects, like the bank's controversial Chad-Cameroon pipeline transaction.

Among these important environmental organizations, I especially gravitated to WRI, with which I shared an affinity in approach and philosophy. Since its incorporation in 1982, WRI had emerged as a serious, sober, and analytical organization with a capacity to execute change. It also didn't lobby or litigate, like the more aggressive and litigious NRDC, instead focusing on policy research and program implementation.[316] In performing the sector's top intellectual and analytical work in the decade since its founding, WRI garnered respect among environmental NGOs, many of whom depended on its research.

WRI's then-president Jonathan Lash, an environmental visionary of his generation, became one of my collaborators and friends. He'd led Vermont's environmental program under Governor Madeleine Kunin and at the time chaired President Bill Clinton's Council on Sustainable Development.[317] Lash's expertise and reasonable nature made him popular on the Hill and in corporate America, where he had strong relationships with industry titans like Jeff Immelt. When I consulted with him over projects like the Chad-Cameroon pipeline, he responded with moderation and understanding, instead of with the shrill statements and threats that emanated from the larger environmental landscape.

Over the course of our discussions, Lash helped mold my thoughts on the environment. When I arrived in Washington, I approached the environment in a local and short-term fashion. When negotiating projects like Tyumen Oil or considering the Three Gorges Dam, I asked whether the project might degrade a natural habitat or ecosystem. The Three Gorges Dam in China was bad, I had reasoned, because of the human resettlement and river-based harm it posed. Tyumen Oil, by contrast, was good because the companies involved used the most modern, environmentally responsible equipment available to help preserve the ecosystem in which they drilled.

But over my talks with the NGOs, and especially WRI's Lash, I began to understand environmental threats in more global ways. "Many people care about the pollution of their nearby lake or their town, but that doesn't mean they have any understanding of climate issues or global sustainability," Lash said. Within the span of a year, I became convinced that man-made carbon was the source of humanity's greatest problem.

Like many, however, I was at a loss for how to decarbonize the world. The 1992 Earth Summit in Rio de Janeiro had eased the way, convening 100 heads of state and many NGO leaders who identified the global threat of a warming planet and committed to addressing it.[318] But when I spoke to leaders in Africa, Russia, or China about the climate problem, they trained their attention on short-term environmental concerns. Completely changing national economies so that they ran on renewables instead of fossil fuels was such a staggering challenge that we made little headway in addressing it.

The climate imperative only heightened my near obsession with reaching harmonized environmental guidelines among the G7. During my tenure at EXIM, I traveled to each of my sister export credit agencies in the G7 and tried to reach consensus on the environment. Many thought I was on a bizarre campaign, but I gradually made headway. When they wouldn't adopt the guidelines in their entirety, I began by asking for more cooperation in project approval. "When a project comes in," I suggested, "let's share it with each partner and discuss its environmental impact." Gradually, we agreed to heightened transparency, committing to share information on every controversial project and discussing its environmental impacts before beginning any financing. My environmental team at EXIM, comprising my highly knowledgeable head of policy Jim Cruse and Isabel Galdiz, the bank's leading expert on export credit policy matters, reported these developments to the Senate. We assured my two worried senators that progress on standards was forthcoming and shortly after I left office, the G7's credit export agencies adopted harmonized environmental standards.

My environmental advocacy was just beginning, and shortly after I left EXIM, I joined WRI's board of directors. When I attended my first board meeting in the fall of 2001, I was humbled to see major veterans of the 1970s environmental movement present.

The organization's founder, Gus Speth, a legend in the environmental community, was a forceful presence. A Rhodes Scholar, Supreme Court clerk, and cofounder of the Natural Resources Defense Council (1970), Speth left the NRDC to serve as President Jimmy Carter's chair of the Council of Environmental Quality in 1977, before founding WRI with a $15 million MacArthur Foundation grant. Political and environmental celebrity Bill Ruckelshaus, a charismatic and good-natured environmental leader and businessman, was also present. He'd achieved acclaim as one of the heroes of the Saturday Night Massacre, refusing the orders of his boss, President Richard Nixon, to fire Watergate special prosecutor Archibald Cox. Ruckelshaus had served as the Environmental Protection Agency's administrator under Richard Nixon (1970–73), and then under Ronald Reagan (1983–85), helping to maintain the reputation of this important agency after congressional and public criticism.[319] With Speth, Ruckelshaus, and Lash, the board meeting was an intellectually engaging, almost university-like affair. But this accord also stemmed from a lack of diversity. I saw mostly older male WASPs at the table, with few women and business leaders present.

Over the following year, I found this generally friendly and academic ethos to permeate the organization. With the research prowess of a university and the policy chops of an activist organization, WRI, to paraphrase Lash, hewed more to the *New York Times* than *Mother Jones*.[320] Instead of the high turnover and internal jockeying that characterized many of its counterparts, WRI was relatively flat and steady. No one had an oversize office or ego or engaged in office politics, choosing instead to battle with industry polluters. It reminded me of serving on the board of trustees at Brown. Because my alma mater's faculty size and financial endowment were smaller than the other Ivies, it had a more cohesive and collegial feel, with less infighting and politics than Princeton, Harvard, and Yale.

But I could still detect a subtle to sometimes overt antibusiness sentiment. The WRI staff accepted me, in large part, because I came out of government and had advocated for environmental guidelines. As I'd come to experience in the coming months, the organization's deep bench of research talent was largely anti–private sector. "I don't see where I fit in," I told Lash that first year.

CAPITALIZING WRI

In the spring of 2004, Lash and Ruckelshaus visited my office in New York, asking me to play a major role in the future of the organization. When they asked me to become chair, I was both taken aback and flattered—and inclined to accept. My time in government had awakened two passions within me: working for the betterment of the developing world and improving the environment. WRI's mission—"to move human society to live in ways that protect earth's environment and its capacity to provide for the needs and aspirations of current and future generations"—seemed to fuse both of my new callings.[321] As we discussed the position that evening, I thought about my recent decision to rejoin the board of Mountain Fuel Supply (renamed Questar). Serving as chair of a leading environmental nonprofit and serving on the board of a natural gas company seemed incongruous. But like many in the country, I believed (or perhaps wanted to believe) that natural gas would serve as bridge fuel on the inevitable path to renewable energy.

Before accepting the offer, I needed to do some due diligence and relationship building. I visited six WRI directors, learning more about the history of the organization and gauging their support for my leadership. I began by driving thirty minutes from my Connecticut home to New Haven to visit Gus Speth, dean of Yale University's School of Forestry and Environmental Studies. Having spent a lot of time on campus with my father, I knew Yale almost as well as Brown. Nostalgic about the time my dad and I had shared here, I parked the car and strolled around, enjoying the beautiful day and scenes of campus life.

Gus and I enjoyed lunch at a restaurant and then sat on a campus bench together, talking about WRI and Gus's research. Having spent most of his life dedicated to environmental matters, Speth was an encyclopedia on the topic and had strong opinions. At WRI program and press events, Speth often gave what I term "parade of horrors" speeches, describing the apocalyptic and dreary future that awaited the planet if we didn't immediately change course on climate policy. He alone could match Al Gore's energy, fluency, and dramatic force when speaking about the earth, arousing sympathy in even the most adamant of climate-change deniers.

My next stop was Denis Hayes, another environmental visionary akin to Ruckelshaus. The founder of the Earth Day Network and leader of the Solar Energy Research Institute, Denis was *Time* magazine's "Hero of the Planet" in 1999. Nine years younger than me, personable and charming, Hayes met me in a relaxing setting in Seattle. I remember thinking that either he looked younger, or I just felt older. Perhaps it was just the exquisite landscape of the Pacific Northwest and his quaint office that appeared to be carved out of a barn. We discussed WRI at some length, and I'll never forget his parting words. "WRI is a great institute, so whatever you do, please don't change the culture."

As I returned from the tour and accepted the chair, I knew the organization had reached an inflection point. After these pioneers of the environmental movement that I had recently visited had helped elevate WRI in its first decade, the organization had now begun to stagnate. WRI's reach and influence had plateaued, donations sagged, and the organization's programs seemed siloed. WRI staff still felt connected to the institute's ambitious vision for the world, charging itself with protecting the capacity of the planet to sustain current and future generations, but they had trouble translating it into actionable programming.[322]

During a staff meeting, years before I arrived, Jonathan Lash did something uncharacteristically dramatic to help inculcate a more practical, results-based approach. On the floor he piled green research reports thirty inches high—studies WRI had drafted. Then he stood on top of them. "These reports are great," he said. "But wouldn't it be better if we could actually *do* something?"

I left Jonathan to continue his work in transforming this research-based advocacy organization from a think tank to more of a "think-and-do tank." He developed an approach that combined analytic excellence with partnerships to forge change. To earn the highest accolades at the organization, it was no longer sufficient to produce excellent scholarship—you had to produce excellent outcomes. The more academically inclined think tank types, doing important science, left the organization, but the activists who wanted to translate research into policy solutions and sustainable programming happily stayed.

While Lash attended to the intellectual side of sustainability, my challenge as chair was addressing the financial sustainability of the organization. My first task was ensuring that we had the budget and fundraising infrastructure to finance WRI's great projects. After reviewing the books, I saw that the budget had stayed at a flat $20 million for years. If organizations don't grow, I have always believed, they wither and eventually die. The fundraising operation, I was shocked to discover, mostly involved various program heads fundraising on behalf of their own projects. You can't run an NGO without a development office and central leadership coordinating with fundraising strategists about where to allocate funds.

Many program heads running their own successful fiefdoms under the umbrella of WRI objected to my proposed changes. Nancy Kete, for example, ran the Embarq program, which helped cities devise sustainable transport solutions. She accused me of trying to undermine her business. Imagine, I said to resisters like Kete, if the history department in an illustrious university raised all its own money but never gave anything to the university at all. It might have a world-class history program, but the university would falter. Many didn't appreciate the analogy, but we created a centralized development office nonetheless, and asked the talented environmentalist and WRI program head Liz Cook to oversee fundraising strategy.

Another key part of successful fundraising involved reinvigorating the board of directors. We needed an environmental star on the board. Many environmental groups invited Hollywood celebrities like Robert Redford, Paul Newman, or Barbra Streisand to their boards. These figures help raise money by attracting donors to galas and elevating the environmental organization's brand in popular consciousness. This was a tempting strategy, and some in the organization urged me to pursue it. Why do you think people showed up to the White House coffee klatches in 1996, they asked, and contributed to President Clinton's reelection? Because they could interact with celebrities like Bill Clinton.

With my wife's background in theater production and cinema, as well as my contacts in the motion picture industry, we could easily have secured Hollywood celebrities. But this ran counter to the spirit of this organization, and it wasn't my style. Instead, I looked for the best intellectual star in the environmental area and decided on Al Gore. Gore was a tough sell. "Every organization, like the NRDC, Environmental Defense Fund, and Nature Conservancy, has asked me to join their boards," he said. "If I join WRI, they'll all be upset. Can I be an advisor instead?"

"I need you to help revive this organization," I said. "We have some terrific people and programs, but frankly we're going nowhere, and you can help us." And then I twisted his arm. "It's just like when you called me and said that the administration needed me in government. I'm now calling you and saying that we need you at WRI." Gore agreed to join in 2006, the same year he published *An Inconvenient Truth*, a milestone in the environmental movement.

Beginning with Gore, the board had star power and became a place of real debate and even disagreement. Gore had deep passion and extensive knowledge about the environment. "Al has more knowledge of the environment than anyone I know," Bill Clinton used to say.

The organization also invited Fernando Henrique Cardoso to join the board. I'd met Cardoso, the thirty-fourth president of Brazil, while I was at EXIM. Everyone had enormous respect for him and was grateful that a former head of state who had overseen Brazilian policies on the Amazon—one of the most critically important environments in the world—had representation on the board. After him, we attracted the former prime minister of Sweden, Göran Persson, a climate warrior who'd enacted more ambitious guidelines in his country than the Kyoto Protocol. The former president of Mexico, Felipe Calderón, also joined the board. His infrastructure and energy reforms had improved the country's sustainability. They all helped us increase our profile in their countries and enabled us to begin attracting sovereign fund support.

But while the environmental community championed climate celebrities like Al Gore and illustrious heads of state, many expressed strong reservations about my courting Caterpillar chair Jim Owens for the board of directors. My relationship with Owens had developed since the Three Gorges Dam fiasco. After EXIM declined financing for the deal, I traveled to Peoria, Illinois, a Caterpillar company town halfway between Chicago and St. Louis. I was sympathetic to the company and believed they were doing a reasonable job trying to maximize shareholder value while keeping jobs from moving overseas. During the trip I met with a reasonable but disappointed management team that led me on a tour of the facilities, including the company's sustainable equipment unit Cat Reman, that offered used but still high-performing equipment at discounts.[323] Instead of recycling used paper and plastics, this industrial machinery giant was recycling engine equipment![324]

To his credit, Owens was sympathetic to my long-term view on the environment and my desire to harmonize environmental standards across the G7 credit agencies. And now that I was at WRI, I knew that his equipment modernization project might attract him to our urban transport program (Embarq), also focused on infrastructure development.[325] After Owens agreed to make a large donation to the program, many at the organization were reluctant to accept it. I then organized another trip to Peoria, this time with Jonathan Lash and Liz Cook. Owens treated us to a lovely dinner at his home overlooking the Illinois river. Then the three of us adjourned to our motel. We devoted the entire next day to touring the facilities. Owens was initially taken aback: "Jim, let me get this straight," he said. "You're telling me that they don't want to take our money? That we have to pass a test?"[326] Owens was a good sport, and we accepted his $7.5 million donation to Embarq.

While my colleagues appreciated his largesse, they didn't welcome him joining the board. A group of senior staff, including Frances Seymour, one of the world's leading voices in forest management and sustainability, was concerned that we were working with *the enemy*. "This will lead to all sorts of industrial companies sitting on our board, as they are polluting the world. This is the wrong move." Some were skeptical because, as WRI staff memorably described it, "[Caterpillar's] big, yellow earthmovers were for many environmentalists the symbol of everything they abhorred."[327]

At WRI, there was certainly precedent for working with the private sector. In 2002, we'd founded the Embarq initiative with financial support from the Shell Foundation. But we typically worked with foundations or charitable arms of companies responsible for offsetting any environmental harm, and not actively with the organizations or leaders themselves. In accelerating our work with private sector power players, I was leading the organization in new directions. And that's because I wanted to change the behaviors of the corporate world. The only way to do that, I believed, was through dialogue with industry leaders, spreading awareness about the dangers of carbon, while also listening to business concerns and needs about shareholder value and maintaining jobs. It was only by bringing the so-called opposition to the table, discussing our joint priorities on business and sustainability, that we could reach common ground.

Owens's joining the board paved the way for other private sector leaders like Michael Polsky, the capable Ukrainian immigrant who was founder, president, and CEO of renewable energy company Invenergy. He was a renewable energy pioneer and after joining the board was generous to WRI. But he too was a controversial pick. He represented the business community and was impatient with government types who didn't understand the private sector. It took time to integrate private sector leaders like Owens and Polsky into the organization, but they enhanced the board. As I've always said, borrowing some terminology from the financial sector, WRI was long on prestige but short on private sector development. Thanks to our cultivation of corporate talent, we attracted eight or nine of our thirty board members from the private sector, bridging an important gap between the public and private sectors and attracting more resources to the organization.

In 2006, I encouraged Liz Cook and Jonathan Lash to launch our first gala, introducing WRI to the New York City donor community. In New York, galas were the primary vehicle for fundraising, as organizations sold tables to different institutions, banks, and friends, while persuading invitees to give more at the event, using memorable headliners and tantalizing auction items. My investment banking colleagues were long accustomed to buying tables at charity galas. Public fundraising dinners were especially great for raising nonprogram funds. WRI had a strong record of securing funds for individual projects but had difficulty generating indirect funds from nonprogram areas for annual reports, staff training, and incubating new initiatives. Though the gala had potential for this form of fundraising, it was WRI's first major dinner and therefore a bit risky. When my wife began theater productions, she tested them out in small not-for-profits before debuting in New York. WRI was opening on Broadway without touring any regional cities.

For our inaugural gala, we honored General Electric CEO Jeffrey Immelt. Immelt and Lash had a strong relationship ever since the GE CEO had approached WRI for advice on reducing its carbon emissions.[328] This industrial giant had generated more pollution than most American cities and secreted toxins into the Hudson River for decades. It was now committed to changing course. Immelt ran the second-most powerful company in the world. Lash persuaded him that increased government scrutiny together with diminishing fossil fuel reserves made greening operations in corporate America's best financial interest.[329] Embracing the motto "green is green" (greening operations actually pays), Immelt had spearheaded the company's Ecomagination initiative in 2005, committing to reducing emissions.[330] Immelt proved a trailblazer because, following the launch of Ecomagination, Walmart, BP, and Goldman Sachs announced their own ambitious corporate environmental programs. As Treasury Secretary Hank Paulson said, "Jeff Immelt is proving by example that the world's best and strongest companies are those that have the best environmental practices."[331] Immelt graciously accepted WRI's award and agreed to assist in raising $500,000 for the dinner.

Former friends and the "who's who" of New York society attended our gala in their cocktail dresses and suits. And we gave them quite a show. Instead of Hollywood headliners, we featured people who matched the intellectual soul of the organization. Al Gore gave a rousing speech, Jeff Immelt graciously received his award, and climate stalwart and *New York Times* journalist Thomas Friedman served as master of ceremonies. After selling out our tables, we raised a stunning $2 million. Most important, the event introduced WRI to a broader demographic, raising our visibility in the business and larger donor communities.

Following the dinner, Gus Speth took Lash aside: "I understand that it makes sense to court people like Immelt," he conceded, "but I don't believe the corporate world has the environmental world's best interest at heart. If the organization continues along this path, I might need to step aside." My friend Steve Ross, a real estate developer and Rockefeller Republican who joined my wife, children, and their significant others at my table, drew the opposite conclusion. As he listened to Immelt speak about the private sector's responsibility to help with climate change and absorbed Al Gore's impassioned remarks, Ross emerged energized and inspired. At one point that evening, he leaned over to Liz Cook and said, "One day, I want to be the Jeff Immelt of the real estate industry."

While we inspired industry leaders like Ross, many of the old guard were uncomfortable with the private sector direction the organization was taking. This was a turning point. We could pursue the idealist approach of the founding generation of luminaries, attracting more heads of state, becoming more of a UN-like organization that continued to generate world-class research. Or we could cultivate a more collaborative approach with the private sector, increasing our global impact. With encouragement from Lash, we took the latter approach, using the event to help WRI attract the buy-in and capital from corporate leaders.

Capitalizing on his enthusiasm for the gala, I turned my attention to Ross, whom I had met in the 1980s. He was a visionary in the real estate business and has amassed a personal empire that would later include the largest private development in US history (Hudson Yards) as well as the posh Equinox fitness studios and the Miami Dolphins football team. It isn't uncommon for people who earn fortunes in unglamourous sectors like real estate development to gravitate to motion pictures or charitable causes. Global developers create 40 percent of global fossil-fuel emissions, I told Steve after the gala.[332] I invited him to join the board and to contribute his insight and finances to spearheading environmentally responsible real estate development. As Ross became an active member of the organization, other corporate leaders followed suit. Michael Bloomberg, a towering business leader doing important political and environmental work, gravitated to WRI's mission, donating $30 million. Dan Doctoroff, a polished and charismatic business leader, private equity manager, and politician, also joined the board. As CEO and president of Bloomberg L.P., and later deputy mayor under Bloomberg, Doctoroff provided important representation from New York City.

But Steve Ross's contribution of $30 million proved a turning point in the organization.[333] In 2014, we used Steve's generous gift and substantial vision to establish the WRI Ross Center for Sustainable Cities. Though originally founded to house and help scale two signature WRI initiatives, the urban transport and sustainable cities programs, Ross's generous core funding has enabled the center to innovate, initiate new ventures, and attract significantly more investment. Under the expert leadership of World Bank alum Ani Dasgupta, the center has created "Ross Center satellites" throughout the world, embedding its mission into the fabric of our global urban landscape. The Ross Center works with over 120 cities across the world and has offices in seven countries and 350 global employees. Just like WRI, the Ross Center is a first-in-its-class research institution, which remains a solution-centered "think-and-do tank."

I'm especially proud that a spirit of friendship suffuses the Ross Center. For me, this has centered on my close friendship with Steve Ross, a friend for forty years, and Ani, the future of the Ross Center and global sustainability. I wouldn't have thought that an investment banker, real estate magnate, and World Bank alum could mesh so seamlessly. Together, we've cocreated a mission to make the Ross Center into the world's biggest and most influential organization of its kind. To accomplish this vision, we speak for hours on end together, considering ideas for funding schemes and discussing whether we should partner with certain companies or NGOs.

During one of these conversations, the three of us brainstormed how we could amplify the center's work, extending its reach and impact to the world's 4,500 cities. During that telephone call we conceived the WRI Ross Center Prize for Cities. This prize aims to uncover hidden knowledge and innovation in global urban sustainability, awarding nonprofits, NGOs, or municipalities for their leadership. In recognizing and rewarding local innovations in sustainability, the prize also seeks to publicize them, bolstering the repertoire of sustainable practices across the world's cities.

We modeled the award on the Pritzker Prize for architecture, and in the tradition of WRI, used excellence in research to distinguish it. To differentiate the prize, we decided to generously fund it, mobilize our marketing and promotional channels to advertise it, and to assemble a juried team of experts to select a winner. For our inaugural prize in 2019, we focused on transformational change, seeking to award and amplify nonprofits and municipalities on the cutting edge of urban sustainability. For our first competition, we expected around thirty or so applications. We received 186.

That year Ross chaired a jury of experts that included community and business leaders, architects, urban planners, mayors, and national government experts. They sifted through these 186 submissions, deciding who should receive $250,000 for the winning urban initiative, and choosing four runners-up. After much deliberation, the jury announced the School Area Road Safety Assessments and Improvements (SARSAI) program, helping children more safely navigate to school in Dar es Salaam, Tanzania, and elsewhere in Africa, as our inaugural recipient.[334] In Africa, children must contend with chaotic traffic patterns, making them twice as likely as their global counterparts to die in transit to or from school. With little money, SARSAI worked with children and families and expertly used data to help create and promote safe infrastructure throughout several African cities.

In 2019, CNN's Sanjay Gupta emceed WRI's "Courage to Lead" dinner in Hudson Yards, praising SARSAI's efforts to create more thoughtful traffic patterns and introduce speed bumps and sidewalks to protect vulnerable children. With so many NGOs and big cities competing, we wanted this small African NGO to send an important message: small groups with slim budgets can create transformational change throughout the world. Given my passion for Africa, I was especially touched that SARSAI won the inaugural award.

Steve Ross has since increased his gift to $100 million, bolstering the impact of the Ross Center/WRI and helping convince others, like Jeff Bezos, that our organization can achieve global impact. I sometimes marvel at how far my friend Steve has come since our initial conversations about greening construction and building developments in 2006. Nearly two decades later, the Ross Center is on the cutting edge of globally sustainable transportation and urbanization. Steve is so much more than the Jeff Immelt of the real estate industry that he once aspired to be. He's a global environmental champion in his own right.

In the fall of 2010, as Jonathan Lash and I drove home from a WRI off-site meeting, he told me that he planned to resign. But given that President Obama was preparing to consider positions for his second administration, Lash agreed to leave only if I planned to continue as WRI's chair, instead of joining the administration. His dedication to the institution touched me, and I confirmed that I had no plans yet to reenter public service.

This marked another turning point at WRI. Its founding generation of environmental leaders—Denis Hayes, Gus Speth, Bill Ruckelshaus, and Jonathan Lash—was departing. In over thirty years, Speth and Lash had expertly helmed the organization, and finding WRI's third president was the most important decision the board would make. As Sue Tierney, a well-respected environmentalist and senior advisor at a Boston-based consulting firm overseeing the search committee, stated it, "It was clear to me that we were not just filling an open position. We were acting as guardians of a trust."[335] She looked for a president who could scale the excellent programs underway and maintain our global reputation while preserving the organization's unique culture. The committee zeroed in on Manish Bapna, who served as a senior economist for the World Bank and executive director for sustainability nonprofit Bank Information Center before becoming WRI's executive vice president and managing director in 2007. Bapna's expertise in international development has been critical at WRI, helping transform the nonprofit's strategic mission, especially ensuring that each program and initiative had measured outcomes.[336]

All of us on the committee favored Bapna, who seamlessly meshed with the leadership and board. But then the committee came across Andrew Steer, a British economist and senior development expert from the World Bank with a forceful presence and sterling reputation. Steer's background at the World Bank, where he served as special envoy for climate change, as well as his work with the World Economic Forum, United Nations, and other important multilateral bodies and organizations, stood to revolutionize the organization, increasing its global diplomacy and visibility among sovereign fund donors in Europe. I still remember the final search committee meeting, when we made an agonizing decision, extending an offer to Steer.

Over our nine years of work together, Andrew proved extremely personable. I well remember one spring evening around 2017 when I joined Andrew and his family for dinner at their Washington, DC, home. The Steers frequently hosted WRI staff, and this day Andrew invited me over when I was in town for a board meeting. Welcoming me at the front door, he turned to his children and said, "I hope you two remember what I've told you."

His son replied, "Yes, this is your boss and he's important to you, so I have to be on my best behavior." Andrew and I both smiled at this youthful sincerity. "You didn't have to recite the whole thing," Andrew explained in mock exasperation, "but I'm glad you remembered." It was an endearing way to begin the evening. Over the years I've been impressed that, despite his demanding travel schedule, Andrew maintains strong relationships with his family.

But it wasn't simply Andrew's charisma, charm, and public-speaking skills that powered WRI's global collaborations and world-class programming during his tenure.[337] Within six months of his arrival at WRI, Andrew doubled down on the organization's global niche in economic development and sustainability. To that end, WRI helped spearhead the Global Commission on the Economy and Climate, uniting a team of distinguished economists and finance ministers under the leadership of Felipe Calderón to help the world understand the economics of the climate transition. The commission's focus on a new climate economy, demonstrating how climate action was essential for economic development, would prove influential and profound. Across the world, countries began reframing climate action from a financial loss to an engine of economic growth and thriving.

I wouldn't realize how influential this commission and WRI's allied partnerships and programming were until March 2021, when I saw President Biden make his first address to a joint Congress. Biden's groundbreaking environmental policy, he announced, would create "jobs, jobs, jobs."[338] For much of the twenty-first century, most businesses and politicians believed that acting on climate change was a noble idea, but that it would hurt economic competitiveness and decrease jobs. Now the world understands that smart climate policy leads to more economic efficiency and drives technological innovation. I smiled as I watched Biden's remarks, realizing how the hard work of Andrew, WRI staff, and the board had helped create this intellectual revolution, which a new American president was translating into landmark national policy. Had I the space, I would recount the major milestones the organization accomplished under Andrew's leadership, detailing the major role that we played in the Paris Climate Agreement (2015), how we forged the Greenhouse Gas Protocol and the Science-Based Targets initiative (SBTi), and our decision to expand into Africa.

In addition to a wealth of experience and accomplishments that he brought to WRI, Andrew's dedication to the mission resulted in significant loyalty from the staff and the board. After quadrupling the organization's budget and increasing our employee ranks fivefold (2012–21), he left WRI in April 2021 to serve as president and CEO of the Bezos Earth Fund.[339] Though we were sad to see him go, this represented a great opportunity for Andrew and the world.

As WRI now looks to the future, with Ani Dasgupta at the helm of the organization, and marks the passage of the three-decade anniversary of the Rio Summit, it has every reason to be optimistic. The size, scale, reach, and budget of the organization have transformed, enabling WRI to build and scale important initiatives. Under Lash's capable leadership, and especially continuing under Andrew Steer, WRI began assuming a truly global presence, opening overseas branches in China (2008), India (2011), Brazil (2013), Indonesia (2014), Europe (2015), Mexico (2016), and Africa (2017). These frontline offices have been talent incubators and innovation centers as well, successfully cloning our programs internationally while tailoring sustainable cities and transportation initiatives to local contexts.

When an organization scales and diversifies so dramatically, growing pains inevitably arise. In the summer of 2019, as Donald Trump and Joe Biden vied for the US presidency, Steve Ross lent his home in Southampton, Long Island, for a Trump campaign fundraiser. Ross's motives were understandable. He gave his home believing that if Trump were reelected, Ross could appeal to his fellow real estate tycoon about the environment and perhaps work collaboratively with the administration. If Trump had a great relationship with one environmental NGO in the country, Ross figured, WRI should be the one.

Ross's decision created a firestorm. High-profile celebrities and angered citizens alike took to social media, declaring they would no longer support his high-end Hudson Yards mall in Manhattan. Others pledged to boycott his posh Equinox fitness clubs and Soul Cycle spin studios.[340] Members of Ross's other nonprofit ventures, like the Ross Initiative in Sports for Equality (RISE), whose mission is to "eliminate racial discrimination, champion social justice and improve race relations," were similarly angered.[341] Taking to Twitter, the Miami Dolphins wide receiver Kenny Stills said, "You can't have a nonprofit with this mission statement," referring to RISE, "and then open your doors to Trump."[342]

Many of WRI's staff agreed with Stills, disappointed that its most generous benefactor was supporting a reelection-seeking president who they saw as deeply hostile to WRI's mission. And they wanted Ross off the board. During this time, I reflected on how difficult morale had been since Trump had catapulted to the presidency three years earlier. The staff had weathered difficult periods before, especially during the George W. Bush administration. After the two-term Obama presidency, which helped WRI raise private sector support from companies eager to conform with the spirit of the administration, Trump's election was a blow. The staff was distraught, many of them in tears, as they watched Trump create policies and espouse values inimical to those to which they'd devoted their life's work.

I tried to give an "up and doing" speech to the organization in 2016, following the election that brought Trump to power. I reminded everyone how we'd endured the Bush years and some of us even the Reagan years. We could survive this too. In fact, I said, we often did better when WRI and the government weren't aligned, as galvanized governments and besieged foundations sought refuge in the NGO space. But this speech was directed as much to myself as it was to WRI staff. I was shocked that this real estate magnate, who'd plastered his name across buildings in my city, had somehow become US president.

Four years later, after Ross's home had hosted a Trump reelection fundraiser, I decided to facilitate a meeting at the WRI auditorium. Three hundred staff must have filed into the theater as I tried to inject some optimism and refocus everyone around WRI's mission. But tempers flared and it proved an unhappy occasion. I felt that despite our best attempts, the meeting wasn't helpful and opinions about the incident only hardened. "We let you move us toward the private sector," one disgruntled staff member said about me, "and now we have a Trump supporter on the board." Luckily, Ani and I drew on our friendship with Steve to defuse the situation. While the world sheltered in place during the coronavirus pandemic in the summer of 2020, we visited Steve's house in the Hamptons, enjoying some socially distanced conversation, but also presenting Steve with new board guidelines to sign.

WRI had used this occasion to help us improve the signature culture that Denis Hayes had sought to protect decades earlier. The board's executive committee, general counsel, and Liz Cook, who worked closely with me on board engagement, used the incident to improve our governance procedures. In a democracy like the United States, board members are free to support any candidate or cause they so wish. But following the Ross episode, board members must now comply with a new code of conduct and disclose major political campaign involvement. This alone has made the board stronger and more cohesive, while demonstrating transparency for WRI staff and other important stakeholders.

WRI has also developed important diversity initiatives. "The Green Movement Has a Diversity Problem," declared a 2019 *Mother Jones* article, "And It's Getting Worse."[343] WRI was no exception to this regrettable industry trend, and we instituted new programming, like the DreamGreen internship initiative, introducing candidates from diverse backgrounds to the organization so that they might pursue future careers in development. In seeking to promote racial diversity among its leadership and staff, I'm hoping that one day, when people join WRI's leadership ranks, they won't see the homogeneous sea of older, nonbusiness-oriented WASPS I encountered in 2001.

We also need this diverse talent because the environmental challenge remains as intractable as ever. In the 1970s, when Hayes, Lash, Ruckelshaus, and Speth joined other environmental visionaries and set out on their pioneering work in sustainability, the world made significant headway. Americans were appalled when they saw the Cuyahoga River catch fire and actively supported events like Earth Day and the incorporation of the Environmental Protection Agency. This decade of progress owed, in part, to the short-term nature of these threats and their solutions. I operated with that same short-termism when I began evaluating environmental threats in finance projects.

But now the threat is global and the health of the planet more threatened than ever. Since the creation of WRI in 1982, carbon emissions have nearly doubled, while the equivalent of fifty soccer fields of forests are cleared every single minute.[344] Urbanization has also proceeded with staggering levels of unsustainability. Of the 3.5 billion people inhabiting today's cities, one billion of them live in slums.[345] Over his tenure at the Ross Center, Ani wants to change that, finding ways to design and manage all of our cities so that their inhabitants have adequate shelter, jobs, and food to feed their families, and a quality of life that comes from good transportation and clean air.

As the world grapples with demographic, agricultural, and energy pressures, occasioned by environmental destruction and increased urbanization, I believe even more in the need for private, public, and nonprofit alignment and collaboration around environmental sustainability. We need more global leaders like Steve Ross and Jeff Bezos to join ranks with heads of state and organizations like WRI and the Ross Center for Sustainable Cities. We need their commitments to greening their industries, and we also need their plentiful resources as we work to reduce global emissions more broadly.

That's why the Earth Fund is such a game-changer for environmental philanthropy. Traditionally, most philanthropic funds enable organizations to perform technical assistance and catalyze change by altering the behavior of an industry sector or influencing a policy. The Earth Fund, by contrast, provides capital at a different scale entirely. Instead of catalyzing investments in a program like Embarq, environmental players can now work to change entire ecosystems. If, for example, New York City, with its 9,000 school buses, sought the Ross Center's support to electrify their fleet, we could partner with the city and bus manufacturers and work with state and federal policy makers to help finance these initial costs. With Andrew Steer now directing these global investments, I'm optimistic about the environmental future. It is only with this multilateral effort that we can meet the sustainability challenges ahead and fulfill WRI's mission to protect the earth's environment and provide for current and future generations.

14

A Democracy Dividend
for Egypt

IN JULY 2013, DICTATORSHIP defeated democracy in Egypt. Or at least that's how it appeared. One year after the popular Arab Spring protests had ended Hosni Mubarak's thirty-year dictatorship, the Egyptian people participated in their first free and democratic election, bringing Mohamed Morsi to office in 2012.[346] But after just one year of tenuous representative democracy, the Egyptian military forcibly removed Morsi, suspending the country's constitution, leaving hundreds of Morsi supporters killed or injured in the streets, and sowing chaos and uncertainty throughout the country.[347]

President Barack Obama expressed deep regret over these events and questioned the future of the country's annual $1.5 billion in economic and military aid.[348] This could have marked a major foreign policy and diplomatic rupture. Since the late 1970s, Egypt was the second-largest recipient of US foreign assistance (only Israel received more), helping to guarantee the Israeli-Egypt peace treaty of 1979.[349] At Obama's request, senators Lindsey Graham and John McCain visited the country in 2013, calling for the release of protestors and the restoration of civilian governance.[350] "We are hopeful that the direction of the transition will be going back to democracy; that is the only one we can support," said Graham.[351]

As Graham and McCain prepared for their Egyptian visit, I recalled my first trip to the country ten months prior. As I describe in the prologue, my 2012 trip to Egypt occurred against the backdrop of a violent uprising in Tahrir Square and the Benghazi attacks. But that trip also cemented my larger vision for the Egyptian-American Enterprise Fund (EAEF) that the Obama administration had tapped me to lead in 2012. Using that fund, I wanted to bolster Egypt's reeling private sector, empower women, and create the economic stability necessary for democratic rule. Following Morsi's ouster ten months after my visit, this fund was needed more than ever.

Though I worried that political developments in Egypt might imperil US military aid to the country, I believed the EAEF's funding remained secure.[352] Many Republicans on the Hill regarded the first generation of ten enterprise funds, created after the dissolution of the USSR, as important milestones—however imperfect they were in execution. Now President Obama and Secretary of State Clinton resurrected this Republican idea, this time deploying enterprise funds to promote private sector development in the Middle East. Bipartisan support for the fund seemed to extend to the chairman, as the Obama administration and congressional Republicans felt that my experience running EXIM and fifteen years of investment experience in frontier and developing economies like Egypt (with my Caravel Fund) qualified me for the job. Chairing the EAEF, I figured, would be similar to running EXIM Bank, where I had autonomy over financial decisions and largely avoided partisan interference and infighting.

As I learned shortly after Graham and McCain returned from Egypt, my reasoning was mistaken. Graham joined several of his colleagues on the Hill in issuing a hold on the fund's money, meaning that I had no capital to make investments or to cover expenses. Although my time at EXIM had acquainted me with power politics on the Hill, I was unprepared for the almighty congressional hold. When members of Congress want to stop an agency or embassy appointment or obstruct a program, they have at their disposal the powerful mechanism of the "hold." By issuing holds, senators prevent bills, ambassadorial candidates, and agency heads alike from reaching the chamber floor for consideration.

My friend Steve Ross, the billionaire turned environmental leader, assured me that Graham was a reasonable man with a good sense of humor. Before he released his hold, Graham wanted an explanation of the fund's proposed investments and more evidence of progress in Egyptian democracy.[353] Confident I could address his concerns, I met Graham and his chief of staff in the summer of 2013.

That day marks one of the worst meetings of my life. After explaining to Graham that his hold imperiled the mission in Egypt, I listened as the senator candidly replied that he didn't care. I conceded that turmoil in Egypt might lead to the suspension of US military aid, but that the EAEF was a purely commercial endeavor that would stimulate free enterprise, create jobs, and possibly make money for the American taxpayer in the process. "If you believe that economic development is essential to the democratic process," I asked, "why would you cut us out?"

President Obama had angered Graham, I learned, and he was going to block the President's objectives until his grievances were resolved. With twenty years of life experience over Graham, I was still confident I could exercise some leadership and manage this discussion. "Let's think this through," I said. "Is there some other way you could express your displeasure with the President without hurting the Egyptian-American Enterprise Fund, the very entity that you and Senator McCain have applauded until now?" To that point, an honest and composed Graham confirmed that his actions were done purely out of spite. But after my admittedly condescending tone, he raised his voice and the conversation deteriorated.

"You've lost your mind," I told him candidly.

"You've lost your mind!" he responded.

"The next thing I know, you're going to tell me that you've decided to close EXIM until Obama makes you happy," I responded.

"Great idea," he replied. "I'll close EXIM!"

"And how about the Overseas Private Investment Corporation?" I added.

"Another great idea!" he said. "I'll close that too."

"Don't stop there. How about the State Department?" I said.

"I'd love to close the f---ing State Department!" he screamed, rising from his chair.

I'm not proud of this childish exchange. In all my days on Wall Street, various corporate and nonprofit boards, EXIM, or as a parent, I'd never had such an appalling discussion. I lowered my voice, told Graham I didn't think he was a reasonable human being, and exited his office. I felt ashamed as I walked out. I'd always prided myself on my interpersonal skills and ability to forge consensus with others. Instead of elevating this discussion and modeling the type of consensus and civility I wished to achieve, I'd lost my temper. To my lasting amusement, Graham's chief of staff met me at the door, saying how happy he was about how the meeting went. "Were you at the same meeting as me?" I responded.

"It was great that you could both express your point of view," he said. "I predict that someday you'll both be friends." I'm still waiting for that day to come.

Over my first two years as EAEF chair, which I narrate in this chapter, my biggest obstacle wasn't contending with violence in Egypt. Instead, it was devising imaginative ways to overcome congressional obstruction, like that from Senator Lindsey O. Graham, and contend with Egyptian resistance to and skepticism about working with the US government. If I could somehow overcome these obstacles and begin the fund from a position of fiscal strength, I knew Egypt would begin to recover. The difficult investment environment in Egypt is precisely what made it an attractive investment opportunity. As Warren Buffett said, "Widespread fear is your friend as an investor because it serves up bargain purchases."[354]

Though I had a hunch that the fund's return on investment would be significant, my commitment to the enterprise fund was based on its nonfinancial ROI. If the EAEF could bolster the private sector against the backdrop of revolution and mayhem, creating jobs, empowering women, and attracting investment, it wouldn't simply change the course of Egyptian history. We could accomplish something important for the Arab and larger frontier and developing worlds.

In the process, we could also revise some common misconceptions about the nature of democratic rule. President Obama and senators Graham and McCain made rousing and noble calls for Egyptian democracy. But before ballots, we needed bread. Developing and frontier countries can't create stable democracies when their citizens lack stable food supplies, secure jobs, and basic necessities like health care. I've long maintained that the only way to secure political stability and achieve democracy in any country is to first ensure economic stability. The enterprise fund was my strategy to achieve that in Egypt.

WRANGLING THE HILL

Only ten days after my trip to Cairo and the Benghazi attacks, another member from the Hill beat Senator Graham to issuing the first hold on the EAEF. On September 28, 2012, Congresswoman Kay Granger, a Republican from Texas and chairwoman of the House Appropriations Subcommittee on State, Foreign Operations, and Related Programs, said, "I am not convinced of the urgent need for this assistance, and I cannot support it at this time. As chair of the subcommittee, I have placed a hold on the funds."[355] Congresswoman Ileana Ros-Lehtinen, a Republican representing Miami who chaired the House Foreign Affairs Committee, placed a hold shortly thereafter. Once again, I called Steve Ross, the owner of the Miami Dolphins, and asked for his help in introducing me to the congresswoman. Senator Graham, as you can imagine, was more difficult to persuade.

It was a surreal time as I worked to overcome these holds while preparing for my Egyptian mission and spending time constituting the EAEF's nine-person board of directors (six Americans, three Egyptians). Among the selections I made was Egyptian American Hythem T. El-Nazer, a fellow Brown alumnus with impressive investment experience whom John Kerry's office recommended. At the time, El-Nazer was a partner at TA Associates, a global private equity firm with $18 billion in investment capital under management, and I later tapped him to serve as my vice chair. My other board members included Sherif Kamel, dean of the American University of Cairo's Business School; Hani Sarie-Eldin, former chair of the Egyptian Capital Market Authority; Neveen El Tahri, chair and managing director of Delta Shield for Investment; and Tarek Abdel-Meguid, founder of asset manager Perella Weinberg.

After assembling a strong Egyptian and Egyptian American board, I noticed that we didn't have a single Republican. Needing bipartisan representation to be effective, I approached Dina (née Habib) Powell McCormick, a well-known and respected Egyptian American who'd worked at Goldman Sachs and served during the George W. Bush administration. Powell and I met for coffee and I found her very personable, agreeing to help coordinate with Republicans on the Hill. Powell knew her way around Wall Street and Washington alike. A few years later, however, we lost a strong board member when White House senior advisor Jared Kushner recommended her for a national security position in the Trump White House.

With the board in place, we now needed funding. In order for the EAEF to begin investing, the government needed to issue its grant agreement, stipulating the mandate, rules, and restrictions pertaining to the new fund. I devoted the better part of September 2012 through the following March to this process, negotiating with a battery of well-meaning government lawyers and USAID officials who knew about the first generation of enterprise funds and were leery of any risks or losses. Their anxiety was understandable, as these first-generation enterprise funds generally had modest returns and lacked strong private sector viability. Congress was unhappy, furthermore, about the United States Agency for International Development's (USAID) management of one of the enterprise funds in the 1990s, citing its unnecessary legal fees and its micromanagement of fund operations.

Many discussions, which sometimes grew heated, concerned the amount of funds we would receive. The White House assured me a fund of $300 million to invest, while the House Committee on Foreign Affairs insisted that Congress had authorized only $60 million. These bureaucratic obstacles were just as discouraging for me as the violence and unrest unfolding in Egypt itself. "The need for the fund is urgent," I pleaded in the summer of 2013. "The Egyptian economy, which has existed for more than two years in a state of suspended animation, is now teetering on the edge."[356]

As I sought to capitalize on the great promise of these funds and begin investing, the Egyptian government and larger business community saw the congressional attempt to strangle the lifeblood of the new venture. This decreased my already slim credibility in a country leery of American influence and "help." Every passing day was painful as I tried to negotiate favorable terms, while Anne Patterson, the US ambassador to Egypt, informed me about the deteriorating circumstances throughout the country.

By March 2013, most reluctant members of the Hill had removed their holds, and we finally signed the ninety-odd-page US grant agreement detailing the major objectives, structure, and restrictions associated with the enterprise fund. The agreement included many restrictions, forbidding our investment in so-called sin industries like weapons and tobacco companies. But it also provided some flexibility in governance. In addition to allowing for a private equity structure, which I describe below, the agreement permitted reflow reinvestment. When the fund sells a business, the proceeds from that sale ("reflows") can be reinvested into the fund. By using a private equity structure with reflows, I knew I could attract the talent needed to make investments substantial enough to help Egypt stabilize.

THE WARREN BUFFETT OF EGYPT

Though the US Congress finally allowed the enterprise fund to invest in Egypt, the country itself didn't welcome our overtures. My time in the Middle East and North Africa (MENA) region always reminded me of *The Ugly American*, a 1958 political novel depicting the failures of US diplomacy.

Since its publication, the stereotype of American insensitivity, incompetence, and arrogance had lingered in the region. The disappointment of the Camp David accords also loomed large among Egyptian government officials, reinforcing the conviction that American "diplomats" like me couldn't be trusted to invest in the country. Over the course of my six or seven meetings with Morsi's successor, President Abdel Fattah Al Sisi, the leader emphasized the inadequacy of my efforts. "We need billions, not millions," he said, believing that America owed the country those vast sums.

Popular conspiracy theories also compromised US credibility. During my first trip to Egypt, I appeared on a popular nighttime program that began at midnight and ran through 2:00 a.m. The anchorman grilled me for two hours about my intentions in his country, suggesting that I was an agent of President Obama who was in Egypt to take over the country. "I'm too old to do that," I said, flashing him a disarming smile. "Give me one reason I would want to do that at my age. I'm here to try and help Egypt's private sector." I didn't persuade him.

Nor did I persuade Sahar Nasr, Egypt's minister of investment and international cooperation, with whom I met during a World Bank meeting in Washington, DC. The meeting was sometime around 2017, and I took Amal Enan, the enterprise fund's first employee whom I'd hired straight out of Harvard Business School. Having grown up in Cairo and participated in the revolution before developing a deep understanding of American business and forming important contacts in the Egyptian embassy and on the Hill, she proved a great fit for the fledgling fund.

Amal had diplomatic finesse, and I was happy that she accompanied me to the meeting. Several Egyptians had warned me that Minister Nasr was a strong personality. We began in a cordial fashion with introductions and small talk about the fund when Minister Nasr reiterated a request that she'd made several times prior in Egypt. "I'd like to join the enterprise fund's board of directors." I once again explained to her that we didn't allow government officials from any country onto the board. "That's unacceptable," she replied. With the assistance of Amal's translation into Arabic, I further explained that this prohibition would have to be acceptable because, while she would be terrific for the post, it was above my pay scale to change US government policy. After a brief pause, Minister Nasr rose from the table and left the meeting as the Egyptian ambassador looked on, a stunned expression on his face. I thought that perhaps she'd gone to the ladies' room, but after the minutes ticked on, I realized the meeting was over. Though this episode stands out in my memory, Minister Nasr's position was typical of many in the Egyptian government who believed, wrongly, that this EAEF's $300 million in investment capital dated back to the Camp David accords and that they had a claim or entitlement to managing it.

Given the anti-American animus among some businesspeople, government officials, and citizens alike, my first objective was to Egyptianize the fund. I'd already assembled a strong Egyptian and Egyptian American board of directors, and I now needed to find a talented Egyptian investment banker to help us run the operation. In April 2013, just after approval of the grant agreement, Ola El-Shawarby, an analyst from the Caravel Fund, and Krishanti Vignarajah, the deputy to Tom Nides at the State Department, joined me on a trip to Cairo, ready to identify our first president and chief operating officer. An immigrant from Sri Lanka, Vignarajah had attended Yale Law School and gone to Oxford on a Marshall Scholarship before joining the government. She was a young, conscientious, and capable diplomat and paired well with El-Shawarby, who grew up in Cairo and was experienced in finance and revolutionary upheaval alike.

In addition to meeting with government officials, the USAID mission, and the embassy, the three of us spent two days meeting with twenty of the brightest Egyptian candidates. After conducting interviews in a somewhat cramped, windowless office, we retired to the central courtyard of the Four Seasons. As explosions sounded off around the city, we discussed the bankers we'd interviewed that day, many of whom worked in New York or London and had what I like to call solid "investment IQs." We made quite a team, with the studious and serious Vignarajah feverishly taking notes the entire time while El-Shawarby smoked flavored tobacco from the hookah.

Though the candidates we met that trip have gone on to form their own private equity businesses, and although I would have hired any of them to work at the Caravel Fund in New York, none had the depth of experience required of this job. We weren't looking for a brilliant analyst to maximize financial returns. We needed someone with the experience, knowledge, and temperament to manage relationships with governments and global businesses all the while devising investment strategies to achieve financial and development success.

After the second day of interviews, we reached a standstill. I remember the sun was setting, and the light reflecting off the courtyard fountain was peaceful and soothing, even as US security details patrolled the area, shielding us from the chaos erupting throughout the city. "Who is the Warren Buffett of Egypt?" I asked El-Shawarby.

"Nassef Sawiris," she replied without hesitation. Sawiris was an Egyptian billionaire who hailed from Egypt's most powerful family. His father Onsi had begun the dynasty with his Orascom Group, while his oldest brother Naguib had transformed telecommunications throughout the MENA region with his Orascom Telecom Holding. But the family belonged to the country's persecuted Coptic Christian community and had decried Muslim fundamentalism and female veiling, while also criticizing Morsi and the Egyptian Brotherhood.[357] The Egyptian government had issued a travel ban against Onsi and Nassef Sawiris, forcing him to work and live abroad. After speaking to Nassef on the phone that day at sunset, Vignarajah and I boarded a direct flight from Cairo to London for a meeting with him the next morning.

It felt good to board a British Airways flight back to London. I booked a room at the Berkeley and enjoyed a run in Hyde Park before my meeting. Nassef's London office was lean and in great condition but modest, and he came quickly to the point. "Who have you considered for the leadership position?" I showed him the list of twenty people we'd interviewed, and he confirmed my analysis: they were great analysts but lacked the capacity and experience to run the fund. "I know the right man," he said. "His name is Ashraf Zaki, and he's been my investment banker." Sawiris called Zaki's office in Cairo and handed me the phone so we could speak. This conversation marks an important milestone in the enterprise fund.

At a meeting in New York the following week, I began a lifelong friendship with this young, talented, terrific man.[358] Direct and honest, Zaki wasn't a salesman and didn't try to impress me. He was focused and serious while still exhibiting a distinctly Egyptian sense of humor. Sawiris was right about Zaki's candidacy. After serving as vice president of investment banking at Morgan Stanley in the 1990s, Zaki moved to Cairo, where he became managing director of investment banking at EFG Hermes, the largest investment bank in Egypt, before founding his own boutique advisory firm. Our chief objective and fondest dream, I told him, was growing Egypt's private sector.

Though Zaki was committed to helping his natal country, very few Cairo-based managers, even those with Western educations and work experience, wanted to work for the US government in any capacity. But directly hiring him was my natural impulse, and I began negotiations by trying to tempt him with a large salary and bonus. "At this stage of my career," Zaki said diplomatically, "I'm more focused on building my own business." If I upped my offering to $1 million a year with a bonus, something I would have done had this been my own firm, the US government would have been in an uproar. Officials would have cited a return to the exploitative or unscrupulous fee schedules of the earlier generation of enterprise funds. I needed a clever way to allure Zaki but steer clear of congressional scrutiny.

Instead of serving in the employ of the US government, I next suggested, how about the US government work for Zaki. As I explained, Zaki could open and operate his own private equity business, and the EAEF, on behalf of the US government, could seed the company, paying him a management and incentive fee based on the realized gains of our investments. We would enact the standard payment structure for private equity managers with one exception. US-based managers typically expect a "two and twenty" arrangement: a 2 percent fee for assets under management and a 20 percent incentive fee on realized gains. I suggested that Zaki receive a 1.25 percent management fee and 12.5 percent incentive fee.

Zaki, I suspected, could make a lot of money with our investments, and when members of the Hill inquired about his profits, I could show them how much below market average the payment structure was. This deal cost Zaki a little autonomy because, at least in the beginning, he didn't have the authority to make investments; instead, I charged Zaki with finding the investments and bringing them before the EAEF's investment committee for approval. But in return, I offered him every private equity manager's fantasy. Most private equity founders struggle to raise their initial capital, spending years and great expense negotiating with institutional investors. Zaki, by contrast, could begin generating millions in annual revenues (1.25 percent on $300 million) the day he began work. Happy to move from an advisory to an asset management role, Zaki created a private equity venture later called Lorax Capital Partners, the US government seeded the fledgling venture, and the two of us agreed to work together to approve every transaction.

For the following three years, I often spoke to Zaki three times a week for hours, creating a friendship rooted in mutual trust and admiration. During our first year together, as I wrangled with the House Appropriations Sub-committee on State, Foreign Operations, and Related Programs and tried to identify our first investments, Zaki performed his work on an advisory basis and earned zero fees. He was focused on becoming acquainted with me and the board and on learning how the fund operated. Our conversations were electrifying as we both discussed the merits of different investments, strategizing about how to transform a lean $300 million into something that could help change the destiny of the country. Because there was no blueprint for how the fund would operate, it was ours to create together.

Zaki and I genuinely like each other and have that "special sauce" of great partnerships. He is a devoted family man, and over the course of our poring over every transaction, he kept me updated on his wife and two daughters. Ashraf's second daughter was born in December 2011, right as revolution spread throughout the country and just as his older child was learning how to talk.

As Zaki and I discussed that first year, when you live in a place convulsed with revolution, people cease planning for the future. While I understood that few foreigners wanted to invest during the upheaval, I was surprised by how risk-averse the Egyptian people were, hesitant to open their own businesses. When I tried to hire someone, I might say, "We're going to develop an incentive plan so you can save over the next five years." Invariably, these candidates looked at me with consternation. "Five years! We're worried about making it through the next five months." Egyptians have a baseline fear that I hadn't witnessed since working in Russia in the late 1990s. Given the ever-present possibility of chaos, I understood the fright and short-termism, and was determined, in the tradition of Warren Buffett, to leverage that fear to create opportunity.

INVESTING IN EGYPT

As I wrestled with the uncertain fate of the EAEF, began organizing the board of directors, and scouted for Egypt's Warren Buffett, I had a clear vision for the fund's first investment. I wanted to buy a small commercial bank and persuade the most capable female financier in all of Egypt to serve as its president. With government interest rates in the mid to high teens, Egyptian banks made few loans to individuals and SMEs. Why risk lending to a small borrower when they could earn over 15 percent by investing in Egyptian treasury bills? With this female-led commercial bank, Zaki and I wanted to change this status quo, leveraging the institution to make small and micro business loans throughout the country.

For the better part of the summer and fall of 2014, Zaki and I discussed, analyzed, and planned for this transaction. After evaluating several Egyptian financial institutions that were small enough for us to purchase, Zaki identified Piraeus Bank, a subsidiary of a Greek multinational financial services company in Athens. Zaki approached the sellers and they expressed interest; he also found a senior Egyptian banking executive with the reputation and domestic and international experience to be our first president.

I also developed a surprising rapport with the man Zaki selected to serve as our first chair. "He's your generation," Zaki told me. "You should talk to him." After getting him on the phone one evening, I immediately went to business, telling him about the high stakes of making our first investment in Egypt, and how he could help us run this bank. But then he surprised me.

"I'm going to tell you where I am," he said. "I'm sitting in my garden, I've just had dinner, I'm smoking a cigar and having some Cognac. I like Cognac. Do you like Cognac?" he asked me. After affirming that I indeed liked Cognac, just as I enjoy a rum punch on the beach sometimes in Anguilla, he continued with a description of his surroundings, describing the beautiful last remnants of sunset filtering into his patio as he relaxed his feet on a table. He then asked me to describe my surroundings and how I felt that evening. His descriptions were so evocative that when I closed my eyes, I could visualize his little garden, with a stone wall and fence enclosure, along with his little foot stool.

We finally returned to the deal, and he confirmed that he'd be chair. He loved that a US government official sought his aid and expressed strong support of the bank's mission to help capitalize SMEs and encourage female leadership. Zaki called me afterward and asked me about the conversation. "I think we fell in love," I said, telling him the story of one of the loveliest and most unusual moments of professional relationship building I'd ever had.

Zaki then prepared an extensive memorandum on the Egyptian banking sector, benchmarking Piraeus to key industry peers. It was every bit as insightful as the best work I've seen on Wall Street. Zaki was confident as he traveled to Athens to negotiate with Piraeus Bank. Prior to departure, we had agreed on a price that was equal to the bank's book value of $85 million. Typically, it's hard to buy a bank without paying a premium to book value. By that I mean that most bank owners enjoy the prestige and income of owning a bank and won't relinquish the company for considerably less than its book value or balance-sheet equity (its net assets minus liabilities). This bank had been stagnant for many years and was making few loans. Like many, the owners feared the chaotic and violent Egyptian atmosphere and wanted out of the country. Having conducted careful due diligence, negotiated a fair price, and garnered the enthusiasm of the EAEF board, I was confident that the bank, the government of Egypt, USAID, and the US State Department would welcome the transaction.

The only hurdle was securing the Egyptian central bank's approval. To help our efforts, the Egyptian ambassador to the United States arranged a dinner at his residence in Washington, DC, inviting leading Egyptian businesspeople working in the United States. About twenty people attended, including Mohamed El-Erian, a distinguished economist and fund manager. He was president of Queens' College Cambridge and also chair of President Obama's Global Development Council. To my surprise and dismay, the chair of Egypt's central bank, seated next to me at the dinner, moved his plate to another table and asked his deputy to take his place. "The governor doesn't want to discuss the bank," the deputy informed me.

During the final phase of negotiations, the governor rejected our proposal, saying he couldn't accept a US private equity company buying an Egyptian bank. He feared we would be too short term in our approach, rushing a sale at the earliest opportunity just to make a profit. There was some truth in his reasoning, as US and European private equity partners have a reputation for seeking short-term profits. But there's a fundamental difference between most private equity managers and the EAEF, I told the chair. Ours was a mission-driven fund with a long-term mandate; we were intent on using the bank to help transform Egypt's financial industry, making loans to Egyptian SMEs and stimulating private sector enterprise. He remained obstinate, saying, "Only a bank can buy a bank."

I felt disheartened. The US State Department had dedicated over two and a half years to mobilizing the EAEF. They didn't just want a transaction—they wanted an investment success story. But after nine months of intense negotiations, travel, and hard work to acquire this bank, we hadn't only failed in my first transaction, but we had also cost the US taxpayer $125,000 in expenses. My vision of a brick-and-mortar bank, with strong female leadership overseeing 125 or so employees intent on promoting financial inclusiveness throughout Egypt, was dashed. In May 2015, less than a year after this failed transaction, Kuwait's Al Ahli Bank purchased Piraeus Bank for $150 million, almost twice our agreed price.

Eager to salvage the reputation of the fund, we turned our attention to Fawry, a large consumer-finance business that Zaki showed me in the spring of 2015. Fawry is an e-payments company and platform similar to California-based PayPal. Since entrepreneur Ashraf Sabry launched Fawry in 2009, it had become Egypt's first and largest electronic-payments network. By 2015, it had over 15 million customers and 50,000 service points that resembled small kiosks throughout Egypt's cities, suburbs, and rural outposts.

Fawry served an extremely underpenetrated Egyptian market. In Egypt, over 80 percent of residents lack bank accounts. To pay utility bills, speak on the phone, or transfer money, most Egyptians had to disrupt their days and part with their limited financial resources, hiring transportation services to visit far-flung agencies and queue in long lines. To overcome this cumbersome and financially limiting status quo, Sabry created a wide range of financial services for all Egyptians. If you needed to buy minutes to speak on the phone, you could head to the local Fawry kiosk and top up your card; if you needed to pay a bill, you could easily do so; and if you needed an affordable loan, Fawry would assess your creditworthiness.[359] By 2015, the company did 1.2 million daily transactions, increasing the efficiency of everyday Egyptians and later extending capital to SMEs on a creditworthy basis.

Both Zaki and my vice chair Hythem T. El-Nazer praised the company as a spectacular investment that met our financial and development requirements. Lacking expertise in technology, I was hesitant and needed some convincing. We had all watched the World Bank and other development agencies struggle for years to reach small and micro enterprises throughout the frontier and developing worlds, and most of their initiatives hadn't succeeded. This fintech company seemed ideally positioned to reach SMEs, and because of its promise to revolutionize economic development in Egypt, everyone on the board wholeheartedly endorsed it.

The one disadvantage about Fawry was that our transaction would represent a "secondary." In the financial community, a primary refers to raising new, fresh capital for a company, while a secondary refers to a transaction among shareholders. Primaries increase growth and inject new energy into a company, while secondaries add little value and provide no additionality. As a former investment banker, I often performed purely secondary transactions because owner-shareholders wanted to liquidate their interest in a company so that they could purchase a home or pursue another business. For each transaction that the EAEF approved, we needed to help grow the private sector, creating jobs and expanding manufacturing instead of making profits for shareholders. It was therefore important to me that our inaugural transaction be a primary.

Given the volatile climate of Egypt, primaries were difficult even for the most promising companies, as most owners and managers sought secondary income to hedge against future political and business volatility. If the EAEF took a position in Fawry, it would replace exiting investors. Even Ashraf Sabry, the ingenious company founder, wanted to sell a minority interest in his company. What a marked contrast to the American culture of bold entrepreneurship and risk-taking. My mind went to Elon Musk, who created the company that would become PayPal, Fawry's US counterpart organization, and leveraged his personal net worth to launch his many other ventures.

I expressed my concern to Zaki, telling him I always felt uncomfortable when the president of a growing company sold shares. He should buy more! If anyone could appreciate Fawry's potential it was Sabry, but he never owned more than 4 percent of the business. For most offerings like this in the United States, I would have generated a stock-option plan for him and other employees so that they could participate in the future growth of the company. In Egypt, I realized, everyone was frightened about another revolution, even the owners of extremely profitable, high-growth companies.

After assessing the drawbacks and benefits, we all agreed that Fawry was an exceptional business. In much of the developing and frontier worlds, banks poorly served the largely cash-dependent, unbanked market. Fintech growth in frontier markets, where people needed access to basic financial services and protections against theft and fraud associated with the cash economy, seemed poised to accelerate. Fawry promised strong financial and development returns, improving the Egyptian quality of life. Zaki organized a consortium, including Helios Investment Partners, a Sub-Saharan private equity fund, and the United Kingdom's Wellcome Trust, and on April 30, 2015, the EAEF acquired 20 percent of the company for $20 million. The consortium acquired 100 percent of Fawry and represented one of the largest transactions for a technology company in African history.

The following three years of managing Fawry were a joy as I watched its technology foster financial inclusiveness throughout Egypt. Farmers on the Nile or in rural Egyptian villages now had banking capacities. When paying bills, people no longer had to rent expensive tuk-tuks to visit a government agency, queue in line for hours, perform the transaction, and rent the vehicles for a return trip. Instead, villagers and farmers descended on a Fawry kiosk, ubiquitous in the country, made a quick, efficient, and inexpensive transaction, and returned to work. This technology improved their lives in concrete ways.

And so did Sarwa, the EAEF's second major investment. Industry professionals created this company in 2001 to finance automobile loans that Egyptian banks routinely refused because of their eagerness to invest in steady treasury bills. When Zaki and I began looking at the company, we loved its excellent management, especially Hazem Moussa, the charismatic and patient son of a famous diplomat. As Moussa showed me, the company had a low "loss experience" in defaults and an impressive network of automobile dealers. By addressing the market gap in consumer finance, the company was also a great development investment as it increased the country's financial inclusiveness. At the time we began surveying it, Sarwa was diversifying its revenue from automobile financing into debt securitization (that is, packaging a group of loans into one financial entity and then selling bonds, secured by automobile loans, to interested investors).

This securitization business had even greater returns than originating auto loans, and it increased my long-term interest in the company. In the coming years, I knew that it would need to pivot from fossil-fuel-emitting vehicles. Because the company wasn't as glamourous and high-demand as the tech-savvy Fawry, we purchased it for a reasonable price, investing approximately $60 million for 74 percent ownership. After the company's 2018 IPO, we sold 20 percent at three times our initial purchase on a per-share basis.

The success of Sarwa and Fawry illustrate the cultural differences about finance in the developed and developing worlds. In frontier and developing economies like Bangladesh, Brazil, Egypt, and Nigeria, most people work diligently to make themselves creditworthy to lenders. They are also loath to default, as this imperils their future ability to borrow money and represents a personal shame and humiliation. With robust financial mechanisms like Chapter 8 and Chapter 11 bankruptcy protection, the United States allows individuals to access fresh capital and rebuild after losses. After Ames Department Stores filed Chapter 11 bankruptcy, the store reopened operations six months later. A former US president filed multiple bankruptcies for businesses he owned, and this pattern has so far posed few lasting personal or financial consequences for him. These cultural differences explain why the loss ratios of Sarwa and Fawry, as a percentage of disbursements, were 1–2 percent, while the equivalent default rate is higher in the United States.

As we now know, Egyptian state-owned banks and JPMorgan Chase alike should have been more aggressive in acquiring companies like Sarwa and especially fintech companies like Fawry. Fintech startups have revolutionized traditional banking and each year claim ever more market share from traditional banks. Smart bankers and investors saw the potential of fintech and offered large sums to secure positions in these companies. Zaki called me somewhat alarmed one day in 2018. As we were planning for Fawry's first IPO, an investor approached him with a staggering offer. A Chinese company offered to purchase a significant position in Fawry for many times its then-current marketplace valuation and join the board of directors.

Chinese ownership would have been inconsistent with the fund's development goals as well as Egyptian national security objectives. By 2018, Egypt's
military and defense departments counted among Fawry's customers, making the government leery of any foreign ownership, including Americans,
who represented the second-largest owners.

Always prescient, Zaki saw the potential for governmental interference and after refusing the Chinese offer suggested that we proactively
include the Egyptian government. If we didn't do so, we risked public officials enacting burdensome regulations or even initiating takeover attempts
under the pretext of national security. We restructured Fawry, inviting two
state-owned Egyptian banks to invest, thereby decreasing the percentage
of foreign ownership. With two state-owned banks controlling 15 to 20
percent in the company, and two foreign-fund owners—Helios and the
EAEF—with reduced positions, Zaki preempted a potential problem in an
elegant and diplomatic fashion. In August 2019, Fawry launched its IPO.
Oversubscribed by 30 percent, it likely marked one of the most successful
IPO offerings in the history of Egypt's capital markets.

After reaching a market value of $1 billion in the summer of 2020,
Fawry became Egypt's first unicorn. Today, around 30 percent of Egyptians
(27 million people) and counting use Fawry's 194,000 kiosks throughout
the country for their daily financial needs. By 2030, I expect its customer
base to include half of all Egyptians. In addition, the company supports
more than 100,000 small and micro enterprises. The company's growth
shows no signs of abating and will soon have the capacity to reach even the
smallest and remotest parts of the country and economy.

It's hard to overstate how much Fawry's technology has revolutionized
financial services in Egypt. Underserved and rural Egyptian areas can now
access point-of-sale (POS) locations to pay bills and add minutes to their
phones. By participating in these POS transactions, Egyptian merchants
now belong to a larger business network, premised on digitization instead of
cash. Egypt's cash economy not only created inefficiencies, tax evasion, and
risk of theft, but it also stymied Egyptian financial growth. When you are

working solely in cash, you have no documentation of your creditworthiness. Fawry's microlending services now allow previous cash-based merchants to establish long-standing relationships with lenders. Instead of doing endless one-off cash transactions, Fawry has a digital overview of a merchant's collections and performance, enabling it to extend working capital. The Egyptian government also has more cash in its coffers, with digital transaction trails allowing them to collect taxes, further encouraging stability and promoting foreign direct investment.

In 2020, I told Sabry that the world was ready to invest in Fawry and suggested that he consider a global public offering so foreign investors could participate in its future growth. At the time of this discussion, I didn't realize that the Ant Group, part of Chinese billionaire Jack Ma's Alibaba empire, was also planning a global fintech IPO, a transaction that would represent the largest IPO in world history.[360] Jack Ma's company presented a sizable threat, however, to the state-owned Chinese banking sector, and Beijing stifled the deal, striking a major blow to fintech and free enterprise in China. Egypt has proven a better investment climate as Sabry worked with JPMorgan Chase, Morgan Stanley, Goldman Sachs, and Citibank to plan a global offering that would show the financial world that Egypt is a worthy destination for capital investment.

One way I could truly overcome US congressional and Egyptian skepticism about my efforts in Egypt was to make an impressive first investment. This was the wise counsel of my fellow EAEF board member Dina Powell, who reminded me of how crucial this first transaction was. By the time of the Fawry investment, frustration had mounted in the State Department and the executive branch. Though Piraeus Bank was a bust, Fawry was the investment home run that we needed.

Fawry's success was further validation of the enterprise-fund model for even the most troubled parts of the developing and frontier worlds. The Bush administration deserves credit for creating these instruments, and the Obama administration and State Department deserve kudos for resurrecting them decades later. Revolution convulsed Egypt in 2011, and in 2013 the Egyptian military deposed Morsi. Egypt's private sector was uneasy about investing capital in the economy. But a $300 million commitment to invest in the private sector made a strong impact, stimulating economic development, cementing important bilateral relationships, and fostering important social and humanitarian outcomes.

Slowly, we've also begun to mend a troubled US-Egyptian relationship. While forming individual friendships with Egyptian business leaders and members of the EAEF's board proved easy and enjoyable, managing the bilateral relationship proved more challenging. Many Americans remain suspicious of Egypt, remembering that the mastermind of the 9/11 terrorist attacks hailed from the country. A climate of mistrust and skepticism about America similarly reigns throughout the twenty-first-century Arab world. Recalling the disappointments of the Camp David accords, many in Egypt strongly distrusted my motives. After first agreeing to chair the EAEF, I knew that to manage this relationship, we needed to "Egyptianize" the enterprise fund, with Egyptians discharging the work in-country and having majority representation on the board.

"Egyptianization" also extended to Ashraf Zaki and my proposal that we seed a private equity fund for him to own and manage. By working with a private equity company, we demonstrated that the US government wasn't dictating terms in Egypt and that Egyptian free enterprise was good for the country. This strategy also allowed Lorax and the enterprise fund to share profits and award salaries competitive with the private sector. Most important, the EAEF's investment in Fawry catalyzed the Egyptian financial sector, changing the lives of millions.

The success of Fawry and Sarwa marked a turning point for the EAEF. Following these fintech and consumer-finance investments respectively, the market value of the fund's assets was much greater than the original USAID grant of $300 million. We'd accomplished this during revolutionary upheaval and a skittish investment climate, inspiring Egyptians to invest with Americans in their own country. As I describe in the next chapter, this success emboldened the fund to make riskier and even more mission-driven investments geared to fostering democracy in the country. While I joined the Obama administration and many other countries in hoping that the Arab Spring protests would produce a stable democracy, the expectation never struck me as reasonable. It's only by providing jobs and bread that we can achieve political stability and democracy in any country. And that's why I am confident that democracy didn't die with the ousting of Morsi in 2012. Egyptian democracy is just beginning.

15

Developing a Better World

AS EGYPT STRUGGLED TO bolster its economy after the Arab Spring turmoil of 2011, it could always count on Saudi Arabia. The Arab world's energy giant injected tens of billions into Egypt's beleaguered postrevolutionary economy and kept the country humming with discounted energy products.[361] But following his vote on a United Nations Resolution on Syria in 2016, President Abdel Fattah Al Sisi ran afoul of his most important and long-standing benefactor. The friendship between the world's two most powerful Sunni nations seemed over, as high-placed Saudi leaders openly mocked Sisi and Saudi-controlled energy giant Aramco declined shipments of discounted petroleum to Egypt.[362]

Prior to this disagreement, Egypt already suffered 15.5 percent inflation rates, currency weakness, a lack of tourism revenue, decreases in money transfers, or "remittances," from the Persian Gulf, and plummeting revenues from its massive Suez Canal expansion project.[363] After Saudi Arabia's withdrawal, Egypt's already reeling economy began to plummet. Everyday staples like sugar, rice, and baby formula began disappearing from Egyptian store shelves.

Sisi absorbed the brunt of the outcry that followed, especially given that his annual budget had decreased the country's extremely popular subsidies by 14 percent.[364] With 88 percent of Egyptians relying on food subsidies, as well as those of oil, gas, and water, the country reached a crisis point. Some feared a return to the dreaded 1997 bread riots that convulsed the city after President Anwar el-Sadat tried to dismantle the subsidy system on which Egypt had relied since World War I.[365] In a 2016 video posted on social media, a man in Alexandria lit his body afire saying, "I can't afford to eat."[366] The Arab Spring was itself set off when a Tunisian street vendor, Mohamed Bouazizi, set himself ablaze in 2010.

Desperate to save his country from collapse, Sisi turned to the International Monetary Fund (IMF).[367] But as a *New York Times* headline read, "Painful Steps Help Egypt Secure $12 Billion I.M.F. Loan."[368] In exchange for the loan, the IMF required a reduction in energy subsidies, the implementation of a value-added tax (VAT), and the freeing or floating of the country's currency.

These reforms struck Egyptians as draconian. Without a well-developed mass transportation infrastructure, Egyptians relied heavily on personal vehicles. With its generous energy subsidies, gas prices in Egypt were among the cheapest in the world, helping fuel the Egyptian economy but creating massive budgetary shortfalls.[369] After Egypt reduced its energy subsidies, increasing the price of gasoline from sixteen to twenty-one cents a liter, already cash-strapped Egyptians were even more impoverished.[370]

The Egyptian government had long struggled to collect income taxes, especially from those working in the country's large and informal cash-based economy.[371] Following the IMF package, Egyptians now faced a 14 percent VAT tax on most of the consumer goods they purchased, decreasing spending power and increasing short-term inflation. November 3, 2016, marked the greatest shock of all, when the Egyptian central bank floated the Egyptian pound, and currency values declined by half.[372] On this day, which one Egyptian referred to as "Black Thursday," many saw the value of their savings cut in half, and many could no longer afford to travel abroad, pay for school, or purchase necessities.[373]

President Sisi worried that these reforms might create a short-term depression and more political instability. Ever since 2014, I'd had regular lunches with Chris Jarvis, a gifted IMF economist who specialized in the Middle East. We would meet at the Hay-Adams Hotel overlooking Lafayette Square in Washington, DC. Over a chef's salad, we discussed Egypt's borrowing of unsustainable sums from its Gulf neighbors and its fiscal deficits that ran as high as 10 percent of its GDP. Jarvis and I were shocked and relieved when, after years of the IMF team's unsuccessful negotiations with Egypt's central bank and ministry of finance, Sisi agreed to the deal. It took courage for Sisi to sign the IMF agreement and enact fiscal discipline. Though I was saddened about the short-term prospects for Egyptians, knowing the hunger and hardship that would visit most people in the country, I was confident that this was the right move. This short-term austerity was the country's only hope for creating a stable economy able to nourish business and attract foreign capital for investment.[374]

In retrospect, the EAEF's decision to invest in Egypt immediately prior to this devaluation was gutsy. The enterprise fund made its $20 million investment in fintech company Fawry and invested $60 million in consumer finance company Sarwa when the country was in an economic tailspin. It's little surprise that the enterprise fund was among the only investors in the country and that some on Capitol Hill were skeptical of the fund's efficacy. If the US government had asked us to liquidate our investments in 2016, we would have lost the US taxpayer a lot of money.

As we anticipated, the IMF program created a bleak year for Egyptian people and their businesses. As borrowing costs soared and inflation rose to 30 percent, many families fell below the poverty line, and many businesses, especially those dependent on imports, shuttered. Anyone who traveled to the United States or Britain had to pay as much as 50 percent more for the expense, while everyone buying imports had to contend with much higher costs. Struggling to stay afloat, businesses borrowed capital at punishing 22 to 24 percent interest rates.[375]

But with the high cost of imports, Egyptian businesses created more locally produced items, stimulating the private sector and increasing employment. Foreign sources could now purchase Egyptian products and services at about 50 percent less than the year prior, further stimulating domestic industry and injecting sorely needed capital into the economy. Egypt's three major sources of revenue—tourism, the Suez Canal, and remittances—also began to rebound. Tourists had fled the country following a series of terrorist attacks after 2011, most notably the bombing of a chartered passenger flight on October 31, 2015.[376] Cheered by Sisi's encouragement of economic and political stability, tourists began returning to discover the treasures of Egyptian civilization and culture at major discounts. Egypt's $8 billion expansion of the Suez Canal, begun in 2015 to help restore the Egyptian economy and elevate the country to an important global trade position, also gradually began to generate profits.[377] Seeing their countrymen struggling, many Egyptian expats increased their remittances to the country, helping families weather this moment of financial hardship.

Even as I saw the market value of the EAEF's investments in Fawry and Sarwa decrease, the IMF program served only to embolden me. After the success of these investments, I started to encourage Ashraf Zaki and the Lorax team to tilt the mission and focus almost exclusively on development goals. During our weekly calls, our conversations began to center on health care, education, and agriculture, and included businesses that might pose certain financial risks but promised significant development returns. With the fund's liquidity able to absorb any losses, our investments now principally focused on increasing the Egyptian quality of life, empowering women, and bolstering democracy.

DEVELOPING EGYPT

Health Care

Knowing of our interest to invest in Egyptian health care, Zaki introduced the EAEF board to entrepreneur Magda Habib in early 2018. Habib had been employee number three and an executive team member at Raya Holding. A Cairo-based diversified investment conglomerate of 7,000 employees, Raya Holding was working to transform the organization into a market leader with a global blueprint.[378] Working with Ashraf Sabry, Habib then cofounded Fawry in 2009, and when the EAEF organized a large consortium to purchase the company in 2015, she liquidated her position.[379] With some capital at her disposal, Habib began to plan her next investment.

Her conversations about developing and improving Egyptian society began to cluster around health care, and she turned her attention to Egyptian clinics, hospitals, and doctors. When most Egyptians experience a toothache or back problem, they can't visit a dentist or orthopedist or even ask a primary-care physician for a referral. Too often, their only options are unreliable public hospitals or expensive private health-care clinics. Most Egyptians can't afford to pay $25 to visit a private clinic every time one of their children contracts a cold. They also chafe at the government-run health-care system. In Egypt, public doctors are notoriously late for appointments and, because they are paid by procedure, sometimes foist unnecessary surgeries on patients.

To reach Egypt's underserved market, Habib and her cofounder worked diligently in 2016 to develop primary care–oriented clinics, hoping to attract investors. But their fundraising efforts coincided with the currency devaluation, and as Habib recalls, "Nobody wanted to take the risk—it was a really, really bad time to be raising funds in Egypt."[380] After managing to secure a round of financing from high-net-worth Egyptians, Habib launched the business in January 2017 and opened the first Dawi Clinic that June.[381]

In several years' time, Habib created a quality, patient-centric series of clinics that were convenient, affordable, and based on international best practices. Every time patients visit a Dawi Clinic, they can expect the same experience: clean facilities, friendly staff, consistent rates ($10 for each appointment), and on-time appointments with internists, pediatricians, and dentists who have access to their digital health records. Because they are full-time and salaried, and their pay isn't linked to procedures, Dawi doctors aren't tempted to offer patients unnecessary treatments. In this way, Habib is at the forefront of a major health-care trend that focuses less on the reputation of doctors and more on creating quality brands.[382]

I was especially impressed that the Dawi Clinic brand espouses relationship building as its foremost value. Habib discourages patient self-diagnosis and initiating appointments with specialists. Instead, she encourages patients to cultivate relationships with primary-care physicians. "Family physicians can diagnose and treat 70–80 percent of any issues you have," said Magda.[383] Primary-care doctors can also prevent illnesses before they take root. Habib is a strong proponent of preventive health care, and that's why every $10 appointment at Dawi includes a ten-minute wellness checkup. At Dawi even if you come in with only a toothache, the dentist still takes your blood pressure and pulse, asks how you are feeling, and makes dietary and lifestyle recommendations.

Supporting a woman entrepreneur dedicated to improving health care was the easiest investment decision we made in Egypt. In October 2018, the EAEF acquired 27 percent of Dawi Holdings with an investment of $3 million. Dawi Clinics illustrate my belief that successful businesses are built around people. In addition to being a great businessperson helping Fawry build a world-class digital payment platform, Magda Habib also has the experience and temperament to make a successful health-care business.

From our first meeting, she demonstrated how she'd expertly studied the market, identifying a gap in health-care needs that could generate a profit. She readily understands, for example, that outpatient services focused on primary care are low margin, so she can achieve a profit only at scale.[384]

And she can achieve scale only by standardizing services and creating efficiencies on the operational side, while also bolstering the Dawi brand on the consumer side, providing Egyptians convenient services, along with patient-driven, safe outcomes.[385] Most doctors' offices in the United States could benefit from someone like Habib managing their practices.

Habib's prudence and thoughtfulness, which I see in evidence during our regular calls, reminds me how skilled women are in managing people. In 2020, for example, I spoke to Habib about Dawi's subscription offering, underway to raise $3–$4 million for the business. "I believe in you, Magda," I advised her, "and I'll buy the entire thing so you that don't have to go through the process of a subscription offering." I reiterated how mission-critical and important her business was.

"I'm so grateful," she said, "but I can't accept." As she explained, investors like Ashraf Zaki and Ashraf Sabry had invested in Dawi Clinics from day one, and it was only fair that she offer them the first investment opportunity. I respected her judgment, and when she called me again, saying that many of her early-stage investors were enthusiastic, but that not all would subscribe, I offered to purchase any unsubscribed shares. "First," she said, "I need to offer the unsubscribed shares to all of the remaining investors. Don't you think so?" I readily agreed. That was the thoughtful, decent, and honorable course.

While Dawi has achieved success in Cairo, the effort of scaling its operations to underserved regions like the Nile Delta poses greater obstacles (but even greater development impacts). I'm confident in Habib's ability to expand Dawi Clinics in a cookie-cutter, Starbucks arrangement throughout Egypt, offering a consistent menu of products and services. I'm also confident that as the footprint increases, providing a greater swath of Egyptians with digitized records, salaried doctors, on-time treatments, and consistent outcomes, Habib will stay abreast of major trends in health care, incorporating AI, digital wearables, and telemedicine into her clinics.[386] Every time I have a call with Habib and listen to her report on the business, I become excited about Dawi Clinics and the future of Egyptian health care.

Agriculture

In the spring of 2018, after Zaki introduced me to Misr Hytech Seed International, I knew that the EAEF had found its second major impact investment. Like Fawry and Dawi Clinics, Hytech's seed business addresses a fundamental gap in the Egyptian economy. The ancient Egyptians built one of human civilization's first large-scale farming projects, using the Nile's fertile shores to raise wheat and other staples.[387] Egypt's growing population has reduced the availability of farmland and transformed Egypt from a site of agricultural productivity to one of the world's leading wheat importers.[388] Egyptian farmers are largely unable to meet the needs of domestic production because most farmers still use traditional methods, like open-pollination farming, which relies on the wind or animals to pollinate seeds. That's why Hytech's high-performing seed technologies were such an appealing solution. Using Hytech's high-yielding seeds, Egyptian farmers could increase their annual yields, allowing the Egyptian economy to lower its reliance on foreign seed imports—an increasingly costly proposition after the 2016 currency devaluation. By increasing domestic farming productivity, Hytech also promised to bolster the country's animal feed and brewing industries while improving food security throughout Egypt.

While researching this company, I was especially impressed with Suri Sehgal, the India-born crop scientist, seedman, and entrepreneur who founded this company in 1993 with his wife, Edda Sehgal. I imagined that this couple had a special affinity for war-torn Egypt given their own upbringings. Suri was only thirteen when the partition of India made him a refugee. He traveled to various refugee camps looking for food and barely managed to survive the violence when he reunited with his uprooted family. Edda Jeglinsky experienced similar upheaval during World War II when she evacuated her native Silesia before the incoming Soviet army and resettled in Germany.[389]

The two met in the United States, when Edda was an au pair to Henry Kissinger, then a professor at Harvard. Her husband, Suri, was working toward a PhD in plant genetics while gaining a diploma in business management.[390] For the next twenty years, Suri developed his expertise in the seed business, developing and producing hybrid seeds of white and yellow corn, grain, vegetables, and sorghum.

When I learned that Sehgal wanted to sell his company in a purely secondary transaction, I wasn't concerned. Suri wanted to spend his time running the S. M. Sehgal Foundation, a globally lauded NGO that he created to champion food security, water availability, and other important development causes in rural India.[391] The agricultural and intellectual property experts vetting the deal confirmed that Suri and his colleagues had created a company capable of addressing food insecurity in Egypt and beyond. Zaki and I were both optimistic that our joint investment with Sub-Saharan private equity fund Helios would ensure Hytech's expansion throughout the African continent. As Suri said, "Misr Hytech, with its strong base in Egypt, is uniquely positioned to establish itself as a leading seed company in the emerging seed markets of Africa. It has the germplasm, the trained people, and contacts of Helios to expand on the African continent."[392] In March 2019, Helios and the EAEF acquired 96.7 percent of the agribusiness, and we anticipate great development returns in the coming years.[393]

Education

With our investments in health care and agriculture underway, I was eager to invest in education. Much to the skepticism of my finance colleagues, I've always argued that teachers should be exempt from taxes. Teachers are critical to our economies and societies and have the power to change the course of a person's life. One reason I joined the board of education in Weston, Connecticut, was because I wanted to evaluate and identify the best teachers for our children. Decades later, I remain a strong believer in public education and am certain it will play a critical role in Egyptian private sector development and future generations' quality of life.

Just as was the case with Egyptian consumer finance, banking technology, and health care, middle-income Egyptians lack affordable, high-quality education. Until recently, most Egyptians sent their children to substandard public schools where teachers are chronically underpaid and inadequately trained, resulting in illiteracy rates of up to a quarter to one third.[394] If parents wanted better for their kids, they had to pay exorbitant rates for private schools. Wealthy Egyptians shell out $2 billion annually for private school tuition to avoid their public schools.[395]

In 2019, Zaki introduced me to the Nermien Ismail Schools Group (NIS), one of Egypt's leading private-school developers and operators, which seemed poised to change Egypt's educational status quo. NIS's eponymous and talented founder, Nermien Ismail, scoured the globe looking for best practices in education. Since launching NIS in 1999, Ismail and her partners have created a school system with one of the largest footprints and greatest reputations in Egypt. At the time that Zaki introduced me to the company, NIS's three campuses, encompassing nine schools and serving over 9,000 students, provided high-quality, affordable education to middle-income families.[396] With millions in need of their services, NIS needed our help to scale.

As I began investigating the company, I was impressed by how prescient it had been about technology. Beginning in 2012, NIS incorporated online curriculum mapping and student information systems, allowing NIS educators to build, design, and prepare curricula against technology-based standards of learning. In 2019, the company was the only fully "blended learning" provider in Egypt, adopting the "flipped classroom" method, in which classroom time is devoted to problem-solving instead of lecturing, and flex models for "self-guided" learning, with an online learning platform that includes over 35,000 videos.[397]

With this infrastructure in place, NIS needed a capital injection so it could open six new schools in Egypt; acquire smaller, distressed local players; and eventually scale operations throughout the MENA region. In so doing, it could also help bolster educational best practices in the developed world. NIS had been exploring a relationship with Florida's Orange County school district, which wanted to accredit, approve, and utilize NIS's online-education platforms in its own schools.

Apart from the wonderful story of Egyptians helping Americans in digital learning, I was even more excited about this company's potential development impact. In 2019, the school served 9,200 students—but it had to reject over 8,000 new applicants each year because it couldn't accommodate them. With our help, the school could expand its reach to an estimated 10,000 additional students over the following year and create more than 2,000 jobs. Egyptians would also save on private tutoring and lessons and possibly funnel that money into household expenses or starting a business.

The Lorax team conducted significant due diligence on NIS and Egypt's larger educational landscape. We documented the Egyptian household education expenditures on public versus private schools and studied the country's English-, French-, and German-language schools, as well as religious and international academies. NIS was unique in this landscape, Lorax concluded, and could expand its geographical presence to other regionally underserved markets. That's because NIS relied on technology and experienced facilitators rather than on gifted teachers. With talented teachers providing in-depth explanations of core concepts and ideas in the videos, NIS staff could facilitate student discussions and engagement. Unlike when my three children came of age, learners now have technology. While teachers and engaged parents still play vital roles in educating children, technology democratizes access to people who lack these personal advantages, allowing ambitious learners to take ownership of their education.

In a mostly primary transaction in 2019, the EAEF invested approximately $32 million in the company. At the time of this writing, this promises to be an excellent financial and development investment, especially when NIS has an initial public offering.

In Egypt, schools and hospitals are integral to the capitalist system, often conducting public offerings that allow them to expand and attract greater human capital. In this way, Egyptians are even more aggressive capitalists than Americans or Britons, who likely think that educational and health-care facilities should be patient- and student-focused, instead of shareholder-oriented. But this system works for Egypt and, unlike in many developed countries, schools and hospitals produce some of the country's most talented entrepreneurs who are committed to increasing revenues and allowing others to participate in their company profits. NIS plans to make its initial public offering in 2025.

Private Equity and Impact Investing

The success of the EAEF across the vital industries of banking, health care, agriculture, and education also helped rebuild the Egyptian private equity business following the Arab Spring. The EAEF's 2014 entry into the market was critical to attracting other foreign investors to Egypt. After seeding Lorax, my long-term mission included supporting other private equity firms that were financially responsible and supported our development goals.

My relationship with private equity manager Ashraf Zaki was unique, both with respect to our commitment to the fund's mission and our friendship, and it proved difficult to replicate this formula. But I've come close with Ahmed El-Guindy, the former head of investment banking at EFG Hermes who went on to found Tanmeya Capital Ventures (TCV), a mid-market private equity fund that invests in SMEs.[398] I think of Guindy as the younger and more aggressive version of Zaki, who instead of pursuing larger investments like Fawry and Sarwa, targeted rapidly growing businesses with $5–$7 million ticket sizes. As with Lorax, the EAEF seeded TCV with $10 million, and I worked with Guindy to invest this money in a way that fit our mission. Our work with TCV has been financially rewarding, and Guindy's assets under management quadrupled over several years, further attracting other important investment partners to Egypt.[399]

In 2020 Egyptian private equity firm Ezdehar Management asked the EAEF to join them in taking a minority position in Al-Tayseer Healthcare Group (THG), the largest health-care provider in the underserved Nile Delta region. The EAEF joined Ezdehar to invest $6 million.

This opportunity helped bolster health care in the Nile Delta region while also allowing the EAEF to invest with a health-care and SME–focused private equity firm. With collaborations like this, along with the help of development funds like the International Finance Corporation (IFC) and the European Bank for Reconstruction and Development (EBRD), the Egyptian private equity ecosystem continues to grow. I hope that these success stories outlive us for generations to come, attracting a stream of global investors to Egypt, transforming it into an economically stable country on the road to an open democracy.

The Future of Enterprise

After signing on the IMF agreement in 2016, Egypt accomplished an impressive turnaround. Though it continues to wrestle with poverty, Egypt is the only country in the entire North African or Gulf region that is growing its gross domestic product, which increased 3.5 percent even during the devastating Covid-19 pandemic.[400] The World Bank agrees, saying "Egypt is the only country in the Middle East and North Africa to witness positive real GDP growth in 2020/2021."[401] By 2018, Moody's Investors Service relabeled its outlook on Egypt from stable to positive, while IMF director Christine Lagarde suggested that the country had achieved "macroeconomic stabilization."[402]

The IMF deserves significant credit for creating a productive deal, helping the country make structural changes that will prepare it for future growth. By 2028, the IMF estimates that there will be 80 million Egyptians of working age, and thanks to the program, the country will be equipped to employ them.[403] Multilateral institutions like the IMF and World Bank don't often receive the kudos they deserve. Constructed after World War II to help rebuild the global financial order, these organizations often enact policies that cause short-term pain. In offering countries capital in exchange for enacting reforms, the IMF makes just as great a contribution to global peace as other important multinational institutions like the United Nations.[404]

When I arrived in Cairo in the fall of 2012, revolution, terror, and bloodshed greeted me in the streets. With the help of the IMF and the wisdom of the US government, the EAEF saw past the tear gas to find talented, experienced investment analysts and corporate finance professionals ready to build a new Egypt.

The success of the EAEF has outstripped even our most optimistic projections. According to EAEF auditors, the fund invested approximately $240 million and in five years' time doubled its size, generating an annual return of over 20 percent. After subtracting administrative costs, we invested $275 million, and the value now exceeds $700 million. Before we liquidate in 2028, I predict that the enterprise fund will have assets that exceed $1 billion.

After shifting emphasis in 2018 to impact-oriented investments, the enterprise fund has demonstrated that we can achieve strong financial returns while making excellent progress on development. If I had the space, I would detail the fund's many additional investments. These might include our 2018 investment in the late Dr. Osama Al-Baz's Orchidia Pharmaceuticals, a business providing Egyptians with ophthalmic solutions like artificial tears while helping the country fight against its tragic levels of preventable blindness. Or I might discuss our investment in Abu Auf—one of Egypt's leaders in specialty foods like nuts, coffee, and cooking essentials—which is promoting healthier eating behaviors in Egypt, or in HA Utilities, an infrastructure and utilities platform making important investments in renewable energy.

Magda Habib's Dawi Clinics and Nermien Ismail's NIS powerfully illustrate how women represent off-balance-sheet assets in developing countries, and that by supporting them we can create much greater business and development outcomes. These women-led companies continue to revolutionize health-care and educational delivery in Egypt. I remain impressed by Habib's managerial acumen and ethics, and was also astounded when, during my preliminary discussions with NIS, I discovered that a school in Florida sought to learn from Egypt's blended-learning platforms. For all the members on the Hill who thought that the EAEF was helping the frontier and developing worlds because they lacked knowledge and experience, here was a school system in Florida seeking to learn best practices from a sister organization in Egypt.

When it came to investing in Egypt, Warren Buffett was right. Revolution is precisely the moment to begin an enterprise fund. We should take the enterprise model to the most troubled parts of the world like Central America, Haiti, and Sub-Saharan Africa and find talented human capital there to lead these funds. We also need to persuade Brazil, Germany, and even China to run their own enterprise funds, working together to grow the private sectors and increase living standards in the developing and frontier worlds.

But such funds can succeed only with the proper approach to relationships. In the future, we need enterprise-fund leaders with experience and the ability to follow through. Managers must be flexible enough to survey the terrain of local countries and to structure fund mechanics in innovative ways, as we did with seeding businesses through private equity. Future fund managers must also "stay the course," as I like to say, always focusing on the long term. Like many in government, past enterprise fund chairs have spent short stints in office. But future managers must adopt a long-term perspective and remain dedicated and patient even if they must wrangle with US government officials over details or encounter opposition and obstruction as I did with Lindsey Graham. It was only after considerable due diligence that we found a man as prescient and talented as Ashraf Zaki. He built a team of dedicated, experienced analysts that not only found our first great investment opportunity in Fawry but also convinced a skeptic like me of its staggering potential.

For the future success of enterprise funds, the US government must commit to cultivating historical memory. When EXIM Bank helped the South Korean economy recover from a devastating financial crisis, no institutional mechanisms existed to memorialize the event so others could mobilize these solutions for the next global crisis. The same is true of the first generation of European enterprise funds. If USAID had recorded some of the milestones it had achieved with the enterprise fund in Poland, under the strong stewardship of John Birkelund, as well as some of the corruption it encountered in the implementation of enterprise funds in South Africa, Central Asia, or Russia, we could have incorporated these lessons when structuring the

EAEF. My hope in writing these chapters on Egypt is that the solutions we devised, like seeding private equity and reaching micro and small businesses through fintech and consumer finance investments, can be passed on to the next generation of enterprise-fund leaders.

As we learned in 2017, the impact of enterprise funds had even more potential than we had ever imagined. That year, Matt Stepan, a man who advised impact investors, joined me in my office. He lit up when he saw a picture of me and Neal Maxwell, the Mormon religion's illustrious twentieth-century scholar. I told Stepan of my unlikely friendship with Maxwell when I worked with an energy giant in Utah, while Stepan described his passion for the developing world that began when he was abroad on his Mormon mission. Stepan wanted to invest in future enterprise funds alongside the US government. "You're creating jobs and improving the quality of life of Egyptians. The EAEF may be the ultimate impact fund!" No one in government had ever conceived of the enterprise fund as representing the public equivalent of a private impact fund.

To scale enterprise funds and increase their future potential, I strongly suggest a marriage between private impact funds and government-sponsored enterprise funds. When I began scouting for opportunities in Egypt (2012) and just prior to our first major investments (2015), the country experienced revolutionary upheaval and a massive currency devaluation. Only sovereign entities could risk investing in this chaotic environment. But as I write this book and the country has stabilized, most large, successful private equity and private impact firms still seek public partnerships. The US government remains sluggish and obstructionist when it comes to such alliances, and I wasn't able to join forces with private funds. But given the increased power of impact investment funds, I predict that the private sector will partner with future enterprise funds, leveraging modest taxpayer funds and private sources to invest in many of the world's poorest countries. It's only with public-private partnerships that we achieve impact on scale. Public officials can take greater risks and ensure that funds stay "on mission," while private entities can leverage their investment acumen to find and nurture the best investments.

I can only imagine what the EAEF could have accomplished with the private resources and support of a powerful Silicon Valley–based technology firm or the Rockefeller or Ford foundations. The private sector controls 90 percent of the world's capital, and private funds offer hundreds of times more than what the World Bank or US Treasury can. If impact investors and socially conscious private equity could join public funds, and if other rich countries followed the United States in creating enterprise arrangements, we could truly create a new world. With such public-private partnerships in Guatemala and Honduras, we could stabilize Central America and avert the current migration catastrophe on the US/Mexico border. If Germany created a series of such public and private funds in the Middle East, it too might prevent the immigration catastrophe on its shores. In Sub-Saharan Africa, such funds could help elevate the poorest parts of the world to the status of middle-income countries.

As I suggested to Hillary Clinton and Delaware senator Chris Coons in the spring of 2021, we could immediately begin to scale enterprise funds with limited taxpayer funding. In 2028, the EAEF will liquidate its funds and either return the original investment capital to the US Treasury or use it to create legacy foundations, helping bolster Egypt's health-care, education, and agricultural sectors. "What if we carved out $200 million from our assets currently under management," I suggested to Coons and Clinton, "and created a new fund to invest in Sub-Saharan Africa?" If we expand the EAEF's mandate to include other parts of Africa, we could scale enterprise funds to troubled regions and countries throughout the continent.

Coons and Clinton liked the idea in part because such partnerships represent our best hope for meeting the rising challenge of China. For decades, China has been active in the developing and frontier worlds, resettling industrious and hardworking Chinese nationals to diverse locations and leveraging large quantities of capital to make local investments and purchase important businesses. Many US policy makers understand that China will outstrip America in global commerce and geopolitical influence if we don't act soon. For many on the Hill, enterprise funds are a strong potential tool for the State Department to meet the challenge of China. But I support them because they create financial and humanitarian benefits that help increase global stability and equality.

As I wrote this chapter, the major news media outlets marked the ten-year anniversary of Egypt's Arab Spring by decrying the political, economic, and human-rights landscape in Egypt. "A Decade On, Silence Fills Egypt's Field of Broken Dreams," read one headline; "A Decade After the Arab Spring, Autocrats Still Rule the Mideast," declared another. It's true that the country is not building a democracy as fast as we might like and that the country's citizens enjoy less freedom than in many Western countries. But as I've undertaken my work in Egypt, I've been chagrined by reporters' consistently negative characterization of Egypt. Few journalists documenting the tenth anniversary of the Arab Spring detail Egypt's successes in democratizing access to health care, agriculture, and education, nor do they describe the country's growing financial literacy, the participation of women in business, and the thriving startup ecosystem nourished in part by socially conscious private equity investors.

These journalists, just like the gifted people working at the State and Treasury departments, expect too much, too soon from the developing and frontier worlds. During my time at EXIM Bank, I was taken aback when high-ranking diplomats lectured countries and heads of state about what they should be doing better, without understanding their history and culture. When directing the EAEF, I shared the desire expressed by senators McCain and Graham and by President Obama for democratic stability in Egypt, while I also joined American progressives like Bernie Sanders who lamented the sometimes-poor human-rights records in these countries. But instead of decrying these imperfections, I worked to address them through bolstering economic development. When working in Egypt or elsewhere, we must establish economic and financial stability before we can perfect the democratic process.

When I think about the prospect of Egypt, my mind returns to January 2011 when I visited Rwanda with my daughter Debbie, my grandson Daniel, and Jamie Odell, my talented portfolio manager at Caravel who specialized in Africa. After landing in Kigali, I was stunned to find a clean, orderly, and efficient airport—such a departure from the rundown facilities and chaotic atmosphere of most regional airports in Sub-Saharan Africa. The taxi departed on freshly paved roads, with LED lights embedded in the tarmac and state-of-the-art traffic lights with countdown timers—innovations the United States didn't yet have. We drove past construction sites for the new Kigali convention center, with a five-star Radisson Hotel and technology park connecting to roads that crisscross the verdant countryside. As we ascended into the mountains, I understood why this country was nicknamed "the land of the thousand hills and mountains." The building lights flickering at dusk revealed a semiurban landscape, nestled in scenic beauty that nearly took my breath away.

As I made my way through this orderly and pristine country, the 1994 genocide was still emotionally palpable. But as in Germany after World War II, you didn't discuss the past openly. Politician and military leader Paul Kagame helped end the catastrophic bloodshed in a military victory, enacting a benevolent dictatorship in 2000. Many observers have since lamented his human-rights record, citing his illiberal treatment of dissenters and political opponents.[405] But fewer have written about the new society he created that emphasized community, patriotism, and civic duty, and his vision for a new country based on self-sufficiency, free-market capitalism, and entrepreneurship. At the time of my visit, fewer still discussed how this African country had become one of the most investor-friendly in Africa. Instead of navigating a byzantine bureaucracy to set up a new business, Odell and I discovered a central office in downtown Kigali where entrepreneurs could efficiently register and file their taxes or licensing materials. We were proud to invest in the only two publicly owned companies in Rwanda and knew they promised great financial and development returns.

After horrific bloodshed in the 1990s, Kagame not only transformed his country into a place of tranquility and technological innovation, but he also championed a society that empowered women. He's consistently promoted girls' education and women in workplace leadership positions, and ensured that the country's 2003 constitution mandated that 30 percent of parliamentary seats be reserved for women.[406] Unlike America's short-lived "Rosie the Riveter" era, after which men returned from the battlefield and displaced women in the wartime workforce, Rwanda's empowerment of women continued after hostilities. Rwanda now leads the world for women serving in government.[407] As I told Kagame during my visit, the best thing we could do for the African continent would be to clone him, so that he could also run Zimbabwe, Niger, and other Sub-Saharan African countries.

Though Rwanda's Paul Kagame and Egypt's Abdel Fattah Al Sisi lack pristine human-rights records, they preside over countries that recently emerged from genocide and revolutionary upheaval and now enjoy stability, job growth, and improved qualities of life. News coverage of both countries, however, continues to overreport negative news, accusing the leaders of rigging elections, assassinating opponents, and muzzling journalists and judiciaries alike.[408] I routinely wonder why Western observers condemn them instead of applauding and encouraging their achievements.

The United States is a place of thriving human rights and, the Trump presidency aside, robust and stable democratic institutions. But it took us two centuries to eliminate slavery and ethnic genocide and engineer the financial infrastructure to achieve this stability—and just as long to have open discussions about our own national divisions and failures. And when it comes to empowering women, we're still lagging far behind Rwanda. We should keep this timetable in mind when we're tempted to criticize other countries, and instead of focusing on abuses, help spur economic development. Economic development is a precondition for human rights and democracy.

And that's why we need more talented young people working in this field.

Most of the brilliant and skilled people destined for public service yearn to enter the State Department and broker peace agreements, like those between the Israelis and Palestinians. Such conflict-resolution accords are of course important because they can result in peace. Embassies, universities, and academic-like bodies and think tanks like the Council on Foreign Relations have focused on high-level diplomacy. Unfortunately, that has sometimes come at the expense of economic development.

Part of this owes to economic development's association with the business community, something that the diplomatic corps, NGO space, and academia have never traditionally embraced. Some of that is changing as the IFC and World Bank have positioned themselves on the cutting edge of measuring economic development and as certain universities and think tanks actively collaborate with private sector initiatives. Throughout my career, and especially during my work with the World Resources Institute (WRI), I've tried to change this status quo and champion public-private partnerships. And though the media rightfully publicizes major peace agreements, I believe that creating jobs is even more important for global sustainability.

I'd like readers to come away from my experience in Egypt with a broader perspective on how to positively impact the world. When Joe Biden became president in 2021, young people inundated me with calls, asking about where they might find work in the new administration, and regaling me with their dreams of joining the White House or State Department. "You should start by dreaming about making a difference in the world," I often suggested, telling them about lesser-known agencies focusing on economic development. "How about joining USAID," I suggested to many, a vital agency that the Trump administration had starved of talent. Or how about staffing any number of advisory committees or agency boards such as the African board at EXIM Bank, which meets every three months to discuss what EXIM and the government are doing in Africa. Or how about contacting your congressperson's local office and speaking to a local staffer about your interests and the needs of your state.

As future generations are now "up and doing," with stronger commitments to having an impact on the world, I encourage them to entertain a broader menu of possibilities. I hope they read my story and resist the seductive allure and glamour of diplomacy and peace negotiations. While Fawry lacks the romance of the Camp David Peace accords, this financial technology has increased the dignity of the Egyptian people and empowered them to lead efficient and productive lives. Economic development remains the best means to create long-lasting social change, and we need future talent to help these efforts. If you want to reach and impact the poorest countries in the world, look to the Development Finance Corporation (DFC), USAID, or enterprise funds. It's only with participation of the young and gifted in economic development that we can truly change the world.

Conclusion

IT IS EARLY MAY 2021 as I write these final words from my study in Connecticut. The days are growing longer, and the forsythia is in bloom. With the new Biden administration in Washington and Covid-19 vaccines available to all American adults, it feels like a season of renewal and a time for cautious optimism after a year of political unrest and pandemic. Like many, I adjusted to the limited travel and state lockdowns by sequestering myself at home, conducting business and board meetings over Zoom. Without a commute, I could begin each workday two hours earlier, something that was especially helpful when working with Egypt, which is six hours ahead of me.

These extra hours were a godsend because my pandemic schedule was as busy as ever. Since I've written my chapters on Egypt, enterprise funds continue to interest the US government. Throughout the spring of 2021, I continued my discussions with Hillary Clinton, Senator Coons, and Biden administration officials about expanding the enterprise-fund model throughout Central America and Sub-Saharan Africa. My idea about harvesting some of the profits of the Egyptian-American Enterprise Fund and using them to seed new funds might first come to pass in Egypt's southern neighbor, Sudan.

I've long eyed Sudan, with its population of 50 million and its extreme debt and hardship, as a unique opportunity for enterprise funds. This is a frontier country with negative growth and, like Egypt following the Arab

Spring, it faces a crossroads. The country might implode economically, fall prey to a dictator, and create regional instability. Or others could intervene with initiatives like enterprise funds to help stimulate the private sector, attract foreign direct investment, and sow the seeds of a stable democracy.

With the Biden administration's new attention on climate and sustainability, my Zoom calls this spring also focused on the environment. As I was drafting the WRI chapter, Jeff Bezos announced his $100 million gift to WRI, and I was thrilled for all of us. But in mid-March 2021, when WRI president and CEO Andrew Steer told me that Bezos had invited him to direct the $10 billion Earth Fund, I was ambivalent. This was a great opportunity for him and for the world, but it meant that WRI would need a new CEO. For nearly every day that followed, I joined our search committee's virtual meetings with global stakeholders and staff, considering this important decision with the team. The market for experienced sustainability talent is very tight, as many foundations, NGOs, and government entities including USAID have begun focusing on building their climate capacities.

While there are countless ways to add value to the world, my two current passions—economic development and sustainability—seem especially promising. As we inch closer to the midcentury mark, troubled parts of the world like Sub-Saharan Africa and Central America must begin developing. For anyone interested in public service and economic development, this is a great time to join USAID, the International Development Finance Corporation, or a fledgling enterprise fund. It's also a great time to work on global sustainability and climate. NGOs and nonprofits like the WRI Ross Center need fresh talent as they develop and scale global initiatives in urban development, clean transportation, and carbon emission reductions.

Apart from allowing me increased focus on enterprise funds and sustainability, the coronavirus pandemic granted me the time to reflect on my life and to complete this book. As I examined my career and determined the episodes that I would include in this memoir, I keep returning to different relationships and collaborations, realizing how they have underpinned any success and joy I've experienced throughout my career.

Relationships loomed large in my twenties when, after graduating from Wharton, I began my career on Wall Street, studying under the brilliant Herbert Wolfe. Under Wolfe's direction, everyone in Hanseatic's research department studied statistics, price-to-book value, and corporate growth, all with an eye to determining strong future investments. Wolfe and Warren Buffett looked askance at me when I said I wanted to visit these companies.

Even at that young age, I believed we couldn't effectively analyze a company without knowing its management. Thereafter, I carved out a finance niche for relationship building. I loved advising Mountain Fuel Supply because in traveling to Salt Lake City, I was able to delve into a cultural environment far different from my own in New York, Los Angeles, or San Francisco. Because I wasn't a drinker or smoker, had a strong work ethic, and loved outdoor sports, I meshed well with the people of Utah and grew close to Mormon leaders and scholars like Neal Maxwell.

When we bought Chappell Music, my colleagues at Wertheim loved what a strong financial investment it was. So did I. But I derived the most pleasure from working with Freddy Bienstock, growing the company's music catalogue through building relationships with new composers. My desire to experience new cultures and understand different people attracted me to motion pictures and people like Arthur Krim. With him and his partners at Orion, I enjoyed their spectacular films like *Hoosiers* and *Amadeus* as I helped them navigate their volatile industry. These executives were so anxious to produce the next Oscar winner that they lost money, and as a financial advisor I wanted to ensure that they could remain solvent and thereby continue to enrich American culture with their movies. No matter the industry or sector that I describe in this book, I've always found more value in people than I have in balance sheets.

Relationship building proved just as critical when I entered the public sector. It was my friendship with David Dinkins and his team, including Bill Lynch, Harold Ickes, and Peter Johnson, that afforded me the opportunity to join the US government. Repotting myself in Washington was an enormously exciting experience because of the different people I met there. I began my journey with Jackie Clegg and Andrea Adelman introducing me to hundreds of members of Congress. I enjoyed meeting these people and finding common ground with them and their wise staff members as I attempted to reauthorize the agency.

This experience of working the Hill was a master class in relationship building. In a highly polarized and rancorous time, I became friends with people as ideologically diverse as Sonny Callahan, Newt Gingrich, Nancy Pelosi, and Maxine Waters. Along the way, I committed some notable errors in human relations, especially with my second-in-command Jackie Clegg, whom I failed to manage well.

My friendship with Bill Clinton facilitated and enabled my early work in government, allowing me to develop personal relationships not just with people but with countries. Without his logistical and moral support, I couldn't have created loan programs in Asia, navigated the Tyumen Oil crisis in Russia, and initiated the reopening of EXIM Bank locations throughout Sub-Saharan Africa. After leaving government, it was my close relationship with Jonathan Lash that led me to WRI and ignited my passion about the environment. Together with that first generation of environmental leaders, we increased the scope and dynamism of this organization, empowering it not simply to conduct world-class research but to effect important change. It was only through close friendships with leaders like Ani Dasgupta and Steve Ross that we later globalized the institution, increasing its stature and visibility to attract the attention and largesse of Jeff Bezos.

My friends and colleagues in Egypt remain critical to our continuing progress in bolstering the private sector there. While so many people in Egypt and the US government contributed to its success, Ashraf Zaki's influence was pivotal. Our collaboration, rooted in our passion for building the private sector of the world's most populous Arab country, powered this fledgling enterprise through its initial hiccups and hardships. Such personal relationships with fund managers and local human talent remain crucial for the future success of other enterprise funds.

As I reflect on my far-ranging career, I've derived the following lessons about life that readers might find instructive. As much as possible, *embrace change*. Many people understandably greeted the pandemic with dread and now refer to 2020 as a "lost year." Others saw opportunity amid the mayhem and, faced with lockdowns, dedicated their efforts to strengthening relationships with loved ones and reevaluating their professional goals and larger purpose in life. I wasn't happy about being sequestered in Connecticut for a year, but without the pandemic, I couldn't have stayed rooted long enough to make significant progress on Egypt and to finish this book.

Given my most significant moments of growth and personal transformation, I'm also a major proponent of "repotting." I consider personal repotting as unrelated to change, because whether you face happiness or adversity, you might still benefit from changing your professional circumstances to maximize growth. I still remember telling my colleagues at Wertheim about how happy I was that we moved our offices from Wall Street to 200 Park Avenue in Midtown Manhattan around 1980. Everyone grumbled about the change and thought my excitement for a new neighborhood was a bit crazy. But we met new people, enjoyed shorter commutes, and discovered new restaurants. This repotting helped our company grow.

Sometimes we repot ourselves when we feel stuck and listless. When my son Doug was twenty-eight years old, he was unhappy with his employer and felt stalled in his career. I suggested that he repot himself to a different city and stop work altogether to pursue an advanced degree. After two years of graduate school at UCLA, a completely different regional and cultural environment, he returned to New York with a fresh perspective (or "root system") and was poised for future success. I was able to advise Doug because something similar happened to me during the late 1990s after I repotted myself in government. I strongly believe that strategic and thoughtful repotting creates the personal growth and transformation that is necessary to making a difference in the world.

But amid change and repotting, it's also important to finish well, carefully managing transitions among different opportunities. I'm proud that I transitioned from Hanseatic to Wertheim in a deliberate way and later left the private sector only after ensuring that the firm was secure without me. I stayed at EXIM even when Rahm Emanuel offered me a career path that may have led to an appointment as treasury secretary. In fact, I violated my cardinal rule and remained in office after the Bush takeover. In my experience, many people in finance and government didn't finish well, leaving their posts under a cloud or amid scandal.

Managing transitions and knowing when to finish is admittedly tricky. We must balance our desire to avoid what my granddaughter Mia calls FOMO ("fear of missing out")—FOMO of ongoing responsibilities to career posts and relationships. People have often approached me for advice about pursuing different career opportunities and how to know when it's right to change course. Before making a change, I routinely ask them to answer the following three questions:

1. Do you like the work, and do you like the people?
2. Are you learning something and gaining value from the experience?
3. Are you compensated, financially or psychologically and spiritually, in a significant way?

Tally how many yeses you have. While it's rare to score a three, you should aim for at least a two. Over the years, many in finance told me that they intensely disliked their jobs and weren't learning anything new. But they felt trapped because the financial reward was so great that they couldn't leave. Others in government, by contrast, approached me with more agonizing decisions. They loved their work and added tremendous value while continually learning, but they struggled with an inadequate salary. If you only score one out of these three, my advice is to seek repotting opportunities. If you score two out of three, you have a difficult choice and should remain open to new opportunities.

And if you score three out of three, you should be extremely grateful. I've been fortunate because for most of my life, I loved my work and colleagues, continuously learned new things, and was adequately compensated for my efforts. My dad didn't score a three for three in his later years, and he repotted himself at fifty, to reread Shakespeare and the history of mathematics.

I often think I am flunking retirement. When you enjoy your work, learn, and add and receive value, it's hard to do something else. And why should you? As I write these words, Warren Buffett is ninety, Henry Kissinger ninety-eight, Nancy Pelosi eighty-one, and President Biden seventy-eight. And they're all doing some of the most important work of their careers.

At eighty-five years old, in what I hope is the seventh inning stretch of a fulfilling nine-inning career, I'm still "up and doing" and couldn't imagine it any other way.

Index

Lewinsky Affair, 231–233
Lewisohn, Oscar, 122
A Life in the Theater, 99–100
Little Italy, 70
Loeb, Rhoades & Co., 58, 60
Loesser, Frank, 75
Loesser, Jo Sullivan, 75, 85
London, 184
Longfellow, Henry Wadsworth, 8
Lorax Capital Partners, 282, 292, 298, 305–306
Los Angeles Times, 78
"lost year" 2020 as, 321
Lott, Trent, 161
Louisville Experimental Kindergarten School, 85
Lucas, George, 89
Lucasfilm movie studio, 89
Luxor Obelisk, 54
Lynch, Bill, 137–138, 319

M
M9 structure, 166
MacArthur Foundation, 252
MacNabb, Katiana Guzman, 242–243
"macroeconomic stabilization," Egypt, 307
Macy's department store, 26
"major bracket" firms, 35
making movies in the 1980's, 89–91
Malaysia, 173
Mallinckrodt, Georg "Gowi" Wilhelm Gustav von, 128
Malliouhana Hotel, 124–125
Mamet, David, 99
Mamaroneck Harbor, 11
managing Mountain Fuel Supply (MFS), 41–48
Mandela, Nelson, 213
Manila, 178, 180
Manilow, Barry, 78
marathon training, 119
Marcos, Ferdinand, 178, 180–181
Marcos, Imelda, 180–181
market mayhem, 126–129
marketing America, 214–217
Marshall Scholarship, 278
Matisse, Henri, 123
Maxwell, Neal A., 43, 49, 310, 319
Maxwell House cans, 37
"May Day" 1975, 55–56, 70
McAuliffe, Terry, 143

McCain, John, 3, 271–273, 275, 312
McConnell, Mitch, 156–158
McCormick, Dina (née Habib) Powell, 276
McDonald, Tom, 212
McFaul, Michael, 194
Medavoy, Mike, 95–96
Mellon family, 33
MENA region (Algeria, Egypt, Libya, Morocco and Tunisia), 210, 280, 304
Merkin, Barry, 16–17, 28
Merrill Lynch, 19–20, 35
"on message," 152–153
Mexican peso, 179
Mexican peso crisis, 1994-1995, 173
Mexico, 244
Miami Dolphins, 260, 266–267, 275
Michael, George, 82
Middle East, 244
Middle East and North Africa (MENA), 277
Midtown Manhattan, 19
Milken, Mike, 46
Millard, Mark, 58–60
Millennials, 8
Millet, Jean-François, 123
Misr Hytech Seed International, 302–303
mission creep, 181, 183–189, 201, 207, 209, 225–227
Mister Ed, 91
moniti meliora sequamur ("Now that we've been admonished, let us follow better ways"), 15
Montedison, 41, 53–67, 69, 71–72, 76, 95–96, 170
Montedison, in Manhattan, 64–66
Montedison, in Milan, 60
Montedison in Manhattan, 63–66
Montedison in Milano, 57–63
Montedison introduction, 53–57
Montedison S.p.A., 57–58
Montgomery Securities, 38
Moody's Investment Service, 307
moral and energy landscape, changes in, 48–51
Morgan, J. P., 200
Morgan Stanley, 6, 26–27, 35, 48, 120, 281, 291
Morin, Bob, 180
Mormon church, 42
Mormon culture, 49
Morsi, Mohamed, 1–2, 4, 271, 278, 280, 292–293
Moscow, 196

Notes

1. Noha El Tawil, "Obama Administration Knew Muslim Brotherhood Has Contacts With Al Qaeda, Yet Objected Its Overthrowing," *Egypt Today*, October 13, 2020, https://www.egypttoday.com/Article/1/93015/Obama-administration-knew-Muslim-Brotherhood-has-contacts-with-Al-Qaeda; Shadi Hamid, "Islamism, the Arab Spring, and the Failure of America's Do-Nothing Policy in the Middle East," *Brookings*, October 14, 2015, https://www.brookings.edu/blog/markaz/2015/10/14/islamism-the-arab-spring-and-the-failure-of-americas-do-nothing-policy-in-the-middle-east/.

2. Erin Cunningham, "Could Morsi Make Peace in the Middle East?" *Public Radio International*, July 17, 2012, https://www.pri.org/stories/2012-07-17/could-morsi-make-peace-middle-east.

3. Technically, Congress didn't pass this piece as legislation, as it was ultimately absorbed in a government funding bill that passed in December 2011 (Consolidated Appropriations Act, 2012, Pub. L. No. 112–74, Div. I, § 7041[b]). Many thanks to Connie Queen for reminding me of this.

4. Throughout this book, I refer to the Export-Import Bank of the United States as EXIM or EXIM Bank. Please note that others adopt different shorthand for the agency, including Ex-Im.

5. Daniel Goleman, "What Makes a Leader?" *Harvard Business Review*, January 2004, https://hbr.org/2004/01/what-makes-a-leader.

6. David Brooks, "A Nation of Weavers," *New York Times*, February 18, 2019, https://www.nytimes.com/2019/02/18/opinion/culture-compassion.html.

7. "Frontier" is a term in the financial community to designate countries at a financial development state prior to emerging markets, like India and Brazil.

8. "How a Couple of Baseball Players Founded Harvey Ltd., Brown's Campus Shop," *Ivy Style*, October 26, 2016, http://www.ivy-style.com/how-a-couple-of-baseball-players-founded-harvey-ltd-browns-campus-shop.html.

9. Ernest Kolowrat, *Hotchkiss: A Chronicle of an American School* (New Amsterdam: 1992), 44. Also note there were contrasting visions for what this school would represent and not everyone agreed to the Yale feeder model. For this section on Hotchkiss, I am indebted to this book.

10. Kolowrat, *Hotchkiss*, 76 *et passim*.

11. Kolowrat, *Hotchkiss*, 25–26 *et passim*; William M. Freeman, "George Van Santvoord Is Dead; Hotchkiss Principal 29 Years," *New York Times*, February 20, 1975, https://www.nytimes.com/1975/02/20/archives/george-van-santvoord-is-dead-hotchkiss-principal-29-years.html.

12. Kolowrat, *Hotchkiss*, 28.

13. Kolowrat, *Hotchkiss*, 26–28.

14. Except for expulsion: Kolowrat, *Hotchkiss*, 26.

15. Kolowrat, *Hotchkiss*, 26.

16. Kolowrat, *Hotchkiss*, 26.

17. Kolowrat, *Hotchkiss*, 25 *et passim*. Please note that there are different ways to render this Latin phrase, and some school literature substituted "advised" in place of "admonished."

18. Kolowrat, *Hotchkiss*, 171.

19. Kolowrat, *Hotchkiss*, 14.

20. "Kurt Grunebaum 76; An Investment Banker," *New York Times*, November 19, 1981, https://www.nytimes.com/1981/11/19/obituaries/kurt-grunebaum-76-an-investment-banker.html.

21. Peter Grant, "New York's Tishman Family Turns to Real Estate Tech Startups," *Wall Street Journal*, November 1, 2015, https://www.wsj.com/articles/new-yorks-tishman-family-turns-to-real-estate-tech-startups-1446430662.

22 "22-Story Office Structure at Park Avenue and 57th Street Awaits Steel Framework," *New York Times*, November 3, 1953, https://www.nytimes.com/1953/11/03/archives/work-is-advancing-on-davies-building-22story-office-structure-at.html.

23 Kelly McCleary and Sahar Akbarzai, "New York City's Iconic 21 Club Is Closing Down," *CNN*, December 12, 2020, https://www.cnn.com/2020/12/12/us/21-club-nyc-closing/index.html.

24 "Maurice Wertheim," Brookhaven–South Haven (blog), accessed April 20, 2020, http://brookhavensouthhaven.org/history/Wertheim/WertheimDegasToMatisse.htm.

25 For this entire Starbucks section, I am indebted to Dan Levitan (cofounding partner at Maveron, a consumer-only venture capital firm), interview with author, February 11, 2021.

26 Scott Austin, "Will the Four Horsemen Ride Again?" *Wall Street Journal*, March 3, 2009, https://www.wsj.com/articles/BL-VCDB-705. These four horsemen "underwrote a large number of the venture-backed IPOs, which averaged about 130 a year before the dot-com bubble."

27 Nathan Buehler, "If You Had Invested at Starbucks' IPO (SBUX)," *Investopedia*, updated May 14, 2020, https://www.investopedia.com/articles/markets/120215/if-you-had-invested-right-after-starbucks-ipo.asp.

28 Technically, the Federal Trade Commission (FTC) originally enforced this securities legislation prior to the creation of the SEC in 1934: "The FTC During the Administrations of Franklin D. Roosevelt (1933–45) and Harry S. Truman (1945–53)," *Federal Trade Commission*, accessed April 21, 2021, https://www.ftc.gov/reports/ftc100-bibliography/1933-1953.

29 Sophia Kunthara, "Why Direct Listings Just Became a Lot More Attractive as an IPO Alternative," *Crunchbase*, August 27, 2020, https://news.crunchbase.com/news/why-direct-listings-just-became-a-lot-more-attractive-as-an-ipo-alternative/.

30 The relationship between the oil and gas divisions was far from seamless: "Corporation Affairs," *New York Times*, May 12, 1976, https://www.nytimes.com/1976/05/12/archives/corporation-affairs-mountain-fuel-holders-support-management.html.

31 Mimi Swartz, "The Day Oscar Wyatt Caved," *Texas Monthly*, November 2007, https://www.texasmonthly.com/articles/the-day-oscar-wyatt-caved/.

32 Reis Thebault, "Who Is Michael Milken, the 'Junk Bond King' Trump Just Pardoned?" *Washington Post*, February 18, 2020, https://www.washingtonpost.com/business/2020/02/18/michael-milken-pardon/.

33 "Mountain Fuel Changing Name to Questar Gas," *Deseret*, August 14, 1997, https://www.deseret.com/1997/8/14/19328382/mountain-fuel-changing-name-to-questar-gas.

34 Jocelyn Mann Denyer, "White House Visit: Pres. Clinton Meets with Pres. Hinckley, Receives His Six-Generation Family History," *Church News*, updated November 18, 1995, https://www.thechurchnews.com/archives/1995-11-18/white-house-visit-pres-clinton-meets-with-pres-hinckley-receives-his-six-generation-family-history-135275.

35 Denyer, "White House Visit."

36 Though, as of 2002, he would continue serving on the board and consulting: "More Than Just Cash," *Deseret News*, April 29, 2002, https://www.deseret.com/2002/4/29/19651864/more-than-just-cash.

37 "More Than Just Cash."

38 Mark Seal, "The Woman Who Wanted the Secrets," *Vanity Fair*, August 2008, https://www.vanityfair.com/news/2008/08/agnelli200808.

39 James Gipson, "NYSE Was Revolutionized by SEC Abolition of Fixed Commissions," July 21, 1985, *Washington Post*, https://www.washingtonpost.com/archive/business/1985/07/21/nyse-was-revolutionized-by-sec-abolition-of-fixed-commissions/8726b8b1-8013-4bcf-aad8-776fcc65f417/.

40 Gipson, "NYSE Was Revolutionized by SEC."

41 "Montedison, S.p.A." *Harvard Business School* Case Study (1984): 1.

42 "Montedison, S.p.A." 1.

43 "Montedison, S.p.A." 1–2.

44 "Montedison, S.p.A." 8.

45 Brian Michael Jenkins, "Does the U.S. No-Concessions Policy Deter Kidnappings of Americans?" *Rand Corporation* (2018): iv, v. Material here cited is from the foreword, "Four Decades of Analysis and Action Frame a Centuries-Old Debate," written by John Parachini, director of Rand's cyber and intelligence policy center.

46 Jenkins, "Does the U.S. No-Concessions Policy Deter Kidnappings of Americans?" v.

47 "Montedison to Expand," *New York Times*, June 1, 1983, https://www.nytimes.com/1983/06/01/business/montedison-to-expand.html.

48 "Montedison to Expand."

49 "Montedison to Expand."

50 I can't independently verify this figure so many years later, but to my best recollection, this was the amount.

51 "The IPO is being reinvented," *Economist*, August 20, 2020, https://www.economist.com/leaders/2020/08/20/the-ipo-is-being-reinvented.

52 Zack Beauchamp, "Bernie Sanders Is Right: Hillary Clinton Praising Henry Kissinger Is Outrageous," *Vox*, February 12, 2016, https://www.vox.com/world/2016/2/12/10979304/clinton-sanders-kissinger.

53 The article makes reference to its profits "last year," which refers to 1986, roughly the time of this meeting: Roberto Suro, "Embattled Executive: Mario Schimberni; The Duel for Dominance at the Top of Montedison," *New York Times*, April 19, 1987, https://www.nytimes.com/1987/04/19/business/embattled-executive-mario-schimberni-duel-for-dominance-top-montedison.html.

54 Suro, "Embattled Executive: Mario Schimberni."

55 Suro, "Embattled Executive: Mario Schimberni."

56 Suro, "Embattled Executive: Mario Schimberni."

57 Connie Bruck, "The Billionaire's Playlist," *New Yorker*, January 12, 2014, https://www.newyorker.com/magazine/2014/01/20/the-billionaires-playlist.

58 Bruck, "Billionaire's Playlist."

59 Ben Sisario, "Warner Music Launches Its I.P.O.," *New York Times*, updated May 28, 2020, https://www.nytimes.com/2020/05/26/business/media/warner-music-ipo.html; Bill Hochberg, "The Record Business Is Partying Again, But Not Like It's 1999," *Forbes*, April 11, 2019, https://www.forbes.com/sites/williamhochberg/2019/04/11/the-record-business-is-coming-back-but-its-not-1999-yet/?sh=3fb7f6683257; Blavatnik's conglomerate made this purchase.

60 Michael DeGusta, "The Real Death of the Music Industry," *Business Insider*, February 18, 2011, https://www.businessinsider.com/these-charts-explain-the-real-death-of-the-music-industry-2011-2.

61 Bruck, "The Billionaire's Playlist."

62 Sandra Salmans, "New Yorkers & Co.; A Song Plugger's Biggest Play: His Return as Boss," *New York Times*, June 4, 1985, https://www.nytimes.com/1985/06/04/business/new-yorkers-co-a-song-plugger-s-biggest-play-his-return-as-boss.html.

63 Emma Vickers and Devon Pendleton, "Blavatnik Is $7.5 Billion Richer After Contrarian Music Bet," *Bloomberg*, updated June 3, 2020, https://www.bloomberg.com/news/articles/2020-06-03/blavatnik-gets-6-6-billion-richer-after-contrarian-music-bet#:~:text=7%2C%202019.,-Photographer%3A%20Stefanie%20Keenan&text=Len%20Blavatnik%20bought%20Warner%20Music,digital%20listening%20dominated%20by%20piracy.

64 Salmans, "New Yorkers & Co."

65 Salmans, "New Yorkers & Co."

66 Salmans, "New Yorkers & Co."

67 Salmans, "New Yorkers & Co."

68 Salmans, "New Yorkers & Co."

69 Kathryn Harris, "Warner Reportedly Will Acquire Chappell: $200-Million Deal Would Merge 2 of 3 Biggest U.S. Music Publishers," *Los Angeles Times*, May 12, 1987, https://www.latimes.com /archives/la-xpm-1987-05-12-fi-7734-story.html; Salmans, "New Yorkers & Co."

70 "How Long Does Copyright Protection Last?" See copyright.gov, accessed December 15, 2020, https://www.copyright.gov/help/faq/faq-duration.html#:~:text=The%20term%20of%20 copyright%20for,plus%20an%20additional%2070%20years.

71 Sisario, "Warner Music Launches."

72 Ben Sisario, "Bob Dylan Sells His Songwriting Catalog in Blockbuster Deal," *New York Times*, updated December 9, 2020, https://www.nytimes.com/2020/12/07/arts/music/bob-dylan -universal-music.html.

73 Sisario, "Bob Dylan Sells His Songwriting Catalog."

74 Though there was significant turnover and industry consolidation, and some spoke of the "Big Three" instead of the "Big Four"; Harris, "Warner Reportedly Will Acquire Chappell."

75 Salmans, "New Yorkers & Co."

76 For this profile of Freddy Bienstock, I am indebted to Salmans, "New Yorkers & Co."

77 Jamie Dimon and Warren E. Buffett, "Short-Termism Is Harming the Economy," *Wall Street Journal*, June 6, 2018, https://www.wsj.com/articles/short-termism-is-harming-the -economy-1528336801.

78 Andrew Wolfson, "Who Really Wrote the 'Happy Birthday' Song?" *USA Today*, updated June 29, 2013, https://www.usatoday.com/story/news/nation/2013/06/29/who-really-wrote-the-happy -birthday-song-/2475837/; Geraldine Fabrikant, "Sound of a $25 Million Deal: 'Happy Birth- day' to Warner," *New York Times*, December 20, 1988, https://www.nytimes.com/1988/12/20 /business/the-media-business-sound-of-a-25-million-deal-happy-birthday-to-warner.html.

79 Wolfson, "Who Really Wrote."

80 Wolfson, "Who Really Wrote"; Fabrikant, "Sound of a $25 Million Deal."

81 Fabrikant, "Sound of a $25 Million Deal."

82 According to all my notes and records, this sold for $18 million. But as I reviewed the *New York Times*, I saw there was some controversy, including an executive at the time who quoted a $25 million price: Geraldine Fabrikant, "Sound of a $25 Million Deal."

83 Benjamin Weiser, "Birthday Song's Copyright Leads to a Lawsuit for the Ages," *New York Times*, June 13, 2013, https://www.nytimes.com/2013/06/14/nyregion/lawsuit-aims-to-strip-happy -birthday-to-you-of-its-copyright.html.

84 Ben Sisario, "'Happy Birthday' Copyright Invalidated by Judge," *New York Times*, September 22, 2015, https://www.nytimes.com/2015/09/23/business/media/happy-birthday-copyright-invalidated -by-judge.html.

85 Ben Sisario, "Details of 'Happy Birthday' Copyright Settlement Revealed," *New York Times*, February 9, 2016, https://www.nytimes.com/2016/02/10/business/media/details-of-happy -birthday-copyright-settlement-revealed.html.

86 "Star Wars," *Britannica*, January 28, 2021, https://www.britannica.com/topic/Star-Wars-film -series.

87 Brian Martin, "Richard Bloch, co-founder of Phoenix Suns, passes away at 89," *NBA*, October 30, 2018, https://www.nba.com/news/richard-block-co-founder-phoenix-suns-passes-away.

88 "Cornelius L. 'Connie' Hawkins," *Hoophall*, accessed January 4, 2021, https://www.hoophall .com/hall-of-famers/connie-hawkins/; Ron Flatter, "Connie Hawkins: Flying Outside," *ESPN*, accessed April 29, 2021, http://www.espn.com/classic/000707hawkins.html#:~:text= Cornelius%20Hawkins%20was%20born%20on,team%20All%2DAmerican%20in%201960.

89 Roger Ebert, "Samuel Z. Arkoff: In Memoriam," *Roger Ebert*, September 18, 2001, https://www .rogerebert.com/interviews/samuel-z-arkoff-in-memorium.

90 Ebert, "Samuel Z. Arkoff."

91 Douglas Laman, "The Highest-Grossing Horror Movies of all Time," *Looper*, updated January 4, 2021, https://www.looper.com/305260/the-ten-biggest-horror-movies-of-all-time/. As for its success, it was the most successful independent film up to a certain point: *The Amityville Horror* was the most successful indie film until the 1990s *Teenage Mutant Ninja Turtles*, and it still maintains its legacy as a perennial Halloween favorite. Sarah Cunnane, "Low-Budget Horror Movies That Killed at the Box Office," *MoneyWise*, December 22, 2020, https://moneywise.com/a/low-budget-horror-movies-that-killed-at-the-box-office.

92 For a full exploration of this movie, please see Troy Brownfield, "Why Was 'The Amityville Horror' So Terrifying?" *Saturday Evening Post*, July 30, 2019, https://www.saturdayeveningpost.com/2019/07/why-was-the-amityville-horror-so-terrifying/.

93 For much of this profile, I am indebted to "Orion Pictures Corporation," *Reference for Business*, accessed January 4, 2020, https://www.referenceforbusiness.com/history2/48/ORION-PICTURES-CORPORATION.html.

94 Aliean Harmetz, "Orion's Star Rises in Hollywood," *New York Times*, April 19, 1978.

95 Mike Medavoy, *You're Only as Good as Your Next One: 100 Great Films, 100 Good Films, and 100 For Which I Should Be Shot* (New York: Atria Books, 2002), 86–87.

96 This is the evaluation of this strong piece on which I also draw: K. Austin Collins, "When the Oscars Chose 'Driving Miss Daisy' Over 'Do the Right Thing,'" *Vanity Fair*, January 22, 2019, https://www.vanityfair.com/hollywood/2019/01/when-the-oscars-chose-driving-miss-daisy-over-do-the-right-thing.

97 She then goes on to note Spike Lee's absence from the list: Collins, "When the Oscars Chose."

98 "Alfred Uhry," *University of Georgia*, accessed December 18, 2020, https://georgiawritershalloffame.org/honorees/alfred-uhry.

99 Please note that after I joined, the corporate headquarters moved to Rocky Hill, Connecticut.

100 "Herbert Gilman, 65, a Marketing Pioneer for Discount Stores," *New York Times*, July 14, 1990, https://www.nytimes.com/1990/07/14/nyregion/herbert-gilman-65-a-marketing-pioneer-for-discount-stores.html.

101 "Milton A. Gilman," *Boston Globe* (obituary), September 30–October 1, 2010, https://www.legacy.com/obituaries/bostonglobe/obituary.aspx?n=milton-a-gilman&pid=145736107.

102 "Milton A. Gilman."

103 "Milton A. Gilman."

104 Alison Leigh Cowan, "Ames to Buy Discount Unit From Zayre," *New York Times*, September 16, 1988, https://www.nytimes.com/1988/09/16/business/ames-to-buy-discount-unit-from-zayre.html.

105 Isadore Barmash, "Ames Stores Appoints a New Chief Executive," *New York Times*, September 24, 1987, https://www.nytimes.com/1987/09/24/business/business-people-ames-stores-appoints-a-new-chief-executive.html.

106 Barmash, "Ames Stores Appoints."

107 Barmash, "Ames Stores Appoints."

108 "The Wal-Mart Cheer" *Walmart China*, accessed March 3, 2021, http://www.trust-mart.com/english/walmart/rule/wmcheer.htm.

109 "The Wal-Mart Cheer."

110 Brent Schlender, "Wal-Mart's $288 Billion Meeting," *CNN Money*, April 18, 2005, https://money.cnn.com/magazines/fortune/fortune_archive/2005/04/18/8257009/.

111 Leigh Cowan, "Ames to Buy Discount Unit."

112 Please note that some news sources list the number of Zayre stores at 388 and others at 392.

113 David Mehegan, "Ames Got an Excedrin Headache After Swallowing Zayre Chain," *Buffalo News*, May 27, 1990, https://buffalonews.com/news/ames-got-an-excedrin-headache-after-swallowing-zayre-chain/article_f8bb0d12-3cb0-5e32-b166-2978334ddab8.html.

114 Louis Uchitelle, "From Income Lost to Real Estate Gained: The Savings and Loan Crisis Leaves Scars," *New York Times*, August 13, 1989, https://www.nytimes.com/1989/08/13/us/ripples-bailout-income-lost-real-estate-gained-savings-loan-crisis-leaves-scars.html.

115 Isadore Barmash, "A Bloomingdale's of Discounting," *New York Times*, October 28, 1979, https://www.nytimes.com/1979/10/28/archives/a-bloomingdales-of-discounting-yet-caldor-has-stores-in-only-3.html; Kenneth N. Gilpin, "Caldor Files for Chapter 11 Protection," *New York Times*, September 19, 1995, https://www.nytimes.com/1995/09/19/business/caldor-files-for-chapter-11-protection.html.

116 Kenneth N. Gilpin, "Bankruptcy Protection Being Sought by Bradlees," *New York Times*, June 24, 1995, https://www.nytimes.com/1995/06/24/business/bankruptcy-protection-being-sought-by-bradlees.html.

117 Mehegan, "Ames Got an Excedrin Headache."

118 The stock was almost $30 in 1987 and in April 1990 was $1.62: Kara Swisher, "Ames Chain Files for Bankruptcy," *Washington Post*, April 27, 1990, https://www.washingtonpost.com/archive/business/1990/04/27/ames-chain-files-for-bankruptcy/878809d8-31a3-4450-97fd-b7fca5f33a6d/.

119 Mehegan, "Ames Got an Excedrin Headache."

120 Kenneth N. Gilpin, "Ames Sues Its Advisers on Zayre Bid," *New York Times*, October 15, 1992, https://www.nytimes.com/1992/10/15/business/company-news-ames-sues-its-advisers-on-zayre-bid.html.

121 Erin N. Berg, "Ames' Acquisition of Zayre Has Proven Disastrous // Sales at Renamed Zayre Stores Down 16 percent," *Tampa Bay Times*, July 6, 2006, https://www.tampabay.com/archive/1990/04/15/ames-acquisition-of-zayre-has-proven-disastrous-sales-at-renamed-zayre-stores-down-16-percent/.

122 Mehegan, "Ames Got an Excedrin Headache."

123 Mehegan, "Ames Got an Excedrin Headache."

124 Berg, "Ames' Acquisition of Zayre Has Proven Disastrous."

125 Harrison Smith, "Melvyn I. Weiss, Class-Action King Felled by Kickback Scheme, Dies at 82," *Washington Post*, February 6, 2018, https://www.washingtonpost.com/local/obituaries/melvyn-i-weiss-class-action-king-felled-by-kickback-scheme-dies-at-82/2018/02/06/8fe2140e-0b4e-11e8-8b0d-891602206fb7_story.html.

126 Gilpin, "Ames Sues Its Advisers."

127 Isadore Barmash, "Bankrupt Ames Hires a Turnaround Expert," *New York Times*, May 1, 1990, https://www.nytimes.com/1990/05/01/business/business-people-bankrupt-ames-hires-a-turnaround-expert.html.

128 Sherri Day, "Ames to Liquidate and Close Stores," *New York Times*, August 15, 2002, https://www.nytimes.com/2002/08/15/business/ames-to-liquidate-and-close-stores.html.

129 Niall Ferguson, *High Financier: The Lives and Time of Siegmund Warburg* (New York: Penguin Press, 2010), 417.

130 Ferguson, *High Financier*, 417-21.

131 Damien McCrystal, "Old Siegmund's Spinning in His Grave," *Guardian*, June 8, 2002, https://www.theguardian.com/business/2002/jun/09/theobserver.observerbusiness13.

132 Daniel F. Cuff, "Wertheim's Chairman Gets Key Job at Ames," *New York Times*, December 22, 1987, https://www.nytimes.com/1987/12/22/business/business-people-wertheim-s-chairman-gets-key-job-at-ames.html.

133 "Stock Market Crashes on 'Black Monday,'" *New York Times* (blog), October 19, 2011, https://learning.blogs.nytimes.com/2011/10/19/oct-19-1987-stock-market-crashes-on-black-monday/.

134 "The Black Monday debacle of 1987 when the stock market turned in a one-day loss that, on a percentage basis, was almost twice as large as the steepest drop in 1929," in Charles R. Morris, "The Day Wall Street Collapsed," *New York Times* (book review), November 17, 2017, https://www.nytimes.com/2017/11/17/books/review/diana-b-henriques-a-first-class-catastrophe.html.

135 "Stock Market Crashes on 'Black Monday.'"

136 The latter is the argument of Diana B. Henriques, *A First-Class Catastrophe* (Henry Holt & Company, 2017); Morris, "The Day Wall Street Collapsed."

137 Morris, "The Day Wall Street Collapsed."

138 Linette Lopez, "The Tisch Dynasty: How Two Boys from Brooklyn Became the Biggest Name in New York," *Business Insider*, May 9, 2012, https://www.businessinsider.com/meet-the-tischs-2012-5.

139 Lopez, "Tisch Dynasty."

140 Lily Rothman, "Read *Time*'s Report on the Crown Heights Riots of 1991," *Time*, August 19, 2015, https://time.com/3989495/crown-heights-riots-time-magazine-history/.

141 Ben Sales, "Ex-NYC mayor Dinkins, blamed over deadly Crown Heights riots, dies at 93," *Times of Israel*, November 24, 2020, https://www.timesofisrael.com/ex-nyc-mayor-dinkins-blamed-over-deadly-crown-heights-riots-dies-at-93/.

142 Steven Erlanger and Marilyn Berger, "Teddy Kollek, Ex-Mayor of Jerusalem, Dies at 95," *New York Times*, January 2, 2007, https://www.nytimes.com/2007/01/02/world/middleeast/02cnd-kollek.html.

143 "Shlomo Lahat, Ex-Mayor of Tel Aviv, Dies at 86," *New York Times*, October 2, 2014, https://www.nytimes.com/2014/10/03/world/middleeast/shlomo-lahat-ex-mayor-of-tel-aviv-dies-at-86.html.

144 Michael Tomasky, "'They Stole That Election From Me,' Rudy Giuliani Said Decades Ago," *New York Times*, December 1, 2020, https://www.nytimes.com/2020/12/01/opinion/dinkins-giuliani-nyc-mayor.html.

145 Tomasky, "'They Stole That Election.'"

146 Tomasky, "'They Stole That Election.'"

147 Sam Kim, "Movie Nights at the White House," *Public Radio International*, August 16, 2018, https://www.pri.org/stories/2018-08-16/movie-nights-white-house.

148 Jeffrey E. Garten, "Opening the Doors for Business in China," *Harvard Business Review*, May–June 1998, https://hbr.org/1998/05/opening-the-doors-for-business-in-china. Brown was the first Black secretary of commerce.

149 Garten, "Opening the Doors."

150 Andrew Glass, "Ron Brown dies in plane crash, April 3, 1996," *Politico*, April 2, 2017, https://www.politico.com/story/2017/04/ron-brown-dies-in-plane-crash-april-3-1996-236759.

151 Glenn F. Bunting and Alan C. Miller, "Clinton Coffee Guests Gave DNC $27 Million," *Los Angeles Times*, January 28, 1997, https://www.latimes.com/archives/la-xpm-1997-01-28-mn-22891-story.html.

152 Bunting and Miller, "Clinton Coffee Guests."

153 Edward-Isaac Dovere, "McAuliffe Looks Past the Clintons, Toward 2020," *Politico*, June 13, 2017, https://www.politico.com/story/2017/06/13/terry-mcauliffe-2020-off-message-239459.

154 Paula Dwyer, "The Ex Im Bank: Caught in the Swirl of Donorgate," *Bloomberg*, March 9, 1997, https://www.bloomberg.com/news/articles/1997-03-09/the-ex-im-bank-caught-in-the-swirl-of-donorgate.

155 Dwyer, "The Ex Im Bank."

156 Dan Balz, "Clinton Wins by Wide Margin," *Washington Post*, November 6, 1996, https://www.washingtonpost.com/wp-srv/national/longterm/campaign/pres96.htm.

157 Though in its first few years, EXIM was dedicated to trade with the Soviet Union. Many thanks to Andrea Adelman for reminding me of this.

158 Dwyer, "The Ex Im Bank."

159 McKay Coppins, "The Man Who Broke Politics," *Atlantic*, October 17, 2018, https://www.theatlantic.com/magazine/archive/2018/11/newt-gingrich-says-youre-welcome/570832/.

160 Coppins, "The Man Who Broke Politics."

161 This number refers to EXIM's program budget. I distinguish program and administrative budgets below. Don Gonyea, "The Longest Government Shutdown in History, No Longer—How 1995 Changed Everything," *NPR*, January 12, 2019, https://www.npr.org/2019/01/12/683304824/the-longest-government-shutdown-in-history-no-longer-how-1995-changed-everything.

162 Coppins, "The Man Who Broke Politics."

163 Andrea Adelman, interview with Dr. William H. Becker (Business History Group), March 20, 2001.

164 Andrea Adelman, interview with Dr. William H. Becker (Business History Group), March 20, 2001.

165 Andrea Adelman, interview with Dr. William H. Becker (Business History Group), March 20, 2001.

166 David Dinkins to Ms. Yvette Hernandez, 1221 Avenue of the Americas (39th floor), New York, New York (March 4, 1997).

167 Many thanks to Jim Cruse for reminding me of this line: Jim Cruse (director of policy at EXIM Bank), interview with author, February 22, 2021.

168 "Congressman Jesse Jackson, Jr., Was Right to Pay His Wife—Sandi Jackson Is Smart, Experienced and a Winner," With Both Hands (blog), May 2009, http://hickeysite.blogspot.com/2009/05/congressman-jesse-jackson-jr-was-right.html.

169 Andrea Adelman, interview with Dr. William H. Becker (Business History Group), March 20, 2001.

170 Andrea Adelman, interview with Dr. William H. Becker (Business History Group), March 20, 2001.

171 Andrea Adelman, interview with Dr. William H. Becker (Business History Group), March 20, 2001.

172 Robert D. Hershey Jr., "Ex-Im Bank's President Is Stepping Down," *New York Times*, November 3, 1995, https://www.nytimes.com/1995/11/03/business/ex-im-bank-s-president-is-stepping-down.html.

173 Steven Pearlstein, "Brody Resigns as Head of Export-Import Bank," *Washington Post*, November 3, 1995, https://www.washingtonpost.com/archive/business/1995/11/03/brody-resigns-as-head-of-export-import-bank/a3496723-9705-4d23-a478-6bf13ec43354/.

174 Pearlstein, "Brody Resigns as Head of Export-Import Bank."

175 "Professor Elaine Kamarck," *Harvard Kennedy School*, accessed March 26, 2021, https://iop.harvard.edu/get-involved/internships-careers/research-assistant-program/professor-elaine-kamarck.

176 "Kamarck Plans to Leave Exim Bank at Term's End," *Wall Street Journal*, December 4, 1996, https://www.wsj.com/articles/SB849661115528091000.

177 "Kamarck Plans to Leave Exim."

178 Hershey, "Ex-Im Bank's President Is Stepping Down."

179 Jim Cruse (director of policy at EXIM Bank), interview with author, February 22, 2021.

180 Jim Cruse (director of policy at EXIM Bank), interview with author, February 22, 2021.

181 Paul Blustein, "Ex-Im Bank, Other Agencies May Merge," *Washington Post*, December 4, 1996.

182 Sam Roberts, "Barry Gottehrer, 73, Lindsay Aide, Dies," *New York Times*, April 13, 2008, https://www.nytimes.com/2008/04/13/nyregion/13gottehrer.html.

183 Al Kamen, "Beckwith: Best Bet?" *Washington Post*, October 20, 1999.

184 Julie Belaga, interview with Dr. William H. Becker (Business History Group), March 23, 2001.

185 Andrea Adelman, interview with Dr. William H. Becker (Business History Group), March 20, 2001.

186 EXIM Bank, "Rita M. Rodriguez Appointed Acting President of Export-Import Bank," press release, March 31, 1997, https://www.exim.gov/news/rita-m-rodriguez-appointed-acting-president-export-import-bank.

187 EXIM Bank, "Rita M. Rodriguez Appointed Acting President."

188 Maria Haley, interview with Dr. William H. Becker (Business History Group), March 23, 2001.

189 Maria Haley, interview with Dr. William H. Becker (Business History Group), March 23, 2001.

190 Julie Belaga, interview with Dr. William H. Becker (Business History Group), March 23, 2001. Please note that Belaga was born in Massachusetts but ran for office in Connecticut.

191 "Four Asian Nations Hit By 1997-98 Financial Crisis Face Vulnerability," *New York Times*, April 19, 2007, https://www.nytimes.com/2007/04/19/business/worldbusiness/19iht-currency.1.5350058.html.

192 For some of the analysis in these paragraphs and throughout this chapter, I am indebted to Antonia Balzas's insightful report: "Averting a Crisis and Promoting Ex-Im Bank—Confidence Boosting in Latin America," July 2001, unpublished.

193 Balzas, "Averting a Crisis and Promoting Ex-Im Bank."

194 Neil Thomas, "For Company and For Country: Boeing and US-China Relations," *Macro Polo*, February 26, 2019, https://macropolo.org/analysis/boeing-us-china-relations-history/.

195 Bruce Gilley, "Reforming Zeal," *Far Eastern Economic Review*, May 27, 1999.

196 William Branigin, "'Crony Capitalism' Blamed for Economic Crisis," *Washington Post*, August 16, 1984, https://www.washingtonpost.com/archive/politics/1984/08/16/crony-capitalism-blamed-for-economic-crisis/d99e8760-087d-4d25-ad66-3d324150dc4d/.

197 Eduardo Lachica, "U.S. Ex-Im Bank's Clout Helps Speed Restructuring," *Asia Wall Street Journal*, May 27, 1999.

198 Gilley, "Reforming Zeal."

199 Lachica, "U.S. Ex-Im Bank's Clout."

200 Steve Hanke, "20th Anniversary, Asian Financial Crisis: Clinton, the IMF and *Wall Street Journal* Toppled Suharto," *Forbes*, July 6, 2017, https://www.forbes.com/sites/stevehanke/2017/07/06/20th-anniversary-asian-financial-crisis-clinton-the-imf-and-wall-street-journal-toppled-suharto/?sh=21514a012882.

201 Balzas, "Averting a Crisis and Promoting Ex-Im Bank," 2001.

202 Alan Friedman, "G-7 Ponders $10 Billion to Insure Asian Trade," *International Herald Tribune*, February 11, 1998.

203 Friedman, "G-7 Ponders."

204 Jim Cruse (director of policy at EXIM Bank), interview with author, February 22, 2021.

205 Balzas, "Averting a Crisis and Promoting Ex-Im Bank," 2001.

206 Balzas, "Averting a Crisis and Promoting Ex-Im Bank," 2001.

207 Gilley, "Reforming Zeal."

208 Seumas Milne, "Catastroika Has Not Only Been a Disaster for Russia," *Guardian*, August 15, 2001, https://www.theguardian.com/world/2001/aug/16/russia.comment.

209 Meeting Schedule and Briefing notes, provided by EXIM Bank to Chairman James Harmon, November 1997.

210 Meeting Schedule and Briefing notes, provided by EXIM Bank to Chairman James Harmon, November 1997.

211 Meeting Schedule and Briefing notes, provided by EXIM Bank to Chairman James Harmon, November 1997.

212 Meeting Schedule and Briefing notes, provided by EXIM Bank to Chairman James Harmon, November 1997.

213 Meeting Schedule and Briefing notes, provided by EXIM Bank to Chairman James Harmon, November 1997.

214 Meeting Schedule and Briefing notes, provided by EXIM Bank to Chairman James Harmon, November 1997.

215 James Harmon, memorandum to Samuel R. Berger, Strobe Talbott, and Stuart Eizenstat, December 1, 1997; James Harmon, memorandum to President Bill Clinton, The White House (1600 Pennsylvania Avenue), Washington, DC, October 13, 1999.

216 James Harmon, memorandum to Samuel R. Berger, Strobe Talbott, and Stuart Eizenstat, December 1, 1997.

217 James Harmon, memorandum to Samuel R. Berger, Strobe Talbott, and Stuart Eizenstat, December 1, 1997.

218 "Russia: BP raises stake in Russia's Sidanco," *Alfa Bank*, April 16, 2002, https://alfabank.com /news/russia-bp-raises-stake-in-russias-sidanco/.

219 James Harmon, memorandum to Samuel R. Berger, Strobe Talbott, and Stuart Eizenstat, December 1, 1997.

220 Please note that these figures represent 2002 data: "Russia: BP Raises Stake in Russia's Sidanco."

221 Terry Macalister, "The Fall of the Sun King," *Guardian*, May 1, 2007, https://www.theguardian .com/business/2007/may/01/bp; David Ignatius, "The Strange Case of Russia, Big Oil, and the CIA," *Washington Post*, January 9, 2000.

222 Ignatius, "The Strange Case of Russia."

223 See for example, David Hoffman and John F. Harris, "Clinton, Yeltsin Gloss Over Chechen War," *Washington Post*, April 22, 1996, https://www.washingtonpost.com/archive/politics/1996/04/22 /clinton-yeltsin-gloss-over-chechen-war/6c51c44b-34b8-4443-b7ba-8d2cee6d0249/.

224 "Human Rights and Other Policy Considerations," *EXIM Bank* (2014 Competitiveness Report Online), accessed February 10, 2021, https://www.exim.gov/news/reports/competitiveness-reports/ human-rights#:~:text=The%20Chafee%20Amendment%2C%20as%20amended,would%20be%20.

225 "Executive Orders," *Federal Register*, accessed February 10, 2021, https://www.archives.gov/federal -register/codification/executive-order/12166.html.

226 James Harmon, memorandum to Samuel R. Berger, Strobe Talbott, and Stuart Eizenstat, December 1, 1997.

227 Douglas Bereuter et al., Letter to Honorable James Harmon, from fourteen signatories from the Congress of the United States, November 19, 1999.

228 Jonathan Peterson, "White House Blocks Aid Package to Russia," *Los Angeles Times*, December 22, 1999, https://www.latimes.com/archives/la-xpm-1999-dec-22-fi-46334-story.html.

229 John Lancaster, "Albright Clears Loan to Russian Oil Company," *Washington Post*, April 1, 2000, https://www.washingtonpost.com/wp-srv/WPcap/2000-04/01/067r-040100-idx.html.

230 Lancaster, "Albright Clears Loan to Russian Oil Company."

231 Rachel Maddow, *Blowout* (New York: Crown, 2021), 28, 31.

232 Maddow, *Blowout*, 28, 36.

233 Maddow, *Blowout*, 38–40.

234 James Harmon to His Excellency Vladimir V. Putin, May 10, 2005.

235 In his "The Strange Case of Russia," David Ignatius draws a similar conclusion.

236 Al Kamen, "Beckwith: Best Bet?" *Washington Post* (In the Loop column), October 20, 1999.

237 Nancy Dunne, "US Eximbank Chief Goes on African Investment Safari," *Financial Times*, May 6, 1998.

238 Peter Baker, "First Lady's Africa Tour Turns Spotlight on Progress, Problems," *Washington Post*, March 18, 1997, https://www.washingtonpost.com/archive/politics/1997/03/18/first-ladys -africa-tour-turns-spotlight-on-progress-problems/ce36f7d4-6747-4dbe-b7b4-f4566b7cb69e/.

239 Steven Mufson, "Ex-Im Bank Aims to Do More in Africa," *Washington Post*, December 16, 1999.

240 These figures are from 1999: Mufson, "Ex-Im Bank Aims to Do More in Africa."

241 James Bennet, "Throngs Greet Call by Clinton for New Africa," *New York Times*, March 24, 1998, https://www.nytimes.com/1998/03/24/world/throngs-greet-call-for-clinton-for-new-africa.html.

242 Paragraph based on James Harmon, "American Interests in Expanding Trade in Africa," Remarks to the Council on Foreign Relations, January 18, 2000; Dunne, "US Eximbank Chief Goes on African Investment Safari."

243 Clyde Robinson, Annemarie Emmet, and Deborah Thompson, "Trip to Africa April 17–25, 1998," EXIM team report.

244 James A. Harmon statement before the House Appropriations Subcommittee on Foreign Operations, Export Financing, and Related Programs, March 2, 2000.

245 Clyde Robinson, Annemarie Emmet, and Deborah Thompson, "Trip to Africa April 17-25, 1998," EXIM team report.

246 Clyde Robinson, Annemarie Emmet, and Deborah Thompson, "Trip to Africa April 17-25, 1998," EXIM team report.

247 Language very similar to various speeches in James A. Harmon, untitled speech, delivered at the United States Nigerian Economic Summit, October 21, 1999; James Harmon, "American Interests in Expanding Trade in Africa," Remarks to the Council on Foreign Relations, January 18, 2000.

248 Jim Cruse (director of policy at EXIM Bank), interview with author, February 22, 2021.

249 Mufson, "Ex-Im Bank Aims to Do More in Africa." *Washington Post*, December 16, 1999.

250 Clyde Robinson, Annemarie Emmet, and Deborah Thompson, "Trip to Africa April 17–25, 1998," EXIM team report.

251 Dunne, "US Exim Bank Chief Goes on African Investment Safari."

252 Clyde Robinson, Annemarie Emmet, and Deborah Thompson, "Trip to Africa, April 17–25, 1998," EXIM team report.

253 Clyde Robinson, Annemarie Emmet, and Deborah Thompson, "Trip to Africa, April 17–25, 1998," EXIM team report prepared for Chairman James Harmon.

254 Mufson, "Ex-Im Bank Aims to Do More in Africa."

255 James Harmon, "American Interests in Expanding Trade in Africa," Remarks to the Council on Foreign Relations, January 18, 2000.

256 "Africa Trip Report," October 15–28, 1999 (prepared by EXIM Bank, authorship and date not specified).

257 EXIM Bank, "Chippewa Falls, Wisconsin, Plants Will Add Jobs to Fill $12.8 Million Fire Truck Order From Ghana," press release, May 28, 1999.

258 James Harmon, "American Interests in Expanding Trade in Africa," Remarks to the Council on Foreign Relations, January 18, 2000.

259 James Harmon to President Bill Clinton, November 9, 1999.

260 Clyde Robinson, Annemarie Emmet, and Deborah Thompson, "Trip to Africa April 17–25, 1998," EXIM team report.

261 Ellen Nakashima, "Clinton Encourages Nigerian Democracy," Washington Post, August 27, 2000, https://www.washingtonpost.com/archive/politics/2000/08/27/clinton-encourages-nigerian-democracy/aa10b974-9bc5-43f8-a787-8292ddb39866/.

262 Clyde Robinson, Annemarie Emmet, and Deborah Thompson, "Trip to Africa April 17–25, 1998," EXIM team report.

263 Clyde Robinson, Annemarie Emmet, and Deborah Thompson, "Trip to Africa April 17–25, 1998," EXIM team report.

264 James Harmon, "American Interests in Expanding Trade in Africa," Remarks to the Council on Foreign Relations, January 18, 2000.

265 Clyde Robinson, Annemarie Emmet, and Deborah Thompson, "Trip to Africa April 17–25, 1998," EXIM team report.

266 James Harmon to President Bill Clinton, November 9, 1999.

267 Clyde Robinson, Annemarie Emmet, and Deborah Thompson, "Trip to Africa April 17–25, 1998," EXIM team report.

268 Clyde Robinson, Annemarie Emmet, and Deborah Thompson, "Trip to Africa April 17–25, 1998," EXIM team report.

269 Bill Brubaker, "U.S. Offers Loans to Fight AIDS in Africa," *Washington Post*, July 20, 2000.

270 James A. Harmon, "A Look At . . . Africa and the AIDS Loan," *Washington Post*, September 17, 2000, https://www.washingtonpost.com/archive/opinions/2000/09/17/a-look-at-africa-and-the-aids-loan/0c3170a1-cf54-4180-b488-6c02a01b3118/.

271 Harmon, "A Look At . . . Africa."

272 Brubaker, "U.S. Offers Loans to Fight AIDS."

273 Brubaker, "U.S. Offers Loans to Fight AIDS

274 Kalumbi Shangula, "We Can't Shoulder More Debt to Treat an Incurable Disease," *Washington Post*, September 17, 2000.

275 Brubaker, "U.S. Offers Loans to Fight AIDS."

276 Brubaker, "U.S. Offers Loans to Fight AIDS."

277 Harmon, "A Look At . . . Africa

278 Brubaker, "U.S. Offers Loans to Fight AIDS."

279 Harmon, "A Look At . . . Africa

280 Mufson, "Ex-Im Bank Aims to Do More in Africa."

281 Jim Cruse (director of policy at EXIM Bank), interview with author, February 22, 2021.

282 EXIM Bank, "EX-IM Bank Supports $114 Million Sale of US Aircraft to Air Namibia," press release, September 17, 1999.

283 EXIM Bank, "EX-IM Bank Guarantee Helps Small Dallas Company to Sell Wireless Cable TV System to Zimbabwe," press release, April 11, 2000.

284 EXIM Bank, "EX-IM Bank-Backed $5.4 Million Sale of Cessna Aircraft to Zambia Enables Doctors to Reach Remote Areas of Country," press release, March 11, 1999.

285 For this discussion of "Boeing's Bank," I am indebted to Jim Cruse: Jim Cruse (director of policy at EXIM Bank), interview with author, February 22, 2021.

286 James Harmon, "American Interests in Expanding Trade in Africa," Remarks to the Council on Foreign Relations, January 18, 2000.

287 EXIM Bank, "EX-IM Bank Guarantee Helps Small Dallas Company to Sell Wireless Cable TV System to Zimbabwe," press release, April 11, 2000.

288 James Harmon, "American Interests in Expanding Trade in Africa," Remarks to the Council on Foreign Relations, January 18, 2000.

289 Marc Lacey, "U.S. Trade Law Gives Africa Hope and Hard Jobs," *New York Times*, November 14, 2003, https://www.nytimes.com/2003/11/14/world/us-trade-law-gives-africa-hope-and-hard-jobs.html.

290 Though this is a journalistic paraphrase of what he said: Lacey, "U.S. Trade Law Gives Africa Hope."

291 James Harmon, "American Interests in Expanding Trade in Africa," Remarks to the Council on Foreign Relations, January 18, 2000; John Dludlu, "US Agency to Take on Africa," *Business Day*, October 26, 1999.

292 EXIM Bank, "200 Million Ex-Im Bank Africa Pilot Program Begins August 1, Short-Term Credit Will be Available in 16 Sub-Saharan Countries," press release, July 20, 1999.

293 William Jefferson Clinton, "Remarks to the Council on Foreign Relations in New York," September 14, 1998.

294 All data and timeline taken from "A Chronology: Key Moments in the Clinton-Lewinsky Saga," *CNN*, 1998, https://www.cnn.com/ALLPOLITICS/1998/resources/lewinsky/timeline/.

295 William Jefferson Clinton, "Remarks to the Council on Foreign Relations in New York," September 14, 1998.

296 "Mission Improbable?" *Project Finance Magazine*, January 2001, 48.

297 For this material about the Jackie Clegg affair, I rely on my memory as well as a memorandum I wrote directly following the incident.

298 "Senator Dodd Marries Bank Executive," *New York Times*, June 20, 1999, https://www.nytimes .com/1999/06/20/nyregion/senator-dodd-marries-bank-executive.html.

299 While this was the date of the election, this outcome wasn't confirmed until the recount later that December.

300 Jim Cruse (director of policy at EXIM Bank), interview with author, February 22, 2021.

301 David Ignatius, "A Different Washington Story," *Washington Post*, December 19, 1999.

302 "Mission Improbable?" 48.

303 Brian Duignan, "Financial Crisis of 2007–08," *Britannica*, accessed May 12, 2021, https://www .britannica.com/event/financial-crisis-of-2007-2008.

304 For this introductory framing language, I am indebted to Robinson Meyer, "The Weekly Planet: How Jeff Bezos Is Spending His $10 Billion Earth Fund," *Atlantic*, November 3, 2020, https:// www.theatlantic.com/newsletters/archive/2020/11/how-jeff-bezos-spending-his-10-billion -earth-fund/616977/.

305 "Bezos Makes First Donations from $10 Billion Earth Fund for Fighting Climate Change," *Washington Post*, November 16, 2020, https://www.washingtonpost.com/climate-environment /2020/11/16/bezos-climate-grants/.

306 World Resources Institute, "Gift from Bezos Earth Fund Will Support Two Major Climate Initiatives at WRI," press release, November 15, 2020, https://www.wri.org/news/2020/11/release-gift -bezos-earth-fund-will-support-two-major-climate-initiatives-wri.

307 These guidelines have been amended several times. For an overview, please see EXIM Bank, "Environmental and Social Due Diligence Procedures and Guidelines" (June 27, 2013, rev. December 12, 2013), accessed February 26, 2021, https://www.exim.gov/policies/ex-im-bank-and-the -environment/environmental-and-social-due-diligence-procedures-and-guidelines.

308 Seth Faison, "Set to Build Dam, China Diverts Yangtze While Crowing About It," *New York Times*, November 9, 1997, https://www.nytimes.com/1997/11/09/world/set-to-build-dam-china -diverts-yangtze-while-crowing-about-it.html.

309 Faison, "Set to Build Dam."

310 Faison, "Set to Build Dam."

311 James B. Kelleher, "Caterpillar CEO: Once Shunned, Now Celebrated," *Reuters*, May 14, 2010, https://www.reuters.com/article/us-manufacturing-summit-owens/caterpillar -ceo-once-shunned-now-celebrated-idUSTRE64D4JR20100514.

312 James A. Harmon, "Preaching Green, Subsidizing Dirty," *Washington Post*, September 1, 1998.

313 Frank Murkowski, "Too Green," *Washington Post*, September 16, 1998.

314 Trip Gabriel, "If a Tree Falls in the Forest, They Hear It," *New York Times Magazine*, November 4, 1990, https://www.nytimes.com/1990/11/04/magazine/if-a-tree-falls-in-the-forest-they-hear-it .html.

315 "A brief history of interrupting public figures," *CNBC*, updated April 15, 2015, https://www.cnbc .com/2011/07/19/A-brief-history-of-interrupting-public-figures.html.

316 "The WRI Story: 30 Years of Big Ideas," World Resources Institute, accessed February 25, 2021, https://www.wri.org/wri-story-30-years-big-ideas. Many thanks to Liz Cook who reminded me that, on rare occasion, WRI does lobby.

317 "Jonathan Lash," World Resources Institute, accessed February 27, 2021, https://www.wri.org/ profile/jonathan-lash.

318 "The WRI Story: 30 Years of Big Ideas."

319 Robert D. McFadden, "William Ruckelshaus, Who Quit in 'Saturday Night Massacre,' Dies at 87," *New York Times*, updated June 12, 2020, https://www.nytimes.com/2019/11/27/us/politics /william-ruckelshaus-dead.html.

320 This was inspired by "The WRI Story: 30 Years of Big Ideas."

321 These data points are taken from "Scaling Our Impact in Urgent Times," World Resources Institute, Strategic Plan 2014–17 (9).

322 For this appraisal, I am indebted to Liz Cook, interview with author, November 24, 2020.

323 Marc Gunther, "Caterpillar Jumps on the Green Bandwagon," *CNN*, May 3, 2007, https://money.cnn.com/2007/05/02/magazines/fortune/pluggedin_Gunther.fortune/index.htm.

324 I paraphrase Gunther, "Caterpillar Jumps."

325 "The WRI Story: 30 Years of Big Ideas."

326 "The WRI Story: 30 Years of Big Ideas."

327 "The WRI Story: 30 Years of Big Ideas." As Jonathan Lash reminded me in a discussion, staff resistance owed to the company making profits selling equipment to coal mining companies that were staunch opponents of climate action.

328 "The WRI Story: 30 Years of Big Ideas."

329 Amanda Griscom Little, "GE's Green Gamble," *Vanity Fair*, October 17, 2006, https://www.vanityfair.com/news/2006/07/generalelectric200607.

330 Griscom Little, "GE's Green Gamble."

331 Griscom Little, "GE's Green Gamble."

332 "The buildings sector alone contributes to 40 percent of global carbon emissions, inclusive of construction and operation": Michelle Bachir and Meadow Hackett, "Decarbonization of Real Estate: End-to-End Business Transformation," *Deloitte*, October 5, 2020, https://www2.deloitte.com/global/en/blog/responsible-business-blog/2020/decarbonization-of-real-estate.html.

333 For this entire section, I am indebted to Ani Dasgupta (Global Director of WRI's Ross Center for Sustainable Cities), interview with author, March 10, 2021.

334 World Resources Institute, "First-Ever WRI Ross Prize for Cities Awarded to SARSAI," press release, April 10, 2019, https://www.wri.org/news/2019/04/release-first-ever-wri-ross-prize-cities-awarded-sarsai.

335 "The WRI Story: 30 Years of Big Ideas."

336 "The WRI Story: 30 Years of Big Ideas."

337 Many thanks to Andrew Steer for helping me with the following profile: Andrew Steer (head of the Bezos Climate Fund), interview with author, June 1, 2021.

338 Alexis Benveniste, "Biden's climate push promises 'jobs, jobs, jobs.' Here's what that might look like," *CNN*, May 2, 2021, https://www.cnn.com/2021/05/02/economy/biden-green-jobs/index.html.

339 World Resources Institute, "President and CEO Andrew Steer to Depart WRI to Lead Bezos Earth Fund," press release, March 9, 2021, https://www.wri.org/news/2021/03/release-president-and-ceo-andrew-steer-depart-wri-lead-bezos-earth-fund.

340 Esther Fung and Andrew Beaton, "Stephen Ross's Planned Trump Fundraiser Draws Calls for Boycotts," *Wall Street Journal*, August 7, 2019, https://www.wsj.com/articles/stephen-rosss-planned-trump-fundraiser-draws-calls-for-boycotts-11565221093.

341 Fung and Beaton, "Stephen Ross's Planned Trump Fundraiser."

342 Fung and Beaton, "Stephen Ross's Planned Trump Fundraiser."

343 Justine Calma, "The Green Movement Has a Diversity Problem. And It's Getting Worse," *Mother Jones*, January 16, 2019, https://www.motherjones.com/environment/2019/01/the-green-movement-has-a-diversity-problem-and-its-getting-worse/.

344 These data points are taken from "Scaling Our Impact in Urgent Times," World Resources Institute, Strategic Plan 2014–17.

345 Ani Dasgupta (Global Director of WRI's Ross Center for Sustainable Cities), interview with author, March 10, 2021.

346 Bret Stephens, "What We Learned From Mubarak," *New York Times*, February 15, 2021.

347 Patrick Kingsley and Martin Chulov, "Mohamed Morsi Ousted in Egypt's Second Revolution in Two Years," *Guardian*, July 4, 2013, https://www.theguardian.com/world/2013/jul/03/mohamed-morsi-egypt-second-revolution.

348 Kingsley and Chulov, "Mohamed Morsi Ousted."

349 Bradley Klapper, "GOP senator holds up $60M in economic aid to Egypt," *San Diego Union Tribune*, October 22, 2013.

350 David D. Kirkpatrick, "2 Senators Visit Egypt with Threat on U.S. Aid," *New York Times*, August 6, 2013, https://www.nytimes.com/2013/08/07/world/middleeast/2-senators-visit-egypt-with-threat-on-us-aid.html.

351 Kirkpatrick, "2 Senators Visit Egypt."

352 Stephens, "What We Learned."

353 Klapper, "GOP senator holds up $60M."

354 Matthew Frankel, "The 100 Best Warren Buffett Quotes," *Motley Fool*, updated August 30, 2019, https://www.fool.com/investing/best-warren-buffett-quotes.aspx.

355 Kay Granger, "Granger Holds Cash Transfer to Egypt," press release, September 28, 2012, https://kaygranger.house.gov/2012/9/granger-holds-cash-transfer-egypt.

356 David Ignatius, "An Egyptian Aid package, Stuck in a D.C. Labyrinth," *Washington Post*, July 19, 2013.

357 "Naguib Sawiris: 'If God Wanted Women to be Veiled, He Would Have Created Them with a Veil,'" *Arabian Business Industries*, November 11, 2019, https://www.arabianbusiness.com/culture-society/432946-naguib-sawiris-if-god-wanted-women-to-be-veiled-he-would-have-created-them-with-veil; "Egyptian Billionaire Sawiris Returns Home to Warm Welcome," *Reuters*, May 3, 2013, https://www.reuters.com/article/us-egypt-orascom/egyptian-billionaire-sawiris-returns-home-to-warm-welcome-idUSBRE9420WW20130503.

358 For this entire section, I am indebted to Ashraf Zaki (managing partner at Lorax Capital), interview with author, January 19, 2021.

359 Please note that Fawry didn't offer all of these services in 2015 but would in later years.

360 Naomi Xu Elegant, "A Jack Ma Company Is Poised to Break the Record for Biggest IPO—Again," *Fortune*, August 21, 2020, https://fortune.com/2020/08/21/jack-ma-alibaba-ant-ipo-biggest-ever/.

361 Nour Youssef and Diaa Hadid, "'We Don't Owe Anyone': Egypt Jousts With Its Chief Benefactor, Saudi Arabia," *New York Times*, November 1, 2016, https://www.nytimes.com/2016/11/02/world/middleeast/egypt-saudi-arabia.html.

362 Youssef and Hadid, "'We Don't Owe Anyone.'"

363 Diaa Hadid and Nour Youssef, "Sweet-Toothed Egypt Endures a Sugar Crisis: 'People Are Going to Snap,'" *New York Times*, October 20, 2016, https://www.nytimes.com/2016/10/21/world/middleeast/egypt-sugar-shortage.html.

364 Hadid and Youssef, "Sweet-Toothed Egypt."

365 Hadid and Youssef, "Sweet-Toothed Egypt."

366 Hadid and Youssef, "Sweet-Toothed Egypt."

367 Diaa Hadid, "Painful Steps Help Egypt Secure $12 Billion I.M.F. Loan," *New York Times*, November 11, 2016, https://www.nytimes.com/2016/11/12/world/middleeast/egypt-gets-final-imf-approval-for-12-billion-loan.html.

368 Hadid, "Painful Steps Help Egypt."

369 "Egypt: A Path Forward for Economic Prosperity," *IMF*, July 24, 2019, https://www.imf.org/en/News/Articles/2019/07/24/na072419-egypt-a-path-forward-for-economic-prosperity.

370 Hadid, "Painful Steps Help Egypt."

371 Eric Knecht and Ahmed Aboulenein, "Egyptian Parliament Approves Value-Added Tax at 13 Percent," *Reuters*, August 29, 2016, https://www.reuters.com/article/us-egypt-economy-tax/egyptian -parliament-approves-value-added-tax-at-13-percent-idUSKCN1141LM.

372 Hadid, "Painful Steps Help Egypt."

373 Mona Abisourour, "The Egyptian Devaluation—One Year Later," *infomineo*, January 2, 2018, https://infomineo.com/egyptian-devaluation-one-year-later/.

374 Nour Youssef and Diaa Hadid, "Egypt Floats Currency, Appeasing I.M.F. at Risk of Enraging Poor," *New York Times*, November 3, 2016, https://www.nytimes.com/2016/11/04/world/middle east/egypt-currency-pound-float-imf.html?action=click&module=RelatedCoverage&pgtype= Article&region=Footer.

375 Abisourour, "The Egyptian Devaluation."

376 Abisourour, "The Egyptian Devaluation."

377 "Egypt's Suez Canal Revenues Up 4.7% in Last 5 Years—Chairman," *Reuters*, August 6, 2020, https://www.reuters.com/article/egypt-economy-suezcanal/egypts-suez-canal-revenues-up-4-7 -in-last-5-years-chairman-idUSL8N2F84GW.

378 "Magda Habib, CEO and Founder, Dawi Clinics," *Enterprise*, November 22, 2018, https:// enterprise.press/stories/2018/11/22/magda-habib-ceo-and-founder-dawi-clinics/.

379 "Magda Habib, CEO and Founder."

380 "Magda Habib, CEO and Founder."

381 "Magda Habib, CEO and Founder."

382 "Magda Habib, CEO and Founder."

383 "Magda Habib, CEO and Founder."

384 "Magda Habib, CEO and Founder."

385 "Magda Habib, CEO and Founder."

386 "Magda Habib, CEO and Founder."

387 Perrihan Al-Riffai, "How to Feed Egypt," *Cairo Review*, summer 2015, https://www.thecairo review.com/essays/how-to-feed-egypt/.

388 Al-Riffai, "How to Feed Egypt."

389 "India Needs to Harvest Water to End Drought Crisis: Indian American Philanthropist Suri Sehgal," *American Bazaar*, November 2, 2019, https://www.americanbazaaronline.com/2016/05/06 /india-needs-harvest-water-end-drought-crisis-indian-american-philanthropist-suri-sehgal/.

390 "Suri Sehgal," *People Pill*, accessed March 21, 2021, https://peoplepill.com/people/suri-sehgal.

391 "Dr. Suri Sehgal Receives American Bazaar Philanthropy Award," *American Bazaar*, November 1, 2019, https://www.americanbazaaronline.com/2016/10/02/dr-suri-seghal-receives-american -bazaar-philanthropy-award/.

392 "Helios Investment Partners and EAEF Acquire Majority Stake in Misr Hytech," *Private Equity Wire*, March 6, 2019, https://www.privateequitywire.co.uk/2019/06/03/276194/helios-invest ment-partners-and-eaef-acquire-majority-stake-misr-hytech.

393 "Helios Investment Partners and EAEF Acquire Majority Stake."

394 "Egypt in Numbers," *BBC*, May 24, 2014, https://www.bbc.com/news/world-middle -east-27251107.

395 "Egypt in Numbers."

396 James Harmon, "Egyptian-American Enterprise Fund 'EAEF' Annual Letter," February 4, 2020.

397 James Harmon, "Egyptian-American Enterprise Fund 'EAEF' Annual Letter," February 4, 2020.

398 James Harmon, "Egyptian-American Enterprise Fund 'EAEF' Annual Letter," February 4, 2020.

399 As of this book's writing, we've attracted one investor, and expect more in the future.

400 For a description of this poverty and how much more work the enterprise fund has to do, please see "Egypt Is Reforming Its Economy, But Poverty Is Rising," *Economist*, August 10, 2019, https://www.economist.com/middle-east-and-africa/2019/08/08/egypt-is-reforming-its-economy-but-poverty-is-rising.

401 "Egypt to Record Growth Rate of 3.5% During 20/21," *Egypt Today*, October 19, 2020, https://www.egypttoday.com/Article/3/93295/Egypt-to-record-growth-rate-of-3-5-during-20.

402 James Harmon, "Egyptian-American Enterprise Fund 'EAEF' Annual Letter," February 14, 2019.

403 Yousef Saba, "IMF Expects Egypt Economy to Grow 5.9% in Year to End of June," *Reuters*, October 15, 2019, https://www.reuters.com/article/us-egypt-economy-imf/imf-expects-egypt-economy-to-grow-5-9-in-year-to-end-of-june-idUSKBN1WU1TG.

404 "What Are the Main Criticisms of the World Bank and the IMF?" *Bretton Woods Project*, June 4, 2019, https://www.brettonwoodsproject.org/2019/06/what-are-the-main-criticisms-of-the-world-bank-and-the-imf/.

405 See, for example, Bert Ingelaere, "Rwanda's Forever President," *New York Times*, August 2, 2017, https://www.nytimes.com/2017/08/02/opinion/paul-kagame-rwandas-forever-president.html.

406 Gregory Warner, "It's the No. 1 Country for Women in Politics—But Not in Daily Life," *NPR*, July 29, 2016, https://www.npr.org/sections/goatsandsoda/2016/07/29/487360094/invisibilia-no-one-thought-this-all-womans-debate-team-could-crush-it.

407 Warner, "It's the No. 1 Country."

408 Tom Zoellner and Keir Pearson, "America's Disastrous Love Affair with Rwanda's Paul Kagame," *CNN*, March 23, 2021, https://www.cnn.com/2021/03/23/opinions/hotel-rwanda-kagame-rusesabagina-trial-zoellner-pearson/index.html.

About the Author

JAMES A. HARMON is chair of the Egyptian-American Enterprise Fund, a private corporation seeded by US government funds to promote the development of the private sector in Egypt. He is the board cochair of the World Resources Institute, a global policy and research institution. In June 1997, Harmon was nominated by President Bill Clinton and confirmed by the US Senate to be chair of the Export-Import Bank of the United States for the four years that ended June 2001. Prior to that he was chair and CEO of the investment bank Schroder Wertheim (1986–96). He lives in Weston, Connecticut.